"Halcomb does the church and academy a great service by answering the big question of why the church needs academic studies . . . This is a good book for all who want to seek the truth behind the text. Whomever 'enters the fray' will come out on the other side a better and more learned student of the Bible."

—Sam Tsang,
Hong Kong Baptist Theological Seminary

"The work of New Testament scholars can be both fascinating and important, but also quite technical. Halcomb has written an accessible and engaging account of several of the key issues discussed among New Testament scholars today. I recommend this book for the clear and succinct ways in which it explains some interesting debates among biblical scholars, debates that have real significance within the life of the church."

—David F. Watson,
United Theological Seminary

"This book aims to not only make the major scholarly issues known to the reader, but to introduce the reader to the scholars who have studied and discussed those issues . . . Halcomb works to build a bridge between the academy and the church, and the result is a unique opportunity for Christians to experience something like a speed-dating round with several centuries' worth of scholars!"

—James F. McGrath,
Butler University

"The church and the academy, no less than the prodigal son and his older brother, have had a rocky history. Like the proverbial father, Halcomb is devoted to both and hopes to bring them together into a peaceable and even amicable relationship. *Entering the Fray* provides a sympathetic introduction to hot topics and prominent figures of New Testament scholarship for Christians who find themselves unsure what all the fuss is about."

—Rafael Rodríguez,
Johnson University

Entering the Fray

Entering the Fray

A Primer on New Testament Issues
for the Church and Academy

T. MICHAEL W. HALCOMB

WIPF & STOCK · Eugene, Oregon

ENTERING THE FRAY
A Primer on New Testament Issues for the Church and Academy

Copyright © 2012 T. Michael W. Halcomb. All rights reserved. Except for brief quotations in critical publications or reviews, no part of this book may be reproduced in any manner without prior written permission from the publisher. Write: Permissions, Wipf and Stock Publishers, 199 W. 8th Ave., Suite 3, Eugene, OR 97401.

Wipf & Stock
An Imprint of Wipf and Stock Publishers
199 W. 8th Ave., Suite 3
Eugene, OR 97401
www.wipfandstock.com

ISBN 13: 978-1-62032-328-1
Manufactured in the U.S.A.

All scripture quotations, unless otherwise indicated, are taken from the Holy Bible, New International Version®, NIV®. Copyright ©1973, 1978, 1984 by Biblica, Inc.™ Used by permission of Zondervan. All rights reserved worldwide.

To Lydia:
One day you'll be one of the greatest women in all of church history.

Contents

Getting Started ix

PART ONE

1. The New Testament and the Others 1
2. Different Methods to the Madness 22
3. From Paul's Gospel to the Four Gospels 42
4. What Do You Mean by "Synoptic Problem"? 54
5. Did Jesus Try to Keep a Messianic Secret? 70
6. ReQuesting Guides on the Quest for Jesus 90

PART TWO

7. Can Luke's Acts be Trusted? 111
8. Paul: Disputed or Undisputed? 134
9. Our Faith(fulness) or Christ's? 154
10. A New Perspective on Paul 176
11. From Peter's House to James's Tomb and Beyond 201
12. Approaching Revelation 236

Conclusion 257
Timeline 259
Notes 281

Getting Started

http://michaelhalcomb.com/enteringthefray-home.html[1.]

FOR THE TYPICAL CHURCHGOER or reader of the Bible, the New Testament is viewed as a sacred and spiritual text. Reading the Gospels, Paul's letters, or other portions of the New Testament during devotion time, hearing about them in sermons, and discussing them within a Sunday school setting or small group gathering is part of the normal life of faith. Occasionally, in such settings laypersons and beginning Bible college or seminary students will read or hear the name of a Bible scholar, perhaps even an academically reputable Bible scholar, and think nothing of it. This is unfortunate because in many ways Bible scholars have been driving forces behind the church and its teachings. Indeed, the average person who totes around an NIV or NASB knows little about the scholars who have participated in bringing such English translations to life.

    1. Scan the QR code or point your web browser to the address given at the beginning of each chapter to access this book's companion website, where you will find additional chapter-specific resources.

Getting Started

To be sure, English speaking Bible readers are inescapably indebted to researchers who have translated ancient texts into modern verbiage. Yet, all translators are forced to make interpretive decisions when they translate and as a result, all translations bear biases. Some of these biases are more difficult to detect than others but even so, they certainly exist. Since this is the case, even preachers and teachers who formulate sermons and lessons based on modern translations have been influenced by Bible scholars, whether they know it or not. To many, this is incredibly frightening.

Indeed, mainstream church culture has often demonized Bible scholars, depicting them as self-serving intellectuals who sit around trying to out-think God by devising new and controversial interpretations. On the other side of things, academics have often leveled harsh critiques against church culture, painting churchgoers as anti-intellectual pseudo-spiritualists. I must admit I am guilty on both counts. Needless to say, in modern times the relationship between the church and the academy has been at its best, strained, and at its worst, antagonistic and dismissive of the other.

Having said these things, this book makes the case that in spite of the wide gap between the academic and ecclesiastical worlds, the modern church needs to be aware of many of the key discussions in which biblical scholars have been engaging. Just to be clear, these scholarly engagements have not been kept secret; they have been promoted in the larger public square, at times with fierce debate. Even so, the average churchgoer has not been tuned in to such conversations. In fact, they may have purposefully tuned out. Some segments of the church population are simply unaware that any such dialogue has taken place, and beyond Google, may not even have the first clue how to explore the details. This work seeks to function as that "first clue."

The aim of this book is to help congregants, pastors, and students of the Bible enter into the fray of the discussions that have shaped the field of biblical studies, and in turn, the church. There are more than a few payoffs for the reader of this book: a greater knowledge of church history, a more circumspect view of the Bible and related interpretive issues, a newfound respect for scholars who have devoted their lives to studying the Bible, a deeper understanding of the role of the Bible and how it has been used—for good or for ill—within modern culture, and a shared discernment of the need to bridge the divide between the church and the academy.

While this book will address a host of issues, they all fall under the rubric of a dozen major discussions that have taken place within the last few hundred years of scholarship. Some of these issues are quite intricate and have been difficult even for scholars to wade through. Therefore, extra care has been taken here to keep the conversations accessible, understandable, and as down-to-earth as possible. Of course, this is not the same as watering down the issues. Yet, there is a sense in which any author must be selective and that is certainly the case here.

Many introductory textbooks, monographs, and academic journals have been written on the issues addressed in this volume. Many such works employ insider academic language and dwell on technical matters at length, rendering them difficult for those outside of the academic world to access, assess, and comprehend. Without a doubt, there is a need for such projects and they have their rightful place within the field of biblical studies. However, this book is purposefully user-friendly and avoids overly technical jargon. This is not to say that because a concept might seem difficult to understand or theologically robust that it will be glossed over.

It is to say, however, that confronting such issues will be done in a way that respects both the scholarly discussions that have taken place and the fact that not everyone who might be interested in them has a background that includes formal training in these areas. For those who take their faith seriously, this book assists you in taking a peek under the hood of biblical studies and seeing the parts of the motor that have been driving the realms of biblical academia as well as the church. The approachable, non-threatening, and non-technical character of this book makes it useful for a wide variety of people who may be interested in Jesus, the Bible, church history, interpretation, and much more, even though they may have never attended Bible college or seminary.

It should be stressed that while this book has a something of comprehensive scope to it, neither every book of the New Testament is covered in detail, nor every interpretive issue that has surfaced since the New Testament was penned is brought into view. This book will not meet every reader's expectations. Where it falls short, perhaps by not entertaining an issue perceived as critical or important, the reader is encouraged to pursue such work and to fill those gaps. Again, this book seeks to function, in the main, as a "first clue" for readers so that they will be able access and make sense of some of Christianity's most important and historic discussions. Throughout this book you will also see a host of "Scholarly Sketches" which will both introduce you to and give you a brief briographical glimpse into the lives of some important researchers in the field of biblical studies.

In closing, I would like to thank my wife for supporting me in this project. In addition, a word of appreciation goes out to Tim McNinch, who helped prepare the manuscript. I would also like to express my gratitude to the library at Asbury Theological Seminary for its help in providing many of the resources used throughout the writing of this book. I am also grateful to Wipf & Stock for taking an interest in *Entering the Fray*. My hope is that this little primer would be beneficial to any and all who read it. This book could be used for a series of Bible studies or even a short sermon series. It could also be used in a college or seminary class, especially a course related to New Testament issues, as it is divided into two major parts and is the perfect length for a semester. It is true that the world of scholarship can be intimidating and off-putting at times; however, it can also be thought-provoking, faith-inspiring and life-giving. So, may this book be an inspiration to you and may it bear the fruit that many years of scholarly toil have sought to produce. May you enter the fray of the field of biblical studies and never be the same, and may the church and the academy be better because of it. May it be!

Michael Halcomb
Pentecost, 2012

PART ONE

1

The New Testament and the Others

http://michaelhalcomb.com/enteringthefray-canon.html

ONE OF THE MOST interesting facts about the beginnings of Christianity is that its founder, Jesus, neither wrote texts nor commanded his disciples to write texts. Yet, for thousands of years, Christians have been text-oriented people. In John's Gospel we catch a quick glimpse of Jesus writing or drawing on the ground but unfortunately, John leaves out precisely what it was that Jesus inscribed in the dirt, leading to a plethora of fascinating and speculative interpretations of this story. Beyond that comment by John, however, we have no biblical account of Jesus writing anything. Despite this, today the church has its own sacred text consisting of twenty-seven highly revered documents. When and how, then, did Christianity—which began with Jesus, who neither authored texts nor commanded his disciples to do so—develop what is now known as the New Testament?

This is an important question for modern Christians for a host of reasons, not least because the Bible itself continues to meet its critics. Ironically, however, many Christians who revere the Bible and possess pet doctrines and theories concerning the nature of the Bible, simply have no idea how it came into existence. When Christians guard their theories without any attempt to substantiate or ground them in history, something has gone terribly wrong. A remedy is needed! The fix may well come from adopting a mentality similar to the slogan of my undergraduate athletics program: "Remember who you are and where you come from." Christians cannot successfully remember who they are without a solid grounding in where they have come from. Our past is invaluable!

During a recent study tour in Jerusalem, I encountered teenagers in military garb carrying around loaded weapons at nearly every ancient site I visited. Eventually, I asked an Israeli native why these soldiers were always out and about, touring the same ancient locations I was. He answered, "When men and women enter the Israeli military they are taken to historical sites of great significance not simply to be educated about them, but to see firsthand what it is they are protecting; it is their history—their inheritance—and they come to embody a deep reverence for these places because of that."

So it should be with Christians. Those who claim to respect and live by the Bible need to know its rich history; they need to know firsthand what it is they are upholding and why. The New Testament is the Christian's inheritance and this fact is not something to be taken lightly. Fortunately, many have dedicated their lives to studying the formation of the New Testament and in this chapter we have the privilege of meeting and engaging some of them. It is my hope that as we explore the development of the New Testament, you will be challenged and edified.

TUNING IN

During one of my seminary courses the professor leading class gave us an assignment that, at the time, I perceived to be quite irreverent. As students, our task was to answer the question: If you could remove one book from the New Testament, which one would it be and why? At that, my doctrinal sensitivities were highly offended. I thought, "Who are we to tamper with and destroy the Bible?" My professor tried to assure me that, in fact, the aim was not to try to destroy the Bible. I remained unconvinced. Needless to say, I did not pass that assignment with flying colors.

Looking back on that experience, I now realize two things. First, the assignment was so upsetting because it challenged the theory of inspiration that I clung to and anxiously sought to protect, and second, I had no idea that until the fourth century CE, the earliest Christians were still attempting to decide which documents should be included in the New Testament "canon." The word canon comes from the similarly sounding ancient Greek term κανῶν (*kanōn*), which means "measuring rod" or "standard." In short, a canon is the standard by which all other things are measured.

For those Christians who lived in the first three to four hundred years following Jesus' life, death, and resurrection, there were a number of developments that led to the eventual formation of the New Testament canon. We would be pulling the wool over our own eyes to ignore such a fact. History shows us that the New Testament neither fell from the sky nor arrived by way of God overtaking the bodies of first-century authors.

The process of canonization occurred outside of Christianity too. Prior to the formation of the New Testament, Greeks, Romans, and Egyptians had canonized the works of their favorite poets, storytellers, orators, grammarians, and historians.[1] Over time, as new works in these categories were created, they were each measured against the initial standardized or canonized volumes. Criteria for including a work within a canon varied greatly, depending on the category. Thus, for rhetorical and poetic works, style was of paramount importance. For historical texts, eyewitness accounts were often of great significance.

Over the course of three to four centuries, Christians developed their own criteria for what should be included in the New Testament canon. Yet, as we shall see, these criteria were not always held with the amount of consistency that we in the twenty-first century would like them to have been. Even before the finalized, written canon of the New Testament, the earliest Christians adhered to another canon,

Entering the Fray

lesser-known among modern Christians, which was called the Rule of Faith (*regula fidei*). In fact, it was this canon that guided the first several centuries of Christians in matters of faith, life, and community.

In a nutshell, the Rule of Faith consisted of the fundamental teachings of Jesus and the apostles by which all Christians were to measure any variety of teachings, doctrines, and lifestyles they might encounter within Christian culture. It must be remembered, however, that one of the most distinct differences between the early church and the church of today is that within earliest Christianity, there was no mentality that the apostolic teachings were confined only to written texts or the pages of a book. The spoken, preached, and confessed word was of the utmost importance. In the mid-to-late second century CE, Irenaeus of Lyons attempted to spell out what he perceived to be the bedrock of the apostolic Rule of Faith. In his book titled *Against Heresies* (3.4.12) he described its principles as follows:

> ". . . one God, the creator of heaven and earth, and all things within them, by means of Christ Jesus, the Son of God, who, because of his surpassing love towards his creation, descended to be born of the virgin, he himself uniting man through himself to God, and having suffered under Pontius Pilate, and rising again, and having been received up in splendor, shall come in glory, the savior of those who are saved, and the judge of those who are judged, and sending into eternal fire those who transform the truth, and despise his father and his coming" (my translation).

Following Irenaeus, others such as Clement of Alexandria (ca. 150–215), Tertullian (ca. 160–225) and Origen (ca. 184–235) offered their nuanced versions of the Rule. Needless to say, it was the firm rooting in these apostolic principles that helped cultivate early Christian culture and pave the way for the written canon of the New Testament. Stated differently, the process of forming a New Testament canon, which took place over hundreds of years, was birthed out of the shared and spoken Rule of Faith. Though there was not always universal agreement among the earliest Christians as to which texts belonged in the canon, there was solid agreement on the Rule of Faith. Grounded in Jesus, it was only by the Rule that texts could accurately be measured and judged.

TAKING NOTE

Near the end of Paul's second letter to Timothy, the apostle instructs the young disciple to waste no time in coming to visit him. Paul also tells Timothy to bring with him a disciple known as Mark and also some books and tablets that he left in Troas with a man named Carpus (2 Tim 4:11–13). Even though this to-do list for Timothy is something readers may easily gloss over, the apostle's choice of words here are not insignificant. When Paul speaks of the "books," τὰ βιβλία (*ta biblia*), and "notebooks," τὰς μεμβράνας (*tas membranas*), we are given a glimpse into the beginnings of two items that helped change the course of world history.

It is likely that when Paul uses the term "books" here, he is actually referring to scrolls. More importantly, however, is that these scrolls were distinct from the "notebooks" that he also speaks of. As you can imagine, it would have been quite difficult for Paul to carry and transport large sets of scrolls as he traveled from city to city. Further, scrolls were very costly and often incapable of being well protected from natural elements. Additionally, scrolls contained the texts of ancient literature and were used for study, not the mundane activities of day-to-day life.

The notebooks that Paul speaks of here were likely made of an ancient type of paper known as parchment, which itself was constructed from ancient papyrus—a thick, paper-like material produced from the papyrus plant. Our first record of parchment being used in a book-like format comes from the first century BCE, found in a work by Suetonius related to the Caesars, one of which was Julius Caesar (Suetonius, *Julius Caesar*, 56.6). It says that Julius folded pieces of papyri over one another, thereby creating a notebook. The first-century CE Latin poet Martial, in his work titled *Epigrams* (24:184) mentions Homer's *Iliad* in book format, describing it as "All locked within several pieces of skin, folded into several little sheets."[2]

Needless to say, these notebooks were precursors to what we now refer to as bound books. In widespread use during the latter half of the first century CE, our earliest actual example is that of a fourth-century CE record of a homeowner's financial transactions over the length of four years.[3] This, of course, is to be expected because these notebooks were precisely what common, literate folks used in the course of their everyday lives. This is important in the study of canonization for a number of reasons, one being that the book format allowed for easier transporting and distributing of Christian writings.

We have no way of knowing exactly how many Christian books were floating around during the first few hundred years of Christianity, but if the book burnings of the emperor Diocletian in 303 CE are any indication, there may have been a considerable number. The church historian, Eusebius, described the atrocities in his book *Ecclesiastical History* (8.2.1), saying, ". . . we saw with our own eyes our houses of worship thrown down from their elevation, [and] the sacred scriptures of inspiration committed to the flames in the midst of the markets." Accounts similar to those of Eusebius suggest that within the earliest Christian communities, books of revered literature had become common.[4] This historical glimpse helps us understand the social and cultural context of the development of the book later referred to as the New Testament.

In addition to the use of the codex, or book format, adopted by early Christians, another factor that helped set the stage for a New Testament canon was the appearance of alternative Christian teachings that began to pop up in religious circles of the second century CE. Chief among these were the belief systems of Docetism, Gnosticism, and Montanism.

In brief, proponents of Docetism taught that Jesus never really lived in the flesh but rather, only seemed to have done so. This, as you might expect, has major ramifications for nearly every major doctrine of Christianity. One of the centerpieces of gnostic belief was that the creator of the world was a demiurge, that is, a villainous deity. Therefore, this world he created is nothing but a trap for humans; it is a mirage. In fact, all humans are really gods who have been deceived into thinking that they are mere mortals. Salvation comes in the realization of one's divinity, a realization that is achieved by receiving a divine spark of enlightenment or knowledge, which lifts the veil of deceit. To be sure, this notion of salvation caused many eyebrows to rise among early orthodox Christians. Additionally, the Montanists were a spring of trouble for several reasons, one being their overemphasis on new prophecies. As a highly charismatic sect, they produced many of their own "inspired" texts alongside those of the apostles and formulated unique and secret interpretations of works like the Gospel of John, Hebrews, and Revelation.

In the midst of these sects and their production of what they believed to be inspired literature, the church began to look inward and conduct self-analysis. By no means was the church forced to develop a canon because of these things, but we would certainly be amiss historically if we ignored them. What we can say is that as the church found itself more and more frequently rejecting teachings from these sects and their favored writings, it also began reflecting, especially in light of the Rule of Faith, on the works that most accurately conveyed its own teachings and expressed its own identity.

The church conducted its collecting and ordering of these texts under at least five principles that, again, were guided by the Rule of Faith: apostolicity, orthodoxy, antiquity, inspiration, and use/adaptability.[5] The belief that the teachings and traditions of the church were handed down directly from the apostles themselves was the earmark of legitimacy. It was the teachings of Jesus and subsequently of his apostles that comprised the foundation of orthodoxy. By orthodoxy, we mean a core belief or set of beliefs, such as the notion that Jesus was raised from death. Certainly, there were not unanimous, across-the-board agreements on every matter between every Christian in antiquity. There was room for disagreement. Yet, in the essentials agreement was always necessary.

In addition to assessing the apostolicity and orthodoxy of a belief, its old age or antiquity was often an important factor. In a context where new sects were being created and their new teachings sometimes flourishing, Christians could challenge these innovative teachings by exposing how disconnected they were from the past. Aged teachings were trustworthy because they stood the test of time. When it comes to the topic of inspiration, a word that, in modern times, carries a lot of theological baggage, it is helpful to realize that for the earliest Christians inspiration was typically viewed as occurring after-the-fact, not before it. In other words, a book or writing was deemed inspired only after it was viewed as aligning with the Rule, not before. Once accepted, a work received the label "inspired." Finally, use and adaptability were helpful criteria in that they allowed the church to question whether or not a certain work met and fulfilled a variety of ecclesiastical needs in a wide array of ecclesiastical contexts. In short, the universality of a work within the worship and teaching settings of the church as a whole was an important consideration.

Entering the Fray

Thus far, it should be clear that the view of a static selection process for the texts to be included in the New Testament was just not in the cards. Instead, the process was very organic and fluid; over the course of hundreds of years, Christians wrestled with social, ecclesiastical, theological, and practical matters, which at various points, contributed to the working out of their Testament. This becomes even clearer when we consider the various opinions put forth by many of the most prominent and respected Christian leaders concerning which texts made the grade and therefore, ultimately deserved to make the canonical cut.

Once the accounts of Jesus' life and teachings and the letters of Paul had been composed, used, and compiled—documents which set the precedent for and foundation of the Rule of Faith—we can confidently say that the church had begun the slow process of canonization. To be sure, there was no preplanned beginning to this! Put differently, in the same way that the writers of the Old Testament documents never expected the coming of a New Testament, neither Jesus nor the writers of the New Testament anticipated any type of formal canon. In fact, as we have seen, a variety of events and circumstances simply and organically led the church in this direction. Thus, even as early as the end of the second century CE, Irenaeus (*Against Heresies*, 4.15.2) is able to refer to a "New Testament" which consists of many of the church's authoritative writings.

Just as well, prior to the year 400 CE, we have at least six lists of books that various leaders and their communities held in high esteem. These were something akin to forerunners of the final or "closed" New Testament canon. Our first example is dated somewhere between the beginning and middle of the second century CE and belongs to Marcion. Of the four Gospels, he included only Luke, and from among the Pauline epistles, he included only Romans, 1 and 2 Corinthians, Galatians, Ephesians, Philippians, Colossians, 1 and 2 Thessalonians, and Philemon.

Also, from either the second or fourth century CE (see the details of note 5 above) we have a portion of the Muratorian canon that, although its beginning lines are missing, includes substantially more than Marcion's list. Named after the historian who discovered it, Ludovico Muratori, this ancient fragment contains the following texts: Luke, John, Acts, Romans, 1 and 2 Corinthians, Galatians, Ephesians, Philippians, Colossians, 1 and 2 Thessalonians, 1 and 2 Timothy, Titus,

Philemon, 1 and 2 John, Jude, Revelation, Apocalypse of Peter, Wisdom of Solomon, and Shepherd of Hermas.

Concurrent with the previous two works, another fragment known as P^{46}, which is missing a handful of leaflets, in its present form contains Romans, 1 and 2 Corinthians, Galatians, Ephesians, Philippians, Colossians, 1 Thessalonians, and Hebrews. From these three texts alone, it is clear that Luke's Gospel and the early letters of Paul enjoyed widespread notoriety. Different compilers and communities often had different reasons for their selections but the similarities are quite striking. It is easy enough to see that within earliest Christianity there was room for unity and diversity to coexist.

In the beginning of the third century CE, the church historian Eusebius also offered a list. Among the works he acknowledged without question were the four Gospels, Acts, the fourteen Pauline works (including Hebrews), 1 John, 1 Peter, and Revelation. The handful of works that Eusebius deemed disputed were James, Jude, 2 Peter, and 2 and 3 John. He viewed as inauthentic a variety of works including Shepherd of Hermas and Didache. Nearly half of a decade later, in the year 367 CE, Athanasius, in his famed *Thirty-ninth Easter Letter*, provided a list of texts which would steer the course for the rest of canon and church history. He included all of the documents that to this day are considered the legitimate twenty-seven texts of the fixed New Testament canon in the West; canonization in the East appears to have a much longer, complex, and diversified history. Thirty years later in 397 CE at the Council of Carthage, these same texts were upheld and agreed upon.

Even in the fourth and fifth centuries CE, at least three other witnesses testify to the canonization of these texts. The fourth-century manuscript of Sinaiticus agrees with the canon of Athanasius but nuances it slightly by appending to it Barnabas and Shepherd of Hermas. Unfortunately, the late fourth-century manuscript of Vaticanus, which follows the outline of Athanasius, is lost to us, so it is unclear whether or not 1 and 2 Timothy, Titus, Philemon, and Revelation were included, though they likely were.

Additionally, the fifth-century Alexandrinus codex, with the exceptions of a portion of John and 2 Corinthians missing, also contains the works listed by Athanasius. Yet, it also contains 1 Clement and twelve chapters of 2 Clement. In the tenth century Pope Damasus, in a letter sent to a French bishop, included only the twenty-seven texts mentioned by Athanasius. Once again, this illustrates that while unity existed within the first ten centuries of church history, even on such an important topic as a literary canon, strict uniformity did not.

Even into the fifteenth and sixteenth centuries, this was still the case. In 1442, the Council of Florence reaffirmed the (by this time) "traditional" twenty-seven. Despite this, major movers and shakers of this era such as Uldrych Zwingli, Martin Luther, and John Calvin questioned the canon. For Zwingli, Luther, and Calvin, Revelation was viewed with great skepticism and its placement in the cannon was met with uncertainty.[6]

In addition, Luther also sought to remove Hebrews, James, and Jude. Calvin also refused to write commentaries on 2 and 3 John. Erasmus also questioned Revelation, denying its inspiration along with that of 2 and 3 John.[7] Even so, in 1546 the Council of Trent affirmed and settled once and for all, the validity of the fixed, twenty-seven book New Testament canon.

> *Johann Salomo Semler was born in 1725 in Saalfeld, Thuringa. He grew up among German Lutheran pietists. Semler published nearly three hundred scholarly works in his life. He both attended and taught at the University of Halle. A controversial figure of his day, he was often referred to as the father of German rationalism.*

It was in the beginning of the eighteenth century that study of the development of the New Testament canon took a critical turn—literally. It was during this time period that Johann Semler began employing modern critical theories and methodologies to the study of canon. His 120-volume study of the canon remains one of the most comprehensive works on this topic to date.[8] Not unlike the reformers before him, he too was skeptical of Revelation. He contended that while it was relevant for the earlier Christians this was certainly not the case for the later church, particularly the church of his era. A controversial figure, he also argued that the lists created early in church history were all of a local and/or regional flavor and therefore, not binding for the universal church across the centuries.

Several decades later, in the first half of the nineteenth century, two influential scholars who helped keep the canonical studies wheel turning were Theodor Zahn and Adolf von Harnack. One of Zahn's most notable contributions to the discussion was his theory that the canon had been completely finalized by the end of the first century.[9]

The New Testament and the Others

However, Harnack argued that this phenomenon took place a century later, near the end of the second century. These two viewpoints are significant because they heavily influenced the next several generations of canonical scholarship.

> *Theodor Zahn was born in 1838 in Mörs. He was a German Lutheran theologian with deep interests in both the New Testament and patristics. He studied and taught at the University of Göttingen in addition to several other prominent institutions. He died in 1933 having published and lectured extensively throughout Germany.*

Zahn asserted that the early ratification of the canon was reached not through a planned and conscious process but rather an unplanned and spontaneous one. Worship and teaching were two of the chief factors that led to the culmination of a New Testament canon prior to the commencement of the second century. The canonical variations after that were mere reflections of local communities working out their social and religious idiosyncrasies.

> *Karl Gustav "Adolf" von Harnack was born in 1851 in Dorpat (Tartu), Estonia. The son of a professor of homiletics and church history, he blossomed as a leading European protestant scholar. He taught at a number of major universities including Leipzig, Marburg, Giessen, and Berlin. He died in 1930.*

Yet, Harnack was not convinced by this thesis. While he applauded Zahn's detailed research, he questioned how the data had been interpreted. One of Harnack's major rebuttals was that Zahn all but ignored the role of the ecclesiastical controversies of the second century. For Harnack, it was simply inconceivable to think that the development of the canon was not shaped in some way by enduring the crucible of early sects and cults that had deviated from orthodoxy. These heretics, whether knowingly or not, forced the church's hand. The result was a secure canon.[10]

> *Walter Bauer was born in 1877 in Königsberg, Prussia. He earned his doctorate from the University of Marburg. He taught in several academic settings but spent most of his career at Georg Augusta University in Göttingen. One of his best-known works, BDAG, is still widely used today. He died in 1960.*

On the heels of these scholars, Walter Bauer was instrumental in sparking a newfound interest in canonical studies as well as the origins of early Christianity.[11] He took elements from both Zahn and Harnack and nuanced them in an incredibly dramatic

Entering the Fray

fashion. For Bauer, it was clear that there were indeed numerous local or regional variations of early Christianity. Unlike Harnack, however, he did not see splintered sects as heretical groups but as legitimate minorities. A uniform and orthodox Christianity did not yet exist. Each divergent form and expression of Christianity was valid. In fact, Bauer asserted that modern scholars were anachronistically reading the later notion of heresy back into these early contexts. By extension, according to Bauer the concept of orthodoxy must be seen as anachronistic as well. These varied and competing forms of Christianity were each legitimate in their own right. The end result is that the entire conversation about canon is a modern concept; it did not exist in antiquity but rather, has retroactively been forced by contemporary researchers back upon ancient history.

> Kurt Aland was born in 1915 in Berlin-Steglitz, Germany. He studied at Friedrich-Wilhelms University and later taught at a number of institutions, including Münster. He was once arrested by the Marxist regime on charges of trafficking watches. He was married twice, had three children, and died in 1991.

Kurt Aland agreed that there were certainly diverse pockets of Christian communities throughout the first several centuries of church history. Yet, he challenged the contention that each of these sects was a legitimate expression of the Christian faith. For example, regarding the teachings of Jesus and the Gospels, Aland wrote, "Each of the four Gospels obtains for itself its own circle of readers and followers. They prevail against the considerable competition of other gospels. . . ."[12] Similarly, he says of Paul's epistles that those "who reject them thereby cut themselves off from the circle of Pauline communities and become a separate community. . . ."[13]

This is especially important to bear in mind for a couple of reasons. First, it shows us that while divergent viewpoints existed within the early Christian movement, there was also an undergirding unity. That unity was located in the person and teachings of Jesus as expressed in the Gospels and Pauline epistles. To reject these was to reject the foundation of the faith and therefore, the faith itself. Second, it was the communities themselves—not church authorities—who gave shape to the process of canonization. As Aland says, "For it goes without saying that the church, understood as the entire body of believers, created the canon. But this canon grew from the bottom upwards, in the communities, among the believers, and only later was officially legitimized from the top. It was not the reverse; it was not imposed from the top, be it by bishops or synods, and then accepted by the communities."[14] This is a salient point that did not go unchallenged by a number of scholars who succeeded Aland.[15]

> Brevard Childs was born in 1923 in South Carolina. He was raised a Presbyterian and earned degrees from the University of Michigan (BA, MA), Princeton Theological Seminary (BD) and the University of Basel (ThD). He was married to Ann, whom he met while studying in Basel. He died in June of 2007.

Decades later, Brevard Childs veered from these topics and chose as his focus what became known as "canonical criticism" or the "canonical approach."[16] Childs's theory was birthed at a time when other scholars had adopted very different and atomistic approaches to the text. We will look at those approaches more closely in the next chapter, but it needs to be pointed out here that Childs's views belonged to a certain context. During his career, numerous researchers were interested in peeling back what they perceived to be layers of tradition beneath the finalized texts of the New Testament. Put differently, they believed that after the initial author penned a text, it underwent modifications and nuances as it was passed on to a variety of communities. The job of the scholar, then, was to strip away those layers and get back to the original, the kernel, which contained the earliest and most authoritative meaning.

For Childs however, placing the emphasis on the original as the most authoritative was problematic. Instead, he contended that interpreters should place emphasis on the final product, that is, the frozen text that was solidified around the fourth century CE. While there were a number of significant implications that resulted from this theory, two of those are important for our purposes here. First of all, by making this move, Childs was attempting to recover the Bible, which had seemingly been taken hostage by specialist scholars, and return it to the church; after all, this is and always has been the church's book! Additionally, in contradistinction to the atomistic approaches, Childs sought to reveal an overarching unity to the Bible. In its finalized or canonized form, these works displayed a deep unity from Genesis to Revelation. To date, many interpreters remain unconvinced by Childs's approach to the canon.

Another influential canon scholar, who was also a student of Harnack, was Hans von Campenhausen. While he built on much of

Entering the Fray

> Hans E. F. von Campenhausen was born in 1903 in Rosenbeck. He studied at Heidelberg, Marburg, and Göttingen respectively. He signed the "Commitment of the Professors at German Universities to Adolf Hitler and the Nazi State" in 1933. He taught at Greifswald, Vienna, and Heidelberg, and died in 1989.

the work of his predecessor, he also critiqued and diverged from certain portions of it. Whereas Harnack delegated the bulk of his attention to the early church's liturgical and didactic contexts as the setting for choosing a canon, Campenhausen rooted the beginnings of canonization in the New Testament itself.[17] For him, Jesus set the canonical process in motion with his teachings. In turn, Paul formulated a corpus of works attesting to the life, teachings, and accomplishments of Jesus. It was Jesus and Paul, then, who initiated and instigated the process of canonization, not the Christians of the second through fourth centuries CE, although they were certainly the inheritors who helped guide the process along.

> Harry Y. Gamble was born in 1941. He earned degrees from Wake Forest (BA), Duke (MDiv), and Yale (MA, PhD) respectively. He has served as Professor and Chair of Religious Studies at the University of Virginia and has published several works related to early church history. He is married to his wife, Tamara.

Harry Gamble, however, has since argued that "During the first and most of the second century, it would have been impossible to foresee that such a collection would emerge. Therefore, it ought not to be assumed that the existence of the NT is a necessary or self-explanatory fact. Nothing dictated that there should be a NT at all."[18] For Gamble, these ancient Christian communities came, over time, to view the Gospels and Paul's letters as on par with the Jewish scriptures. This took place, in the main, within the context of worship or liturgy.

In fact, "None of the writings which belong to the NT was composed as scripture.... The documents which were eventually to become distinctively Christian scripture were written for immediate and practical purposes within the early churches, and only gradually did they come to be valued and spoken of as 'scripture.'"[19]

Lee McDonald, who has researched and written extensively on matters pertaining to the canon and canonization, shares a similar view. He writes, "No conscious or clear effort was made by these authors to produce Christian scriptures. It is only at a later stage in the second century, when the literature they produced began to take on the function of scripture within the Christian community, that its status as scripture began to be acknowledged."[20]

> Lee Martin McDonald was born in 1942. He earned his ThM from Harvard University and his PhD from the University of Edinburgh in Scotland. He has authored/edited over twenty books and hundreds of articles. He has served in several American Baptist churches as well as the U.S. Army Reserve's chaplaincy.

In light of all his research into the corridors of canon history, McDonald's ultimate conclusions are twofold. First, echoing Aland and Campenhausen among others, he asserts that the one "true canon of faith for the church" is the "Lord Jesus Christ."[21] Of course, in no sense is McDonald attempting to rule out or downplay the role and significance of the Bible in the life and history of the church. He still goes on to say, secondly, that "The Bible is still the church's book, without which the Christian faith would be a blur. Without it, Christians would have difficulty in articulating their identity and mission. Without it, there could be little basis for renewal of the believing communities around the world."[22]

> Elaine Pagels was born in 1943 in Palo Alto, California. A student of the history of religions, she also studied dance at Martha Graham's studio. However, she earned her PhD from Harvard University where she studied under Helmut Koester. She teaches at Princeton Theological Seminary and is married.

Such claims and ideas have not gone unchallenged, however. In recent history, two researchers, Bart Ehrman and Elaine Pagels, have questioned the current canon which has been handed down through the centuries. Particularly interested in gnostic texts, these two claim that a rediscovery of early Christianity also leads to the reshaping of the traditional canon. You will recall the booklist belonging to the *Easter Letter* of Athanasius in 367 CE, mentioned above. During that time, Athanasius, who was also the bishop of Alexandria, Egypt, banned books smelling of heresy. This prohibition led many in gnostic communities to stash away or hide their texts.

In December of 1945, some of these texts were rediscovered in the Egyptian library now known as Nag Hammadi. For Ehrman, these lost books also represent lost Christianities. Pagels believes that, in fact, these texts reach back to an earlier and more authentic version of Jesus'

Entering the Fray

> Bart D. Ehrman was born in 1955. He studied at Wheaton College (BA) and received both his MDiv and PhD from Princeton Theological Seminary, where he studied under the renowned text-critic, Bruce Metzger. Ehrman has two children and is married to Dr. Sarah Beckwith, an English teacher at Duke University.

life, message and vision. Against Aland's notion that the canon was formed from the bottom to the top, from the people to the leaders, Pagels argues that it was the church authorities who not only gave shape to the now traditional canon but also suppressed other voices and texts like those of the gnostic communities. For them, what is needed today then is a reconsideration of the contents of the canon.

To be sure, Ehrman and Pagels have earned themselves abundant amounts of attention for making such claims. Their work has elicited a host of responses, and among evangelicals most of those responses have been intensely negative. This is very interesting in light of the observation that throughout church history there have been diverse views about the canon. Again, even as recently as the Reformation era we read of Luther, Calvin, and Zwingli all questioning the canon's contents. Perhaps there are numerous factors that play into the intense reaction to Ehrman and Pagels, for example, the way media slants such discussions, or the fundamentalist culture of anti-intellectualism. Or, perhaps, it is simply a mirroring of Athanasius's actions. After all, the bishop did ban these texts.

> Luke Timothy Johnson was born in 1943. A native of Park Falls, Wisconsin, he studied at Notre Dame Seminary (BA), St. Meinrad School of Theology (MDiv), Indiana University (MARS), and Yale University (PhD). He also served as a monk for nearly a decade. He has seven children and is married to Joy.

So, the converse of the question asked by my professor a number of years ago may be asked here: Should we add any texts to the canon and if so, why? Or we might ask the more general question: Should the canon remain closed? Perhaps the thoughts of Luke Timothy Johnson are helpful in this regard. He writes:

> "It is the nature of the canon to be closed. An unlimited canon is no canon, any more than a foot ruler can gain inches and still be a foot ruler. Because it is closed, the canon is able to perform its function of mediating a certain identity through the successive ages of the church. Because the church today reads the very same

The New Testament and the Others

writings as were read by Polycarp and Augustine and Thomas and Luther and Bonhoeffer, it remains identifiably the same community. Only such a steady measure can provide such continuity. If a lost letter of Paul's should be discovered, there would undoubtedly be great excitement, but there should be no expansion of the canon, for that letter never, from the time of its composition to now, shaped the identity of the catholic church."[23]

> William J. Abraham was born in Northern Ireland in 1947. He is ordained in the United Methodist Church and teaches at Perkins School of Theology. He earned his BA at the Queen's University of Belfast, his MDiv from Asbury Theological Seminary, and his DPhil at Regent's Park College.

This sentiment is echoed in a way by William Abraham, who contends that the canonical heritage of the church has always shaped, is shaping, and will continue to shape its being and identity. For Abraham, if you "Take away the instruments, the players, and the score" then you "take away the orchestra."[24] If you "Remove the various components of the canonical heritage of the church" then "you systematically dismantle the life of the church as a whole."[25] Further, if you "remove" or "drastically change the canonical heritage once it is up and running" then you are essentially reconstituting "the church along radically different lines."[26] Perhaps this is much of the reason for the church's widespread backlash against scholars like Ehrman and Pagels; their mission, in the end, is viewed by many as wholly and ultimately an attempt to dismantle the church.

TAKING ACTION

Throughout this book, at the end of each chapter we will ask the "So what?" question. By that, we simply mean: So what does all of this scholarly stuff have to do with the church? Our answers to these questions should lead us toward certain courses of action. When it comes to the topic of the New Testament canon and its formation, there are a handful of responses we might offer.

As humans, we tend to love stories. Even more, we love juicy stories. Further still, we love stories with thick plots. We love conspiracy theories. In the wake of the Nag Hammadi findings in Egypt in 1945, the world has seen a number of these theories surface. In America, books like *The Da Vinci Code*, a bestseller that eventually went on to become a box office hit, prove this fact. Yet, some have argued that it is no great leap from the conspiracies embedded in a popular work like this one by Dan Brown to those espoused by Bart Ehrman or Elaine Pagels.

Indeed, the theories put forth by these authors have, in recent times, put canonical Christianity under fire. While some agree with the interpretations of the data put forth by these writers, others have vehemently disagreed. The discoveries of these so-called "lost Gospels" is certainly interesting on a historical front, and without a doubt, they can aid us in better understanding the various social contexts with which earliest Christianity interacted. Yet, these gnostic texts lack coherence and cohesiveness with the Old Testament, the saving work of Jesus the Messiah, and his redeeming work, which will finally and fully be consummated upon his return. In the absence of this coherence, Gnosticism is found wanting.

Further, nowhere in our canonical heritage do we find the gnostic texts judged to be reflective of the earliest canon and subsequent church history. This may seem like something of a circular argument but really, much of one's opinion on this matter may rest in whether or not they believe the canon was generated by Christians or Christian leaders. In other words, there is much riding on whether or not the canon was initiated and settled by the people or by the powers, that is, by the laity or church authorities. It would appear, however, that Kurt Aland was right on this matter. While gnostic texts reflect serious matters worth dealing with, in terms of potential for inclusion in the canon they were never serious contenders.

As we have seen, the development of the canon happened over the course of centuries within a host of contexts. This long process reflects a real diversity within the earliest Christianity. Different booklists and different interpretations of texts were not uncommon. Among all of the diversity, however, there was a deep unity. Despite the picture that some would like to paint, the first few centuries of Christianity after Jesus' death were not ones where an "anything goes" mentality prevailed. No, the first Christians had a baseline against which they measured any variety of teachings, doctrines, or lifestyles that they might encounter in Christian communities, namely, the Rule of Faith.

The Rule itself was grounded in the self-authenticating person and teachings of Jesus, which were further hashed out in the gospels and epistles. These things formed and stimulated the essence of the church;

The New Testament and the Others

they helped create and maintain its identity. In turn, the apostles advanced these ideals and in time, a canon of texts was fixed. We must always take pains to remember, however, that it is Jesus with whom the textual canon started and it is Jesus himself who is the underlying standard for every Christian.

Perhaps from our predecessors who lived in the era of canonization, today's church can learn the principle of unity amid diversity. In our era, the H-word (heretic) is thrown around rather easily and haphazardly. Some folks believe that they have Christianity solved and that anyone whose views differ from their own are either heathen, wayward souls, or in the grip of the evil one. This type of stiff fundamentalism is not only unhealthy, it is dangerous. Furthermore, it is not in keeping with our heritage.

It is not being suggested here that all beliefs are created equal or that all teachings are relative. It is also not being suggested here that Christians simply keep quiet about their beliefs. I am suggesting, however, that Christians need to be as eager to show grace and dignity to those with whom they disagree as they are to challenge them. There is a time and a place to express doubts, worries, concerns, and challenges. But there is also a proper way to express them. Embracing a stance or apologetic of humility is a great place to start. Sometimes, the difficult result of agreeing to disagree has to be an option. We must not clutch our pet doctrines so anxiously that we turn away a brother or sister in Christ when their view may differ somewhat from our own.

Finally, it should always be kept in mind that our true common denominator in the faith is that Jesus is the Messiah who has wrought salvation for all of humanity. It is on this rule that we stake our faith and lives. As we sit thousands of years removed from the era when Jesus walked the earth, we have the privilege not only to see the reach of his life but also to study the textual canon he presaged. What a privilege, indeed!

2

Different Methods to the Madness

http://michaelhalcomb.com/enteringthefray-methods.html

Israeli airport security is no joke! Beyond the high-tech baggage and body scanners, one traveling in or out of Israel can expect multiple full-body pat-downs, armed guards at every turn, detailed luggage swabbing, ethnic profiling, cross-interrogation, and more. Israeli airlines are serious business. I suspect that the intensity level at the airport is much of the reason that, when facing two interrogators—one a top-ranking official—and an Israeli policeman holding an AK-47, I kind of missed the punchline of a joke.

Different Methods to the Madness

I was being repeatedly questioned about my intentions for traveling to Israel. So, I repeatedly told them that the purpose of my visit was for study. Having answered that question nearly a dozen times, finally the official asked what my interests were in learning an ancient language. I started to explain that I was studying and preparing to be a Bible scholar when he interrupted me and said, "A Bible scholar? You'd be better off being a chef!"

As I said above, it took me a bit longer than usual to get the joke. Besides, I did not want to appear to laugh too quickly in such a serious situation, at such a serious man about such a serious topic. Eventually, a short grin appeared on my face and he belted out a jolly laugh and placed his hand on my shoulder. He said, "Here's your passport, Mr. Halcomb. Step right inside that doorway, have a seat, and wait for your name to be called." Really, that was code for, "Have a seat over there and wait for the next two men to rip your bags apart, swab everything you have, and interrogate you again."

Of the many airport experiences I've had, this is definitely one of the most memorable. The official's statement that I would somehow get more enjoyment out of life by being a chef rather than a Bible scholar has stuck with me. Not because I question my pursuit of biblical scholarship but because it reminds me that many people have no clue how fulfilling and meaningful a life of studying the Bible in-depth really can be.

The more I've thought about that man's comment, the more I've come to realize that his contrast was not as stark as he might have thought. That is particularly true when applied to the contents of this chapter. Here, I take on the role of a chef who opens up the kitchen doors and lets you have a peek at all of the behind-the-scenes action. I reveal, if you will, the recipe of the last several hundred years of biblical scholarship. I show for example, just what a hint of textual analysis here and a dash of narrative analysis there can contribute to the full course meal. So, wait no longer, let's dig in!

TUNING IN

It is not difficult to find bad interpretations of the Bible. In fact, the internet is like the operating headquarters for people who think they know how to interpret and explain the Bible but often really have no clue. Much of what one reads online is, to borrow a word from the apostle Paul, dung! This is the case because many readers approach the text without any consideration of history, ancient social context, or original languages. They substitute in place of these types of things their own emotions, modern social contexts, and local languages. This is a recipe for interpretive disaster.

Yet, misreading and misinterpreting the Bible is far from novel; it has been going on for centuries. One of the goals of modern biblical scholarship has been to lay down some ground rules for approaching the Bible. Of course, Bible scholars are people too and therefore, they are not infallible interpreters. Time has proven this over and over again. However, just because there have been scholars who have made terrible interpretive judgments does not render the whole enterprise worthless.

As interpreters ourselves, the aim is to come to the text with a realization of our own subjective tendencies so that we might see more clearly the text and its own tendencies. The issue has to do, in many ways, with integrity. For what reasons are we approaching the text and when we do so, what sort of attitude or stance do we have towards it? At the bare minimum, it seems to me that a responsible interpreter will approach the text with at least the same attitude as its writer or writers, namely, with integrity.

The fact is, the writers of the New Testament documents were not attempting to dupe or trick people. They were not simply making things up out of thin air; they were not concocting fairy tales. Instead, they approached the writing task with honesty and sincerity. Certainly, they aimed to be persuasive. Yet, this was never at the cost of genuineness and truth telling. To be sure, the New Testament authors were products of their times and cultures, and had agendas. Even so, as writers with integrity, they are clear about those agendas. Further, their cultural contexts are not something to be hidden, but exposed and put out in the open.

Some of those cues, however, are easily missed by the untrained eye. If you've ever been led by a tour guide on a trip, you can relate to this. For example, several years ago when I was walking through the ancient ruins of Ephesus, all I saw were lots of stones, statues, and buildings. But at every turn my tour guide pointed to a statue and explained the history behind it; he situated it in its proper context so that I could understand it. For every ancient column or bust, he did the same. Had

Different Methods to the Madness

he not done this, very little would have had any significance to me. His trained eye, however, helped bring the ancient city to life for me.

Many Bible scholars seek to do something similar. The aim is to bring to life for modern readers what is already there in the text. Over the last several centuries, much attention has been given to the matter of interpretation and the most fruitful ways of going about such a task. What has been discovered is that there is no one, monolithic approach that can resolve all of our interpretive questions. Put differently, there is no "one size fits all" approach to interpreting the Bible. Just as well, there is no foolproof guarantee attached to scholarly interpretations. For all the work that scholars have done and will do, they have not and never will eradicate irresponsible interpretations. The goal, however, is to help curb them.

Now, one of the complicating factors with all of this is that many Bible scholars are specialists. In the same way that doctors, lawyers, and engineers tend to specialize in the various subsets of their respective fields, so do Bible scholars. In any field that has a variety of specializations, technical insider language develops. Terms are created, adopted, and used that those outside of the specialist circle have difficulty understanding. Not only does this create confusion when scholars attempt to speak about their findings to outsiders, it also creates resistance. More often than not, when a scholar begins using insider language with a non-specialist, that person quickly loses interest and tunes out. Perhaps, then, some of the reason so many irresponsible interpretations of the Bible exist is due to the failure of scholars to communicate in a way and on a level that non-specialists can relate to.

Even the modern starting point for in-depth study of the Bible proves this. It all began with what scholars refer to as "historical criticism." Now, to the average Christian layperson, that is a problematic phrase. Immediately upon hearing it, walls are put up and defenses raised; criticizing the Bible is not something that most Christians want to invest their time in. Yet, the word "criticism" here, when used by scholars, does not mean to negatively evaluate the Bible. Instead, it is a scientific term that means to examine, or analyze, or look closely at. From the beginning, then, there is a communication failure between specialists and non-specialists; this is a confusing term.

Even so, the confusion escalates. Initially, under the banner of historical criticism were the two categories, "higher criticism" and "lower criticism." There again we see the word criticism. This time, however, there seems to be a nuance to the category. Perhaps higher criticism has to do with criticizing more and lower criticism has to do with criticizing less. Nothing could be farther from the truth. For scholars, lower criticism has to do with analyzing the syntax, grammar, and words of the text. In short, it is a close look at the ground-level elements of the text, what one can see on the page.

Higher criticism, on the other hand, deals with the elements behind or outside of the text. For example, the historical setting, authorship, dating, audience, and social aspects are all outside forces that gave shape and contour to the text. Therefore, these are all characteristics that someone using higher criticism would be interested in studying. Thus, neither higher criticism nor lower criticism has anything to do with the degree of negativity or criticism that one might have towards the Bible. To avoid confusion and resistance, I propose here that it would be much more helpful for scholars to adopt the titles "historical analysis," "higher analysis," and "lower analysis" when speaking of these concepts.

Further, I suggest that for each of the specializations within biblical scholarship, we replace the word "criticism" with the word "analysis." Thus, specializations such as form criticism, redaction criticism, and narrative criticism would fare much better if titled form analysis, redaction analysis, and narrative analysis. In fact, throughout the rest of this book, I will aim to adopt my own proposal. In the end, the goal is not to build up resistance in the non-specialist towards scholarship but rather to make scholarship accessible. If people believe that right out of the gate the Bible is being criticized, they will not likely have an interest. If we can do away with that resistance by appropriately nuancing our language, we ought to do so.

TAKING NOTE

In reworking names and ideas, we are not the first generation to do so. Bible scholars have a long history of this, in fact. This is especially true of our predecessors in the faith who lived in the eighteenth century CE. It might be premature to begin there, however; we need to step back at least two hundred years farther. Our landing pad is the Reformation era, the period instigated by the desire for religious fervor and freedom, the era when Martin Luther nailed his ninety-five theses to the doors of the Catholic Church and sparked a revolution.

In a nutshell, Luther, a German friar and theology professor, had become upset with Catholicism's practice of selling indulgences to pardon sins. He was adamant that God's forgiveness could not be purchased with money. In a moment saturated with righteous indignation, he drew up ninety-five reasons against this practice and attempted to outline the ways and means of true repentance and forgiveness. From this point on, there would no longer be one ruling Catholic Church. Those who agreed with Luther would identify themselves as Protestants.

With Luther, Christianity had been forever changed. Unfortunately, deep divisions were drawn between Christians who identified themselves as Catholics and others who identified themselves as Protestants. Heresy hunting and damning ensued from both sides of the divide. This historical moment also had a profound impact on biblical interpretation. Protestants and Catholics had very different views about the Bible. For Catholics, church officials were to interpret the text. Luther had wrestled that authority away from church leaders so that among Protestants everyone was invited to read and interpret the Bible. One of the collateral byproducts of this division was the way that society in general began to grow skeptical of the Bible's authority and relevance.

Whereas the Bible had held a place of nearly unquestioned authority in the Western world from the time of Constantine, that is, for around twelve hundred years, this was no longer the case. The Bible had been the church's sacred scripture for over a millennium, but now, in a world touched by the Enlightenment, which valued reason and science, it was coming under scrutiny. By the time of the eighteenth century, people had become disenchanted with the Bible. The Catholics used it to promote their views while the Protestants did the same. The Bible was used, so to speak, as confessional propaganda. This was a huge religious turn off to many.

While the Bible's authority and relevance were being shoved to the margins of society, thankfully it was still being studied in the academy. In a most ironic turn of events, those studying the Bible within the university realized that in order to preserve any of its authority and relevance for modernity, the Bible must ultimately be situated in ancient history. During this Enlightenment era, Greek and Roman classical literature was being widely studied. Scholars used the findings of their research to illustrate how ideals from ancient history could be helpful in the present day. This was especially true in the realms of politics, society, and morality.

What had separated these classics from the Bible was that they had never really enjoyed the status of sacred scripture. Yet, these works were providing meaningful and relevant ideas for contemporary society and in doing so, were achieving a status upgrade that imbued them with a certain amount of authority. The methods and approaches used to study these ancient works were scientific in nature and therefore, trusted and respected. If there was any hope of wresting the Bible from the grips of death, it seemed that the way to do so was to show that it too, was an ancient text, written in ancient languages, and firmly rooted in history. Enter: biblical analysis (or, traditionally, "biblical criticism").[1]

It should be noted at this point and before moving on that, in order to keep this chapter from becoming a book in and of itself, it seems best to mention only one or two modern scholars who have earned a reputation as specialists in their field of analysis. You can easily consult the contents of their works for more detailed descriptions and their bibliographies to find related resources. The goal here, as throughout the book as a whole, is to provide you with a "first clue" concerning these matters. Just as well, in order to illustrate how the various approaches work, I will use Mark 1:1 as an example. We will run this verse through the host of interpretive filters described below.

We wade into the waters of biblical analysis by way of the method known as "historical analysis." Historical analysis, also known as higher analysis, is concerned, as we have already mentioned, with the world behind the text. Two of the trailblazers for this approach were Johann D. Michaelis and Johann G. Eichorn (or Eichhorn). Both of these men practiced textual analysis as well and were predominantly Old Testament scholars.

> Johann David Michaelis was born in 1717 in Halle, Germany. He was the son of C. B. Michaelis, a prominent professor at Halle. He was an extraordinary philologist and linguist who exerted much influence in biblical studies. He taught at the University of Göttingen for many years. He died in 1791.

Both Michaelis and Eichorn set the trend for historical study by using ancient literature and findings outside of the Bible to help shed light on the biblical text. For example, they used ancient Semitic inscriptions and Ancient Near Eastern writings

Different Methods to the Madness

> Johann Gottfried Eichorn was born in 1752 in Dorrenzimmern, Germany. He studied under Johann D. Michaelis at Göttingen, where he would later assume the role of professor. He was a prominent OT scholar but also lectured on the NT and in fact, published an introductory textbook on the NT. He died in 1827.

comparatively with the Old Testament. This approach essentially created the mold for every biblical commentator who followed. Indeed, one could pick up any commentary written by a scholar today and find within it citations of historical resources outside of the Bible, that help make sense of the text at hand. These types of findings might be interpreted so as to shed light on the date, setting, or author.

For instance, when using historical analysis to understand Mark (Mk) 1:1, some questions that could be asked are: What might this verse tell us about the author? What might this verse tell us about the context out of which the author wrote? Might this verse provide us insight into the beliefs and practices of the community or communities to which the author belonged and/or was writing? Does it tell us anything about the author's own beliefs or practices? In terms of dating this text, does this verse give us any information about the time period when this may or may not have been written? Do other ancient texts resemble Mk 1:1, and if so, what might that suggest about the work itself and even the author?

> Morna D. Hooker was born in 1931. She earned her Doctor of Divinity from Cambridge (the first female to do so). In addition to being bestowed with numerous scholarly awards such as the Burkitt Medal, she has held a number of academic positions and has been an active preacher within the Methodist Church.

In her commentary on Mark, Morna Hooker writes, "With this somewhat abrupt introduction we may compare the LXX version of Hosea 1:2, which reads, 'The beginning of the word of the Lord through Hosea'; instead of introducing the word of God, spoken through a prophet, however, we have [here] the good news of Jesus Christ."[2]

What Hooker has done here is a result of the process initiated long ago by Michaelis; she compared Mark with another ancient text, which helped her draw conclusions about the author's intentions and background. The author, then, is rooted in the history of Israel's prophets and frames his own telling of Jesus' story in that way. Further, he seems to assume that his audience has some familiarity with the prophets too. Historical analysis has taken data from behind the text and helped shed some interpretive light.

Yet, a foray into the text itself is also important. "Textual analysis," a branch of lower analysis, seeks generally to recover or retrieve the originally authored version of a text, or as close to that original as possible. This is often done by looking at a variety of ancient manuscripts of the same text and comparing their variations. It also utilizes the analysis of grammar and syntax. Over the course of the last century, the name Bruce Metzger has nearly become synonymous with textual analysis. Metzger has helped develop and refine this aspect of scholarly study in many ways. He has also helped bring this highly specialized approach to non-specialist audiences.

> Bruce Manning Metzger was born in 1914 in Middletown, Pennsylvania. He earned his BA from Lebanon Valley College and his ThB, MA, and PhD from Princeton, where he taught. His wife Elizabeth's father was the third president of Princeton. He had two sons, John and James. He died four days after his birthday in 2007.

In Mk 1:1, for example, there is an important difference in some of the ancient manuscripts available to us. Some of the oldest and best-preserved manuscripts, which are marked with the symbolic abbreviations ℵ*, Θ, and 28ᶜ, do not contain the phrase "Son of God," υἱοῦ θεοῦ (*huiou theou*). Metzger's interpretation of these absences leads him to suggest that this "may be due to an oversight in copying."[3] However, he points out that "there was always a temptation (to which copyists often succumbed) to expand titles and quasi-titles of books." Metzger concludes that since other manuscripts, marked with the symbolic abbreviations B, D, and W all include the phrase "Son of God," it is not "advisable to omit the words altogether" in a translation. "Yet because of the shorter reading and the possibility of scribal expansion," Metzger chooses to enclose the words within square brackets in his final translation.

In addition to historical analysis and textual analysis, many scholars have also found value in the interpretive method or specialization known as "source analysis." A much more detailed description of this method is given in chapter four of this book but it is still worth mentioning in brief here. When it comes to the New Testament, source analysis deals predominantly with the Gospels of Matthew, Mark, and Luke (referred to as the synoptic Gospels). Researchers using this approach

Different Methods to the Madness

have been interested in the fact that the Gospels tell many of the same stories, yet have significant differences.

How are these similarities and differences to be accounted for and understood? It has long been suggested that the similarities come from shared oral or written sources, while the differences often have to do with a writer's style. This has led some to suggest that the sources Mark used when he was writing were from oral tradition as well as a hypothetical written source known as "Q." Matthew and Luke both used Mark and Q as source documents, but in addition, had their own special sources (referred to as "Special M" and "Special L"). Today, Mark Goodacre is one of the leading researchers using source analysis to examine the Gospel accounts. When it comes to Mk 1:1, we might ask the question: How it this introductory verse both similar and different from the beginnings of Matthew and Luke? Can those observations supply us with any information about potential sources these writers may or may not have used?

> *Mark Goodacre was born in 1967 in Leicestershire, England. He earned his DPhil at the University of Oxford. He has taught at the University of Birmingham (England) and also Duke University (North Carolina). Goodacre has published extensively on the synoptic Gospels and Q.*

Whereas source analysis endeavors to uncover potential sources used in the production stages of a text, "form analysis" is more concerned with the end result. In many ways, form analysis has to do with questions of genre. Is the form that this writing takes a poem, letter, song, parable, sermon, etc.? Each form belongs to a particular life setting, what German scholars referred to as a *Sitz im Leben*. Thus, a text's genre or form, when situated in its proper life setting, can often give rich detail about the author and the social context into which the writing was birthed.

For example, imagine you were reading a letter from a relative who was telling you about a recent event that happened in their child's life and you came across this sentence: "They were singing, 'Red Rover, Red Rover, send Tommy over.'" You would recognize this form as a chant. It is not, however, a religious or political chant. Therefore, its life setting (or *Sitz im Leben*) is not a liturgical or a political context. Instead, it is a playground chant; it something kids yell when they are playing a game. Therefore, you would situate the chant in the setting of a playground.

Entering the Fray

Even if you did not know a lot about the relative who sent you the letter, you could glean from these observations that the child of your relative is likely school-aged. It might also tell you that they either live near a park or frequently go to a park. In turn, this may suggest that they value fun and place some priority on their children having friendships and being active.

> Dennis Eric Nineham was born in 1921. He is an ordained priest and chaplain and studied at The Queen's College (Oxford). He has held positions at Keble College (Oxford) and the universities of Bristol, Cambridge, and London respectively. He has a wide range of expertise in both theological and biblical studies.

One scholar who has used form analysis to understand Mark's story is Dennis Nineham. In his view, the various forms throughout Mark's account reflect the fact that he was a collector of materials who was writing from the standpoint of the church around 75 CE. Therefore, the concerns and beliefs expressed in the Markan narrative are reflections of the Christian community. When it comes to Mk 1:1, Nineham includes it in a larger section, which he extends to 1:14.

Nineham refers to this as a prologue. The prologue is a form that is found in a drama. Nineham says, "when the curtain goes up at the beginning of v. 14, he [the reader]—unlike most of the actors—knows who the principal character is and can follow the full meaning of the action."[4] The form, then, is a prologue whose *Sitz im Leben* is the theater where great dramas take place and narrators, actors, and audience members alike find themselves caught up in the story.

Another approach used by New Testament scholars is known as "tradition analysis." This method often overlaps with other approaches but on its own, it is interested in the history of traditions before they were set to writing. For those scholars who believe that one of Mark's sources came from oral traditions that were passed down to him, the goal is to uncover what these traditions were and to discover traces or residues of them throughout the Markan narrative.

Looking at Mk 1:1, it could be asked, for example: Was there an oral tradition of referring to Jesus as "Son of God?" Once this is asked, in light of what is known about the two manuscript traditions—one group containing the phrase and one group not containing the phrase—it might be asked whether or not there were two competing traditions in the early church, one that knew and referred to Jesus as Son of God

Different Methods to the Madness

and one that did not. Uncovering these traditions may grant us insights into the contexts of various early Christian communities as well as the life of the author. As an example, what might it suggest about the author of Mark if he chose one of these traditions over the other?

In recent times, Rikki Watts has suggested that in and behind Mark's story rests a new exodus tradition, patterned on the Old Testament book of Isaiah. In a nutshell, the prophet Isaiah used a threefold template to tell his story. This pattern is, first, deliverance from the nations and from idols; second, Yahweh leading his people in "the way of the Lord"; and third, Yahweh leading his people to and vindicating them with a great triumph in Jerusalem. Essentially, it is Isaiah taking the Exodus story of God's deliverance and reframing it for the people of his time. Watts suggests that the Markan author and the community with which he was affiliated embraced and adhered to this tradition of Isaiah's "new exodus." Even more, when Mark finally draws up his own account of Jesus' life, he uses Isaiah's new exodus tradition as the template for his own narrative.

> Dr. Rikki E. Watts is a native Australian who holds several degrees, including one in aeronautics. He traveled for some time with Cirque du Soleil conducting scientific analyses for their shows. He has also worked with IBM. He holds degrees in Philosophy, Art history, and Sociology. He teaches at Regent College.

Watts makes the point that Mk 1:1 must be connected to verses two and three, which immediately follow. Therefore, Mk 1:1–3 forms the opening of the entire work. Further, Watts notes, "It would be most unusual if the themes evoked in the opening sentence were fundamentally different from those dealt with in the body of the work. Clearly then Mark's citation is crucial. As part of the heading it is programmatic for the prologue and therefore the whole Gospel. . . ."[5] Watts, then, has uncovered a tradition behind (and within) the Markan account, which he believes sets the thematic stage for the remainder of the story.

Next in our survey of biblical interpretive specializations is "redaction analysis." Related to source analysis, this approach is interested in the editor(s) of a text. If the author of Mark used a number of sources, how exactly did he compile them? What did he include from those sources and what did he leave out? What were his biases and what was his agenda? What theological motivations can be identified in the author's choice to rearrange, edit, and create new materials out of older ones? Imagine, for instance, that a person named Emperor Marcus wrote a document in 5 CE that contained the phrase "God is good." Then, another document, dated to around 20 CE, written by a man named Phaedrus was discovered. In the work of Phaedrus the following statement is found: "As the beloved Marcus once said, 'Our God alone is very good.'" It appears that the quote is not exact and therefore, Phaedrus took some editorial liberties. The scholar using redaction analysis would seek to unearth the motivations and reasons for these edits.

Willi Marxsen is heralded by many as the one who introduced redaction analysis to the field of biblical studies. In considering Mk 1:1, Marxsen notes that the word εὐαγγέλιον (*euangelion*), or "gospel," is basically synonymous with the terms that both Matthew and Luke use in their accounts. Matthew uses the term βίβλος (*biblos*), "book" or "recording," and Luke uses διήγησις (*diēgēsis*), "story" or "account."[6] For Marxsen, one must question why, if Mark was written first and both Matthew and Luke used his text, did they each choose similar yet different terms? What were the motivations for this? One of the answers for Marxsen has to do with focus. In Mark, "Jesus is the subject of the gospel" while Matthew is interested in making him "proclaimer of the gospels."[7] In short, Mark is the first to tell the story about Jesus, which he calls the "gospel." By the time we get to Matthew, who reworks Mark's story in his own way, the term gospel ultimately "becomes the designation for a book" (βίβλος). Luke's understanding of the word gospel is similar to Matthew's, but more so than Matthew, "he writes a life of Jesus in a historicizing fashion."[8] Thus, as Marxsen sees it, "As it turned out, Mark provides an important key" to the development of the theologically loaded term, gospel.

> Willi Marxsen was born in 1919 in Kiel. He served as a soldier in WWII and later studied theology in Kiel, where he earned his doctorate. He was active in the church and held several academic positions. Marxsen was interested in the relationships between the church, Christian identity, and Christian living.

One of the fastest growing methods among New Testament interpreters today is "literary" or "narrative analysis." The idea of this approach is to focus on both the individual literary devices at work in the text as well as the overarching framework that cohesively pieces together the story and gives it its flow. The literary analyst might focus on devices such as rhyme, repetition, climax, comparisons, contrasts, irony, etc. Each of these mechanisms gives shape to the story and signals that it is meant to be read and understood in a certain way. The same analyst may also focus on major ideas or themes that seem to link the entire narrative together.

Jack Kingsbury provides readers with an excellent example of this approach. When engaging Mk 1:1, Kingsbury speaks purely in literary terms. He says, based on 1:1, "The personal name of the protagonist of Mark's story is 'Jesus'. Mark not only introduces Jesus to the reader by this name but also, as narrator, regularly uses it himself. Indeed, there are only three instances in which Mark permits characters in his story to address Jesus as such. Twice it is demoniacs (1:24; 5:7), but once it is blind Bartimaeus (10:47)." It is easy to see from these few remarks that Kingsbury's main interest is the role of Jesus' identity over the course of the entire narrative, beginning with 1:1.[9]

> Jack Dean Kingsbury was born in the 1930s in California. He earned his doctorate from the University of Basel. He has served much of his career as a professor at Union Theological Seminary (VA) and has written extensively on the Gospels. Kingsbury is heralded by many as a pioneer in biblical literary criticism.

Also interested in big-picture ideas is the method known as "canonical analysis."[10] This approach was popularized at a time when other many methods had become incredibly reductionist or atomistic. Instead of stripping away different layers of perceived traditions behind a text so that they could get back to an original, those using canonical analysis want to focus on the text in its finalized or completed form, as preserved in the biblical canon. In doing this, an overarching unity can be discovered. A leading scholar in this area was Brevard Childs.

When Childs read Mk 1:1, he saw it as a title. Yet, he also saw much more than that. It was a title that characterized the entire message of the Markan account. Childs wrote, "This gospel is the proclamation of the saving work of Jesus Christ which had been promised by the prophets of Israel. Mark is not offering a report of Jesus' own preaching, but rather a theological construal of the meaning of his entire ministry."[11] In these two sentences,

> Brevard Childs was born in 1923 in South Carolina. He was raised a Presbyterian and earned degrees from the University of Michigan (BA, MA), Princeton Theological Seminary (BD), and the University of Basel (ThD). He was married to Ann, whom he met while studying in Basel. He died in June of 2007.

Childs was able to sum up not only the whole of Mark's story but the whole of Jesus' ministry. Further, he was able to suggest that the roots of Jesus' ministry reached all the way back to Israel's prophets.

Childs parsed this out a bit more when he wrote, "Mark's reference to the 'beginning of the gospel' is not a chronological designation of when his public career began, the first phase of an historical movement, but the beginning of God's saving acts which continue to exert power in Jesus Christ."[12] He continued, "The Marcan [sic] introduction thus establishes the canonical perspective for the entire book. . . . From this canonical perspective the Jesus of the Synoptics and the Christ of Paul do not stand in opposition, but both bear witness to the true theological significance of his life and death as God's saving acts for the redemption of humanity."[13] In other words, the message of Mark can be found across, and is in concert with, the rest of the New Testament canon. Just as well, it shares a unified message with the whole of the Old Testament canon.

In the last few decades, "social-science analysis" has become very popular. The group of scholars working in this area are concerned with studying, locating, and explaining the New Testament in its ancient cultural environments, in particular, the ancient Mediterranean world. These specialists strongly stress that this ancient context is in many ways, the very opposite of the modern Western context. Thus, in the ancient Mediterranean world, focus on honor/shame, limited good, patronage, kinship, purity rites/rituals, collectivism, and other socio-cultural mores and practices are the lenses through which the New Testament must be viewed. At the helm of the social-science analysis ship stands Bruce Malina.

In commenting on Mk 1:1, Malina has some interesting insights. In the ancient world of Jesus where kinship and honor/shame were pillars of society, both of these can be seen in Mark's opening verse. In Jesus' world, honor was to be preserved at all costs. When a person committed a shameful act, shame fell upon the entire family. Shame was to be avoided at all costs. Honor and shame could either be acquired or ascribed. One could acquire

> Bruce J. Malina is a professor at Creighton University. He earned his Doctor of Sacred Theology from the Studium Biblicum Franciscanum in Jerusalem, as well as a Doctor of Theology from the University of St. Andrews (Scotland). He is a founder of The Context Group and has published extensively.

honor through good deeds, winning challenges, or through fame and wealth. Ascribed honor is simply inherited honor. There is no seeking it or vying for it; it is, without question, ascribed to a person. Thus, a son not born into a royal family might spend his life trying to acquire honor. Yet, a son born into a family of royalty, by default, has honor already ascribed to him.

In Mk 1:1, when it is noted that Jesus is the Messiah, the Son of God, we see both kinship and honor codes at work. Had Mark simply stopped at the phrase "Jesus is the Messiah" ancient listeners would have likely asked how he received such a high place of honor. However, in adding the phrase "Son of God" the author answered that question. God is the being with the most honor and therefore his son, by default, is ascribed this honor. The kinship link is not a one-way street, however. Just as God can give Jesus honor, so also Jesus, through his life and acts, can bring his father honor. The kinship bond is incredibly tight. Malina says, "In that society, public authority always derived from one's status or honor rating. That rating in turn was dependent on the stand of one's father. . . . Mark immediately identifies Jesus as the Son of God [and] . . . thereby asserts the basis for the authority of Jesus as quickly as the question arises in the mind of the reader."[14]

"Socio-rhetorical analysis" is another tactic for interpreting texts. Today, there are two camps that claim this title but they are each using very different approaches. When Ben Witherington III describes socio-rhetorical analysis he is referring to the use of modern social sciences (anthropology, etc.), social history, and ancient rhetorical devices to engage the text. However, when Vernon Robbins speaks of socio-rhetorical analysis, he is talking about an all-encompassing approach to the text; one that can end up using every type of analysis listed in this chapter. He describes it as "an approach to literature that focuses on values, convictions and beliefs both in the texts we read and the world in which we live."[15]

> Ben Witherington III, was born in North Carolina in 1951. He earned his DPhil from Durham University (England) and is a prolific publisher. He has written a commentary on every book of the NT and appeared on many major television networks. Currently, he teaches at Asbury Theological Seminary.

There is not ample space here to discuss the many nuances between these two different approaches, which share the same name.

Entering the Fray

In reviewing the works of both Witherington and Robbins on Mk 1:1, those nuances are not necessarily easily discerned either. For both scholars, 1:1 is part of the Markan prologue and a precursor to what comes later in the story. In Robbins's estimation, 1:1 can be identified as the ancient rhetorical device known as "exergasia" (Latin: *expolitio*). The exergesia was a procedure by which one could elaborate or dwell on an idea or topic without seeming repetitive. As the ancient rhetorical treatise known as *Ad Herennium* (4.42.54) says, exergesia "consists in dwelling on the same topic and yet seeming to say something ever new. . . . We shall not repeat the same thing precisely—for that, to be sure, would weary the hearer and not elaborate the idea—but with changes." For Robbins, 1:1 states the topics that will be elaborated throughout the beginning of Mark's narrative, namely, Jesus (1:14), the gospel (1:14, 15) and God (1:15).[16]

> Vernon K. Robbins was born in 1939. He earned both his MA and PhD from the University of Chicago. He is currently a professor at Emory University in Atlanta, Georgia but has also taught in Norway and South Africa. He currently leads the Rhetoric of Religious Antiquities (RRA) group.

For Witherington, the rhetorical nature of 1:1 is to be found in the fact that this verse forms an "inclusio" that goes to 1:15. Further, this is an ancient biography and therefore, it focuses on identity. Mark's story contains a line that is similar to a phrase found in the Priene Inscription, which is about the emperor Octavian. A portion of the Inscription says, ". . . since the birthday of the god [Octavian] was for the world the beginning of his good news . . ."[17] The term "good news" is the same term as "gospel" in Greek (εὐαγγέλιον, *euangelion*). Witherington states, "The birthday of the emperor was celebrated throughout the empire and was the occasion of festivals called evangels. What is different about this announcement is that Mark wishes to begin with Jesus' coming on the public scene as a historical figure, not his actual birth."[18] Both scholars, then, pay attention to both the rhetoric and language of Mark's account, as well as the rhetoric and rhetorical devices found in works prior to and contemporary with the New Testament era.

Our final close-up look at New Testament methodologies brings us to "imperial analysis." This approach has changed the entire landscape when it comes to reading Revelation, which many now view as anti-imperial literature. It is also prominent among Pauline and Gospel

Different Methods to the Madness

studies. In a few words, imperial analysis seeks to explore the ways in which the New Testament intersects with the ancient Roman empire. In most instances, where connections with the empire are discerned, they are inherently subversive, that is, they are meant to criticize and challenge it. Sometimes these challenges are overt and sometimes they are cloaked in code.

In Mk 1:1, Ched Myers contends that there is a very overt imperial critique. Thus, whereas Witherington recognized a loose connection to the emperor, Myers places much more weight on this relationship. Myers writes, "Roman propaganda focused on eulogizing Caesar as the 'divine man.' This ideological strategy is well documented in coins of the period, and of course in the later emperor cults of Asia Minor."[19] He makes the link even more explicit stating, "From this (εὐαγγέλιον) there emerges yet another dimension of Mark's title. He is serving notice that he is challenging the apparatus of imperial propagation. His dramatic prologue . . . heralds the advent of an 'anointed' leader, who is confirmed by the Deity and who proclaims a 'kingdom.'"[20] In short, "Mark is taking dead aim at Caesar. . . . From the very first line, Mark's literary strategy is revealed as subversive . . . the 'good news' of Mark does not herald yet another victory by Rome's armies; it is a declaration of war upon the political culture of the empire."[21]

> Ched Myers is a native Californian. He earned a BA from the University of California at Berkley and an MA from Graduate Theological Union. He has served as adjunct faculty at numbers of institutions including Fuller Theological Seminary. He and his wife Elaine work with Bartimaeus Cooperative Ministries in California.

As you can see, there are many different approaches that scholars have employed to help them uncover and understand what is in the Bible. Of course, some interpretations are more sound and probable than others. Even so, looking at the New Testament from all of these different angles has the potential to enrich one's Bible study. Beyond the methods mentioned above, there is a plethora of remaining approaches. Among the many other approaches used by researchers are performance analysis, psychological analysis, reader-response analysis, minority analysis, mnemo analysis, gender analysis, eco-theological analysis, economic analysis, Bakhtin analysis, and post-colonial analysis. For those just entering the field of biblical studies, seeing all of these approaches can seem a bit overwhelming. The advice I give to folks is

39

to pick one that interests them and stick with it. Once you have a good grasp, try to use other approaches. The mistake that many people make, especially students, is to try to master them all at once. This is impossible, not to mention unintelligent. To get the most of these methods, pick one and run with it for a while.

TAKING ACTION

As one who will always be a student of church history and the history of biblical interpretation, I must say that I feel incredibly privileged to be part of this rich heritage. I am tremendously glad that I did not take the airport official's advice and try my hand at being a chef (not that there's anything wrong with being a chef, it's just not for me). I stand in a long line of some of the world's most creative and brilliant thinkers; scholars who helped shape entire generations and in some cases, even centuries. If you are a Christian, that is part of your heritage too!

One of the most fascinating things about being a reader and interpreter of the Bible is that I am always learning new things about it. Two thousand years after its composition, it continues to brim with fresh, life-giving insights. I am grateful to those researchers who devoted portions of their lives to developing methods that help me deeply engage the Bible. When I first became a Christian, I only knew how to read the New Testament devotionally. I would simply open it up, read for a bit, try my hardest to understand and then close it. More often than not, I was just "putting in my time." Now, however, those flat types of readings have been given color and contour. Likewise, your time in the New Testament can really come to life when it is approached from many of the different angles mentioned here.

As much as I get joy from reflecting on the history of modern biblical interpretation, there is something that bothers me as well. We live in an age where it is very easy for Christians to be dogmatic about their own interpretations of the Bible. When someone questions or challenges those interpretations, massive disputes or arguments break out. Sometimes, churches divide. I cannot help but think that much of this is due to arrogance and ignorance. The arrogance prevents one from maintaining a posture of gracious and loving humility, while the ignorance prevents one from acknowledging the history of interpretation.

Different Methods to the Madness

The fact is, Christians need to be more circumspect. Christians who have a handle on the history of interpretation are much less likely to lay down quick and hateful judgments. As we have seen here, there is always more than one way to look at or understand a verse or passage. Different interpretive methods may either affirm or challenge one's conclusions but as Christians, we must remain in the mildly vulnerable state of being willing to hear the views of others—particularly those with whom we may disagree.

Finally, the point should be made that students, pastors, and laity need not fear Bible scholars. The majority of scholarly interpreters are not out to discredit or destroy the text. In fact, what we have seen here shows quite the opposite. Fresh and creative approaches to the text can inject new life into communities. Of course, we must guard against being novel for novelty's sake and we must take care not to ordain every interpretation as equally valid. Even so, we must also remain open to each new generation of God's people hearing the Bible anew in their various contexts.

I am only speculating, but perhaps the airport official who made the comment about being a chef had discerned the church's resistance to biblical scholarship. Maybe he had come from a background where he felt that the rigid literalism or fundamentalism of his faith community had held him captive as an interpreter. Perhaps he had grown tired of chewing on stale Sunday morning sermons. I suppose that if this was the case, there are many who can relate to him. If indeed that was his story, I wish I had said to him, "Why would I want to be a chef when I can feast on God's word? By the way, I want to give you an invitation to the party, here's a book for you."

3

From Paul's Gospel to the Four Gospels

http://michaelhalcomb.com/enteringthefray-gospels.html

AFTER MY GRANDFATHER PASSED away, the one possession of his that was handed down to me was his poetry collection. This collection, brought together in two tiny, very beat-up books, was written on the road during his travels as a truck driver. Since his death, I have read through these memoir-like books numerous times. One of my favorites is a poem he titled "Her Moving Moods."

In this piece, he marvels at my grandmother's ability to have the living room furniture rearranged every time he comes back home from a trip. In the last lines of the poem he humorously says, "She may be very clever in her decorating schemes, but they disturb my leisure and they haunt me in my dreams / I wish I had the nerve sometime when she is out of town, to place the furniture myself and nail the pieces down."

I love this poem; it reminds me of my grandparents and their distinct quirks and personalities. The irony in this piece also strikes me because Grandpa, who was always on the move, simply wanted stability when he returned home. Yet, Grandma, who was for the most part a stay-at-home wife, found that rearranging the furniture could break up the monotony of life. For her, the continual change of perspective was necessary while, for Grandpa, the rearranged furniture was often disorienting; he just wanted his chair to be in the same spot as it was when he left.

When we enter the fray of New Testament studies, we can often begin to feel like my grandpa: disoriented. For instance, did you know that even the order or arrangement of the New Testament has been debated for nearly two thousand years? Hearing this can be quite surprising, especially for new Christians. Then, it can be even more disorienting to hear New Testament experts suggest that the four Gospels (Matthew, Mark, Luke, and John) were not written first but instead, that Paul wrote some of the earliest documents.

Since we live in a world driven by calendars, a world where things are orderly and happen in order, we tend to think that the New Testament is also arranged in chronological order. To put it differently, we often think that because the four Gospels are placed at the beginning of the New Testament, they must have been written first. Research shows, however, that the apostle Paul wrote first. Some Bible scholars have suggested that Paul may have written within a decade after Jesus' crucifixion, whereas the Gospels were likely penned about twenty to forty years after Jesus' death.

If you are feeling a little disoriented from this rearrangement, take a moment and pause; you will be okay. Perhaps you are thinking, "How could the Gospels have come after Paul's letters when the letters focus so much on problems within churches, while the Gospels focus on Jesus' life, death, and resurrection? Christ came before the church, right? So, wouldn't it make more sense that the Gospels came before the letters?" These are all great questions. Even more, they are very important questions.

Entering the Fray

Certainly, it is true that Christ preceded the church. But that does not mean that the Gospels had to precede the letters. The fact is, while Paul's letters or epistles do focus a lot on various issues within the congregations that he writes to, those issues are always addressed in light of the person of Jesus. Paul's conclusions were always informed by the significance of the life, death, resurrection, and return of Jesus.

Thus, while at first glance there might seem to be a huge canyon that stands between the letters and the Gospels, that gap may actually be much smaller than we realize. Thankfully, scholars have devoted time to thinking about and discussing this issue. Listening in on their conversations may help relieve some of the tension of having had our mental furniture rearranged.

TUNING IN

It makes sense that in attempting to overhear the scholarly discussion about the movement from Paul's gospel to the Gospel accounts, the word "gospel" itself needs to be understood. What does the word gospel mean? Where does the word come from? A scholar by the name of Graham Stanton has done quite a bit of digging and has unearthed some interesting answers to these two questions.

In his book *Jesus and Gospel*, Stanton suggests that the English word "gospel" is the translation of the Greek compound word εὐαγγέλιον (*euangelion*). In this word, *eu* means "good" and *angelion* means "message" or "tidings." This is also where the English word evangelism comes from. But where does this Greek word come from?

Stanton, having looked at this word and its usage throughout ancient literature, including literature outside of the Bible, traces its origins back to the emperor cult of the Roman empire. Christians did not invent this word. Gospel was a word that emperors like Gaius used to describe their political ideals and goals.

Therefore, when Christians began using the term gospel, they were essentially borrowing it. Or, as Stanton suggests, they adopted it

> *Graham N. Stanton was born in 1940 and passed away in 2009. He earned his PhD at Westminster College and served as a professor at Cambridge University. Stanton wrote broadly on Jesus, the apostle Paul, and second-century literature. He received numerous awards and was highly esteemed among his peers.*

From Paul's Gospel to the Four Gospels

and assigned it new meaning. No longer was this term assigned to emperors, now it belonged to Jesus. In other words, when early Christians began using it, they did so as a challenge to the emperor cult; they were attempting to make a type of counter-cultural statement. As Stanton argues, for the earliest Christians, the word "gospel" was "honed in the teeth of the rival 'gospels' of imperial propaganda."[1] In Christian circles, then, it no longer referred to the good tidings of the emperor, but instead to Jesus Christ.

From this, we gather that when the earliest followers of Jesus first started using the word gospel, it referred to a body of content about Jesus. More particularly, it referred to an oral or spoken body of content about Jesus. It was only later, however, that this content began to be written down and preserved. Stanton suggests that around 150 CE, the middle of the second century, when the transition from scrolls to bound books (also called "codices") was taking place, the four distinct Gospel stories were melded together. It was only after this that these combined accounts became known collectively as "the Gospels."

Now that we have some orientation to the word gospel and the different meanings that it took on in its early stages, we are in a better position to explore the relationship between Paul's gospel and the Gospel accounts. So, let's turn our attention to this matter and see what scholars have been saying.

> Wayne A. Meeks was born in Aliceville, Alabama in 1932. He earned his PhD from Yale University and has taught, among other places, at Indiana, Emory, and Yale Universities respectively. He has published extensively in the area of NT studies and has remains active in the Presbyterian Church.

Nearly twenty years ago, a Bible scholar by the name of Wayne Meeks wrote a book titled *The Origins of Christian Morality*. In his book, Meeks made the following important statement: "We have not thought of Paul as a storyteller, for the Jesus stories of the Gospels are absent from his letters."[2] While this assertion seems true enough, it was not the final word on the matter. Meeks and many others began suggesting that while Paul's letters seemed to lack explicit stories about Jesus on the surface, just below the surface there is an underlying story.

Think about meeting a person for the first time. In that initial meeting, you typically get to see and know the individual in a surface-level sort of way. Yet, you realize that there is more to them; they are the product of a rich story. The various components of that underlying story have shaped who they are today. The more time you spend with that person, the more of their underlying story you will come to know. Judge them by their cover and you will miss out on hearing and sharing their life's story.

Meeks was suggesting that, for too long, Paul's readers have judged his letters by their covers; they have merely read them on the surface level. If we lean in and look more closely and listen more attentively, we can find an underlying story that has shaped Paul's own story. That story is none other than Jesus' story; it is the narrative of the Messiah. In the same way that a frame sits below the exterior of a car and functions as its structural base or substructure, the Jesus story that Paul tells sits below the surface of the words on the page and serves as its base; scholars refer to it as a narrative substructure.

Just like a car's frame, this below-the-surface story of Paul's has many nuts and bolts to it. This is the case because Jesus, while a simpleton on the surface, had a rich and complex background story to him. Paul dug deep into the inner-workings of Jesus' story and in turn, scholars have been digging deeply into the ways Paul does this. So, let me introduce you to a number of these scholars and what they have to say about Paul's use of Jesus' story.

TAKING NOTE

I should say from the start that for the sake of space and clarity I am forced to be quite selective about whom to introduce in this section. Ockham's Razor suggests that we should keep things short, sweet, and to the point. Perhaps the "first clue" to getting into the present conversation is the statement made in 1983 by professor Richard Hays (see biographical details below): "The narrative structure for which we are searching is the structure of the Gospel story, not of Paul's personal story."[3]

The search among Bible scholars for a core story in Paul's letters has been a long and trying one; even today, the case is not closed on this matter. The hunt is still on to discover parallels between the story of Christ that Paul presents and those that the Gospel accounts present. Now, before we jump the gun and try to connect the dots by say, chain-linking verses like a *Thompson's Chain Reference Bible*, we should

From Paul's Gospel to the Four Gospels

remind ourselves that such an approach will likely get us nowhere fast. A more sound approach would be to evaluate Paul's work on its own merit first and then to assess the ways in which we think the parallels or comparisons with the Gospels are functioning.

Paul and the Gospel authors are indeed engaged in conversation about Christ. But to hear the conversation we must allow each to speak with their own voice, otherwise we cut off the conversation and manipulate the texts into an awkward uniformity. Imagine taking a chapter from a novelist and a single article from a journalist, and attempting to reconstruct an entire, coherent belief system based upon them. Now, imagine looking at the full body of work that each author has done, one at a time, and then attempting to make parallels. Which approach would bear the most fruit? The second, of course!

This is the approach that many scholars have taken when it comes to studying the core of Paul's letters in relation to the Gospel. Yet, we have reached an important intersection here where we must ask the question: Is that core made up of many smaller chunks or is it one big chunk of its own? Or, the way scholars have asked the question, Does the core have one big, controlling story, that is, a metanarrative, or does the core consist of many little narratives?

> Nicholas T. Wright was born in 1948 in England. He received his PhD from Merton College (Oxford) and has served as the Bishop of Durham. Wright has written a number of highly influential books and has appeared on many major television networks as a historical and theological consultant.

While there is indeed a central, underlying story, it is helpful to attempt to separate this large core into smaller chunks so that we can see each of the pieces more clearly. This is the view that a number of researchers have taken as well, yet, with some nuances. For example, the respected scholar, N. T. Wright, has identified three pieces to this larger story: the story of God, the story of Israel, and the story of the world.[4] Wright suggests that Paul takes these three elements or micro-stories and presses them together to form the larger story, or macro-story, which is the story of Jesus.

Ben Witherington agrees with Wright for the most part. However, he sees four smaller stories: the story of a world gone wrong, the story of Israel in a world gone wrong, the story of Christ (which grows out of both Israel's story and God's own story), and the story of Christians (which arises out of all of the preceding stories).[5] If you compare

47

Entering the Fray

> Ben Witherington III was born in North Carolina in 1951. He earned his DPhil from Durham University (England) and is a prolific publisher. He has written a commentary on every book of the NT and appeared on many major television networks. Currently, he teaches at Asbury Theological Seminary.

> James D. G. Dunn was born in 1939 and studied at both Glasgow and Cambridge. He has become an incredibly influential scholar within the field of NT studies. He is widely published and perhaps best known for his work on the "new perspective" on Paul.

Wright's views with Witherington's, you see a lot of overlap as well as some distinct nuances.

Whereas Wright has emphasized a three-piece band and Witherington a four-piece band, another scholar, James Dunn has suggested a five-piece band. Dunn's five pieces are: the story of God and creation, the story of Israel, the story of Jesus, the story of Paul, and the story of believers.[6] Again, if you compare this view to the other views above, it is similar with some nuances. Now, before you conclude that this entire discussion is pointless because even the scholars cannot agree with one another, I would ask you to see it not so much as disagreement but rather, postive and healthy conversation. Each of these scholars is building on and interacting with the works of others, and the very fact that they can do this should be far more encouraging than discouraging.

> Richard Hays was born in 1948. He earned his PhD from Emory University in NT and has received a couple of honorary doctorates. He has an extensive lecturing and publishing record and has received numerous prestigious awards. Hays has also taught New Testament studies at Duke University.

Without a doubt, there are many voices that have gone unmentioned here that have contributed in very important ways to this discussion. One we should turn our attention to is Dr. Richard Hays. It is important to hear Hays out because his explanation, while similar to some of the ideas suggested above, seems to capture the core elements in the richest way yet. Hays identified three elements: Christ's death and resurrection (which, for Paul, is the climactic point of Israel's story), the future resurrection and judgment, and participation in God's transforming story (essentially a reenacting of Christ's pattern of faithful suffering and death).[7]

From Paul's Gospel to the Four Gospels

As you can see, this discussion is not too difficult to follow and even makes a lot of sense. I think it is also important to point out here that these scholars have not simply isolated themselves in an office somewhere, writing about matters totally detached from reality. In fact, as we shall see in just a moment, this conversation has very important implications for today's church.

> Michael Gorman was born in 1955. He received his MDiv and PhD from Princeton Theological Seminary. He is currently acting Raymond E. Brown Chair in Biblical Studies at St. Mary's Seminary in Baltimore. He is a well known and respected Pauline scholar who lectures and teaches in churches worldwide.

Before moving on, however, there are two more scholars that deserve to be heard. The first of these is Michael Gorman. In 2001, Gorman wrote something of a groundbreaking book, which he titled *Cruciformity: Paul's Narrative Spirituality of the Cross*.[8] As you can see, the term "cruciformity" is a hybrid or compound word, which solders together the concepts of crucifixion and conformity. In a nutshell, Gorman suggests to readers that according to Paul, the implications of Jesus' death—the event which puts his life and resurrection in proper perspective—are that believers' lives must conform to his pattern of faithful suffering and death. This, of course, echoes what the scholars mentioned above suggested.

Yet, Gorman presses this view out a bit differently than the others. He decides, based in large part on Philippians 2:6–11, that there are four fundamental elements giving shape to Paul's master story: cruciform faith, cruciform love, cruciform power, and cruciform hope. Certainly, Gorman is on to something here. In his book, he connects Paul's own life and story to the story of Jesus by way of what he refers to as a "cross-narrative pattern." More simply, this pattern is based on the example of Jesus, who was a suffering servant put to death on a Roman cross. Paul imitates Jesus and adopts this very same pattern for his own life. Yet, he does not stop there but rather, exhorts all believers to do the same. Bearing and embodying the cross is a core element of both Paul's gospel and the synoptic Gospels.

Gorman also emphasizes the concept of cruciform love. Again, this is rooted in the life and even more, the death, of Jesus the Messiah. In the same way that Jesus' life was patterned after self-emptying and self-giving, so too should the lives of believers be patterned in this manner. This is equally true of cruciform power, the idea that when one, like Christ, empties themselves in self-giving to the point of weakness, they find God's sustaining presence or power.

The fourth pattern, cruciform hope, focuses on the forward-looking aspects of Jesus' crucifixion and the cruciform lifestyle. Stated differently, Christ's crucifixion itself anticipated his resurrection; it anticipated hope. Thus, for those who have adopted the cruciform pattern(s) of Jesus, their present sufferings act as a type of prelude of hope to the future song of promised resurrection.

Now we are beginning to get to the heart of our original question about the relationship between Paul's writings and the Gospels. We are seeing that for Paul, this master story has at its core, the suffering Messiah and his death. It is only a small step from here to the Gospel accounts.

> Luke Timothy Johnson was born in 1943. A native of Park Falls, Wisconsin, he studied at Notre Dame Seminary (BA), St. Meinrad School of Theology (MDiv), Indiana University (MARS), and Yale University (PhD). He also served as a monk for nearly a decade. He has seven children and is married to Joy.

One more Bible scholar who may help us accomplish that step is Dr. Luke T. Johnson. I have in mind here, a particular book of his titled *The Real Jesus*.[9] There is much that could be said about this thought-provoking work of his but there is one matter in particular that further accentuates the discussion we are having here. Johnson argues, "The Gospels of Matthew and Luke develop the image of Jesus in a distinctive way. Yet each keeps the same fundamental image of Jesus as the suffering Son of Man."[10]

Johnson's observation, as you can see, fits well with what others like Richard Hays and Michael Gorman have suggested about Paul's writings. It would seem, then, that at least one answer to the question of how the movement from letters to Gospel accounts came about is found in the story pattern of Jesus' death. In retrospect, this might even seem obvious.

Now, before we end this chapter, one more word is in order, namely, a word about the "Christ Hymn" in Philippians 2:6–11. It is not by accident that Michael Gorman has structured a big part of his argument around this handful of verses. This is the case because what we have here may well be the earliest reflection of Christian literature (and liturgy!) in the New Testament canon.

In short, Philippians 2:6–11 conforms to the structure of an ancient Christian hymn, a song used in worship settings.[11] The very fact that it was used within the context of worship gatherings suggests that it would have been familiar and recognizable to a large number, if not all, of the earliest Christians. I draw attention to this because it seems to further substantiate our findings. In other words, to the first Christians, the canyon-like divide between Paul and the Gospels that some have envisioned would have been non-existent. For them, the same narrative pattern that was evident in worship was also evident in, and the basis of, both Paul's writings and the later Gospel accounts.

At the end of the day, all Christians should be grateful for the labor-intensive work that scholars have offered up. By thinking deeply and critically, these scholars have not only solved a riddle, they have been able to reconstruct a more accurate picture of Jesus, the Gospels, Paul and his letters, and also the earliest church. Of course, we have only scratched the surface here; we have not taken a deep plunge into all of the details but then again, that was neither the purpose of this chapter nor is it the aim of this book. Indeed, we are simply getting our feet wet by getting oriented to the discussion. This is a "first clue." Yet, the invitation is always there for you to do some more excavating.

TAKING ACTION

There are at least four significant implications that this scholarly discussion brings to bear on the lives of those who make-up Christ's church today. The first of these is that by appealing to this conversation, you can challenge the claims of those who have suggested that Paul created or invented Christianity. For example, in 1986 a book was released which bore the title *The Mythmaker: Paul and the Invention of Christianity*.[11] In that book, it is suggested that Paul, a man whom many Christians have been misled to believe was a devout Jew, was in fact a thoroughgoing Hellenist. It is precisely from this background that he borrows myths and legends to help set the invention of Christianity in motion.

While we have not yet discussed Paul's life, what we have heard discussed, that is, the cruciform pattern underlying Paul's letters, flies directly in the face of such claims. For starters, items like the Christ Hymn may suggest that a movement patterned after the cruciform life of Christ existed independent from Paul, lending credence to the suggestion that he did not just invent Christianity. The same could be said of the Gospel accounts, which share this same pattern and are attributed to at least four different authors.

Additionally, while there were ascetic movements in the ancient world, no religious movement, especially a movement the size of Christianity, can be found promoting a way of life patterned on crucifixion; that dog simply will not hunt. There is a certain unity and coherency to early Christianity and its origins, especially at the level of story, that penetrated every aspect of life—from hymns to letters to Gospels.

Now that you know this, you are in a better position to respond clearly and respectably and even with a certain level of sophistication, to claims that Christianity was simply invented. The pastor or Bible study leader who can help their congregation or class members hear these truths are sure to gain respect and appreciation. How bad does it make the church look when a pastor or leader is asked a question like this and instead of providing an answer, the pastor simply shrugs the question off, acting as if it is unimportant, tries to explain but falls all over his or her words, or appears to have never even thought about it?

Another payoff of listening in on this scholarly dialogue is that you now have at least one way to accurately measure the texts of the Bible against other ancient sources. For example, many of us have seen the holiday television specials that attempt to debunk the New Testament or prove that some other ancient text deserves the same status as the canon itself, or the various texts which make up the canon. Certain skeptics continue to overemphasize the gnostic Gospels, such as the Gospel of Thomas or the Gospel of Peter, and now you can confidently show why it is that such texts should not be included: They do not bear the underlying cruciform pattern of the canonical New Testament texts. When the big religious holidays such as Christmas and Easter come around, people seem to become instantly intrigued by such matters. As a Christian who needs to be prepared in season and out of season to give an answer regarding matters of faith, you will now be more equipped to do so.

This relates to another issue, a critique that has been leveled repeatedly by naysayers of the Christian faith: Since the Gospels were written twenty to sixty years after Jesus died, there is no way they can be accurate, they must have been changed. Such a claim, however, holds no water. We could appeal to the fact that when the Bible is set beside other ancient writings, in terms of manuscript evidence, there is really no comparison; the New Testament blows every other ancient text out of the water in this regard. However, that line of reasoning only gets us so far and may not carry much weight with questioners. Instead, by hearing this scholarly discussion, what we can now appeal to is the fact that within early Christianity there was a unifying thematic pattern that provided coherency throughout all of its writings, religious practices, and ethics. The cruciform pattern is precisely what provided consistency within the Christian movement not only with the first sixty or so years, but even to this very day.

Finally, a very practical result of eavesdropping on this scholarly discussion is that as a believer, it should influence your commitment to Christ. More pointedly, scholars have issued a call for Christians in this age to get back to the roots, so to speak, and to begin re-patterning their lives and their congregations after the cruciform pattern of Christ. For the first Christians, in whose songs, stories, and letters we find an intentional focus on a cruciform way of life, this was the core of their faith. This should be no less true of us.

4

What Do You Mean by "Synoptic Problem"?

http://michaelhalcomb.com/enteringthefray-synoptic.html

AT A CHURCH WHERE I once served as a minister, it was tradition to invite a musical group to the annual holiday banquets. Being a rural church, bluegrass and southern gospel were the genres of choice. Personally, the groups I enjoyed the most were of the *a cappella* stripe. Perhaps this is because I have always marveled at the ways in which people can relate to one another through music. I have often noticed a connection between musical harmonizing and real relational harmony.

Indeed, there is something incredibly rich and appealing about harmony. Whether it is musical, relational, or when everything in life

What Do You Mean by "Synoptic Problem"?

seems to be fitting together just right, harmony has a calming peace about it. When things are in harmony things are in order; order gives us a sense of stability and a certain level of comfort. When things are not in harmony, life's tune can be painful to deal with.

Early in church history, in the second century CE to be precise, a man by the name of Tatian sensed a certain amount of discomfort when he encountered the Gospel accounts of Matthew, Mark, Luke, and John. For him, engaging these four different stories was something like listening to four terrible singers attempting to harmonize with one another—it was brutal. So, he decided that he would take these four discordant Gospels and boil them down into one. He called his work *Diatessaron*, which is simply a Greek compound word where *dia* means "by" and *tessaron* means "four"—thus, one book by way of four.

In the third century CE another thinker, Ammonius, did something similar and in the fourth, Eusebius picked up the baton. Augustine, from the fifth century, can also be included on this ledger. So, what was it about the four Gospel accounts that these readers found so bothersome? What was the problem? In a nutshell, the issue had to do with why on the one hand, the Gospels of Matthew, Mark, and Luke were so similar, yet on the other hand, they were so different. The problem, so to speak, was a harmony problem. To put it in musical terms, we might ask: Why do these Gospels often sing in tune with one another, but at other times, sing out of tune with one another?

That question is the focus of this chapter. For the last several hundred years scholars have referred to this as the "synoptic problem." The "synoptic Gospels" are Matthew, Mark, and Luke—John is excluded because when set alongside the former three, there is little literary similarity. As you probably already know, to give a synopsis just means to place items side-by-side with the intent of comparing and/or contrasting them.

Thus, the so-called synoptic problem is rooted in placing these three texts together and looking at them comparatively and contrastively. Yet, the very question that needs to be asked up front is: Is there *really* a problem? As we explore this topic we will meet a number of researchers who have much to say about it. I think that you if you listen with intent, this scholarly conversation has the ability to deeply enrich your faith-life. So, let's tune in.

Entering the Fray

TUNING IN

One of the biggest charges leveled against Christianity within the last few centuries has had to do with the trustworthiness of the New Testament. The claim that the Bible is full of contradictions is a perennial argument raised by skeptics to knock the legs out from under the Christian faith. For the naysayers who put forth such challenges, the synoptic Gospels are something akin to a breeding ground of contradictions.

So, we need to see right from the start that this is not simply an issue that scholars have dreamed up. No, this is an issue for skeptics too. For this reason alone, it should be an issue that concerns all Christians. I want to draw attention to the fact that I used the term "issue" in the preceding sentences purposefully. I did so because it is misleading in light of the evidence to say there is actually a "problem," but there certainly is an issue that needs to be addressed.

Okay, enough beating around the bush; it is time to get to the heart of the matter. The best place to start is with Luke, who explicitly mentions other sources or resources. In Lk 1:1, the text says that prior to writing up his own account, Luke knew of many others who had sought to do the same thing. He goes on to say in 1:2 that many eyewitnesses of Jesus' life and many servants of the gospel were taking the initiative to pass on their knowledge to others. Some, he says in 1:1, were attempting to gather or compile knowledge from these various sources into one central location. Then, in 1:3, Luke says that this seemed like a good idea to him also and so, he followed suit.

There are a number of significant things that these remarks convey, but two deserve our direct attention here. First, Luke, like others, felt it necessary to write an account of Jesus' life, and second, Luke was aware of other sources or resources that were already in existence prior to his own document. In short, Luke was not only familiar with other sources/resources but modeled his own writing project on the approaches that others had been using, namely, compiling stories about Jesus into a single location.

Well, to what sources might Luke be referring? Additionally, what sources might he be modeling his own project after? For many, this is where the issue starts to get a bit hairy. Part of the reason for this is that a veritable smorgasbord of answers has been suggested. Yet, there is no need to get stuck in the swamp of suggestions; there are a handful of ideas that have gained prominence, and having a good grasp on those will help put us in a position to better educate believers and skeptics alike.

What Do You Mean by "Synoptic Problem"?

TAKING NOTE

The so-called synoptic problem is really, as we have seen, more of a synoptic issue or synoptic question that is concerned with the similarities and differences between Matthew, Mark, and Luke. The ongoing discussion between scholars has to do, in large part, with the idea that the elements of these stories are alike and unalike because they share some of the same resources but use their own distinct sources as well. An analogy may prove helpful here.

When going through my PhD program, prior to taking my final exams, one of my requirements was to submit a reading list consisting of one hundred books. Of these one hundred, the seminary had already chosen thirty for me, they referred to these as the "core thirty." This meant that every New Testament student had to include these core thirty books in their list. In other words, we shared at least thirty of the same sources.

Yet, each student was required to choose seventy sources that they thought would help prepare them both for their exams and their dissertation writing. Therefore, each student had similar and dissimilar resources. If asked the same question on an exam, there would surely be some overlap in our answers. Yet, there would also be differences because not only did we select different sources, we are individuals who think and write differently.

Scholars of the Synoptics are interested in which sources each of the Gospel writers used; the answer to this "synoptic question" resides in the sources. Intense researching, careful reading, and creative reasoning have all borne a number of fruitful suggestions. Some bear more fruit than others and some are certainly more plausible than others. So, let's pick a handful of the ripest fruits from the giving tree of scholarship and sink our teeth into them.

> *Burnett H. Streeter was born in 1874 in London. He received his PhD at Queen's College (Oxford) and later became a professor at Oxford University. His works on the synoptic Gospels, ancient manuscript traditions, and text-critical matters have all been widely influential in the field of biblical studies.*

Probably the most suggested answer to the synoptic question is what is known as the "two-document theory" (or alternatively, the "four-source theory"). One of the foundational and foremost advocates of this idea was a scholar by the name of B. H. Streeter who presents this theory in his work *The Four Gospels: A Study of Origins*.[1]

Entering the Fray

I find it easiest to understand the logic of this view when it is broken down in segments. The two-document theory begins with a timeline, which spans a period of about forty to seventy years:

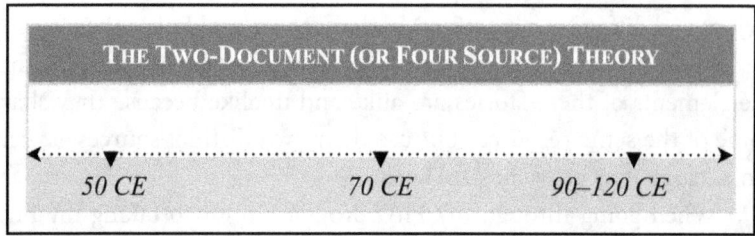

These are the relative time periods attributed to the Gospels and the resources used to help shape them. Streeter suggested that Mark was written first, somewhere around 50 CE. During this time period he also thought that another source existed, which was essentially a collection of stories, teachings, and sayings of Jesus all gathered into one location. German scholars referred to this with the very vague and general term "Quelle" (German for "source"). This was later abbreviated as "Q." (For a different view on the origins of the term "Q," however, see note 1 mentioned above.) Thus, Mark and Q were written around the same time, as the chart below suggests.

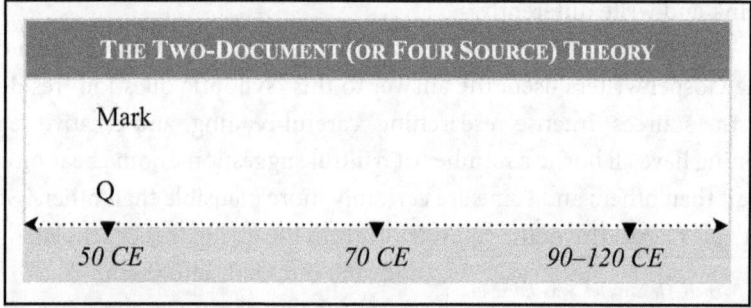

As time passed, other writers such as Luke and Matthew undertook the task of drawing up their own accounts of Jesus' story. Their projects were completed around 70 CE, that is, a decade or two after Mark and Q. One of Streeter's main reasons for placing Mark first was that both Matthew and Luke include almost all of Mark's content—about 90–95% in fact. Yet, as we shall see in just a moment, the key word there is "almost."

What Do You Mean by "Synoptic Problem"?

THE TWO-DOCUMENT (OR FOUR SOURCE) THEORY
Mark   Matthew
Q   Luke
◄┄┄▼┄┄┄┄┄┄▼┄┄┄┄┄┄▼┄┄┄►
50 CE   70 CE   90–120 CE

In a very general sense, both Matthew and Luke follow Mark's storyline. In essence, they simply copied his content, with nuances here and there. In antiquity the modern concept of plagiarism was practically non-existent, which meant that copying and editing was not an issue. In fact, as Luke suggests, the goal was to share the stories and details so that they could be copied and preserved. Thus, it is safe to conclude that Matthew and Luke used Mark as one of their major sources and they did so without any hang-ups about plagiarism.

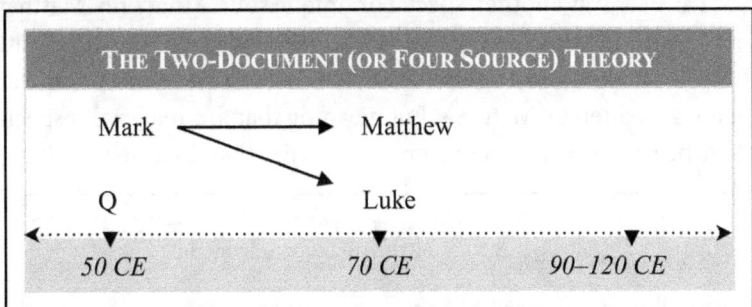

So, Mark accounts for many of the similarities that exist between the Synoptics. However, there are parts of the story where Matthew and Luke are similar, that are not found in Mark's version. For example, you probably know that Mark's Gospel has no story about Jesus' birth. Yet, both Matthew and Luke do tell about Jesus' birth.

Streeter was interested in the question of how Matthew and Luke could have ended up with similar content, when that content was not found in Mark. For Streeter, the answer was found in another resource, a general source that has come to be known as Q. Therefore, in addition to Matthew and Luke using Mark, they also both drew material from Q.

Entering the Fray

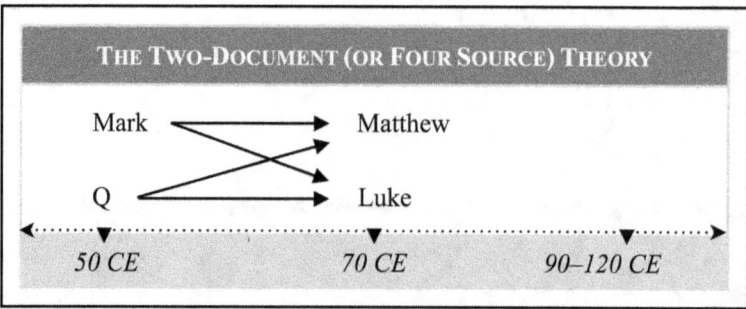

Still, this answer was insufficient for Streeter. Why? Well, despite all of the similarities between Matthew and Luke, which could be accounted for by Mark and Q, there remained some differences between them. Therefore, the question now was how exactly to account for these dissimilarities. For example, neither Mark nor Q included Jesus' famous Sermon on the Mount in their accounts. Luke did not include it either. However, Matthew decided to include it in his. But if Matthew did not get the Sermon on the Mount from Mark, Q, or Luke, where did he get it? The answer was another, special or unique source that only Matthew was aware of. For this reason, this source has been given the generic title "Special Matthew," or in abbreviated form "Special M"—not to indicate that it was written by Matthew, but meaning that this material is special *to* Matthew's Gospel, written sometime earlier than Matthew itself.

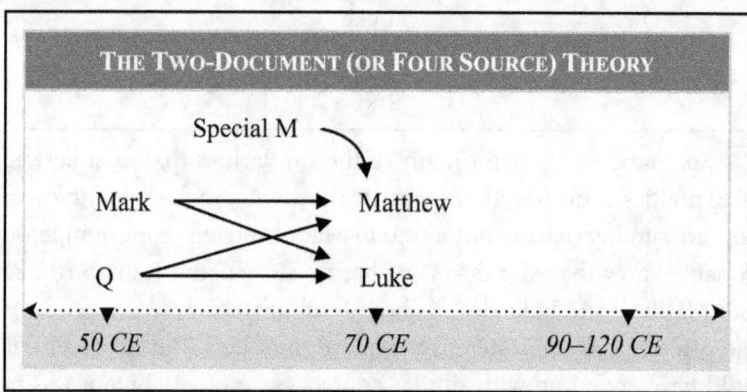

There is at least one more portion of this theory that we must attempt to make sense of, namely the material in Luke's account that is unique to Luke. To put it differently, if the content of Matthew that is only found in Matthew is attributed to Special M, then what about the unique content of Luke? For instance, neither Mark, nor Q, nor Matthew

What Do You Mean by "Synoptic Problem"?

included Jesus' famous Sermon on the Plain in their accounts. However, Luke did. Therefore, this material unique to Luke must have come from somewhere. Can you guess the name of the suggested source? If you said "Special Luke" or "Special L" you are right! Like Special M, it is suggested that Special L was in existence before Luke wrote.

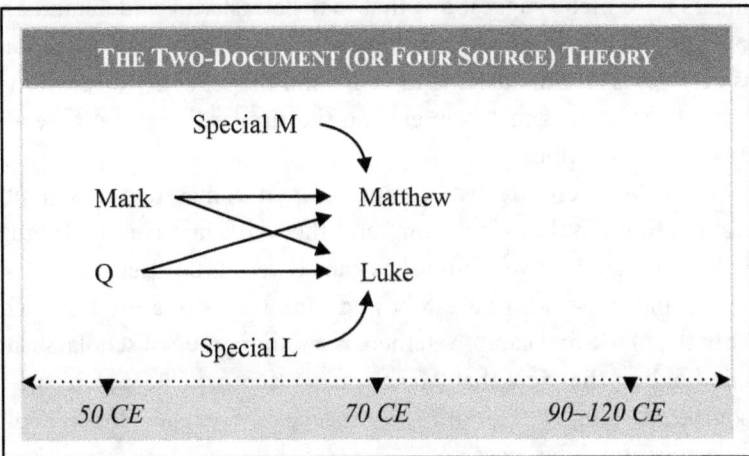

As for the Gospel of John, it is all but left out of this conversation. That is attributed to a number of things, such as the fact that it is so different in arrangement, contains material not found in any of the Synoptics or their related sources, and because it is believed to have been written at a much later date. Therefore, it has no bearing on the synoptic question.

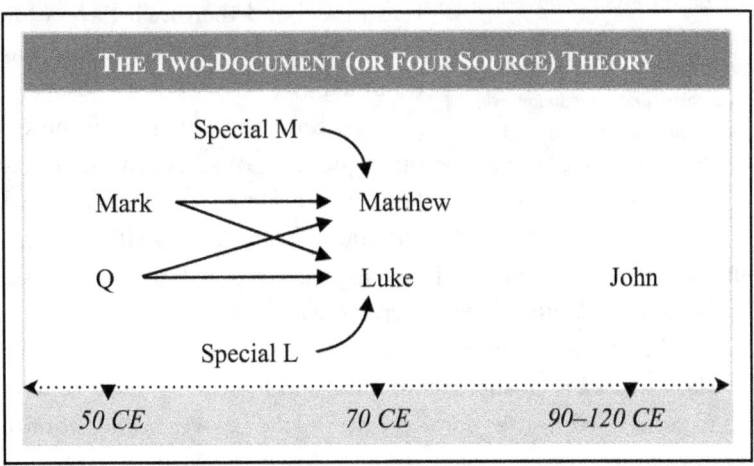

Entering the Fray

If you were able to digest this piece of data, then the other pieces of related inforation should be no problem. In all reality, Streeter's idea is not too difficult to follow and the logic, at least on the surface, seems quite sound. Perhaps this is why so many researchers have adopted it as their own means of answering the synoptic question. Even so, other scholars have made suggestions that may be easier to understand and more plausible. The important thing to realize as we explore these various theories is that the driving force behind the scholarly discussion is the hunt for sources that help explain the similarities and differences between the Synoptics.

Basically, there are two camps when it comes to the synoptic question: The Matthew-first camp and the Mark-first camp. (There is a Luke-first camp as well, but it has gained very little attention.) B. H. Streeter and those who have followed him are, as one might expect, within the Mark-first camp. Yet, there is another group of scholars who, while holding the view that Mark was written first, do not resort to resources such as Q, Special M, or Special L to explain the synoptic similarities and differences.

Known first as the "Farrer theory" because it was developed by Bible scholar Austin Farrer, this approach is now also known as the "Farrer-Goulder-Goodacre theory." This is the case because researchers Michael Goulder and Mark Goodacre have, in their own ways, adopted and modified this view. Let's start with Farrer's model and then we'll have a look at how Goulder and Goodacre have modified it.

> Austin M. Farrer was born in 1904 in Hampstead (London, England). He studied at St. Paul's School in London. He was a prominent and often controversial Anglican theologian and churchman who served as a deacon, priest, and chaplain. He and the theologian C. S. Lewis shared a close friendship.

Within the discussion on the synoptic question, Austin Farrer is perhaps best known for his concept of "Mark-without-Q," or "Mark-without-other-sources" for that matter. This idea was first promoted in his 1955 essay "On Dispensing With Q."[2] For Farrer, the answer to the synoptic question is to be found within the Synoptics themselves. His explanation is that Mark wrote his Gospel account first and then, Matthew who wrote second proceeded to use Mark's story. Finally, Luke was the last of the Synoptics to be written; Luke used both Mark and Matthew as the image below illustrates.

What Do You Mean by "Synoptic Problem"?

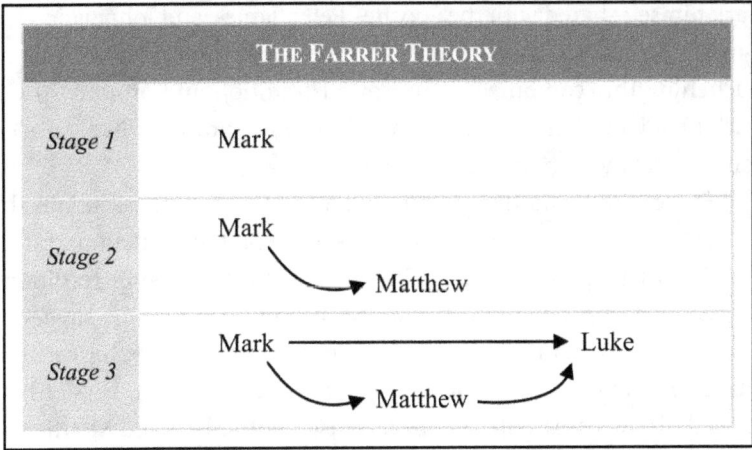

As you can see, when it comes to processes and charts, Farrer's idea seems much easier to take in than Streeter's. However, we should consider that there is more going on here than initially meets the eye.

Michael Goulder recognized this when he was developing an answer, and his example of attention to detail is a model for us all. In elaborating on Farrer's thoughts, some of Goulder's main contributions came in the areas of dating the Gospels and drawing attention to traditions that he believed influenced them.³ Let's look at several of these issues in turn.

> Michael D. Goulder was born in 1927. He was educated at Trinity College (Oxford) where he studied under Austin Farrer. He was awarded an honorary doctorate from Trinity College during a lecture series on the synoptic Gospels and Q. He spent most of his academic career at the University of Birmingham.

In terms of dating, one of the major differences between Goulder's ideas and Streeter's ideas is that for Goulder, the Gospel accounts are all written later. However, Goulder suggests that it is precisely these later dates that allow time for a variety of traditions about Jesus to develop. The term "traditions" seems to refer to largely oral sources in existence prior to and during the time when the canonical Gospel accounts were composed.

We might imagine a core, foundational set of stories being shared orally prior to any of the Gospels being written. This group of core stories may be referred to as the "Jesus tradition." At some point prior to 70 CE, Mark, who was aware of this tradition, decided to compile these loose stories into one large, coherent story. Thus, the much broader Jesus tradition became narrower within the Markan tradition, which

Entering the Fray

Mark himself shared with the apostles Peter, James, and John, who were living in Jerusalem. These church leaders spent time crystallizing and sharpening this combined or narrowed tradition and around 70 CE, Mark finally put it into writing. Mark's account, however, likely underwent several more crystallization periods.

In fact, when Matthew wrote around 80 CE, he was essentially doing just that—crystallizing and/or expanding on the Markan narrative. Goulder believed that Matthew did not use other sources or traditions, only Mark and his own creativity and ingenuity. In fact, he suggested that Matthew structured his account around a type of worship or liturgical cycle. Finally, Luke wrote his Gospel around 90 CE. Like Matthew, he used his own creativity. Yet, he also used both Mark and Matthew in conjunction with the Hebrew Bible or Old Testament. Luke may well have been aware of the traditions that preceded Mark's written account.

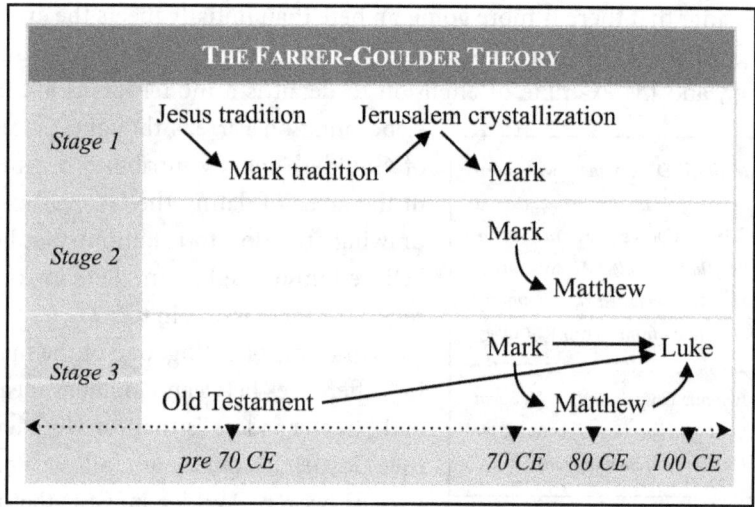

Without a doubt there is much to commend when it comes to Goulder's elaborations. While he does actually posit the use and existence of other sources in the writing of the Synoptics, unlike Q, Special M, or Special L, they are not influential—with the exception of Luke's use of the Old Testament—in the writing process. Mark Goodacre has built upon the suggestions of Farrer and Goulder, offering some of his own fresh insights. While much could be said in the way of Goodacre's contributions, that which is arguably his most significant contribution will receive attention here.

What Do You Mean by "Synoptic Problem"?

In the spirit of Farrer's "On Dispensing With Q," Mark Goodacre has mounted the largest and most recent assault on the concept of Q.[4] He has written numerous works that challenge the bulk of B. H. Streeter's hypothesis. Where he does align with Streeter is that he agrees that Mark wrote first. But beyond that, there is little similarity. For Goodacre, Q does not exist.

> Mark Goodacre was born in 1967 in Leicestershire, England. He earned his DPhil at the University of Oxford. He has taught at the University of Birmingham (England) and also Duke University (North Carolina). Goodacre has published extensively on the synoptic Gospels and Q.

This is incredibly significant because it dethrones what has likely been the dominant view taught within seminaries (and therefore churches) over the last several generations. It also challenges an entire branch of scholarship that has been taken up with Q research. For starters, Goodacre reminds readers that Q is an entirely hypothetical document; an actual manuscript or fragment has never been seen or heard of. Even more, Q creates many more problems than it solves.

> John S. Kloppenborg was born in 1951. He earned his PhD from the University of St. Michael's College. He has taught in a number of academic institutions throughout the world, with much of that time being spent at the University of Toronto (Canada). He is a general editor of the IQP (International Q Project).

This flies in the face of the work of scholars like John Kloppenborg, whose scholarly career has been based around Q.[5] Kloppenborg and others have not only reconstructed Q—which has been edited several times—but they have also reconstructed an entire ancient community that they imagine to have produced and used Q. Again, nowhere in ancient literature and nowhere in archaeological findings has any such thing ever been proven—there is not one shred of evidence for this. Goodacre, then, is one of the leading voices against Q and the concept of Mark-first in a Mark-without-Q world.

It was mentioned above that there are basically two camps when it comes to the synoptic question: the Matthew-first camp and the Mark-first camp. Besides dividing these groups on the bases of Matthean priority (Matthew first) or Markan priority (Mark first), we can also divide them up between ancient and modern thinkers. Whereas the Mark-first discussion was borne out of the context of the nineteenth century, and

65

therefore consisted of only modern scholars, the Matthew-first discussion can be traced all the way back to St. Augustine in the fifth century CE.

A quote from Augustine himself will set us about in the right direction: "Therefore the four evangelists who are well-known to the whole world and who are four in number . . . are said to have been written in this order: first Matthew, then Mark, thirdly Luke, lastly John. . . . it is believed that Matthew wrote in Hebrew and the others in Greek"[6] (*The Harmony of the Gospels*). Additionally, Augustine suggested that Mark was the abbreviator of Matthew's Gospel. Augustine's theory, which has the backing of early church history behind it and which appears—on the surface at least—to be the simplest of all suggestions is depicted in the diagram below.

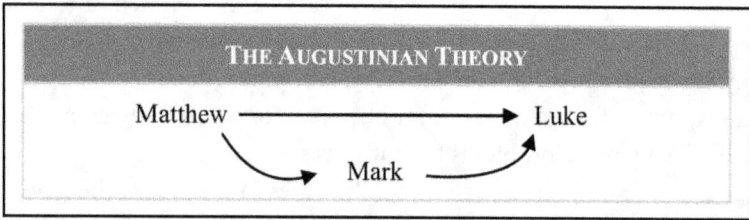

It is not the case that Augustine developed this idea. It is the case, however, that he was the first to attempt to give a type of scholarly explanation for it. Indeed, both Irenaeus and Origen before him held this view. What is of great significance for the synoptic question has to do not only with the fact that Matthew was claimed to have written first, but two of the points used to substantiate this: that Matthew was written in Hebrew (or more particularly, Aramaic), and that each of the names attributed to the Gospels are associated with the persons who actually wrote them.

Both of these arguments have faced tremendous challenges. In terms of the first point, no Aramaic text of the Gospels has been recovered from the first-century CE. The overwhelming majority of proof based on manuscript evidence is that the original Gospels were all composed in Greek. Further, because the Gospels were not known with names until well into the second-century CE, it cannot be proven—by way of manuscript evidence or earlier tradition—that the Synoptics (and John) can, without a doubt, be traced back and assigned to the names that were later attached to them.

What Do You Mean by "Synoptic Problem"?

If these two proofs alone are not enough to persuade someone that Augustine's theory is mistaken, the more strenuous and difficult part would be to explain why Mark chose to delete so much of Matthew's story, why Mark's writing style is not more refined, why Mark tends to contain many of the more difficult wording and ideas, and further, why Luke would tend to copy or follow the more problematic text of Mark over and against a smoother, more polished copy of Matthew.

> Johann J. Griesbach was born in 1745 in Butzbach, Germany. He earned several degrees and spent the majority of his career at the University of Jena. In 1976, two hundred years after the publication of his Greek synopsis of the Gospels, scholars remembered him by hosting the J. J. Griesbach Bicentenary Colloquium.

These and other issues found a modern advocate willing to take them up, in the scholar Johann J. Griesbach.[7] Like Augustine before him, he was not the first to propose his view but was the first to really popularize it in his era. One of the biggest differences between the Griesbach and Augustinian views, however, is that Griesbach chose to depart from the order that Augustine espoused. For him, Matthew wrote first, then Luke, and then Mark.

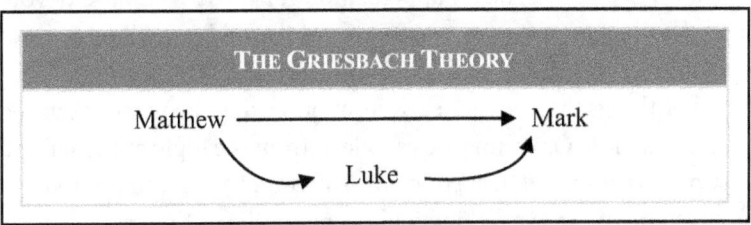

One of the biggest problems that this theory faces, however, is why Mark, which is the shortest of all the Gospels, would on the one hand delete so many of the stories from these accounts and then take the leftovers and expand them. Such questions have been raised by Robert Stein, who has striven to refute such views, especially by contending that a late dating of Mark is simply implausible. For Stein, Mark was written in Rome in the 60s CE, by John Mark, who based at least some of his account on the eyewitness testimony of Peter.[8]

> Robert H. Stein was born in 1935. He earned his doctorate from Princeton Theological Seminary. He has written many works on the Gospels and Jesus. He has taught in a number of institutions including Bethel Theological Seminary (Minnesota) and Southern Baptist Theological Seminary (Kentucky).

Entering the Fray

TAKING ACTION

If we return to the beginning analogy of harmony after having surveyed the leading scholarly answers to the synoptic question, it might appear that Bible scholars are not simply out of tune but singing completely different songs. To be sure, we can choose to hear these discussions in a negative way. However, there is another option: We can choose to hear them as band mates playing different instruments but having the same goal of mastering the song. Even more, we can come to the realization that they are inviting us to join the band, to hone our skills and to make fruitful contributions.

In addition to helping readers understand the synoptic question, I also hope that you have been able to recognize that scholars, who have given so much of their lives to attempting to clarify issues surrounding the Gospels, are not evil people trying to distort or destroy the Bible. They were not attempting to overturn the church or church history. Deep scholarship often asks questions of and challenges deeply held consensuses with Christian circles, but that does not necessitate an unhealthy reaction or response from churchgoers. There should, at some level or another, be an appreciation for those who have devoted themselves to attempting to make sense of the Bible's intricacies.

There are some things that we can learn from the discussion itself and other things that we can learn from observing the persons engaged in the discussion. One thing we can glean from the topic of the synoptic question is that too often skeptics who attempt to use it to discredit the New Testament are overstating and oversimplifying the issues.

The fallacy of exaggeration or oversimplification suggests to us that these critics have not done their homework; if you need proof, check YouTube! By being out-of-the-loop of this discussion, they tend to be reductionistic to the point of overlooking the connection between the Gospels and all of the expert research conducted on them. Having listened to what scholars have suggested, we can offer several plausible answers, all of which are likely stronger than their pretentious claims.

For the pastor or Bible study leader who is confronted by the person whose trust in the New Testament may appear to be threatened by the differences in the Synoptics, taking the time to show them a few plausible answers may bring them a sense of peace. One great resource worth pointing laity toward is William R. Farmer's book *The Gospel of Jesus: The Pastoral Relevance of the Synoptic Problem*. Here, Farmer shows how the synoptic question has immediate implications for Christian beliefs about Jesus' death, the origin of the church, saying the Lord's Prayer, God's love for the poor, and a number of other significant issues.

From observing the overall conversation one of the things that we can learn is that just like the Synoptics themselves, there is room for difference among God's people. In fact, there is a profound beauty in the freedom of being able to having room to question, explore, and offer different points of view. Of course, this is always done with an eye toward orthodox core beliefs as well as the preservation of the church's unity.

Finally, we must not overlook the fact that the scholars we have been listening to have provided the church and academy with a good example of the value of in-depth and close readings of the New Testament. The invitation is there for us to follow suit and to participate. Approaching the Bible with interpretive integrity and creativity has the potential to shed further light on discussions like this one. Who knows, if you put your mind to it, maybe you could be the one to provide a definitive answer to the synoptic question!

5

Did Jesus Try to Keep a Messianic Secret?

http://michaelhalcomb.com/enteringthefray-secret.html

THROUGHOUT MY YEARS OF pastoring and teaching in the church, some of the biblical passages I have seen laity most struggle with are those in which Jesus commands persons not to tell anyone about him. For evangelicals and missionaries in particular, passages like Mk 1:40–45 or 8:23 are not only challenging, but even bewildering. And why, after the transfiguration, does Jesus to forbid his disciples to tell others about the things they saw (Mk 9:9)? New Christians, many of whom have come to faith through some sort of evangelistic outreach or special event, often believe that they are expected to begin immediately replicating the evangelistic trends that invited them in. However, when they open the New Testament and find Jesus forbidding any kind of talk about his identity, disequilibrium sets in.

TUNING IN

For a few hundred years scholars have been attempting to make sense of the seemingly contradictory expectations of the Great Commission (Mt 28:16–20) and Jesus' demands to maintain silence (e.g., Mk 8:23). On the one hand, the Great Commission is evangelistic and missional in nature and on the other hand, silence about Jesus seems non-evangelistic or non-missional in nature. In this chapter, we will put our ears up to the doors behind which this scholarly dialogue has been taking place. We will hear from a host of important researchers who have weighed in on the issue of the Messiah's desire to keep his identity on the down-low. We would all do well to listen closely, for some of the implications may come to bear directly on our own faith. We might even recognize the roots of some of our deeply held views about Jesus.

TAKING NOTE

Attempting to understand who Jesus was and who Jesus perceived himself to be has long been of interest to scholars. As we shall see in the next chapter on the "historical Jesus," many suggestions have been made in this regard. It is worth pointing out here, however, that to those standing outside of these conversations among biblical researchers, it might appear that scholars have had something of an identity crisis on Jesus' behalf; they've had a hard time deciding who he was!

Which of Jesus' identity markers were the most prominent? Was he first and foremost a Messiah, Son of Man, servant, Son of God, teacher, prophet, philosopher, rabbi, sage, or king? Or, was his primary identity rooted in something else? Whatever that main identity was, why did he mandate silence about it?

Perhaps one of the best places to start when attempting to hear this conversation is with the research of Wilhelm Wrede. In 1901, Wrede published a book titled *The Messianic Secret*, which would prove widely influential for many years to come.[1] In sum, he argued

Entering the Fray

> F. G. E. Wilhelm (or William) Wrede was born in 1859 in Hanover. He grew up a Lutheran and like his father, served in Lutheran ministries. Wrede both studied and taught in Göttingen and was a member of the History of Religions School, which consisted of many prominent theologians of the 1800–1900s.

that Jesus himself did not believe that he was a messianic or divine figure, but the early church came to believe he was both. Thus, Wrede became interested in how the first church arrived at these conclusions, when Jesus himself had not shared them.

Though he believed Mark was the first of the Gospel accounts to have been written, Wrede suggested that at some point prior to the composition of Mark another tradition had been floating around. The creator of this earlier tradition came up with the idea that, despite the fact that Jesus never identified himself as a messianic or divine figure, he privately or secretly thought of himself as such. Before Mark wrote his story, according to Wrede, he had become aware of this tradition that had been floating around. Even more, it became the framework that Mark adopted and used to shape the whole of his narrative.

To substantiate this thesis, Wrede compared Mark to the other Gospel accounts. As far as Matthew and Luke, he noted some differences but it was the contrast with John that stuck out to him. For Wrede, John was the last of the Gospel accounts to be written. Further, the major difference between John and Mark was that in John's story, Jesus is open to sharing his messianic identity whereas in Mark, Jesus is not. So, Wrede's question was: If Mark was the first to write his story about Jesus and in that story Jesus is keeping his identity a secret, while John is the last to write his story about Jesus and in it Jesus is open about his identity, how do we account for this?

The answer rests, to a great degree, in discerning the author's intent. For Mark, the earliest Gospel author, the point was to stress the personhood of Jesus *prior* to the crucifixion and resurrection. This time period was marked with confusion among Jesus' followers and the wider populace about Jesus' precise identity. Scholars have often referred to this pre-resurrection time as the pre-Easter period; a point in time when Jesus existed without all of the church's post-resurrection theology hoisted upon him.

In contrast, John's narrative is patently from a post-Easter perspective. John is very theological in form and content and he desires

Did Jesus Try to Keep a Messianic Secret?

to stress the personhood of Jesus *after* the crucifixion and resurrection; he is viewing Jesus through a resurrection-shaded lens. We might say that he is looking at the life of Jesus in retrospect. The things that Jesus said and did prior to his death that had previously made no sense, now make sense in light of the resurrection. Thus, it was over time, through a process of slow development, that Jesus came to be recognized as a messianic figure in the earliest days of the church.

> Adolf Jülicher was born in 1857 in Falkenberg, Germany and grew up as a Lutheran. He studied at the University of Berlin and later spent most of his academic career teaching at the University of Marburg. Jülicher is perhaps best remembered by scholars for his rejection of allegorical interpretations of parables.

Despite his groundbreaking research, Wrede's thesis was not readily accepted by everyone. Some adopted portions of it but called other sections into question. Quickly, debate ensued. In the late 1800s and the early 1900s, a scholar named Adolf Jülicher, who had a major research interest in parables, took a middle-ground approach.[2] Jülicher, like his contemporary Albert Schweitzer, drew attention to the fact that Jesus' parables in Mark's story contained a tint of secrecy to them. However, where Jülicher differed with Schweitzer was in his contention that Jesus' parables could be traced back to a Jesus who knew that he was indeed a messianic figure. Just as well, for Jülicher, Mark's post-Easter story could also be traced back to the real, historical figure of Jesus.

> Albert Schweitzer was born in 1875 in Germany and was raised a Lutheran. He was broadly educated and earned his doctorate from the University of Strasbourg. He was a major contributor to historical Jesus studies but perhaps best remembered for leaving his life of biblical scholarship to be a medical doctor in rural Africa.

Albert Schweitzer, who had published on the messianic secret theory in 1901—on the same day as Wrede, in fact—proposed a different theory regarding Jesus' self-understanding. Schweitzer believed that Jesus' secrecy went beyond his potential messianic identity. Jesus also kept secrets about suffering and God's kingdom. Jesus' means of keeping these three secrets was by referring to himself not as the suffering Messiah of God's kingdom, but as the "Son of Man."

As the Son of Man, Jesus believed that he was an end-of-the-age prophet who was sent to usher in God's return, particularly at his death. With this at the fore of his mind, over time he grew anxious, and in an

Entering the Fray

effort to force God's hand in bringing his kingdom sooner, he went up to Jerusalem, as Mark's story suggests, "solely in order to die there."[3] Therefore, according to Schweitzer, Wrede was wrong to suggest that the secrecy motif is rooted in the story itself; it is not a literary theme that holds the story together. Rather, Jesus' secrecy has its origins in his concept of the end-of-the-age or the "eschaton." Jesus was an anxious eschatological prophet who, while disclosing his identity privately to his disciples, was quick to keep others on the outs lest they interrupt his plan to usher in God's kingdom.

Whereas Jülicher and Schweitzer found at least some common ground with Wrede, one of Wrede's first major challengers, William Sanday, really did not. Sanday was quick to try to knock the legs out from under Wrede's messianic secret theory. When speaking of Wrede's hypothesis, Sanday noted that he could not "conceive of anything more utterly artificial and impossible."[4] For Sanday, Wrede's theory was wholly inconceivable on at least two accounts: For one thing, it requires the belief that those writing in the first century chose a more difficult means of explaining Jesus' life over a less difficult one, and for another, it hinges too much of subsequent Christian belief upon the single event of Jesus' resurrection.

> William Sanday was born in 1843 in England. He taught at Oxford and also served at Hatfield Hall (Durham) in the late 1800s until he moved on to Christ Church where he stayed until his passing in the early 1900s. Sanday was well known in Anglican circles and is remembered as a tenacious speaker and author.

In regard to the first point, Sanday offers an analogy. He asks readers to imagine an ancient scribe who is given two items, a blank writing pad and a bunch of facts about Jesus' life. This scribe is then asked to compose a story about Jesus' life. What course of action does the scribe take; does he take the facts and muddy them up with all sorts of confusing details and ideas or does he "boldly go in and fill up the blank with the facts required?"[5] Of course, Sanday believes that the second line of action is the one that would have been taken. For him, then, Wrede's theory is simply too convoluted to be plausible.

Wrede's theory is also found wanting, at least for Sanday, in the fact that it places all of the stress on the resurrection. It will be helpful to cite Sanday at this point. He says, "It is true enough that the belief in the resurrection bore a great weight of superstructure in apostolic times.

Did Jesus Try to Keep a Messianic Secret?

But I doubt if at any time, from the first century to the twentieth, it has ever had so much weight thrown upon it as in this theory of Wrede's.... Supposing that the resurrection accounts for the rest of Christianity, what is left to account for the resurrection?"[6] Sanday goes on to ask, "The elephant stands on the tortoise; but what does the tortoise stand upon?"[7] It made sense to Sanday that Jesus must have declared to his disciples prior to the resurrection that he was the Messiah.

> Johannes Weiss was born in 1863 and was the son of the noted NT exegete Bernhard Weiss. He was also the son-in-law of the prominent liberal theologian Albrecht Ritschl. He both earned a degree from and taught at Göttingen. Weiss helped pave the way for future discussions of eschatology and Christian origins.

In 1911, a scholar by the name of Johannes Weiss, who shared Schweitzer's view that Jesus was an end-times messianic figure, also contended that Jesus' claims must reach back to the historical Jesus. One of his contributions to the discussion, not too far from Sanday's contentions, was that it would have been next to impossible for Jesus' disciples to simply invent these messianic claims. How could "the Crucified" have been interpreted by the disciples as "the Messiah, the King of Israel" unless Jesus himself had mentioned it beforehand?[8] They could not have created this claim out of thin air, and then persuaded themselves of it.

> Martin F. Dibelius was born in 1883 in Dresden in the church parsonage where his parents lived. His mother died while he was a young boy, which drew him close to his father. He earned a PhD from Tübingen and a ThD from Berlin, where he also taught. He is also remembered for challenging Nazi dominance.

In that same year, Martin Dibelius, who also held the view that Jesus was an eschatological messianic figure, approached the discussion by way of his studies on John the Baptizer. Dibelius attempted to show that the wider populace viewed John as an eschatological figure too, whose main role was to prepare the way for the Messiah. However, when John baptized Jesus he had not yet realized that Jesus was the Messiah; that thought finally crossed his mind while John was sitting in prison. Dibelius attempted to prove this argument by isolating Jesus' sayings about John from the larger narrative (this act of isolating sections of the text is known as "form analysis").

Entering the Fray

Dibelius reasoned that since the early believers were very interested in preserving the words of Jesus, Jesus' sayings—along with a few narrative portions—were the earliest materials within the Gospel accounts. For him, the other sections of the Gospels were later additions, included to fill out and smooth out the story. This logic led Dibelius to subsequently label Mark's account "unliterary" and nothing more than "collections of materials."[9]

> *Karl Ludwig Schmidt was born in 1891 in Frankfurt. He earned his doctorate from Berlin University. He served in the Polish army and was badly injured, which led to his discharge and return to academia. Schmidt is remembered as both a founder of the Form Criticism School and as an anti-Nazi protestor.*

Not long after this, in 1919, Karl Schmidt also considered Mark's story through the lens of form analysis.[10] Like Dibelius, he pressed the notion that Mark's account had originated from sayings of Jesus, and that those sayings were later linked together by Mark, like a string of pearls on a necklace. Therefore, Schmidt concluded, Mark's story cannot be read thematically as a whole, and the so-called messianic secret was not in the mind of the composer of the Gospel. This also implies that the suggestions about Jesus developing an awareness of his messianic identity do not hold water. Schmidt proposed that the isolated pearls of the Gospel accounts reveal, instead, facts about the communities who believed them.

> *Rudolf Bultmann was born in 1884 in Germany and raised as a Lutheran. He studied at Tübingen, Berlin, and Marburg. He researched under J. Weiss and is remembered by many for his demythologizing (removing of the mysterious/myth-like portions) of the NT. Bultmann has long been viewed as a polarizing scholar.*

This all led Rudolf Bultmann, in 1921, to return to and adopt Wrede's thesis, albeit with some nuances.[11] Whereas Wrede suggested that Jesus did not know about his identity as a messianic figure, with the concept of Jesus' developing knowledge now out of the way, Bultmann was able to claim that Jesus actually rejected such claims outright. Like many before him, Bultmann accepted the idea of Jesus as an eschatological figure. However, Bultmann detached from that identity any links to messianic thought. He concluded that the messianic secret motif was the result of the later Christian community intertwining its own theology of Jesus with the earlier sayings of Jesus, which

Did Jesus Try to Keep a Messianic Secret?

(once disentangled) actually reveal Jesus' own rejection of a messianic identity.

As you can see, in the first two decades of the twentieth century, the concept of the messianic secret was receiving great attention. While the hypothesis received challenges, by the time of Bultmann it had not yet been extinguished. In fact, Bultmann did much to revive it. Clearly, the theory brought on many questions about the historicity of Jesus as well as Jesus' identity and it drew much attention to Mark's Gospel account. Up to this point in church history Matthew's narrative had received pride of place because many believed that it was written first. However, research on the synoptic question brought Mark to the fore, so that it no longer played second fiddle to Matthew.

> Arthur S. Peake was born in 1865 in Leek, Staffordshire. He was raised a Methodist and continued in that tradition throughout his life. He studied at Oxford and taught at a number of colleges and universities, including the University of Manchester. Peake was also active in the 1927 Lausanne Conference.

Enter: Arthur Peake. In 1924 Peake pushed back against Bultmann and others who rejected the concept of Jesus' developing awareness of his messianic identity. In reintroducing this idea, he contended that while Jesus knew he was the Messiah, his silence "was due to his own uncertainty. Only when his ministry was far advanced did he become sure in his own mind."[12] Therefore, instead of prematurely revealing and forcing this information upon his followers "it was better that Jesus should lead them through intimate familiarity with him, through watching his actions and listening to his words to form their own judgments of him. . . ."[13] It was only after the resurrection, in retrospect, that the members of the Christian community were able to grasp the meaning of Jesus' messianic claims.

We need to take note that Peake, while rejecting the bulk of Wrede's thesis and while opposing many of Bultmann's arguments, had also adopted elements from both to formulate his view. He accepted Wrede's stress on the resurrection and saw some value in Bultmann's emphasis on the early Christian community. Yet, he nuanced both of these views to a great degree and added his own emphases. Peake went on to recycle Schweitzer's notion of Jesus' use of the title "Son of Man," as well. For Peake, "Son of man is necessarily equivalent to Messiah. . . . both were fulfilled in him just as he was at once Messiah and Servant of Yahweh."[14]

Entering the Fray

> *Julius Daniel Schniewind was born in 1883 in Elberfeld. He studied in Bonn, Halle, Berlin, and Marburg. He earned his doctorate from Halle in 1925. He served as a WWI chaplain and later, after much theological and religious controversy, as a hospital chaplain. He taught in a variety of universities and colleges.*

Peake's view was later modified by Julius Schniewind, whose agenda was to emphasize two things: that Jesus fulfilled the Jewish expectations of the awaited Messiah, and that it was the content of Jesus' messianic campaign that was veiled or kept secret, not the fact that he was the Messiah.[15] The secret, in large part, had to do with the fact that these two things merged together in one individual, one man. Thus, with the double emphasis on the messianic expectations of the people as well as the messianic identity, Schniewind's views helped add steam to Peake's arguments, which emphasized the one, special, messianic Son of Man.

In my estimation, the importance of Peake's reuse of this idea cannot be overstated. This is the case because the "Son of Man" concept would reemerge in 1936 with the groundbreaking work of Ernst Löhmeyer. In his monumental work *Galilee and Jerusalem*, Löhmeyer made the case that Mark was attempting to preserve the tradition that Galilee was the land of messianic revelation while Jerusalem was the land of messianic rejection. Thus, the secret of Jesus' identity was being revealed to those in Galilee while it was purposefully being kept secret from those in Jerusalem. For Löhmeyer, this accounts for how all of the miracles, exorcisms, and healings, save one, occur in Galilee. Further, Galilee functions as the "holy land of the eschatological coming" of the Son of Man.[16]

> *Ernst Löhmeyer was born in 1890 in Dorsten, Westphalia. He was raised a Lutheran and later earned his ThD at Berlin and then a PhD at Erlangen. In 1946, Soviet NKVD agents kidnapped Löhmeyer, imprisoned, tried, and later executed him on false charges. After being kidnapped he was never seen again.*

Löhmeyer had found the proverbial string that held Mark's pearls together in the concept of geography (Galilee and Jerusalem). This attention to geography opened up new ways for understanding Christ, or what scholars refer to as Christology. Yet, the emphasis was no longer on one community but two, each with a different understanding of Jesus. Galilee accepted him as the messianic Son of Man, while

Jerusalem deemed him blasphemous and sought to kill him. This, of course, shares some affinity with Peake's work where proper and improper understandings between various communities come to the fore.

> Hans Jürgen Ebeling was a German theologian and philosopher. He was heavily influenced by Immanuel Kant and is one of the lesser-known voices among modern scholars within messianic secret research. Ebeling was very active in speaking out against Communist Socialism in his day and was a devout Catholic.

In 1939, H. J. Ebeling weighed in on the messianic secret motif. Ebeling did not really build on the work of Löhmeyer but rather Bultmann.[17] One of Ebeling's main contributions to the question was to suggest that the secret was meant to emphasize the mysteriousness of Jesus' identity. It was this mysteriousness that drew readers and listeners into the story. Despite the fact that Ebeling constructed his argument by way of Bultmann over against Löhmeyer, his approach to Mark as literature with a theological or more specifically a Christological purpose, would soon cross paths with Löhmeyer's work and help pave the way for later literary approaches to Mark.

> Frederick C. Grant was born in 1891. He earned his Sacred Theology Doctorate from and served as a professor at Union Theological Seminary and later became president at Western Theological Seminary. He published widely on the Gospels and was a pioneer in researching Mark in relation to orality. He also served on the translation board of the RSV.

Some of this was intuited in 1940 by Frederick Grant, who, although he accepted much of Wrede's original thesis, offered some significant modifications.[18] Here, just before the middle of the century, Grant challenged the predominant view of the previous forty years by suggesting that Jesus' messiahship was not eschatological, but rather social in nature. This was a radical departure from the norm, especially from the claims of interpreters such as Schweitzer. No longer was Jesus to be viewed as ushering in God's end-time kingdom but rather God's kingdom here-and-now, in Palestine. Here, we can see strands of influence from both Schniewind and Löhmeyer, who emphasized the Jewish and geographical elements in their own works. Finally, Grant argued that this fact became clear to Jesus at his baptism, which marked the beginning of the proclamation of a kingdom of God that was deeply social.

Entering the Fray

> *Alfred E. J. Rawlinson was born in 1884. He studied at Dulwich College and Oxford. He taught at Keble College and Christ Church, both in Oxford. He underwent ordination in 1910 and served as the Bishop of Derby for over two decades. He was a renowned NT scholar, Anglican churchman, and theologian.*

In 1949, Alfred Rawlinson picked up on the social aspect of Jesus' proclamation that Grant had proposed, but he took a different tack and began suggesting that while Jesus revealed to pockets of society that he was the Messiah, he rarely, if ever, qualified his identity in any specific regard.[19] Stated differently, Jesus was purposefully vague or ambiguous about what *type* of messiah he was. The people were expecting a nationalistic messiah but that was not his role. Yet, in order for them to arrive at this conclusion, he could not just come out and say it; they had to experience his life, teachings, miracles, and resurrection. Had Jesus revealed that he was not a nationalistic messiah too early in his campaign, the people may have refused to hear him out and/or let his ministry run its course. Rawlinson's perspective balanced out the earlier view of Grant who put the focus on messianic *content* over and against messianic *type*.

If we pause and take stock, we realize that in the first half of the twentieth century there was no shortage of discussion about the messianic secret. The second half would prove to be just as abundant, if not more so. Scholars took this matter seriously. There was much more riding on Wrede's theory and its subsequent manifestations than just a good, scholarly, fireside chat.

It should be clear by now that the key issue in all of this was whether or not Jesus claimed a messianic identity for himself and if so, what type of messiah he understood himself to be, and what content constituted that understanding. Riding on that question's coattails were inquiries about the earliest Christian community and what they also believed about these things. Therefore, while many have questioned Wrede's hypothesis, it is clear that at the least he was wildly successful in opening the floodgates for generations of scholarly questions and investigations.

Additionally, he and those after him helped pave the way for later views of Jesus as a social prophet and end-times figure, concepts that have become quite mainstream in many Christian circles today. Indeed, there is a good chance that you have heard pastors emphasize at least

Did Jesus Try to Keep a Messianic Secret?

> Vincent Taylor was born in 1887 in Lancashire, England. He earned his doctorate from the University of London and later taught at Wesley College (Leeds). He was a very active Methodist preacher and teacher. In addition, he was a member of the prestigious Fellowship of the British Academy.

one of these identities of Jesus. You now have an idea of where such concepts may have formed some of their modern roots.

By the time the middle of the twentieth century had arrived, Vincent Taylor was becoming an active voice in the messianic secret conversation. One of his main contributions to the dialogue, following the likes of Bultmann and Dibelius, came by way of form analysis. However, he broke ranks from those two scholars by showing that the isolated stories did not detract from the validity of either Jesus' words or Mark's overall story, but rather affirmed it. In other words, he flipped the approach of Bultmann and Dibelius on its head. These were not sayings or stories that when isolated simply formed a "heap of unstrung pearls."[20] Instead, Mark's narrative is "a collection of self-contained narratives, many of which are grouped topically and others chronologically."[21] In this comment, we also see the literary approaches of earlier interpreters coming to the fore. It cannot be stressed enough just how influential these early approaches were to understanding Mark's Gospel as a carefully and purposefully structured piece of sacred literature.

In terms of the messianic secret, then, Taylor saw it as a literary theme rooted in the historical Jesus. Thus, Mark did not simply make it up but rather, was offering what Jesus really said. Jesus knew that he was the Messiah, but he also knew that it would not be accepted as valid until after the resurrection, therefore, he imposed silence. He did not want to put the cart before the horse, so to speak. Part of what Taylor helped accomplish here was to bring Mark into the spotlight, and also to urge researchers to reject the earlier claims that Mark's account was completely incoherent in its arrangement. As we shall see, approaching Mark as a coherent text with a fixed order would soon become a common presupposition.

> Willi Marxsen was born in 1919 in Kiel. He served as a soldier in WWII and later studied theology in Kiel, where he earned his doctorate. He was active in the church and held several academic positions. Marxsen was interested in the relationships between the church, Christian identity, and Christian living.

In 1956, Willi Marxsen, who was indebted to those who used form and literary analyses before him, attempted to bridge these approaches with redaction analysis.[22] In a nutshell, a redactor is a type of editor. Now, do not think of an editor as someone who toys haphazardly with the text, pasting blots of white-out over this word or that and then adding his own. Instead, think of a redactor as a preservationist; an editor who seeks to preserve the text. For Marxsen, it was important to understand why the redactor chose the isolated units that he did and why he arranged them in the order that he did.

To answer these questions, one has to consider three things. First, attention must be given to the specific social contexts out of which the isolated sayings or stories arose. For example, a prayer would have belonged to a worship context whereas a quote about buying and selling would have belonged to the context of the local market. Second, the literary arrangement and function of the story are highly significant. For example, a parable was likely meant to teach and when it was used, it typically followed a certain format. Third, the background or life setting of the author/redactor should be acknowledged. For instance, can knowing whether or not the redactor of Mark wrote from Rome in a hostile situation give us clues as to why he chose the sayings and stories that he did and then proceeded to order them in a specific way?

Research into these questions led Marxsen to suggest that the Markan redactor may have been active in several early Christian communities. This may account for some of the more or less coherent portions of the overall story. When it comes to the messianic secret, it is not merely a motif used to help bind the Markan narrative together but also a reflection of traditions about Jesus from a variety of communities brought into cohesion. Once again we see the attempt to bridge the gap between Jesus himself and the later literature of the church about him.

> Karl Adam was born in 1876 in Bavaria. He received his doctorate from the University of Munich and was ordained into the Catholic priesthood in 1900. He has left a controversial legacy as many have acknowledged a pro-Nazi agenda in his works. He published frequently and held several academic positions.

In 1962, Karl Adam sought to add another extension to the bridge by revisiting how the Son of Man title related to the messianic secret. Adam contended that Mark's story directly reflected Jesus' own goal, which was to use the Son of Man label to help keep the secret about his messianic identity. Stated differently, this mysterious title drew the attention of those who had ears to

Did Jesus Try to Keep a Messianic Secret?

hear, while at the same time keeping it secret to those who did not. As Adam wrote, "The phrase was a circumlocution for his messianic secret . . . that he was at the same time Lord of the future and Redeemer of the present."[23] It is here that we should note the shifting tides among interpreters. Whereas much of the discussion had previously called into question whether or not Jesus' ministry was messianic, scholars were now becoming surer that, indeed, it was.

> Ben Meyer was born in 1927. He studied all over the world and received his doctorate from The Universita Gregoriana. He held positions at several esteemed institutions including McMaster University. He wrote several significant works on the historical Jesus, hermeneutics, and philosophy.

Ben Meyer held this position firmly. For Meyer, Jesus absolutely knew that he was the Messiah. Further, the literary structure of Mark's story only served to prove this fact. Meyer vigorously showed, in his book *The Aims of Jesus*, that Jesus understood himself to be the coming restorer of Israel whose messianic destiny would be fulfilled in his overturning of repudiation, suffering, and death.[24] As the rebuilder of God's temple into the community or kingdom of God, Jesus viewed the Davidic kingship passage in 2 Sam 7:12–14 as a reference to himself:

"When your days are fulfilled and you lie down with your fathers, I will raise up your offspring after you, who shall come forth from your body and I will establish his kingdom. He shall build a house for my name and I will establish the throne of his kingdom forever. I will be his father, and he shall be my son." As Meyer would later say, "Jesus' whole public performance was meant to be deciphered. His public life was accordingly a lived parable. It was designed to supply Israel with data apt to generate the conclusion: This is indeed 'the coming one!'"[25]

> Jack Dean Kingsbury was born in the 1930s in California. He earned his doctorate from the University of Basel. He has served much of his career as a professor at Union Theological Seminary (VA) and has written extensively on the Gospels. Kingsbury is heralded by many as a pioneer in biblical literary criticism.

In 1983, Jack Kingsbury, who did not at all engage Meyer's work, suggested that the whole discussion of the messianic secret up to this point was built on the wrong foundation.[26] For Kingsbury, the focus was not on Jesus the Messiah but rather Jesus the Son of God. He attempted to prove this point by suggesting that the author of Mark's Gospel was telling the story from God's point of view. In the Markan account, God speaks of Jesus as a son and at the climactic point of the story, the Roman centurion describes Jesus as the Son of God as well. Therefore, what we have in Mark should be referred to as a sonship secret, not a messianic secret. It is this sonship secret that is held from human lips until the climax of the story, and the sonship secret that moves the story along. While Kingsbury's claims received much attention from scholars and his detailed literary approach was warmly welcomed, over time his solution to the riddle of the messianic secret lost traction.

> Burton L. Mack was born in 1931. He earned his PhD in NT Studies and the History of Religions from the University of Göttingen. Mack held a position for a number of years as the John Wesley Professor of NT at Claremont School of Theology (CA). Mack has been a controversial scholar throughout his career.

Another literary approach to the matter, one which actually resurrected Wrede's thesis and attempted to build upon it, was offered in 1988 by Burton Mack. One of the more controversial parts of Mack's thesis was that Mark knowingly and purposefully blended stories of Greek myth, drawn from the wider culture, with the stories he knew about Jesus' life. Jesus, then, became like the heroes of Greek myth, embodying many of their miraculous and divine attributes. Further, the messianic secret "scenario took its rationale from the popular meaning of the Christ title...."[27] Mack also proposed that the author of the Markan narrative was a literary genius whose story embodied a "complexity of narrative designs" and is "amazingly unified and coherent."[28] Not only was this a major distancing from predecessors such as Schweitzer, but

> Heikki M. Räisänen was born in 1941 in Helsinki, Finland. He earned four degrees, including his ThD, from the University of Helsinki, where he also served as Professor of NT Exegesis for over three decades. Räisänen has written extensively on the life of Paul and has received numerous awards as an outstanding Finnish scholar.

it was also an incredible contribution to literary analysis; Mark was no longer viewed as a rote assembler of sayings, with hardly any capability of storytelling. He was beginning to be recognized as a sophisticated author in his own right.

In 1990, Heikki Räisänen also lent credence to the notion of the creativity and literary sophistication of the Markan author.[29] For Räisänen, the key to understanding the messianic secret

Did Jesus Try to Keep a Messianic Secret?

was not to be found by lumping all of the secrecy passages together as a whole. Instead, he suggested that the silence commands to demons served a different function than the silence commands to humans. The result of Räisänen's perspective is that Mark ends up having many different motifs and themes, not simply one large messianic secret. This being the case, the so-called messianic secret loses its force and becomes something of a bench warmer among other thematic players.

> Morna D. Hooker was born in 1931. She earned her Doctor of Divinity from Cambridge (the first female to do so). In addition to being bestowed with numerous scholarly awards such as the Burkitt Medal, she has held a number of academic positions and has been an active preacher within the Methodist Church.

Only a year after Räisänen's project was published, Morna Hooker's work came out. Hers was another work that contributed to the discussion of Mark's literary genius. While somewhat indifferent on the matter of whether Jesus was knowingly messianic or not, Hooker chose to emphasize that the messianic secret was a literary device that drew the audience into the story in a most unexpected way. For her, the messianic secret, which is found "on every page of the gospel" is precisely and ironically the very thing that keeps the "truth about Jesus" hidden from plain view.[30]

> Nicholas T. Wright was born in 1948 in England. He received his PhD from Merton College (Oxford) and has served as the Bishop of Durham. Wright has written a number of highly influential books and has appeared on many major television networks as a historical and theological consultant.

If Hooker was unsure of whether Jesus presented himself as a messianic figure or not, N. T. Wright's mind was settled. In 1996, Wright, who was deeply influenced by Meyer, leveled powerful blows to Wrede's thesis.[31] Of the many holes he poked in Wrede's argument, his two biggest had to do with how convoluted the theory was and how it would have taken much more than the forty years Wrede posits for it all to have taken place.

In Wright's mind, it is simply inconceivable that Jesus did not understand himself as messianic. Jesus certainly claimed to be the Messiah, but he instructed his disciples to keep quiet about it so that they did not attract unwanted attention to him; this could bring a quicker end to his messianic campaign than he desired. To be sure, Jesus' campaign was social, religious, and political in nature. To some degree, he was redefining the concept of Messiah; however, he was doing so tactfully so as to keep the messianic ship from running aground. If we look closely at Wright's claims, which have gained a lot of momentum within the last decade, we can see a brilliant synthesis of much of the work that preceded him.

> David Watson was born in 1970. He has served in the Methodist Church as an ordained minister. He studied at Texas Tech, Perkins School of Theology, and went on to earn his PhD from Southern Methodist University (TX). He has served as a professor of NT and academic dean at United Theological Seminary (OH).

Most recently, in 2010, David Watson published a book titled *Honor Among Christians*.[32] In this work, he took a patently different approach to the messianic secret. Watson's main argument was that in the ancient world, secrecy was viewed differently than it has been in the last couple of centuries. In reviewing ancient literature, he shows that secrecy was actually understood as concealment or even more, resistance. While on the surface there may seem to be little difference, when understood within an honor/shame cultural matrix, there is in fact, a great difference.

In a world where honor was to be sought and preserved at all costs and shame to be avoided at all costs, Jesus sought to redefine the honor/shame codes that persons lived by. In Mark, Jesus is an example of someone who is not out to seek honor for himself—though he easily could have. Instead, he is often caught mingling with the shameful of society. In doing so, he is actually subverting the dominant honor/shame system and redefining it. In God's eyes, it is honorable to be in the presence of the shameful. Yet, it is shameful to go about seeking honor for the societal or religious promotion of one's self.

Therefore, when it comes to the messianic secret, first of all, the term "secret" is misleading. Second of all, in every instance where previous interpreters have been troubled by Jesus' seemingly contradictory messianic claims, approaching them through an honor/shame paradigm relieves the tension and reveals that Jesus is actually resisting the honor that persons are attempting to place upon him. This also has to do with the honor/shame society being run by the patronage system. In the patronage system, when someone pays you honor, you must accept it and honor them back; this is known as reciprocity. This was, in large part, the way that ancient society functioned. Jesus, the Messiah, resisted being ascribed such honor and attempted to offer his own honor/

shame system. Without a doubt, Watson's work marks a tremendous turn in studies of the messianic secret and may well be the study that paves the path for the next century of research on this topic.

TAKING ACTION

In this chapter we covered over one hundred years of conversation on the messianic secret. In doing so, we listened to nearly two dozen Bible scholars as they sought to work through this issue. History reveals that this has been a tension-filled and difficult subject matter. Yet, its implications for biblical scholarship, theology, and the life of the church must not be overlooked; there is much to glean from this incredibly dense dialogue. Here, I want to offer three very practical examples of how and why being aware of this topic is important for modern Christians.

The easiest place to start is with Watson's work. While his work is still new, it is also quite revolutionary and it is likely to become a mainstay within messianic secret research. One of the most important results of Watson's project is that it pays close attention to the cultural practices of the ancient world. He takes modern readers back into the first century and helps them understand societal practices, expectations, and codes. In this regard, he accomplishes two things: He avoids forcing his own modern cultural expectations and views upon the text, and he helps locate Jesus within his own social, cultural, and religious contexts.

In our modern, Western world we are often arrogant when it comes to culture; many of us believe that we stand at the apex of human history. For example, we find televangelists and false prophets reading Revelation and ripping it from its original, ancient context and acting as if it was written for us moderns. While it is absolutely still significant to us and carries relevance and meaning for us, it was not addressed *to* us. It was addressed to seven ancient churches in Asia Minor and we must recognize that. When we ignore this, we fall into the errors of historical and theological arrogance, both of which lead to ignorance.

The fact is, so many of the seemingly odd things described within the Bible make complete sense when situated in their ancient settings. Pastors and teachers must take proper care to understand ancient cultural codes and practices when attempting to interpret the Bible in today's world. Not only will this help temper the triumphal and arrogant attitudes that Christians often have today, it will remedy some of the biblical illiteracy and ignorance that exists as well. Perhaps if Wrede had attempted to do this in the early 1900s, the discussion of the messianic secret would have taken a completely different route.[33]

This all leads into the second point, which is that even before Watson published his work, scholars were already wrestling with how to set Jesus within his own Jewish context. While we will get into this more in future chapters, it does deserve to be mentioned here that this is critical in any conversation we wish to have about Jesus. Living in a post-Holocaust world where the sufferings of Jewish people course through the veins of world history, a world that is deeply aware of the fact that Jewish persons' identities were stripped from them by a Nazi regime, we as Christians must be sensitive to this. The best place to start may be with the respectful recognition of Jesus' own Jewishness.

At the same time, we need to be aware that while we Christians claim Jesus as the true Messiah, we are not called to be arrogant and hurtful as we do so. To be sure, Jesus' messianic identity has long been under attack and without a doubt, it will continue to be interrogated. Even so, one thing that all of this research on the messianic secret might reveal to us is that in the end, it can stand on its own; it will outlast its naysayers. Thus, we need not go around preaching a replacement gospel, that is, one that claims that the truth of Christianity has replaced the truth of Judaism. Instead, we would do better to call ours a gospel of completion, a gospel that completes or fulfills the first covenant. The ramifications of all of this in modern Jewish-Christian relations may be very fruitful.

A final lesson from our survey of research on the messianic secret shows us the value of seeing the Bible as literature. Of course, it is sacred literature but it is literature nonetheless. On the level of reading, being able to acknowledge the outlines of larger narratives, the various types of genres, etc., are all important. Attention to these signals prevents us from forcing wrong literary types upon the text. It is important to read a parable as a parable and not as a historical account. It is important to read a prayer as a prayer and not a joke.

In all reality, being aware of the literary dimensions of the text should only heighten our respect for the Bible and those who composed it. We can see that they took great care when shaping their stories and sought to preserve and deliver them using all of the creativity with which the Creator of the universe had endowed them. Next time you open your Bible, take time to marvel at its literary sophistication; revel in its literary brilliance. Pastors and Bible study leaders, do not let your congregants go on reading the Bible without taking note of its rich literary diversity and features. Show them these riches and they will be edified for a lifetime.

Looking back on all this, we can see the power and significance of a theory. One question set hundreds of years of scholarship in motion. Many think themselves incapable of being influential in the world of biblical studies. Even though Wrede himself wrote soon before his death that he no longer agreed with his original hypothesis but did in fact, think that Jesus understood himself to be the Messiah, his question outlived him.[34] None of us should underestimate the power of our questions and studies. With that therefore, I say, never be afraid to ask questions of the Bible. Questions are not irreverent and God is not afraid of your questions! Ask them, because you never know how that inquiry may just take on a life of its own, leading you and many others deeper into the mystery of the Bible and the mystery of God, and that is a secret worth sharing.

6

ReQuesting Guides on the Quest for Jesus

http://michaelhalcomb.com/enteringthefray-jesus.html

TUNING IN

A NUMBER OF YEARS AGO I lived in a small town located near a major interstate. While this provided easy access for travel, one of the more annoying results of living there had to do with radio frequency. I'm referring specifically the radio frequency known as the Citizens' Band. In America, it is predominantly cargo truck drivers who use this frequency. Installed in their rigs are devices known as CB Radios or CBs for short. Much like walkie-talkies or phones, these CBs allow truck drivers to communicate with one another.

The problem that I continually encountered was that because I lived so close to the interstate, whenever I used a cordless phone, it would cross frequencies with the Citizens' Band. The conversations of the truck drivers were often so loud or static-ridden that I would be unable to hear the person on the other end of my call. All I could hear were a bunch of different voices, jumbled and confusing.

When it comes to the topic of the "historical Jesus," it can often seem like little more than a jumbled-up, confusing conversation. If we listen to Christian radio, we hear musicians singing about a Jesus who deserves to be glorified. If we watch Christian television, we hear speakers talking about a Jesus who wants to bless you with health and wealth. If we read pop-Christian literature, we find a Jesus who is meant to inspire us to achieve greatness. If we go to church we often encounter a Jesus who has only one goal: to save us. If we go to youth conventions we find a Jesus who yearns to be our homeboy. If we read scholarly works, we often find an incredibly complicated Jesus who is difficult to understand.

The fact is, understanding Jesus is no simple task. When we attempt to describe Jesus to others, we often end up painting a portrait of a Jesus who looks, thinks, speaks, and acts like us; we create Jesus in our own image and likeness. Yet, there must be a better way, right? There must be some way to move beyond our own modern, self-styled Jesuses and back to the original Jesus, right?

Well, the answer to such a question is not so easy. This is something that scholars have wrestled with for centuries. It is likely that much more than you know it, the view or views of Jesus that you hold can be traced back to some particular point in the dialogue that researchers have been holding. The aim of this chapter is to help you sort through what, from time-to-time, appears to be a static-ridden, jumbled-up, scholarly conversation about the historical Jesus. Our guides on this quest have many fruitful and challenging things to say. So, get ready to journey through one of the most intriguing discussions known to modern human history.

Entering the Fray

TAKING NOTE

When we tune in to scholarly dialogues about the historical Jesus, we quickly learn that the heart of the conversation is not so much about who Jesus is, but rather, who Jesus was. In other words, the issue is one of the past more than it is of the present. Yet, within scholarship the question of what we can know about the historical figure of Jesus of Nazareth did not become central until the late 1700s. We might even pinpoint a more precise date to 1774.

The era is important to demarcate because it was at this point in history that The Age of Reason or The Enlightenment was taking place. The Enlightenment was a period of history during which science, reason, intellect, exploration, and an escape from irrationality, church dogma, and ignorance were vigorously sought after. Today, all of us in the West are children of this age; it is part of the foundation of our intellectual history. This, of course, has carried over to the field of biblical studies.

> *Hermann Samuel Reimarus was born in 1694 in Hamburg. He served most of his professional career at the Gymnasium Johanneum in his hometown, where he taught oriental languages. He was an avid Deist and challenged the historical foundations of the traditional Christianity of his day.*

We also draw attention to 1774 because that is when the influential work of a man by the name of Hermann Reimarus was first published.[1] Though he did not live to see the publication of his work, the last of which entered the public domain in 1778, Reimarus set in motion what would prove to be one of the most important ideas in all subsequent eras of religious history, especially that of church history. His main claim was that the historical Jesus, that is, the Jesus that existed prior to formation of the church, was not the same person as the Christ who was taught and proclaimed by the church.

To state the matter differently, Reimarus argued that Jesus' cry of forsakenness to God from the cross proved that his mission failed. In this, the disciples who had followed him found their hopes and dreams shattered. Their only reaction was to steal his body from the tomb, create a story about his resurrection and proclaim it throughout their world. In sum, the disciples invented or reinvented Jesus as "the Christ" to suit their own desires, needs, and agendas. It is here, with Reimarus that, for the first time in history, a historical-theological wedge is driven into Jesus so that we no longer have just a Jesus of history but also a Christ of faith.

After Reimarus, a windfall of research would ensue, which attempted to tackle this topic. This pursuit is what Bible scholars refer to as the "first quest" for the historical Jesus. All in all, we can identify three quests, or waves of scholarly research and dialogue, each with their own driving forces. In the remainder of this chapter we will highlight some of the key voices and views within each of these quests. This is necessary because as Albert Schweitzer once noted, "No one can justly criticize, or appraise the value of new contributions to the study of this subject unless he knows in what forms they have been presented before."[2]

The First Quest

> *Heinrich Paulus was born in 1761 in Leonberg, Württemberg. He served as a professor of exegesis, church history, theology, and oriental languages at a variety of institutions including the universities of Jena, Würzburg, and Heidelberg. Paulus was a Lutheran rationalist and a very controversial figure in his day.*

While there are many significant pieces to the puzzle of the first quest, the big picture emphasis was on the life of the Jesus of history, that is, Jesus the man from Nazareth. To uncover what this man was really like, researchers began attempting to reconstruct Jesus' life by writing biographical-style accounts. One of the first of these was penned by a rationalist, Heinrich Paulus, who sought to offer a different approach to Jesus' miracles.[3] If you have ever heard someone say about Jesus' miracle of walking on water that he was simply walking near the shore or in a shallow portion of the lake, you have Paulus to thank for that.

For Paulus, the Gospel writers were men of their time who did not know the modern laws of science and therefore, could only explain these phenomena surrounding Jesus in supernatural terms. Thus, in Paulus's reconstruction of Jesus' life, Jesus was not a miracle-worker but a regular man whose acts were interpreted by his disciples supernaturally and theologically. So, the events recorded in the Gospels were likely actual, historical events, however they were described supernaturally for lack of available modern reasoning.

Entering the Fray

> David Friedrich Strauss was born in 1808 in Ludwigsburg. He studied at Tübingen and then returned to his alma mater, Stift, where he taught philosophy. He was a pupil of the famed F. C. Baur and is remembered as one who, in his day, challenged the traditional views of the foundations of Christianity.

David Strauss built upon the work of Heinrich Paulus, sharing his rejection of the notion of miracles and asserting that the ancients simply used non-modern, non-scientific modes of thinking and language to describe Jesus' miracles.[4] However, he pressed this issue a bit further than Paulus. For Strauss, the language that the Gospel writers used was imaginative and poetically descriptive; it was a means of imbuing the events of Jesus' life with meaning and significance. He referred to this as mythological language. By myth he did not simply mean that the stories were made up and had no historical basis, instead he believed that whatever did happen historically, could only be uncovered once the miraculous, fanciful, or mythical language was stripped away.

For Strauss, the miracle or myth language was evidence of the Gospel writers' theology. It was their post-resurrection belief that led them to paint Jesus' life with such charming and magical strokes. Or, stated differently, it was the disciples' post-Easter faith that took the human Jesus, the Jesus of history, and made him into the Christ of faith—a character who shared qualities with those in the ancient myths. Strauss's work hammered deeper the wedge between the historical Jesus and the Christ of faith. If you have ever heard someone say that the stories about Jesus are legends or myths, well, now you know just who helped bring that view into the world of scholarship and mainstream society. A great many people who make these claims today do not realize just how indebted they are to a pre-modernistic mindset.

> Ernest Renan was born in 1823 in Tréguier, France. He studied at the Issy-les-Moulineaux Seminary and later accepted a teaching position at Vendôme. From the early years of his teenage life, Renan was marked as a sophisticated thinker. Like many of his contemporaries, Renan became a controversial figure.

Following Strauss was a scholar by the name of Ernest Renan. In 1863, Renan published a book titled *The Life of Jesus*, which was quickly popularized because of its easy-to-read, imaginatively colorful, and controversial nature. An excerpt brings the emotional and novelistic tendencies of Renan's work

ReQuesting Guides on the Quest for Jesus

to light: "[Jesus'] imagination and his love of nature found themselves constrained within these [Jerusalem Temple] walls. True religion does not proceed from the tumult of towns, but from the tranquil serenity of the fields."[5] Notice in this quote the way in which Renan seeks to penetrate Jesus' thoughts and emotions; he is psycho-analyzing Jesus and his actions.

Bringing together the processes of psychology and imagination, Renan sought to reconstruct the life, or better yet, the personality of Jesus. Yet, the Jesus portrayed in the Gospels was, Renan asserted, the Jesus of legends and fables and not the Jesus of history. For example, Renan wrote "The legends about him were thus the fruit of a great and entirely spontaneous conspiracy, and were developed around him during his lifetime. No great event in history has happened without having given rise to a cycle of fables; and Jesus could not have put a stop to these popular creations, even if he had wished to do so."[6]

Part of Renan's agenda was to help make Jesus accessible and relevant. His aim was to portray Jesus in a very romantic light, as a loving man and an upright, moral teacher. As such, he was neither Lord nor God. Yet, Renan's book sold rapidly and was a best-seller in its day. Perhaps it was Renan who helped set the precedent for much of the pop-Christian, positive-thinking work that flourishes today. Whether or not this is the case, the fact remains that Renan's work lodged the argument deep within the psyche of his age, greatly influencing the generations that followed. He argued forcefully that the Gospel accounts were mere legends of Jesus' life and that viewing Jesus as a good man and teacher is what is important. This remains a popular perspective still today.

> Albert Schweitzer was born in 1875 in Germany and was raised a Lutheran. He was broadly educated and earned his doctorate from the University of Strasbourg. He was a major contributor to historical Jesus studies but is perhaps best remembered for leaving a life of biblical scholarship to be a medical doctor in rural Africa.

Not too long after this, Albert Schweitzer began teaching and publishing. Schweitzer brought the first quest to a close with at least two very important points. The first of these was a common thread that he noticed running through all of the reconstructions of the historical Jesus up to 1906: Jesus always ends up resembling the scholars who reconstruct his life.[7] In a nutshell, these reconstructed Jesuses always ended up taking on the attributes and desires and mindsets of the interpreters.

This was substantiated by his second point, which was that the Jesus of history was simply irrelevant to modern humanity. If historical Jesus researchers were being forced to create a variety of Jesuses in their own images to meet their own needs, then there must be something lacking about the original Jesus. Schweitzer's explanation was that Jesus was a failed end-times moralist who, based on his belief that the world's end was on the horizon, urged his followers to sell everything they had to follow him, to divorce under no circumstances and to live pure moral lives. Jesus' moral agenda, then, having been driven by a failed end-times anticipation, is irrelevant and useless in the modern world.

> Rudolf Bultmann was born in 1884 in Germany and raised as a Lutheran. He studied at Tübingen, Berlin, and Marburg. He researched under J. Weiss and is remembered by many for his demythologizing (removing of the mysterious/myth-like portions) of the NT. Bultmann long been viewed as a polarizing scholar.

If the historical Jesus was irrelevant, there could be little reason to study him. This line of thinking moved Rudolf Bultmann to take up an interest, then, in the Christ of faith. For Bultmann it was the Christ figure that was important to and for theology, not the Jesus of history. In his 1926 work titled *Jesus*, Bultmann remarked, "We can now know almost nothing concerning the life and personality of Jesus, since the early Christian sources show no interest in either, are moreover fragmentary and often legendary."[8] Here, we can see a clear pushback against the scholarship that preceded him. For Bultmann, the historical Jesus was only important and meaningful to the degree that he provides us with Christian theology, that is, a faith that is centered on the post-Easter Christ of faith. Therefore, the emphasis is not on the proclaimer but the proclamation; the focus is not on the preacher but what is preached.

Thus, it was in the early twentieth century that the first quest came to an end. The various lives of Jesus that had been reconstructed had their fifteen minutes of fame but were ultimately exposed, and collapsed in on themselves. This backdrop of historical Jesus studies is important for every contemporary Christian, if for nothing else than to recognize the origins of common beliefs about Jesus. Yet, there is a lot more riding

ReQuesting Guides on the Quest for Jesus

on the line here, from the validity of the Gospels, to the veracity of miracles, to the humanity and divinity of Jesus.

When we stop and look back at these issues, we can see how they might be perceived as threatening to the faith. Certainly, a large number of present-day Christians are ill equipped to answer many of the questions raised during the first quest, even though they were raised hundreds of years ago. Yet, most of these scholars were not seeking to destroy the Christian faith; they were simply attempting to understand it within the social, spiritual, and intellectual contexts of their day. Thus, hearing them out with a bit of patience and humility is the way to go. The fact is, none of these scholars had the last word. To be sure, subsequent generations would produce scholars who would step up to the microphone and make their own contributions to the quest.

The Second Quest

> Ernst Käsemann was born in 1906 in Westphalia, Germany. He earned degrees from the universities of Bonn, Tübingen, and Marburg respectively. He was a student of R. Bultmann, and often remembered for resisting German socialism and Hitler. This led to his arrest and imprisonment by the Gestapo in 1937.

It is well documented among biblical scholars that the second quest or the "new quest" for the historical Jesus, which lasted about three decades, began in 1953 with one of Bultmann's students, Ernst Käsemann. As with the first quest, understanding the social context behind this quest is important. There are four factors, in particular, that need to be noted. First, the breeding ground for the new quest was post-WWII Germany. Following the evils of the Holocaust, scholars were highly sensitive to the fact that Jesus' human identity was important because when lifted out of his original context, any type of Jesus can be created to suit any type of agenda—even an anti-Semitic, murderous agenda. One of the hallmarks of the second quest, then, was a purposeful search for the Jewishness of Jesus.

Second, in the late 1940s, the Dead Sea Scrolls were discovered in the caves of Qumran. While the scrolls contain no texts of the New Testament, many of the nearly 1,000 manuscripts contained portions of the Old Testament, Apocryhpa, and Pseudepigrapha. However, these works were still invaluable to New Testament scholars because they helped fill out a much broader picture of ancient Jewish society and culture. Put negatively, scholars came to recognize many of the grave deficiencies inherent within previous historical reconstructions.

Third, the second quest was influenced by the onslaught of new methodologies and approaches to studying the Bible. Form analysis, redaction analysis, source analysis, and other similar paradigms were providing interpreters with new tools to unravel the mystery of the Jesus of history (for more on this see chapter four). These methodologies gave the field of biblical studies a refreshing boost of confidence. This was especially true in the case of historical Jesus research.

Fourth, Ernst Käsemann commenced the new quest with a lecture he gave on October 23, 1953 at the University of Marburg, the institution where he had studied under Bultmann. Käsemann addressed a group of colleagues, alumni from Marburg, who had also sat at Bultmann's feet. His lecture was titled "The Problem of the Historical Jesus."[9] In that piece, he issued a call for new questers and challenged them to recognize that continuity between the proclaimer and the proclaimed did in fact exist. If the Gospel writers cared enough to write about the man Jesus and sought to take his life seriously, then his life is still relevant for people and as such, the historical Jesus should be taken with the utmost seriousness, especially by Bible scholars.

> Günther Bornkamm was born in 1905 in Görlitz, Germany. He earned his PhD from the University of Marburg where he studied under R. Bultmann. He was a member of the Confessing Church, which spoke out against the Nazi regime. He served as a soldier in WWII and later taught at the University of Heidelberg.

With Käsemann, the previous rupture between the Jesus of history and the Christ of faith became much less prominent. Following his lead, a number of scholars began publishing influential works that would help guide the second quest along. In 1960, Günther Bornkamm published a book titled *Jesus of Nazareth*, in which he stated, "No one is any longer in the position to write a life of Jesus."[10] A clear rejection of the aim of the first quest, Bornkamm was not interested in the emotional and psychological interpretations of Jesus. For him, it was the uncontested historical facts about Jesus that were of the utmost importance; these were the foundation upon which new questers should build.

ReQuesting Guides on the Quest for Jesus

Jesus was a Jew from the town of Nazareth who spoke the Aramaic language, worked as a carpenter, and underwent a baptism by John. Jesus taught in parables, challenged the religious establishment of his day, went to Jerusalem, and was crucified on a Roman cross. Jesus proclaimed an apocalyptic, end-time judgment, which emphasized the reality of God's presence in the here-and-now as well as the future. As one would expect, Bornkamm's work is a reflection of many of the contextual aspects that gave rise to the second quest.

Over the next two decades, Norman Perrin produced at least two highly influential works for the new quest.[11] For him, the key to getting back to the Jesus of history was found in the sayings of Jesus, which were preserved in the Synoptics. His tool of choice for determining the genuine sayings was redaction analysis. In biblical studies a redactor is viewed as a preserver of data, such as texts or stories or sayings, who then takes that data and arranges it in a purposeful manner to make a theological point. Thus, when a modern scholar utilizes redaction analysis he or she is seeking not only to uncover that theological point but also to isolate the individual elements that contribute to making that point.

> Norman Perrin was born in 1920 in England. He earned his ThD from the University of Göttingen, where he studied under Joachim Jeremias. Perrin taught at Emory for a short time and then moved to the University of Chicago Divinity School. He died at the age of fifty-six as a revered interpreter of the Gospels.

So, Perrin combed the Synoptics and isolated all of the sayings of Jesus. Following this, he began to differentiate between Jesus' own thoughts and the sayings that were likely shaded by the Gospel writers themselves. In this, Perrin developed the criteria of the "irreducible minimum," meaning that unless a saying within the Synoptics could be identified with complete certainty as belonging to Jesus, then it must be attributed to either Christian traditions that had preserved and embellished these sayings, or to the Gospel authors or redactors themselves. Perrin had several other sub-criteria that helped him reach his conclusions.

If we think of a baseline where one end represents the extreme of being consumed with the miracles of Jesus, then the new questers may be on the other extreme where they are consumed with the teachings of Jesus. Lost somewhere in the middle seem to be Jesus' deeds. This is not to say that what the Jesus of history did was totally and completely lost on scholars but rather, that it had not assumed priority.

> Hans Georg Conzelmann was born in 1915 in Talifingen, Germany. He earned his doctorate from the University of Tübingen. He served in WWII and afterward, taught at a number of respected institutions, including Zurich and Göttingen. He is remembered for his pioneering work in redaction analysis.

This is true of Hans Conzelmann's work as well.[12] His contribution to the second quest came by way of emphasizing the eschatological and existential facets of Jesus' teachings. In other words, Jesus proclaimed a message that was future oriented; its significance was relevant for the present in that it was preparatory for the future. To this end, the historical Jesus and his "kerygma," that is, his proclamation of God's imminent kingdom, remain significant. Jesus' importance as a historical figure is to be located in the fact that he is the one who brought forth the kerygma.

Another prominent figure associated with the second quest was Rudolf Schnackenburg. In his view, a completely accurate view of the historical Jesus is impossible. Even with Perrin's various criteria, he asserted that it is simply too difficult to distinguish between what belonged to Jesus, whether in part or in whole, and what belonged to the Gospel writers. All that can be salvaged is a faithful interpretation based on and resulting from the writings of those closest to him. For Schnackenburg, then, the study of the historical Jesus remains important most of all "for theology and the church."[13]

> Rudolf Schnackenburg was born in 1914 in Würzburg, Germany. He earned his PhD from Breslau. He was a respected scholar and Catholic priest, who taught at a number of institutions but spent most of his career at Maximilians University in Würzburg. Upon retirement he served as a nursing home chaplain.

> Edward C. F. A. Schillebeeckx was born in 1914 in Antwerp, Belgium. He earned his doctorate from Sorbonne and later assumed a number of teaching roles at various academic institutions including the Catholic University of Nijmegen in the Netherlands. He is remembered as a creative and controversial theologian.

While there are many others who could be mentioned within this section, we round out our review of the new quest with Edward Schillebeeckx.[14] Like many of his contemporaries, Schillebeeckx drew a distinction between the Jesus of history and the Christ of faith;

however, he was not willing to leave the distance between the two at that. He believed that it is the duty of every Christian faith community in every generation to deal seriously with the matter of the historical Jesus. As we do, we follow the example of the earliest Christians, who preserved and passed on their experiences of Jesus. It is thus the "tradition of Christian experience" side-by-side with our own "present-day experiences" that affirm and confirm the words of the historical Jesus. The result is less of a focus on the Jesus of history over against the Christ of faith, and more on living in continuity with what the authors and/or redactors of the Synoptics passed on. This being the case, serious study of the historical Jesus remains absolutely necessary because he is the one who influenced the writers and the faith communities of which they were a part.

At the end of the day, the second quest was incredibly different from the first. The new quest did not reject miracles outright, and resisted dogmatic approaches or pigeon-holing itself into one interpretive paradigm. The second quest's agenda, while focused, was broad enough to welcome various critical approaches and data from outside of the Bible (e.g., the Dead Sea Scrolls and other archaeological finds), which helped reconstruct the ancient Jewish world of Jesus. The second quest's emphases on the kerygma, eschatology, and the human experience were significant enough to shape decades of scholarly study and leave an important mark on the field of biblical studies.

The Third Quest

The third quest inherited from the second its openness to new methods of interpretation. As the third quest was beginning, Bible scholars were becoming familiar with and starting to employ approaches from anthropology and the social sciences. This marked a dramatic change in historical Jesus studies. Whereas the previous two quests provided researchers with tools to analyze biblical and extra-biblical sources from the ancient world from a literary perspective, the social sciences allowed them to investigate the cultural words behind and within these texts.

Of course, the second quest had already attempted to locate Jesus within his ancient Jewish context. However, the third quest was able to fine tune these readings with much more precision by exploring the particularities of ancient societies and cultures. For example, whereas

Entering the Fray

the second quest was able to situate Jesus within a context where various Jewish sects such as the Pharisees, Sadducees, and Essenes existed, the third quest was able to examine each of these factions in terms of ancient rituals, notions of purity, group structures, and social mores. The ultimate goal of the third quest is to create a portrait of Jesus that places him in a world where for the most part, his ideas, values, and concepts share continuity *with* and make sense *in* the context of the surrounding culture.

> Géza Vermes was born in 1924 in Hungary. He studied in Budapest and later earned his ThD from the Catholic University of Leuven. He was raised Roman Catholic and even served in the priesthood, but left the church in 1957 to reaffirm his Jewish identity. He taught for over two decades at Oxford University.

Géza Vermes acts as a sort of bridge between the second and third quests. He has published a number of widely influential works on the Jewishness of Jesus and his gospel.[15] Throughout these volumes, Vermes has attempted to reveal how Jesus and his teachings were both products of the ancient Jewish world.[16] For Vermes, Jesus was neither a messiah nor a deity but rather a Jewish holy man, much like the ancient figures Honi the Rain-maker and Hanina ben Dosa. According to Vermes, both John and Paul are responsible for transforming Jesus from this Jewish holy man into an "other-worldly savior figure." Along with Vermes, scholars of the third quest would now begin to develop portraits of Jesus the Jew from social and cultural perspectives.

It was N. T. Wright (see below) who, in 1992, gave the third quest its name. However, the beginning of this third phase is often traced back to 1985, a year in which E. P. Sanders published his monumental work *Jesus and Judaism*, and when the controversial Jesus Seminar convened its first meeting. For Sanders, the Seminar, and all researchers to follow, if the goal is to locate Jesus in a culture where his words and deeds make sense contextually, then the challenge is to accurately reconstruct those social and cultural worlds. For Jesus to have had any success, his life and preaching must have made sense to those around him.

> Ed Parish Sanders was born in 1937 in Texas. He earned his ThD from Union Theological Seminary (New York) and has received numerous honorary doctorates. He has taught at McMaster, Oxford, and Duke and has lectured throughout the world. He is a highly respected scholar in the field of NT studies.

Sanders, for example, wondered how Jesus, who lived as a Jew, could have spawned a movement that became distinct from Judaism. The answer, he suggested, is to be found by fitting Jesus "realistically into his environment."[17] For Sanders, Jesus was a prophet who boldly proclaimed the reign and inbreaking of God's kingdom. Sanders's portrayal of Jesus as a prophet, as we shall see, has remained influential throughout the course of subsequent historical Jesus research. At the end of his study, Sanders concluded that:

> Jesus saw himself as God's last messenger before the establishment of the kingdom. . . . Sociologically and psychologically Jesus and his movement are quite comprehensible. In fact, we cannot say that a single one of the things known about Jesus is unique. . . . What is unquestionably unique about Jesus is the result of his life and work. They culminated in the resurrection and the foundation of a movement which endured.[18]

The next four researchers, Robert Funk, Marcus Borg, John Crossan, and Burton Mack are all members of the Jesus Seminar. Together, they and other members of the Seminar seek to uncover the real Jesus from beneath the layers of theology and dogma placed upon him by the church and Christian interpretation. Funk, the founder of the Seminar once said in an interview, "The only Jesus most people want is the mythic one. They don't want the real Jesus. They want the one they can worship. The cultic Jesus."[19] For Funk and the Seminar, situating Jesus within his ancient Jewish social and cultural contexts means undressing him from the Christian garb hoisted upon him by later interpreters.

Burton Mack, in his book *A Myth of Innocence*, attempted to reconstruct the processes by which Jesus was transformed by early believers from a Jewish sage into a Christian deity. He proposed that there were two religious

> Robert "Bob" W. Funk was born in 1926 in Indiana. He studied at Butler University, Christian Theological Seminary, and earned his PhD from Vanderbilt University. For the majority of his career, Funk was a polarizing and controversial figure, a mantle that his Westar Institute and The Jesus Seminar carry on today.

> Burton L. Mack was born in 1931. He earned his Ph.D. in NT Studies and the History of Religions from the University of Göttingen. Mack held a position for a number of years as the John Wesley Professor of NT at Claremont School of Theology (CA). Mack has been a controversial scholar throughout his career.

groups devoted to Jesus: the Jesus movement and the Christ cult. The former strove to keep the "memory of Jesus alive and thought of themselves in terms of Jewish reform" while the second views Jesus as "the Lord of a new religious society that called for abrogation of the past."[20] Ultimately, the Christ cult won out and the Jewish Jesus, that is the historical Jesus, gave way to the divine Christ.

> *John Dominic "Dom" Crossan was born in 1934 in Ireland. He earned his Doctor of Divinity at Maynooth College, whereafter his studies led him around the world and to resign from the Catholic priesthood. He taught at DePaul University for two and a half decades.*

Dom Crossan, while sharing affinities with Mack, nevertheless produced his own reconstruction of Jesus the Jew. For Crossan, use of the social sciences is the key to unraveling the cultural Jesus. In his view, Jesus was a Jewish cynic philosopher, with a high degree of interest in magic. He believes that this comports well with the social setting out of which Jesus emerged, namely, that of Jewish peasantry. While these notions may not seem highly controversial, other portions of Crossan's work have led many scholars to vigorously reject his claims. Many have rejected his conclusions, claiming that the sources he uses in his reconstruction are unreliable. For example, he claims, based on the texts of Josephus as well as the Gospel of Thomas that after the crucifixion, Jesus' body was not laid in a tomb but rather eaten by wild beasts, most likely dogs.[21]

> *Marcus J. Borg was born in 1942. He earned his DPhil from Oxford University. He taught for decades at the Oregon State University and has held the position as Canon Theologian at Trinity Episcopal Church in Portland. As a prolific member of the Jesus Seminar, Borg's work has been very controversial.*

Marcus Borg veers away from the notion of fitting Jesus into one role or character slot. Thus, Jesus is not simply a messianic figure, teacher, or philosopher but takes on a host of identities such as charismatic sage, healer, social prophet, spirit person, and wisdom teacher.[22] In Borg's work, there is a clear break from mainstream scholarship as he gives very little attention to matters of eschatology and the resurrection. For him, these elements have more to do with the future and as such, shed very little light on the historical events of Jesus' life. More than anything, Borg's work seems to emphasize the ways in which the social aspects of Jesus the Jew were incredibly threatening to the social powers, forces, and structures of his day. In the end, it was the response to this threat that resulted in Jesus' death.

> Ben Witherington III was born in North Carolina in 1951. He earned his DPhil from Durham University (England) and is a prolific publisher. He has written a commentary on every book of the NT and appeared on many major television networks. Currently, he teaches at Asbury Theological Seminary.

Stepping back outside of the Jesus Seminar we encounter one of the most prolific writers in all of NT studies: Ben Witherington.[23] In 1990 and 1994, Witherington produced two studies, both of which aimed at showing that Jesus thought of himself as a wisdom figure, or more particularly, a sage. Further, Jesus, who followed in the footsteps of the prophets, was a "prophetic and eschatological sage." As such, he understood himself to be the Wisdom of God who was the only one capable of revealing God and God's ways to humanity. While Borg also viewed Jesus as a sage, Witherington is much more open to the idea that the future was significant to Jesus and his proclamation. On these grounds and others, in 1995, Witherington offered a strong rebuttal to the portraits of Jesus espoused by the Jesus Seminar.

> John P. Meier was born in 1942 in the Bronx, New York. He earned his Doctor of Sacred Scripture from the Biblical Institute (Rome). He has spent most of his academic career at the University of Notre Dame (Indiana). Meier is a Catholic priest and a highly respected scholar in NT and theological studies.

For John Meier, another influential third quest scholar, the evidence seems to suggest that Jesus was a marginal Jew, whose life and message had both continuity and discontinuity with the surrounding culture and various Jewish sects. Something of a poster boy for the third quest, in the sense that he is open to all sources and a wide variety of interpretive approaches, in his works Meier forcefully reiterates the push for understanding the social and cultural contexts of Judaism within Jesus' day. Indeed, between 1991 and 2009, he published four large volumes on the historical Jesus in which the first explores sources, the second covers miracles, the third analyzes ancient social persons and groups, and the fourth focuses on Jesus' sayings and teachings in relation to the Mosaic Law. As Meier has noted, "The word became truly flesh insofar as the word became truly Jewish. No true Jewishness, no true humanity."[24]

Entering the Fray

> Nicholas T. Wright was born in 1948 in England. He received his PhD from Merton College (Oxford) and has served as the Bishop of Durham. Wright has written a number of highly influential books and has appeared on many major television networks as a historical and theological consultant.

N. T. Wright enters the conversation by suggesting that this Jewish Jesus is best understood as an eschatological prophet. He agrees with Meier that Jesus was viewed by his contemporaries as one "possessed of remarkable powers."[25] As such, Jesus used these powers, in conjunction with his proclamation, to perform prophetic acts. In fact, these acts often substantiated the prophetic message. Despite the fact that Jesus is rarely referred to as a prophet in the NT, Wright still presses the issue arguing that, "Jesus was seen as, and saw himself as . . . a prophet like the prophets of old, coming to Israel with a word from her covenant God, warning her of imminent and fearful consequences of the direction she was traveling, urging and summoning her to a new and different way."[26]

Taking a different route, in 2008, Pieter Craffert published his work *The Life of a Galilean Shaman*.[27] The title, a giveaway of the portrait that Craffert attempts to paint of Jesus—a shaman—while provocative, is not new. In fact, Vermes had suggested this nearly three decades earlier. However, what Craffert does offer is a new approach, which is spelled out in the book's subtitle, *Jesus of Nazareth in Anthropological-Historical Perspective*.

> Pieter F. Craffert was born in Natal, South Africa. He earned his doctorate from the University of South Africa (Unisa). He has also studied with Gerd Theissen at the Karl Ruprecht University in Heidelberg, Germany. Craffert is an active member of the Context Group.

While Craffert's work has not had time to receive a lot of attention, it is certainly controversial.

Craffert uses the social sciences and anthropology to explain Jesus' altered states of consciousness, the disciples' so-called post-resurrection experiences, and other events. In the main, Jesus was a shaman-like visionary, who, during the course of being possessed by visions, conducted his mission. Within this study, Craffert concludes that events such as the resurrection, therefore, were not historical in the strict sense, but were believed by Jesus' followers as they had visionary experiences within an altered state of consciousness. One of the major takeaways from Craffert's work is the way in which he exposes many of the methodological flaws of the earlier quests for the historical Jesus.

> Anthony Le Donne was born in 1975. He earned his PhD from the University of Durham where he studied with James D. G. Dunn and John Barclay. He has taught NT and Second Temple Judaism at Lincoln Christian University and has an interest in historiography in relation to historical Jesus research.

While incredibly different than Craffert's work, Anthony Le Donne's 2011 publication *Historical Jesus: What Can We Know and How Can We Know It?* contains a similar agenda, namely, to challenge the methodological approaches of the third questers. Le Donne creatively seeks to reorient discussions of the historical Jesus by reframing the concept of how to do historical research. Using postmodern-friendly analyses, Le Donne looks at the family, politics, and death of Jesus, suggesting that these accounts of Jesus' life are records of memories about Jesus. His approach then, is to suggest that the historical Jesus was, is, and always will be a historical memory.

This is not to say that the events described did not happen. It is to say, however, that the events described are memories, which readers are left to interpret with social and cultural sensitivity. To do this, Le Donne provides some introductory principles of Memory Theory. Much of his agenda is to get readers to question how, what, and why they remember about Jesus. This, then, opens the way for asking the same questions of the Gospel writers. One of the most fruitful aspects of Le Donne's study is that, unlike the questers before him such as those of the Jesus Seminar, he does not seek to separate the historical Jesus from his religious context. Le Donne writes, "Those who attempt to arrive at a non-religious historical Jesus do not follow the advice of any contemporary philosophy of history. These interpreters do not strip away religious elements from the gospels because they are hostile to Christianity; they do so because they are poor historians."[28] It remains to be seen, of course, what sort of reception Le Donne's work receives from the wider scholarly world and what influence, if any, it might have on the future of historical Jesus research.

As we reflect on the course of historical Jesus studies, we can highlight several important matters. First, from the beginning there has been an emphasis on the relationship between Jesus and eschatology. Was his proclamation end-times oriented or not? Second, there has always been an emphasis on identity. Whereas the first questers constructed "lives of Jesus" even while overlooking many of the cultural cues and details of ancient context, the second questers began to tune in to those contexts. For many of them, writing out of a post-Holocaust setting turned their attention to the Jewishness of Jesus. The third questers were able to supplement the previous studies on the Jewishness of Jesus by paying close attention to the particularities of ancient context. This brings us to a third matter: sources and methods. One of the great ironies of biblical studies seems to be that as we move further away from the first century, we actually move closer to a fuller understanding of the historical Jesus and the society and culture of which he was a part. Advances in the social sciences and anthropology, as well as literary studies and the humanities, have made it possible to comprehend Jesus with more precision and sensitivity.

TAKING ACTION

The writer of Ecclesiastes once stated, "There is nothing new under the sun." When it comes to historical Jesus research, this is especially true in terms of asking questions about who and what type of person Jesus was. The Jesus of the New Testament has proven to be one of the most, if not the most, exciting and controversial figures of world history. At a bare minimum, this is one reason for exploring who Jesus was. Along the way, being able to recognize yours or others' presuppositions about Jesus and where those beliefs might have come from is incredibly important. This is simply part of what the Apostle Paul referred to as being ready in season and out of season to give the reasons why we believe what we do about Jesus.

As an outsider looking in at the world of biblical studies, many times it seem like researchers are simply sitting around waiting to have a flash of brilliance so that they can offer the next innovative theory on Jesus. Indeed, some might even be pressed to ask of scholars, "What have you done with Jesus?" The answer to such a question is not easy. Yet, it might be summed up in the reply, "We've attempted to understand him." As this chapter shows, there are layers and layers of information and data that must be worked through before anything truly meaningful can be said about the historical Jesus. With certainty, we can say that Jesus has not been lost, nor has he been buried under the pages of scholarship.

While finding the original Jesus involves rigorous study, it is not simply rote academic work; it is the work of faith! It is a way of loving God with our minds. It is a means of giving the Holy Spirit more to work with. It is a duty of the faithful follower of Jesus to take these matters seriously. Professors, pastors, and Bible study leaders need to be willing and able to walk others through this history of interpretation so that they can wrestle with these issues, know their own religious heritage, and firm up their faiths.

Just as well, in a society where the end-times are all the rage, knowing some of the history behind this can go a long way. For centuries, NT scholars in general and historical Jesus scholars in particular have been attempting to work through the relationship between Jesus and eschatology. Some views have been more sound than others, and some, regardless of how sound they may or may not be, have gained a lot of ground within mainstream society.

The ability to temper the apocalyptic fervor displayed by many in the *Left Behind* camp is much needed today. Likewise, the church needs to expose the errancy of false prophets like Harold Camping, whose numerous predictions about the end of the world were dead wrong, though they persuaded many. Christianity needs those who can access the history of interpretation to help shed light on such issues. Having a handle on historical Jesus research, and understanding the various nuances of Jesus the eschatological prophet may prevent others from buying into, or even becoming the next, Harold Camping. Seen in this light, we can all be especially thankful for the research on this topic given to us through the diligent work of Bible scholars.

Many scholars have spent their entire working lives studying the historical Jesus. Even so, despite the variety of things that have been said about Jesus, they are not equally valid or equally plausible, and within the field of biblical studies, it is not as if anything goes. The reality of the matter today is the same as it was when Jesus asked Peter, "Who are people saying that I am? And who do you say that I am?"

It is worth noticing that even for Jesus, knowing what others have said about him is important. Just as well, knowing what you yourself have to say about him is important. In fact, that age old question confronts us all. One of the great benefits of studying the historical Jesus

Entering the Fray

is that, to some degree, we are in a much better position to answer his question than if we had not studied at all.

At the end of the day, many will be tempted to look at the long tradition of scholarship on the historical Jesus and say, "If scholars cannot decide who Jesus was, then how can I?" or "There are so many views suggested by scholars that I don't even know where to begin!" or "How can we trust scholars when they cannot agree with one another?" These are all remarks that I've heard, and at one point or another have had cross my own mind. But the fact is, we cannot push the blame for our own ignorance onto others. We should all assume responsibility for studying to show ourselves approved before God and others, not by complaining but by knowing why we believe what we believe.

So, as you continue to study the historical Jesus, whether it be from the vantage point of a student, pastor, preacher, or layperson, do not get bogged down in the swamp of pointless excuses. Instead, humble yourself and carve out time to immerse yourself in these explorations of the most interesting man to ever walk the earth. Allow the Bible scholars mentioned here and the countless others who have worked through this topic to be your guides. If you listen closely, they just might help you hear a fresh word from God.

PART TWO

7

Can Luke's Acts be Trusted?

http://michaelhalcomb.com/enteringthefray-acts.html

"Your Bible is nothing to me; nothing more than information anyway." Just before writing this chapter, I had a conversation with an acquaintance about our respective views of faith. I had asked him his opinion of the Bible, and—without skipping a beat—he replied with this rather bald and sobering remark.

His statement is interesting because it suggests that the Bible, a text that has shaped much of world history, is rather trivial. If you have ever watched television quiz shows you have probably been amazed at the massive amounts of trivia that some contestants know. At the end of the day, however, if the great majority of persons viewing these shows are anything like me, they will remember neither the questions that were asked nor the answers given. While the game show was important to the contestant, to viewers like me it was nothing—nothing more than inconsequential information anyway.

It is both fascinating and unsettling to me how some people can approach the Bible with such nonchalance—even to the point that it is comparable to game show trivia. Isn't it interesting that the same book that is sacred to one person can carry little meaning for another? On many levels, the issue really has to do with meaning. It is one thing to say that the Bible is informative, yet it is another thing to personally accept or reject the meaning of that information.

In this chapter we will encounter a wide variety of readers who have interpreted the very non-trivial information of Acts in different ways. The result, of course, is the perception of different meanings. Yet, this is no small matter because in a very real sense, Luke's (the author of Acts) credibility is on the line. In the main, we are concerned here with the question posed in the title of this chapter: Can Luke's Acts be trusted? Yet, there is an immediate follow-up question that should be asked: Trusted in what way?

Over the course of the last several hundred years scholars have tended to discuss Luke in a twofold manner, namely, as a theologian and as a historian. We will devote our attention here to the latter. In light of this, we might refine our initial question and ask: Can Luke's Acts be trusted in terms of historical accuracy? As it turns out, our answer to this question is intimately related to whether or not we believe that Paul was historically accurate when he wrote accounts of his own travels in his epistles. Therefore, our entry into the terrain of Acts must necessarily overlap with the landscape of Paul's undisputed letters.

While we shall discuss the so-called "disputed" and "undisputed" letters of Paul in chapter eight, a brief word about this matter is in order here. It has been suggested that from the earliest days of church history there are several canonical letters attributed to Paul, that some interpreters believe Paul himself did not write.[1] One view is that after Paul's death some of his closest associates, those who carried on his torch, so to speak, wrote letters on his behalf, which he never had the chance to compose. Among other reasons, this notion has led some interpreters to place these letters in the category of "disputed," meaning that it is unclear and therefore disputed as to whether or not Paul himself wrote them.

Can Luke's Acts be Trusted?

The epistles falling under this disputed label are: Ephesians, Colossians, 2 Thessalonians, 1 and 2 Timothy, and Titus. Some would include Hebrews in this group. In turn, this means that there are seven undisputed letters: Romans, 1 and 2 Corinthians, Galatians, Philippians, 1 Thessalonians, and Philemon. Again, these letters are generally accepted as authentically Pauline, that is, from Paul himself. Since these letters are authentic they are the letters that can be trusted when seeking to reconstruct a chronology of Paul's life. The fact is, however, that they offer very little in the way of specifics when it comes to this topic.

Yet, Acts offers quite a bit of detail about Paul's travels. Thus, for many, placing Acts and Paul's undisputed letters side by side is the natural course of action. Surely, they compliment and substantiate one another, right? It is precisely at this point where many interpreters, asking this very same question, find themselves bewildered. Squaring Paul's statements with Luke's is no easy task; some have even declared it impossible. Oddly enough, it is at this breach where we tune in to the matter of whether or not Luke's Acts can be trusted in terms of historical accuracy.

TUNING IN

I rarely watch televangelists; I'm not really a fan. Recently, however, I was channel-surfing and happened upon a show titled "It Is Written." A pastor by the name of John Bradshaw was attempting to give a defense for the reliability of the Bible and in doing so, he appealed to the historical accuracy of Acts. He said, "And keep in mind, Dr. Luke has been called by many, 'One of the most accurate historians you could ever read.'"[2] On the one hand, this televangelist was correct: Luke's accuracy as a historian has been championed by many.

One the other hand, this televangelist conveniently leaves out hundreds of years of interpretive history. In doing so, his claim is very one-sided. The fact is, there are also many who have not only questioned Luke's historical credibility but have found his work completely unreliable in terms of history; he has been dubbed one of the worst and least accurate historians you could ever read.

In no way, shape or form did Bradshaw acknowledge the plethora of arguments that have called his viewpoint into question. In short, he was telling his own version of history to validate his own beliefs. Thus, people who are familiar with the interpretive history of Acts realize that this televangelist has lost a lot of his credibility; if he cannot accurately describe what has been said about Luke in the last four centuries, then there is likely no way that he can speak with any precision about Luke and his over two-thousand-year-old document.

This televangelist is but one example of why some people do not trust Christians and especially those who call themselves preachers. When important details are glossed over, significant pieces of history conveniently ignored, dissenting voices muted, and only one point of view allowed, people begin to worry. This worry is not unfounded, however, because like many religions, Christianity has been used as an oppressive device. What is needed is transparency. In terms of the historical trustworthiness of Acts, that is precisely what the remainder of this chapter seeks to provide.

TAKING NOTE

As I noted above, over the span of the last several centuries biblical researchers have put forth many different views about Acts.[3] Here, I will divide the varying voices into two groups: the dissenters and the advocates. Roughly, we may say that the dissenters belonged to the geographical regions of Germany, associated with the "Tübingen School," and the Netherlands, which was associated with the "Dutch Radical School." The advocates may be associated with British and American schools. Certainly, there is some overlap between the views of these two parties; in fact, many scholars are hybrids in one way or another, but there are also very marked differences. Here, we shall draw attention to a number of the most prominent interpreters from each group and note their contributions to the topic under review.[4]

It should be pointed out that the interpreters mentioned here are not listed in any sort of detailed chronological order. While there is a loose chronology at work, the overall aim here is to show how the scholars and their views are related to one another. Our starting point is with the dissenters and one of their most elite researchers, Wilhelm de Wette.

A sort of biblical jack-of-all-trades, de Wette was a prominent Old Testament scholar who was also well known and respected in the field of New Testament studies. We begin here because de Wette's *Introduction to the New Testament* was one of the foremost works of his era that challenged the historical accuracy of Acts. A few examples are in order.

In both Acts 11:25–30 and 15:1–2, we read that Paul made visits to Jerusalem. If read in narrative order, Luke is clearly describing two separate visits. For de Wette, however, this is nothing more than a literary device, a doublet; Paul actually visited Jerusalem once, not twice and therefore, Luke simply told the story a first time and then modified and reused it again later.[5] In addition to this and against the traditional consensus of the day, de Wette contended that the "*we* passages" of Acts (16:10–17; 20:5–15; 21:1–17; 27:1—28:19) did not include the author Luke.

For example, in Acts 16:6, the author mentions that "Paul and his companions" were traveling together throughout the region of Phrygia and Galatia. In narrating this, the author is speaking as one outside of that circle of companions. In grammatical terms, he is speaking in the third person (they). However, just four verses later, the author switches from the third-person (they) to the first-person tense (we). Now, instead of speaking as an outsider, the author says, "But after he [Paul] saw the vision, immediately *we* sought to leave to Macedonia." The "we" here seems to indicate that whereas earlier the author was not directly involved with Paul, he now is. This is a recurring feature throughout the remainder of Acts.

> Wilhelm M. L. De Wette was born in 1780 in Ulla, Germany. He was raised Lutheran as his father was a pastor, but later in life Wilhelm defected from the faith. He remarried after his first wife died during childbirth. He studied at the University of Jena and later taught at the University of Basel.

For de Wette, the author simply could not be the eyewitness; he could not have been a firsthand observer. For starters, the author had already contrasted himself with the eyewitnesses (Lk 1:1–4). Further, the author is biased when it comes to the miracles in the "*we* passages"; he is very one-sided. Therefore, one should be skeptical of his accounts because much of what he writes should be viewed as incomplete, false, and overly prejudiced.[6] Much more could be said about de Wette's views but these will suffice for now. It is important for our purposes to note that he challenged the longstanding consensus of the historicity of Acts and as a result, set off a domino effect.

Entering the Fray

> Ferdinand Christian Baur was born in 1792 in Schimden, Germany. He was a professor of New Testament at the University of Tübingen for nearly three and a half decades. Both he and his father were pastors. Baur was (and remains) a controversial figure within the fields of biblical studies and church history.

It was F. C. Baur, a monumental German Bible scholar and founder of the infamous Tübingen School of New Testament studies, who played a major role in shaping Acts research for many years to come. In brief, Baur's view was that the earliest Christians were divided into two major and competing sects, one devoted to Peter and the ways of Judaism, and the other devoted to Paul and friendly to the ways of Gentiles. It was through this split lens—based on his interpretation of the factions within the congregation at Corinth (1 Cor 1:11)—that Baur interpreted Acts.[7]

Baur's thinking was that if there were two parties that were antagonistic toward one another this meant that each group had its own beliefs and biases. As a reader, Baur sought to uncover and expose the (theological) biases of biblical writers, including those inherent to Acts. He referred to this approach as "*tendenz* analysis," which we will refer to here as "bias analysis" or "tendency analysis." When analyzing Acts, Baur noticed that the author had a tendency to compare Peter and Paul. Throughout the story both apostles are, among other things, shown performing miracles, giving public speeches, rebuking and correcting false teachings, and imparting the Holy Spirit to believers.

For Baur, however, this bias or tendency was something of a scandal. In fact, Baur leveled the charge that the author of Acts was falsely and deceitfully attempting to portray harmony between the leaders when, in all actuality, none existed. This is even more evident, he believed, when Acts is set beside Paul's epistles. In this case, there are two incredibly different portrayals of Paul; they are simply not the same person! Thus, Baur's conclusion was that on a historical level, the author of Acts simply could not be trusted as an accurate historian; he was too biased.[8] From this point forward in critical scholarship, two Pauls, or one Paul with a split personality, would be a major topic of discussion.

One of Baur's students, Matthias Schneckenburger, built upon his famed teacher's research. By the time he began publishing his own work, the idea that the author of Acts was an advocate of Paul had become

Can Luke's Acts be Trusted?

> Matthias Schneckenburger was born in 1804 in Talheim, Germany. His father was a farmer and businessman and his brother, Max, was a well known scholar. Matthias was a prominent Lutheran pastor and theologian in his day. He taught New Testament and theology at the University of Bern.

prominent among the members of the Tübingen School. For Schneckenburger, this was to be seen most clearly in the plethora of parallelisms that were used to place Paul on par with Peter. One of Schneckenburger's major contributions to Acts studies was to provide a thorough and detailed analysis of these comparisons.[9]

While his own study led him to the conclusion that Baur was right that the author had biases, in the end, he disagreed with the conclusion that this meant that Acts was historically untrustworthy. For Schneckenburger, the reason that the Paul of Acts and the Paul of the letters seem so different is due to context. In the epistles, Paul goes into detail about his life and thought, whereas in Acts, generalities rule the day. Further, in the epistles Paul can defend himself, in Acts he cannot and thus, the author does on his behalf. In fact, the author of Acts writes, in the main, to defend Paul and his apostolic endeavors. Thus, while many of the historical details of Acts could be readily accepted and others directly challenged, it remained that the central point of the writing was not history but persuasion. This conclusion of Schneckenberug's was, of course, very different from that of his predecessors.

> Eduard Gottlob Zeller was born in 1814 in Kleinbottwar, Germany. He studied under Georg W. F. Hegel at the University of Tübingen. He taught at the universities of Bern, Marburg, and Heidelberg respectively. He was an ardent opponent of Christianity during his lifetime. He died at Stuttgart in 1908.

However, Eduard Zeller, a student and son-in-law of Baur, carried on and championed some of his father-in-law's ideas.[10] The first to analyze Acts as a whole with the Tübingen School's bias analysis approach, it has been suggested that Zeller's major monograph was "the only really thorough study of Acts ever produced by the Tübingen School."[11] For our purposes here, it is important to know that Zeller believed Acts to be completely unreliable in terms of historical accuracy.

All of Acts's miracle stories were something akin to theological propaganda. Zeller claimed that there were internal inconsistencies, contradictions, and errors all over the place. Further, he heavily

119

exploited the notion that since the author of Acts was clearly biased, he should not be trusted on historical matters. In addition, he claimed that the Paul of Acts did not resemble the true Paul of the epistles, despite the attempt of Acts to make it seem otherwise. Never before had a scholar published with such fierce skepticism toward the historicity of Acts and its reconstruction of Paul as had Zeller.

Aside from imparting skepticism down through the Tübingen ranks, one of Zeller's other lasting offerings was the notion that in addition to Acts being a pro-Paul apologetic, it also had a second and very political purpose: to prove beyond the shadow of a doubt that Christianity was a legal religion that was not a threat to Rome.[12] Although later understood in a number of different ways, this contextual observation by Zeller would be examined by many scholars to follow and become a major focal point in many studies on Acts.

> Martin Dibelius was born in 1883 in Dresden, Germany. He earned a PhD from the University of Tübingen and his ThD from the University of Berlin. He was a professor of New Testament at the University of Heidelberg for over three decades. A very influential scholar, Dibelius died in 1947.

Another major Acts scholar among the Germans was Martin Dibelius. If for Baur, tendency analysis was the primary mode through which to engage Acts, for Dibelius it was "style analysis."[13] In other words, Dibelius was highly interested in the author's style and how it shaped the framework of Acts. One of Diebelius's main arguments was that while the early Petrine-focused portions of Acts were only loosely tied together, the remaining Pauline-focused chapters were tightly linked by way of a source—one of Paul's itineraries.

Yet, even with this source available, Dibelius contended that the style of the author of Acts reveals that historical accuracy was never really part of the compositional equation. Instead, the writer was simply and creatively formulating his own story; he was arranging, rearranging, adding, subtracting, and modifying the data available to him so as to create an engaging narrative. This is especially true of the speeches, which Dibelius believed contrasted with other ancient speeches.

When placed next to speeches given in trusted historical works of antiquity, Dibelius believed the speeches of Acts shared little affinity with them. Dibelius's conclusion, then, was that Acts is meant to be encountered as literature, not history. Therefore, he paid little attention

Can Luke's Acts be Trusted?

to the matter of historical accuracy or to his scholarly contemporaries who were concerned with this topic.

> Philipp Vielhauer was born in 1914 at Cameroon, to pietistic missionary parents from Switzerland. He studied under Rudolf Bultmann and Martin Dibelius, among others. He was put out of his church in Baden when, in the 1930s, he refused to take Hitler's oath. Later drafted and wounded in war, he had a plate placed in his head.

Another significant German interpreter of Acts was Philipp Vielhauer. His publications have received much criticism despite having an extended and influential reach. One scholar has even suggested that Vielhauer's work opened up an entirely new era of research among interpreters of Acts.[14] Vielhauer was interested in the theology of Paul and whether or not there was consistency between the Pauline theology found in Acts and in the epistles. His conclusion was that Luke's theological portrayal of Paul could not be squared with that of the letters.[15]

In particular, Vielhauer argued that in the categories of natural theology, law, Christology, and eschatology, there was no cohesiveness between Acts and the writings of Paul. For example, in Paul's Aeropagus speech (Acts 17), the concepts of sin, grace, and cross are all but missing. Yet, in Paul's letters these are all central elements![16] This proves that the author of Acts had a theological agenda and therefore, cannot be trusted on historical grounds. Now, the dual Pauls that Baur had earlier introduced were even farther separated. Just as well, the trustworthiness of Luke as an accurate historian was called into question at an even greater level.

> Hans Georg Conzelmann was born in 1915 in Talfingen, Germany. He studied at the universities of Marburg and Tübingen, earning his doctorate from the latter. He taught at Tübingen, Heidelberg, Zurich, and Göttingen. He fought in World War II where he received serious injuries. He died in 1989.

For Hans Conzelmann, historical approaches to Luke had simply missed the point. Luke was not a historian, he was a theologian. Hence the title of one of Conzelmann's most influential works: *The Theology of St. Luke*.[17] In this book, Conzelmann argued that the context of Luke-Acts was one in which Christians had become worried about the return of Christ; the delay caused tremendous amounts of stress and concern. In an effort to remedy these anxieties, Luke sought to provide his fellow believers with "salvation history," which began in the time of Israel, was realized during the life and ministry of Jesus, and is continuing in the interim period but requires patience.

For the author of Acts, history is the handmaiden of theology; in Luke's retelling, history serves the purposes of theology. As one scholar has suggested, "According to Conzelmann, the service of history to theology is so complete that Acts can no longer be considered 'history' in the traditional sense at all."[18] Luke's theology is that, in this waiting period, the church is "a place where the world is at home." The apostle Paul, however, sharply rejected such a notion.[19] This is where the fissure already split open by other interpreters seems to have been laid bare; now, the Paul of Acts and the Paul of the letters might as well be cracked mirror opposites.

> Bruno Bauer was born in 1809 in Eisenburg, Germany. He studied at the University of Berlin and was classmates with the controversial Karl Marx. Bauer was very conservative at the beginning of his career, but over time became a very controversial figure himself, especially when, in 1852, he rejected the historical Jesus.

Next in view is Bruno Bauer—not to be confused with F. C. Baur mentioned above—a scholar who was a very controversial figure in his time. Since their inception, his works have repeatedly earned the label "radical" (which he viewed in a positive sense, much like the term "innovative" today) and on at least one occasion, even led to his removal from university faculty. Bauer was an ardent opponent of Christianity and sought to deliberately discredit it by attempting to call into focus the untrustworthiness of the Bible. For Bauer, Acts was fertile stomping ground.

Very much could be said regarding Bauer's scholarship but it is significant for our purposes here to note the fact that he was an advocate of the popular "two Pauls" view of his day. Even so, he could hardly conceive of trusting Acts, much less Paul's epistles, for an accurate view of the real Paul. Instead, he asserted that Acts was written in the East and that all of Paul's letters, which were forgeries, were written in the West and were meant to function as correctives to the presentation of the apostle in Acts. This ultimately led Bruno Bauer to reject the Tübingen hypothesis espoused by F. C. Baur regarding Christian origins.

During this era, Willem van Manen arrived at the eventual conclusion that Luke sought to write a religious or sacred history, based on his own interpretation of the historical events mentioned. By the end of

Can Luke's Acts be Trusted?

> Willem Christiaan van Manen was born in 1842 in Noordeloos, Netherlands. He, his father and grandfather were all pastors in the Dutch Reformed Church. He studied at Utrecht and was later a professor in Early Christian literature and New Testament Exegesis at Leiden University. He died in 1905.

his career, van Manen had become even more skeptical than Bruno Bauer about the authenticity of Paul's letters and asserted that none of them, not even the so-called "undisputed letters" could be trusted. Further, because Acts used the Pauline epistles (alongside texts such as the Acts of Paul, the Acts of Peter, the Pauline Itinerary, and Josephus) it too, could not really be trusted in terms of historical accuracy or factuality.

> Franz Camille Overbeck was born in 1837 in St. Petersburg, Russia. He was a close friend of Friedrich Nietzche and a protestant theologian. He studied at the universities of Leipzig, Göttingen, Berlin, and Jena respectively. His antagonism toward Christianity made him a very controversial figure. He died in 1905.

Franz Overbeck, owing much to de Wette, was just as adamant about the historical unreliability of Acts as many of his predecessors.[20] In fact, for Overbeck, it was viewed as a settled matter among serious interpreters that the whole of Acts was not to be trusted in terms of history. He reasoned that the author lacked sound sources and wrote out of historical ignorance. The "we passages," for example, may have come from a companion of Paul's but they were still modified so much that their trustworthiness cannot withstand critical scrutiny. Further, following Zeller, Overbeck asserted that one of the purposes of Acts was to show Christianity's validity in Rome's eyes. Another purpose of Acts was to show that Christianity is valid because of its ancient ties; Acts desires to show how second or third-century Christianity is intimately connected to its religious past.

> John Knox was born in 1900 in Frankfort, Kentucky. He studied and taught at both Emory University (BD) and the University of Chicago (PhD). In addition, he taught at Union Theological Seminary. Originally a Methodist pastor, later in life he was ordained in the Episcopal Church.

John Knox also concluded that Acts could not be looked to for historical accuracy, especially in relation to a chronology of Paul's life and travels. He went to great lengths to argue this point. He asserted that while the author of Acts likely had sources available to him while he was writing, in the end, they were tremendously reworked to fit his own narrative and point of view. This is clear, for Knox, particularly in the case where Luke mentions five visits to Jerusalem whereas Paul himself only mentions three. Therefore, "we can justly say that a fact only suggested in the letters has a status that even the most unequivocal statement of Acts, if not otherwise supported, cannot confer."[21] Yet, Knox was not willing to completely throw Acts out. He wrote, "We may, with proper caution, use Acts to supplement the autobiographical data of the letters, but never to correct them."[22] The distinction between Paul's firsthand chronology and Luke's secondary sources only helped further the divide between a Lukan chronology and a Pauline chronology.

> Jonathan L. Reed was born in the 1963 in Minneapolis. He earned his PhD from the Claremont Graduate School, where he studied with Burton Mack. He has taught in numerous academic institutions and has appeared on many major television networks such as ABC, CNN, and NatGeo as an archaeological consultant.

Our last two interpreters to be mentioned here are John Crossan and Jonathan Reed. Together, these two wrote the book *In Search of Paul: How Jesus's Apostle Opposed Rome's Empire with God's Kingdom*.[23] Given the interpretive history up to this point, one can likely glean from the subtitle that Crossan and Reed rehash the claim that within Acts, Christianity—with Paul at the heart of it—is portrayed as a non-threat to Rome. For Crossan and Reed, not only is this bias problematic, it simply cannot be squared with the Paul of the (undisputed) letters.

> John Dominic "Dom" Crossan was born in 1934 in Ireland. He earned his Doctor of Divinity at Maynooth College, whereafter his studies led him around the world and to resign from the Catholic priesthood. He taught at DePaul University for two and a half decades.

Crossan and Reed repeatedly and aggressively push the thesis that when writing, Luke "emphasizes certain elements with regard to Christians, pagans, Jews, and Roman authorities that reflect his own, much later views rather than Paul's much earlier experiences."[24] For these commentators, Luke consistently misunderstands, misinterprets, and erroneously reworks the truth about Paul. For them, it is even problematic that within the New Testament, Luke's Acts is situated before Paul's epistles. They claim that in the present sequence, "you meet the Lukan Paul before you meet the Pauline or historical Paul," and as a result, from the start, "Paul gets colored Lukan."[25] Because of this, when Acts is critically sifted for accurate details about Paul and Pauline chronology, little to nothing of historical value will be extracted.

Looking back on some of the conclusions of the dissenters, one can see that there are a number of characteristics that are rather consistent throughout: skepticism toward Luke as a historian because of his apologetic biases, socio-political agendas or authorial styles and tendencies, an emphasis on Lucan theology (over against history), and a focus on literary details (over against historical details). It should be kept in mind that alongside these movers and shakers in Acts studies, many other names were left out of our survey; this is but a sketch of a much larger picture.

Now we turn our attention to the advocates. As with the previous group, we shall pay close attention to prominent trends among this lineup of interpreters, especially on points where they agree and disagree with their dissenter colleagues.

> Albrecht Benjamin Ritschl was born in 1822 in Berlin. His father was an evangelical pastor. Ritschl studied at the universities of Bonn and Halle, receiving his doctorate from the latter. He lectured at Göttingen for twenty-five years, where he taught church history and the history of dogma. He died in 1889.

One of the most forceful rejections of the Tübingen view came from a former student of F. C. Baur, Albrecht Ritschl. A leading theologian of his era, Ritschl challenged Baur's thesis on a number of levels. One of the major cracks that he exposed in Baur's view was that it was much too indebted to the philosopher Georg Hegel's idea of dualism. Put differently, Baur took Hegel's philosophy, which—explained rather simplistically and crudely here—understood the world as arranged in opposing pairs (e.g., left/right, black/white, wrong/right, etc.) and superimposed it back on the ancient church and its texts. This is precisely how Baur arrived at his conclusion of the dueling factions of the Peter and Paul parties. Thus, one of Ritschl's claims was that Baur's theory owed more to this modern philosophy than to sound exegesis and historical research.

After leveling this strong critique, Ritschl believed he had also put himself in a position to show that harmony actually existed among the apostles. For him, Peter and Paul certainly had some tensions between them. However, these were mainly social or practical differences, not necessarily theological ones and certainly not differences of core theological belief.²⁶ This was especially potent in Ritschl's claims that the Jerusalem Council (which he identifies in both Acts 15 and Gal 2) revealed "essential agreement" between Peter, Paul, and those involved. Again, while there may have been practical differences between those in attendance at the meeting, in theological essentials all were on the same page. This is a markedly different interpretation than those of Ritschl's German colleagues.

Eduard Lekebusch and Ernest Renan (see below) contested the allegations of many of their Tübingen and Dutch colleagues. For Lekebusch, this occurred in his work, *A New Investigation into the Composition and Origin of Acts*.²⁷ The genius of this in-depth work is that unlike a great majority of his predecessors, Lekebusch did not approach Acts with a ready-made theory of choice. Instead, he sought to approach it on its own terms, as a piece of ancient literature. Through a close examination of the Greek texts of both Luke and Acts and their linguistic tendencies, Lekebusch found that the two were incredibly cohesive. Importantly, Acts was not simply strung together haphazardly.

> *Eduard Lekebusch was born in 1830. He was a pastor of two churches in the northern state of Schleswig-Holstein in Germany. Lekebusch earned a doctorate in theology and it is unclear whether he published much beyond his book investigating the composition and origin of Acts. Lekebusch died in 1892.*

Lekebusch concluded that the linguistic tendencies and style of the author of the "*we* passages" were consistent with the remainder of Acts. He argued that this author was Luke, who also penned the third Gospel. Even more, this is the same Luke mentioned in Paul's epistle (Col 4:14), who was one of Paul's companions. Lekebusch earned a fair amount of credibility in his field for not shying away from building on the work of Baur and his descendants. Although he held great disagreements with many of the dissenters, he did not simply stick his head in the sand or cover his eyes and ears, acting as if those scholars and their works never existed. Rather, his courteous, detailed, and scholarly interaction with these interpreters went a long way.

Next, we look at Ernest Renan, who was also being taken seriously by many of his contemporaries.²⁸ While he was not in agreement with Lekebusch on much, he did agree that the "*we* passages" of Acts were historically reliable. He believed that Acts 1–12 was historically unreliable due to the legendary sources used to reconstruct it, as well as

> Ernest Renan was born in 1823 in Tréguier, France. He studied at the Issy-les-Moulineaux Seminary and later accepted a teaching position at Vendôme. From the early years of his teenage life, Renan was marked as a sophisticated thinker. Like many of his contemporaries, Renan became a controversial figure.

> Joseph Barber Lightfoot was born in 1828 in Liverpool. He graduated with a Doctor of Divinity in 1851 from Trinity College in Cambridge. He served as the Bishop of Durham for a decade. He helped produce the Revised Version of the Bible as well as a translation of the Apostolic Fathers. He died in 1889.

the author's overly apologetic agenda. However, chapters 13–28 were solid because they were based on trustworthy sources. In short, the portions of Acts directly related to Paul could, for the most part, be trusted on historical matters. In addition, noting Acts's setting within the context of the last two decades of the first century CE, Renan drew on Zeller's theory to propose that Luke wrote to help prove that Christianity was no threat to the Roman Empire.

Around this same time, J. B. Lightfoot, who wrote a number of commentaries on the Pauline epistles and a few articles on Acts, sought to show how archaeology validated Luke's geographical and historical accuracy.[29] In addition to the many seemingly incidental coincidences between the epistles and Acts as well as the likeness of the speeches between Paul on the one hand and Peter and James on the other, Lightfoot believed that a close inspection of historical and archaeological data could reveal that the Paul of Acts and the epistles were one and the same.

For example, Luke's claims that Achaia was ruled by a senate-sent proconsul, and that in Cyprus the proconsulate was assumed by Sergius Paulus, could both be substantiated by textual and archaeological evidence.[30] These are but two examples illustrating the detailed historical accuracy of the author of Acts. Lightfoot also shows how Corinthian, Ephesian, Athenian, and Philippian finds help substantiate Luke's work. Despite never having written a full commentary on Acts, through his other works, Lightfoot vigorously challenged the views of the dissenters. For him, Luke is faithfully accurate and has no agenda driving him; his purpose is simply to edify the church and provide it with a history from its beginnings up to the present.[31]

Like Lightfoot, Sir William Ramsay bolstered claims about the historical accuracy of Acts based on geographical and archaeological

Entering the Fray

> Sir William Mitchell Ramsay was born in 1851 in Glasgow, Scotland. He studied at the University of Aberdeen as well as St. John's College, Oxford. He taught at the former for twenty-five years. To this day, Ramsay's work remains influential. He died in 1939.

evidences. Early on, Ramsay was a skeptic of Luke's reliability, however, after studying in the Mediterranean basin and taking on detailed research there, his views changed. For instance, he noted that Luke's description of Paul's travels between Phrygia and Lycaonia in Acts 13–14 is meticulously correct.[32] Ramsay reasoned that "there is a certain presumption that a writer who proves to be exact and correct in one point will show the same qualities in other matters. No writer is correct by mere chance, or accurate sporadically."[33] For Ramsay, logic suggested that if Luke was so detailed in speaking of minor matters, then it stands to reason that the same would be true of more prominent matters.

Throughout his work, Ramsay endeavored to show that this was indeed the case; Acts can be trusted in the smallest and greatest of details. Ramsay wrote, "Luke's history is unsurpassed in respect of its trustworthiness.... I was finding from day to day other unused ancient evidence on a small scale; and if Luke's narrative was trustworthy, it was for me exceptionally valuable, as giving evidence on a larger scale. There was nothing else like it."[34] In terms of Acts's accuracy in relation to Paul's movements, Ramsay devoted much attention to developing what is known as "the South Galatian hypothesis."[35]

In the first two chapters of Galatians, Paul mentions two visits to Jerusalem. In Gal 1:17–20, Paul says that after his Damascus Road encounter, he visited Jerusalem once. Fourteen years after that visit, he notes in 2:1–10 that he visited Jerusalem again. Many interpreters have suggested that the first visit mention in Galatians may be paired with Acts 9:26, while the second one fits with Acts 15. It is precisely because these connections and the details within them cannot seem to be squared that many have been led to believe that Luke was historically inaccurate. Ramsay, however, held that Gal 1:17–20 should be linked to Acts 9:26, and likewise that Acts 11:30 and 12:25 should be viewed as the counterpart of Galatians 2:1–10. For him, this was not the Jerusalem Council but rather a gathering between Paul and the Jerusalem apostles to discuss famine relief. Acceptance of this view relieves many of the tensions between Acts and the epistles.

Can Luke's Acts be Trusted?

This would also lead to the conclusion that Galatians was written just prior to the Jerusalem Council narrated in Acts 15, which took place shortly before 50 CE. In turn, this makes Galatians the earliest of Paul's letters and suggests that Paul's first missionary journey included visits to the cities of Lycia, Perga, Psidian Antioch, Iconium, Lystra, Derbe, and Attalia. All of these cities were in the southern region of Galatia, not the northern. This theory would allow that both Paul's account of his visits to Jerusalem, and Luke's, are historically accurate. Thus, these Galatians passages are not depicting Paul's second missionary journey (Acts 15:39–18:23), as many have suggested. Were this the case, Ramsay believed, Luke's historical accuracy would have been greatly compromised.[36]

> Karl Gustav "Adolf" von Harnack was born in 1851 in Dorpat (Tartu), Estonia. The son of a professor of homiletics and church history, he blossomed as a leading European protestant scholar. He taught at a number of major universities including Leipzig, Marburg, Giessen, and Berlin. He died in 1930.

Adolf von Harnack, however, held to "the North Galatian hypothesis" while at the same time asserting that in Acts, Luke is, for the most part, historically accurate. He certainly believed that there were discrepancies between Acts and the epistles but in his study of the language, style, "*we* passages," and Pauline travels, he found that the agreements far outweigh the supposed contradictions.[37] On social and theological levels he also showed that the portrayal of Paul in both Acts and the letters coincide. Harnack's research led him to conclude in the second work of a three-volume series that, "From almost every possible angle of historical criticism [Acts] is a solid, respectable, and, in many respects, an extraordinary work."[38] For Harnack, Acts is not a political defense of Christianity, nor is it primarily a defense of Paul; rather it is a continuation of the third Gospel (Luke) and seeks, in the main, "to present historically the power of the Spirit of Jesus in the apostles."[39]

> Henry Joel Cadbury was born in 1883 in Philadelphia. He was raised within the Quaker tradition. He earned his PhD from Harvard University, where he later taught for two decades. He accepted the Nobel Peace prize in 1947 on behalf of a British humanities organization he had served alongside. He died in 1974.

Henry Cadbury, an incredibly influential commentator on the interpretive history of Acts, has claimed that while Luke's work may appear to have a number of confusions, in all reality, "Taken as a whole . . . [Acts] commends itself at once as a generally historical narrative."[40] One of Cadbury's major contributions to Acts studies has to do with his striving to situate the text and its author within the proper ancient contexts. In other words, Cadbury strove to show how Luke was in keeping with other ancient historians and their approaches to writing historical accounts. While this has not settled the matter on whether or not Luke is finally and always historically accurate in his storytelling, it does show that modern interpreters must judge him by practices and techniques common to history writers in antiquity, not those of modernity.[41] It is simply inappropriate to use modern standards for writing history to measure ancient authors like Luke. With this insight, Cadbury became something of a game-changer in Luke-Acts studies.

> Colin John Hemer was born in 1930. He earned his doctorate under F. F. Bruce at the University of Manchester in 1965. He taught at Manchester as well as Sheffield and served as the librarian at Tyndale House for a few years. He also lectured in Turkey and Australia. He was an avid birdwatcher. He died in 1987.

Colin J. Hemer has forcefully argued this point as well. He goes to great lengths to show that Luke fits nicely and comfortably within the setting of other ancient historians. Further, he dismantles the widely held assumption that in terms of historical accuracy, the ancients "had no standards of their own."[42] Drawing on the likes of Strabo, Dionysius of Halicarnassus, Dioscorides, Josephus, Philo, Chrysostom, Epictetus, Plutarch, Livy, Polybius, and many more, he shows that in fact, ancient historians had very exacting standards for writing historical accounts. Additionally, he knocks the legs out from under the argument that ancient accounts such as Luke's cannot be trusted because they contain biases.

Hemer writes, "It would be an extreme position to suggest that history is so far written in the historian's image that no sufficient deposit of hard truth is left. . . . If then our modern house is in considerable disorder . . . we cannot pass comprehensive judgment on the ancients for not being exempt from the problems with which we are afflicted."[43] Further, the presence of biases "in an ancient source does not invalidate that source; it merely requires the proper exercise of critical judgment upon it. No source is 'pure history' in the sense some theologians demand; all are to some extent interpretive and therefore open to the problem of bias. But they are not necessarily unusable for that reason."⁴⁴ In the end, Hemer concludes that Luke's Acts and Paul's epistles do not contradict one another, rather they are highly complementary of each other; both are historically accurate and trustworthy.

> Frederick Fyvie Bruce was born in 1910 in Elgin, Scotland. He was heavily influenced by William Ramsay while studying at the University of Aberdeen. He later started the biblical studies department at the University of Manchester. A prolific author, he published thousands of works. He died in 1990.

F. F. Bruce was another advocate of the historical reliability of Acts. He had studied ancient classical works prior to focusing on New Testament, which provided him with the skills to rather easily make connections between the two. Bruce viewed Acts as "a historical document" that belonged to "the line of descent from Thucydides."⁴⁵ As such, Bruce argued that the so-called contradictory Pauls of Acts and the letters are not grounded in history but scholarly creativity. Therefore, Acts and the epistles can be read in tandem and illumine one another. Luke writes both with a concern for historical events as well as to offer a rebuttal to the "Imperial City" against "the popular charges brought against Christianity by insisting on its complete and acknowledged innocence before the law of the Empire."⁴⁶

> I. Howard Marshall was born in 1934. He earned his PhD from the University of Aberdeen, Scotland, where he later taught and became Professor Emeritus. Marshall has lectured all over the world including in Prague, Cairo, and the Ukraine. His wife Maureen Yeung, is president of Evangel Seminary in Hong Kong.

Finally, we consider the influential interpreter I. Howard Marshall. Once again, a tremendous amount could be said concerning Marshall's work but for our purposes here, only a few items will be discussed. Synthesizing a number of the views of his predecessors, Marshall contends that Luke was a historian but that he also had his biases, particularly those of the theological sort. In his view, then, "Luke is *both* historian *and* theologian" and by that he means, "as a theologian, Luke was concerned that his message about Jesus and the early church should be based upon reliable history."⁴⁷ Further, in agreement with Cadbury and Hemer, Marshall asserts that Luke makes use "of the common literary pattern of his time to express his own particular sentiments. The point in the adoption of the conventional form is that Luke was claiming for his work a place in contemporary literature and thereby commending it to the attention of his readers."[48]

In the end, Marshall concludes that Luke is the beloved physician mentioned in Colossians and that he was a traveling companion of Paul's. Marshall rejects the notion that Acts cannot be used to reconstruct Pauline chronology and asserts that, while "there are differences between the picture of Paul in Acts and that in his own letters . . . this does not mean that the two pictures are irreconcilable. . . . We believe that the two can in fact be harmonized in general terms."[49] Here, Marshall provides an aggressive disputation of blanket claims against Luke's capability to compose accurate history.

Reflecting on the advocates, we note several important details. First, over time, the scholars listed here became more aware of pushing their own biases about writing history back on to Luke (and Paul). This caused them to reach back to the ancient world to see if examples of Luke's history-writing contemporaries could shed light on Acts. Second, the interpreters within this group made it a point to avoid ruling out theories and possible evidences, whether textual or archaeological, before examining them closely. This was not always the case with the dissenters. Third, the advocates were much more inclined to give Acts the benefit of the doubt as opposed to relegating it to the realm of "historically unreliable" right out of the gate. Fourth and finally, it should be recognized that many of the gains made by the advocates were likely only possible because of the challenges from their dissenter colleagues. It is quite likely that had the challenges from the Tübingen and Dutch schools never been raised, much of the hard research used to validate Luke's historical credibility would likely still be unknown.

TAKING ACTION

A professor of mine once shared with me a formative piece of advice his father gave him as a child: "Take your work very seriously, but don't take yourself too seriously." Working through the incredibly tangled history of the interpretation of Acts is a challenge but at the end of it, as interpreters, we are reminded to take both it and our own work of engaging the Bible very seriously. There is too much riding on the line to not do so. Critics and dissenters will always emerge. Yet, there is a sense in which, while their claims need to be taken with much seriousness, they might also be viewed as a gift. Without their critiques and questions, many of history's most salient points would go unnoticed. In their own way, dissenters have often contributed to the validation of Christianity's trustworthiness.

On this matter, we might take notes from J. B. Lightfoot who, while disagreeing with some of the dissenters of his day, did so in a non-hostile way. He respectfully engaged their work and systematically offered his own counterproofs, all the while maintaining an air of graciousness and humility about himself. Far too often modern Christians are quick to dismiss the views and questions of those with whom they disagree. The litmus test of a mature faith is not writing-off one's challengers but rather hearing them out, loving them regardless, and offering reasoned responses. It was this approach that earned Lekebusch much credibility among his peers. This is no easy task, of course, and I confess I have fallen flat on this principle from time to time. Yet, it is a goal worth reminding ourselves of, and straining toward.

For the Bible study leader or pastor who aims to teach Acts, it might be very beneficial to walk together through the interpretive history laid out here. Not only will this give the group some firm historical grounding to stand on, but inevitably it will raise many questions. Dealing with matters of how to define terms such as "history," "interpreted history," "reliability," "accuracy," "biases," "tensions," "contradictions," and more will urge congregants to take Acts seriously. Additionally, it could be shown that even after centuries of scrutiny, the Bible remains a force to be reckoned with. Each generation is not only entrusted with the task of passing on the interpretive history preceding it, but also responsible for exposing its truths and weaknesses. Even more, every era needs to raise up sound interpreters who will draw out the Bible's relevance for today and help enact its "salvation history." Indeed, these are serious matters and they are simply too important to leave to the pens of radical revisionist historians. Had our predecessors left Acts in the hands of such revisionists, we would have nothing but disregard for Luke and his work today. Thankfully, devoted interpreters have not let that happen and now, we can say with confidence that, indeed, Luke's Acts can be trusted.

8

Paul: Disputed or Undisputed?

http://michaelhalcomb.com/enteringthefray-paulines.html

THROUGHOUT MY MIDDLE SCHOOL years my pals and I became interested in what FBI specialists refer to today as graphology, that is, the study of signatures. Now, this was not a natural interest of ours, rather, it just sort of happened. It may have even been inevitable. Yet, as mischievous teenage boys, we were not interested in the science itself or just anyone's autograph; we were interested specifically in our parents' signatures.

You see, whenever our middle school sent our term grades or report cards home with us they wanted proof that we had shown them to our parents. For our teachers, that proof was denoted by a parental signature. For some students (not me, of course!), however, the thought of showing midterm grades to their parents was particularly frightening. Thus, the way to avoid a potential catastrophe was to study the signature of a parent, practice writing it, and then take it upon oneself to sign their name.

Today we refer to a composition that is signed in the name of someone who did not actually write it as a forgery. Producing forgeries is nothing new; this practice has been around for thousands of years. Yet, when thinking about the concept of forgery in the ancient world, we might try to see it from two different angles, one positive and one negative. Let's start with the positive.

In antiquity, students often took courses on rhetoric, the art of persuasion. In these classes they would study renowned rhetoricians and public speakers, how to structure speeches rhetorically, and the use of important rhetorical devices. One of these devices was known as *prosopopoeia*. This is a Greek compound word that, in modern verbiage, might be translated as "make a face." We may think of this rhetorical device as making the face of someone else come to mind through your own work. Put differently, today we could even liken it to putting (your own) words into someone else's mouth.

In learning how to use prosopopoeia, an ancient schoolboy might have been assigned the task of writing a rhetorical piece about a political issue. Because the student had no real political clout or status, to make his speech more persuasive, he could write the speech as if Cicero or some other prominent figure were delivering it. This idea is not all that far from when, in my childhood days on the basketball court, I wore a Michael Jordan jersey, Air Jordan shoes, stuck my tongue out, and attempted to mimic Jordan's moves every time I took a jump shot or drove to the hoop; I believed that portraying myself as Michael Jordan was sure to convince my friends that I was an excellent basketball player.

In this sort of way, writing under the name of someone else in the ancient world was not only accepted, it was viewed positively. Yet, there was another practice in antiquity that, for the most part, was viewed negatively because it was perceived as inherently deceitful. While some scholars have suggested that pseudonymity was perfectly acceptable by ancient standards, we should likely call a spade a spade and stick with the term forgery for this type of document.¹ 2 Thess 2:2 refers to these types of texts when it warns congregants not to become easily alarmed by "a spirit or by a message or by a letter" sent "as if it were from us" but which is, in reality, from someone else.² These types of documents are forgeries.

Comments such as these in 2 Thess have led scholars down the road of analyzing ancient texts to determine whether or not they are forgeries. Such undertakings have taken place on both biblical and extra-biblical documents but, of course, for our purposes we are interested in the former. It might actually be surprising to learn that some scholars have sought to examine the New Testament documents in an effort to see if signs of forgery are evident. It might be even more surprising to discover that many scholars hold the view that six letters of Paul fall into this category.

These six letters, which I alluded to briefly in the previous chapter, are: Ephesians, Colossians, 2 Thessalonians (this is very ironic, given the statement of 2:2 cited above as well as 3:17 where Paul says that he signs the letter with his own hand!), 1 and 2 Timothy, and Titus (these last three are often referred to together as the "Pastoral Epistles"). Of the twelve major topics discussed in this book, I would venture to say that it is this issue that has likely caused the greatest breach between the church and New Testament scholars. There is a sense in which this matter is perceived as directly calling into question not only the trustworthiness of the New Testament, but also and even of God himself.

Taking their cues from 2 Thess 2:2, modern laity are frightened by the fact that through tinkering with what they believe to be an inspired text, they themselves might be perceived as false prophets, deceivers, rebels, and men or women of lawlessness. This, therefore, is how they categorize scholars who conduct this type of research. Such reticence is wholly and completely understandable. Further, laypersons typically shirk at this because it appears to fly in the face of the concept of scriptural inspiration. How can these texts be inspired if they are forgeries or frauds? Even more, this would either suggest that God, on the one hand, used deceit for his own gain, or on the other hand, that his sovereignty amounts to little because he has evidently had no superintending hand in the creation of New Testament documents.

This claim that nearly one fourth of the New Testament's twenty-seven documents are forgeries cuts to the core of some of Christianity's most deeply held beliefs. The typical reaction from a layperson is to simply shake their head at the issue and walk away or to begin condemning those who make such inquiries. Given that this is the usual response, and given that this is the issue under review throughout the remainder of this chapter, my hope is that you will not put the brakes on at this point and stop reading.

I am not going to argue here that the six letters mentioned above are forgeries. The evidences of these disputed texts, as many scholars would prefer to label them, can ultimately speak for themselves. Just as well, you can come to your own conclusions about whether or not you think they are disputed or undisputed. What I intend to do here is to acclimate us to the conversation by looking at how researchers from both sides of the matter assess the evidence. In other words, after getting tuned in a bit more to the conversation, we will work through each of these six texts by letting one scholar from each side make their case. In my view, this is the fairest way of helping folks enter the fray of this very important discussion.

TUNING IN

Throughout many of the letters bearing Paul's name, the apostle is found telling his congregants to mimic him, that is, to be like him.[3] Two of the best examples are found in the epistle to the Corinthians. In 1 Cor 4:16 he says, "Therefore, I exhort you to become imitators of me" and in 11:1, "You all become imitators of me, just as I am also [an imitator] of Christ." For the most part, these rhetorical statements have a practical aim: They are used to persuade congregants to hold correct beliefs, which will, in turn, shape their liturgical and ethical behaviors. What we never find Paul saying, however, is "You all become imitators of me in terms of letter-writing," or "Write letters in my name, acting as if you were me." Certainly, just as it is the case today, imitation was a form of flattery in Paul's era. Yet, when it came to writing epistles, Paul never admonished the laity of his congregations or his coworkers to write in his name.

Further, Paul suggests that when he cannot be physically somewhere, his letters should not simply be considered the next best thing, but a realistic representation of himself.[4] To help that process along Paul invests a certain level of authority in his coworkers and letter-carriers who, upon arrival at the churches he has overseen, deliver and perform his letters thereby giving voice to them. For Paul, this type of delivery was a valid means of putting his own words in someone else's mouth. What is not clear or evident, however, is that Paul himself encouraged, permitted, or even tolerated the creation of documents under his name.

Additionally, no examples of forged ancient religious letters in general, or Christian letters in particular, have ever been found.[5] Yet, other types of ancient forgeries have certainly been uncovered. In the academic world, scholars refer to this phenomenon as pseudepigraphy. This compound term comes from the two Greek words "pseudēs" and "graphē," which taken together mean "false writing." The related term pseudonymous, also a Greek compound word from the terms "pseudēs" and "onoma," means "false name"; thus, these were texts that, while claiming authorship by a specific person, were actually written by someone else under a false name. Many of the writings that fall within this category are narratives and novels, but not letters, and especially not religious or Christian letters. This makes it all the more puzzling to many, especially non-specialists, that researchers can place so much stock in the idea that six of the letters attributed to Paul are pseudonymous.

It may be the case that there are several reasons for this. One of these reasons is that over time, a handful of respected scholars have championed these views. For the most part, these scholars have conducted detailed analyses that have led them to such conclusions. What happens, then, is that these views get picked up and adopted by other authors. Instead of doing thorough research of their own, they simply consult a handful of works and pay lip-service to the work of others. I refer to this as scholarly regurgitation. Truth be told, scholarly regurgitation is widespread within academic circles!

This also happens in the church, however, because pastors buy commentaries that make bald statements such as "the majority of scholars believe" this view or that. Not wanting to appear unscholarly and not wanting to conduct original research, they simply adopt and regurgitate the views in sermons and Bible studies. In short, laziness, in the form of not doing thorough research, and fears of not being taken seriously or perhaps even mocked or bullied by the majority of scholars are powerful driving forces. Blindly or fearfully subscribing to the

Paul: Disputed or Undisputed?

views of others and reproducing them without having done thorough research only damages the academic guild and the church.

As a note of caution, it is a good practice—and one I adhere to myself—that anytime you find someone appealing to the majority rule, a red flag should go up in your mind. Not only is this type of appeal a logical fallacy, in reality, there is no way that one scholar has any means of quantifying what the majority of Bible scholars worldwide believe. Further, it may often be the case that those researchers who make claims about the majority view are later shown to have been incorrect. For our purposes here, all one needs to do is place any number of commentaries on the Pastoral Epistles next to one another and they will see that sweeping claims about pseudonymity are often made, all the while offering no substantive evidence. In fact, it is quite common to read remarks such as, "The majority of scholars believe that the Pastoral Epistles are pseudonymous. We accept this view too; however, we will not cover the topic of pseudonymity in any depth here." Again, blanket statements such these, which are not backed by strong research, should raise every reader's suspicions.

TAKING NOTE

> Edward Evanson was born in 1731 in Warrington, Lancashire. As a child, he was educated by his uncle and in his teenage years, studied classics at Emmanuel College, Cambridge. He was an ordained minister but after preaching a controversial Easter sermon in 1771, he lost that post. Evanson died in 1805.

In 1792, a scholar by the name of Edward Evanson wrote a controversial work that set in motion much of today's debate about the disputed and undisputed Pauline epistles. Near the end of his book, he stated that "not one of these Epistles contains in it that necessary internal testimony of the divine authority of the writer, the spirit of prophecy; whilst Paul's epistles to the Corinthians, Thessalonians, Galatians, and Timothy, have the historic testimony in their favour, strongly corroborated by that and every other internal evidence of authenticity."[6] Needless to say, Evanson's examination was highly critical and for that very reason, quite controversial.

One to never miss a good controversy, several decades later, the famed scholar of the Tübingen School, F. C. Baur, put forth a redressed version of this view—though he never cited Evanson as a source—and

Entering the Fray

> Ferdinand Christian Baur was born in 1792 in Schimden, Germany. He was a professor of New Testament at the University of Tübingen for nearly three and a half decades. Both he and his father were pastors. Baur was (and remains) a controversial figure within the fields of biblical studies and church history.

asserted that with the exception of Romans, 1 and 2 Corinthians, and Galatians, all of the Pauline epistles were pseudonymous. This type of examination appealed to many, and through Baur and his colleagues the question of pseudonymity became incredibly popular. Following this, it became standard among a number of scholars to refer to the disputed epistles as pseudo- or deutero-Paulines (where "pseudo" means "false" and "deutero" means "secondary").[7]

At this point, we turn our attention to the six disputed Pauline epistles. As has already been noted, we shall allow interpreters from both sides of the fence to have their say. Of course, these are only two variations among a mass of nuanced views. Further, it should be kept in mind that the works of these scholars are being introduced as "first clues" not the final word; these are gateways, if you will, that can set you on the way to successfully navigating this topic at a more in-depth level. It would be highly beneficial after reading this chapter to consult the bibliographies of these works and dig deeper into the topic. For now, however, let's turn our attention to Ephesians.

> Andrew T. Lincoln was born in 1944 at Wolverhampton, England. He earned his BD from Westminster Theological Seminary, Philadelphia and both his MA and PhD from Trinity College, Cambridge. He has taught at several prominent universities such as Sheffield, Toronto, and Gloucester.

In a number of works on Ephesians, Andrew T. Lincoln has argued that the letter does not come from the hand of Paul. He has a number of reasons for this view, two of which interest us here. The first is linguistic in nature while the second is related to theology. Here, Lincoln also appeals to the supposed majority rule, stating, "The view that the implied author, Paul, is not the real author reflects the consensus in New Testament scholarship."[8]

In terms of language, Lincoln contends that the style of Ephesians varies greatly from the undisputed letters, that there are many unique terms found here that are not present in the others, and that the method of argumentation is characteristically unPauline.[9] For example, the very lengthy sentences of Ephesians (1:3–14, 15–23; 2:1–7; 3:1–7, 14–19; 4:11–16; 5:17–14 and 6:14–20) do not mirror Paul's undisputed letters. Additionally, Lincoln contends that there are a host of irregularities when it comes to the grammar and syntax of Ephesians; these are patently out of keeping with the habits of Paul.[10]

The seemingly unusual language contributes to an atypical Pauline theology. Thus, Lincoln contends that where the undisputed epistles focus on the death of Christ, justification in relation to works of the law, and specific congregations, here the emphasis appears to be on the exaltation of Christ, Christ's cosmic lordship, a realized eschatology, and a universal church. These and other ideas lead Lincoln to conclude, "Connected with these changes of emphasis in thought is a perspective which appears to be later than that of Paul." The author, then, who wrote Ephesians after Paul's death, was a member of a "Pauline school" that sought to carry on the apostle's mission in Asia Minor.[11]

Perhaps one of the things we should notice about this view is that it does not seem as damaging as one might think. Put differently, Lincoln's view has the capability of removing some of the initial fears associated with pseudonymity. The notion of one of Paul's disciples or co-workers carrying on his teacher's legacy through letter writing does not come off as too threatening. Even so, some would contend that there is still a lot riding on the line and that beneath all of Lincoln's conclusions, there are many important historical, ethical, and theological questions that need to be addressed and answered.

> Markus Barth was born in 1915 at Safenwill in the canton Aargau. The son of the Reformed pastor and incredibly influential theologian Karl Barth, Markus made a name for himself within the field of New Testament scholarship and theology. He taught at the University of Basel in Switzerland. He died in 1994.

An interpreter who argues against the view that Ephesians is pseudonymous is Markus Barth. Directly challenging Lincoln's view, he stresses that "the internal evidence which the epistle gives for Pauline authorship is rather impressive."[12] Even more, he alleges that no student of Paul's could have written Ephesians because it is too different from the undisputed letters. Put differently, had a disciple of Paul's written the epistle, he "would probably have kept closely to his master's teaching. He would have avoided going beyond what his master had said."[13]

Like Lincoln, Barth acknowledges that the language of Ephesians is somewhat different than in the undisputed texts. However, as we have seen, he interprets the evidence as proof of Pauline authorship, rather than pseudonymity. Just as well, Barth contends that it is unlikely that an imitator could have written this. As with a Pauline disciple, an "imitator would have wished to give the impression of being a true Paulinst."[14] Further, the theology displayed in Ephesians is not so divergent from Paul's earlier works that it can just be assumed to be from someone else's hand. Instead, the theological aspects of Ephesians should be seen as "emphatic accents" of the other epistles.[15]

Without a doubt, this is a very brief look into what some scholars would define as an intricate problem. Yet, this short example is illustrative of how two interpreters can interpret the same evidence in different ways. As interpreters ourselves, we have to ask if either of these has stronger evidence in its corner and if so, proceed on those grounds. Or, if neither of the options appears to stand to reason, we must take it upon ourselves to offer correctives that are backed by proofs. With this in mind, we give our attention to Colossians for a few moments.[16]

> Margaret Y. MacDonald earned her BA from Saint Mary's University (1983) and her doctorate from the University of Oxford (1986), where she held a Commonwealth scholarship. She has taught at the universities of Ottawa and St. Francis Xavier.

We begin with the work of Margaret MacDonald, who advances the view that Colossians was not authored by Paul and therefore, is pseudepigraphal. Her view is that it comes from a circle of Paul's co-workers. Similar to what Lincoln says about Ephesians, MacDonald writes, "The authenticity of Colossians has been questioned on the basis of language, thought, and style. For example, Colossians includes many long sentences and demonstrates a tendency to heap synonyms together. In comparison to the undisputed letters it contains a greater number of relative clauses and is notably heavily infused with liturgical influences."[17] Here again, the varied grammar and syntax of Colossians has given a scholar reason for pause.

Yet, MacDonald builds on this idea. Drawing on the social-science concepts of charismatic authority and group theory, she pays particularly close attention to Col 1:6–8 and 4:7–18. In both of these sections the letter mentions a number of Paul's underlings. In the wake of a major crisis, namely, the death of their charismatic leader, the group forms and aims to carry on Paul's mission. Thus, MacDonald sees the epistle's opening and closing sections as an attempt to "reinforce the authority of Paul's co-workers" at Colossae by emphasizing "their connection with the apostle."[18] Even beyond this, MacDonald contends that, "Perhaps the strongest evidence of the need to exert authority in community life in a new way . . . is the use of the household code in Col 3:18—4:1."[19]

> Craig L. Blomberg was born in 1955 at Rock Island, Illinois. He earned his PhD in New Testament from Aberdeen University, Scotland. He has taught at Palm Beach Atlantic College and Denver Seminary. He was also a research fellow with Tyndale House, in England. He has a wife, Fran, and two children.

While Craig Blomberg agrees that the language and style of Colossians stands in somewhat of a stark contrast to that of the undisputed letters, his view is that the particular social context is the reason for this. From his perspective, the Christians in Colossae were in danger of being subsumed by a syncretistic religion. By "syncretistic," Blomberg basically means a mixture of ancient Jewish and Hellenistic beliefs, which when brought together, constituted a heresy that undercut the divinity of Christ and his saving work, and placed the burden on humans to justify themselves. Thus, "the specific diction clearly reflects Paul's need to reply to the Colossian heresy. . . ."[20]

On another note, "Colossians and Ephesians turn out to be remarkably similar in style and content. Each resembles the other more than any other letter attributed to Paul."[21] If Colossians was written after Ephesians, wouldn't it have made more sense for the forger to mimic an undisputed epistle? In addition to this, Blomberg points out that Paul did not plant or start the church in the tiny town of Colossae. Thus, "It is also worth asking if the pseudepigraphic writer would choose a church Paul did not found to address in attempting to pass off his letter as Pauline. . . ."[22] Additionally, it is well known that around 61–62 CE, an earthquake destroyed Colossae and to this day, it has never been rebuilt. This would mean that the letter was penned circa 61 CE or earlier. Is it conceivable, therefore, that Paul, who died in the mid-sixties, would have allowed a false letter written in his name to circulate within the churches? Just as well, if it was common in pseudepigraphal literature to write in the name of a deceased person in order to make them a hero and/or to contemporize them for new situations and audiences, would this not rule out pseudepigraphy?[23]

Entering the Fray

> Maarten J. J. Menken was born in 1948 in Leiden, Netherlands. He earned both an MA and PhD in theology from the University of Amsterdam. He has taught at several institutions such as Tilburg University (Netherlands) and Catholic Theological University (Utrecth). His research focuses on the NT's use of the OT.

Turning now to 2 Thessalonians,[24] we begin with the work of Maarten Menken. We have already noted above some of the ironies of this epistle having been called into question, most notably that it warns against forged letters, and that it claims to contain Paul's own signature. Yet, Menken contends that the evidence still argues against Pauline authenticity. As Lincoln and MacDonald did with Ephesians and Colossians, Menken calls 2 Thessalonians into question on the basis of style—to which he appends the notion of "tone"—and theological differences. He also argues that 2 Thessalonians was too dependent upon its predecessor, 1 Thessalonians, with some nuance, to be an original Pauline letter. Ironically, this is precisely the principle that Barth uses to argue that Ephesians is *not* a forgery, and that likewise Blomberg employs to show that Colossians is original. Unlike these two letters however, 2 Thessalonians, according to Menken, is mimicking an undisputed epistle (1 Thessalonians).

In fact, in terms of outline, Menken strives to show that there is little difference between the two Thessalonian letters. After offering a side by side comparison of the two epistles, Menken concludes that, "From this survey, it is evident that there is a very large degree of agreement between 1 and 2 Thessalonians; almost all parts of 2 Thessalonians have parallels in 1 Thessalonians. . . . There are of course, several points of agreement which are not very impressive when taken in isolation, but one should pay attention to the cumulative impact of major and minor similarities."[25] Menken concludes that there is "only one explanation for all of these similarities," and that is "literary dependence" and "because 2 Thessalonians is . . . the later one of the two letters, it means that 2 Thessalonians is literally dependent upon 1 Thessalonians."[26]

Furthermore, if "Paul wrote the second letter shortly after the first one," we must consider that it is possible that he kept a copy of 1 Thessalonians and used it as a template. If that were the case, why would he have written "a second letter to the same addressee which is so remarkably alike the first one"?[27] Stated differently, in Menken's view it is inconceivable that Paul would have wasted time writing a letter so similar to the one he had just sent because he would have known that it would not have accomplished much.

Even more, given that the major theme of the two letters is the "parousia," that is, the return of Christ, it is hard to conceive of Paul having such a dramatic theological shift in such a short amount of time. In other words, it is hard to make sense of the differences between Paul's belief in 1 Thess 4:15–18 that Christ's return is soon to take place and the claim in 2 Thess 2:1–12 that it will not soon take place. It is highly unlikely, suggests Menken, that Paul would have had such a dramatic theological shift in such a short time span that he writes 2 Thessalonians to correct himself.

Similarly, it is hard to account for the dramatic change of tone from the first to second epistle. Menken says, "From 1 Thessalonians, one gets the impression of a warm, personal relationship between Paul and the Christian community at Thessalonica. . . . The tone of 2 Thessalonians is much more formal and distant."[28] Menken continues, "The difference of tone per se is not a sufficient reason to deny Pauline authorship to 2 Thessalonians, but in combination with other factors, it has some weight."[29] One of these other factors is style. "In 2 Thessalonians, there is a relative large number of parallelisms . . . and a relative lack of antithetic wordings and of triadic formulae. Wordings in the letter are at times somewhat 'overdone', such as the excessive use of 'all,' 'every,' . . . or the coupling of substantives. . . . Several typical features of Paul's style are missing in 2 Thessalonians."[30]

These and other problems meet resolution, asserts Menken, when one acknowledges a pseudonymous hand behind the epistle.[31] In fact, this is "the only possible explanation" and is the "decisive argument against Pauline authorship of 2 Thessalonians."[32] Indeed, "it was not written by Paul himself, but its author passes himself off as Paul. . . . 2 Thessalonians can be considered as a reinterpretation of the eschatological teaching of 1 Thessalonians."[33] Despite the confidence and assuredness with which Menken writes, this view has not gone unchallenged.

One interpreter who holds the view that 2 Thessalonians is authentic is

> Donald Guthrie was born in 1915 in England. He earned all of his degrees (BD, ThM, and PhD) from the University of London. He was a lecturer and principal at London Bible College (now London School of Theology) and published a number of prominent New Testament works. He died in 1992.

Donald Guthrie. In answering the question as to why Paul would have penned two letters so close to one another on the same subject, he appeals to the notion that "the changed situation demanded a similar yet different approach.... These similarities and differences are adequately accounted for by the practical demands of the church at the time."[34] It is a "psychological fallacy" to assume that one man cannot write two similar letters in a limited amount of time, especially if the situation has changed and calls for such actions.

Context also can account for the change in tone. Guthrie writes, "Paul is having to deal with a different situation and probably write in a different mood. He is warmer towards them in the first Epistle because of the great encouragement news of them had brought him. But he must have been a little perplexed . . . at the turn of events."[35] Further, "It is a fallacy to assume that any writer must also write in the same tone, since tone is very much a matter of mood which is in turn easily affected by prevailing circumstances."[36]

Regarding the matter of the parousia, again Guthrie emphasizes context. For him, "a sufficient explanation of the different eschatological emphasis is the need to answer a misunderstanding which had not yet arisen when 1 Thessalonians was written."[37] Perhaps in the interim a forged letter with faulty teachings about Jesus' return had made its way into the Thessalonian congregation. If this is the case, this may be connected to the statement in 2 Thess 2:2. Thus, "The change is not in eschatology but in viewpoint due to changing circumstances."[38] In the end, Guthrie contends that "Not one of these objections is seen to possess real substance. . . ."[39] Even more, "we may conclude that 1 Thessalonians was not as effective as Paul had hoped in dealing with the problem of idleness and that fresh misunderstandings had arisen concerning the *parousia* . . . and such an impression obviously needed to be corrected."[40]

At this point we bring into focus the triad of letters often referred to as "pastoral epistles." This specific label, which may find its roots in Thomas Aquinas, was popularized through the centuries by a number of early interpreters such as Abraham Scultetus, David Berdot and Paul Anton.[41] While early on this notion had the idea of a "pastoral rule," today the phrase is taken to mean that these letters were written and addressed to pastors. Thus, one of the major differences between these epistles and the others is that they are more individual-centered and less congregation-centered. Stated differently, they were originally more exclusive than inclusive or more personal than universal. Turning our attention to these texts, we will deal with them as a unit, rather than individually.

> *I. Howard Marshall was born in 1934. He earned his PhD from the University of Aberdeen, Scotland, where he later taught and became Professor Emeritus. Marshall has lectured all over the world including in Prague, Cairo, and the Ukraine. His wife Maureen Yeung, is president of Evangel Seminary in Hong Kong.*

We begin with the work of I. Howard Marshall, who begins with the assumption that "the three letters are by one author" and "Any differences in character between them are due to the different situations addressed rather than to differences in authorship or thinking."[42] With this in mind, he further contends that the pastoral epistles "fit well into the period around the death of Paul and the transition to the period in which he was no longer there to lead the congregations which he had planted."[43] Thus, these texts "reflect an undeveloped ecclesiology that more naturally belongs to the earlier part of this period."[44] The period he is referring to, the so-called "tunnel period" of early church history, begins around 70 CE and carries through to the end of the first century. In sum, these three letters are not written by Paul, but by someone else, after Paul's death; it is "a significant minority of scholars" who hold the view that Paul wrote these works and "most other scholars now take it as an unquestioned assumption that the PE are not the work of Paul."[45]

Marshall, however, is not completely comfortable with the term pseudonymity because of its inherently negative qualities. He opts, therefore, to use the term "allonymity."[46] Literally, this Greek compound word means "other name." For Marshall, this removes the pejorative sense and the notion that these texts were written with the intent to deceive. This scenario, he says, "can be positively defended" and "offers the most plausible solution to the enigma" of the origins of these letters.[47] One has to question, however, whether or not Marshall's label changes are legitimate. For example, given the fact that Christians did take issue with certain pseudepigraphal practices in antiquity, is Marshall's renaming actually anachronistic?

Marshall proceeds to argue that "It is most reasonable to associate the letters with the leaders of the congregations in the two areas mentioned in the PE, Crete and Ephesus/Asia Minor." Unlike many scholars have done when attempting to prove non-Pauline authorship for Colossians, Ephesians, and 2 Thessalonians, Marshall alleges that when it comes to the pastoral epistles, one cannot base their conclusions on style, word count, or statistical analyses, but mainly setting or context.[48] Marshall's reconstructed scenario, which he believes provides the evidence for the contention that Paul did not write these three works, is seen in the following two statements:

> ". . . Somebody produced letters written allonymously in the name of Paul, addressed to his immediate helpers and with the implicit rubric: 'These letters represent the kind of thing that I think Paul would have to say to our churches today if he were still alive. Consequently, I have not simply repeated the actual things that he said, but I have had to think how he would have reacted to present circumstances.'"[49]

> "[The letters], especially 2 Tim, are based on authentic Pauline materials whose extent cannot now be traced precisely. . . . The stimulus came from the existence of the authentic letter behind 2 Tim, which was already beginning to face up to the problems of the opposition, and led to the composition of 1 Tim and Titus to deal more explicitly and fully with the problems caused by opposition and heresy in Ephesus and Crete. The letters were intended to give Pauline backing to Timothy and Titus and associated church leaders in their work of calling the congregations back from false teachings and practices. They are examples not of psuedonymity but of allonymity. Their composition was accordingly in no sense deceptive. . . ."[50]

Another scholar who has written on the pastorals is Luke Timothy Johnson. Unlike Marshall, however, he accepts Pauline authorship. In what is likely the most vigorous critique of the "consensus" to date, Johnson charges that, "For many contemporary scholars . . . the inauthenticity of the Pastorals is one of those scholarly dogmas first learned in college and in no need of further explanation. . . . Contemporary critics are heirs to a constantly reinforced tradition of reading from the perspective of authenticity."[51]

> Luke Timothy Johnson was born in 1943. A native of Park Falls, Wisconsin, he studied at Notre Dame Seminary (BA), St. Meinrad School of Theology (MDiv), Indiana University (MARS), and Yale University (PhD). He also served as a monk for nearly a decade. He has seven children and is married to Joy.

Further, decisions concerning whether or not Paul wrote these works should "be based on the cumulative effect of specific lines of argument rather than on the weight of opinion."[52] Johnson, agreeing much with the position of Marshall, writes, "the various criteria that were developed willy-nilly—placement in Paul's career, style, church order, consistency in theme—increasingly appear to be simplistic and possibly even misleading."[53]

In contrast with Marshall, Johnson believes that much of the reason that these texts are often attributed to a pseudonymous hand comes from the fact that they are grouped together. This means that scholars analyze them together. Yet, Johnson contends that they should be held as distinct from one another and analyzed in this way as well. This prevents interpreters from drawing broad characterizations from the letters as a whole and then pitting that evidence against each of the letters individually so as to show contrasts. "Thus the position that 'the Pastorals' evince a more elaborate church order than that in the undisputed letters is false when applied to either Titus or 2 Timothy. 2 Timothy has nothing on the subject, and Titus has at most a few (not altogether clear) lines."[54] Such generalizing serves to "blur the distinctions among the three letters" and as a result, strengthens "the perception of them as a single literary production."[55] Once this has been done, scholars proceed to contrast this group of texts with the undisputed documents, which, in turn, often leads to the contrasting of the authentic Paul with the unauthentic Paul. This is the same type of approach that Marshall takes. For Johnson, this is too problematic and therefore, he reads the letters as singular entities, not as a group.

Despite the fact that Johnson believes it is impossible, beyond the shadow of a doubt to prove the authenticity of these three letters, he does believe it wholly possible to negate the claims that they are inauthentic. He does so not only by dealing with the accusations against Pauline authorship, but also offering alternative reasons regarding the validity of such claims. For Johnson, this comes by way of illustrating that the letters fit within the time and shape of Paul's ministry. He argues that Paul was "a pastor more than he was a theologian" and as such may be designated "a practical theologian."[56] Further, each of these letters in its own way actually aligns with the typical character of Paul's other correspondences in that they are each interested in and emphatic about matters of moral character. Even so, they must remain unique; they

Entering the Fray

cannot be collapsed in on one another and seen as one large epistle. "No more than we can collapse Romans and Galatians and pretend that they are 'saying the same thing ... can we be allowed to collapse 1 Timothy, 2 Timothy, and Titus, declaring them to be 'saying the same thing.'"[57]

Additionally, whereas those who reject Pauline authorship typically consider the mentions of Paul's co-workers as incidental, Johnson places much value on this factor. After working through these connections, he writes, "Any attentive reader must be struck by the remarkable correlation between these random notes concerning Timothy in the authentic letters of Paul and the portrayal of him in the two letters addressed to Timothy."[58] Finally, Johnson draws attention to the literary form of the letters. In opposition to those who read these as fictitious letters, concocted narratives, or pieced together fragments, Johnson states that, "It matters, in reading Paul's other letters, that we read them first of all as real letters than as narratives, fictional correspondence, or philosophical treatises posing as letters."[59] Reading these texts in any of the three ways just mentioned "tilts the question [of authenticity] in the direction of pseudonymity."[60]

Yet, Johnson asks, "What if there were well-established letter forms that were available to Paul in his lifetime that these letters resemble even more? ... In fact, such letter types were available and do fit the form of the pastorals." Johnson sees 2 Timothy as "our most perfect example from antiquity of the personal *paraenetic* letter." Further, 1 Timothy and Titus "fit the form of a royal correspondence called the *mandata principis* (literally, 'commandments of a ruler') letter."[61] Even more, these two particular types of letters mirror the specific types of relationships that Paul had with the addressees, Timothy and Titus, so that they "fit the social circumstances of his relationship with his delegates perfectly."[62] In this way, they "render intelligible virtually every detail" in these epistles and therefore, "ought to be of the greatest significance in evaluating the authenticity of these letters."[63] In the end, Johnson argues that these three letters were originally "regarded as real letters, written to real people" and therefore, they are still "to be interpreted, as the rest of Paul's letters, with reference to the situation described in the letters and to the rest of the Pauline corpus."[64]

The whole topic of the so-called disputed and undisputed Pauline letters is not something to be taken lightly. This is an important matter. One thing that should be immediately realized from this chapter, however, is that one should neither be bullied into accepting a view, nor do so simply because it is in line with the house majority. As Johnson reminds us, many scholarly arguments perpetuate themselves "mainly by force of inertia," even when they are "based on an unexamined majority vote by an increasingly uninformed electorate."[65] There is not much to commend in letting others do our thinking and voting for us! Besides, taking that route only takes the fun out of digging into the Bible—perhaps that's much of the reason why it is such a stale, lifeless book to so many these days.

TAKING ACTION

Once again, we have seen a diversity of opinions from respected scholars and how, despite interpreting the same evidence, they often arrive at opposite conclusions. I remember how frustrating I used to find this when I first entered the fray of biblical scholarship. I wanted so badly for someone to settle matters like those mentioned in this chapter, and finally just tell me what to believe. Even today, I still hear students new to the field, and laity in various church settings, voicing these same thoughts. Yet, there is something to be said for arriving at an informed conclusion without simply buying wholesale what one or more commentaries might suggest. I call this "owning your interpretation." When you own it, you are much more likely to take action on it and live in light of it.

The truth is, biblical interpretation is and always will be an ongoing process. All of the answers are not figured out. We will always have to readjust and reorient our claims based on new evidence and ideas. It has been written that, "The history of exegesis is, in a great measure, a history of errors."[66] While this is certainly true, it is also the case that significant and stable ground is rarely reached without trial and error. Every interpreter of the Bible will necessarily make interpretive mistakes. Yet, many mistakes and pitfalls can be avoided through patience, endurance, and perseverance in disciplined study.

So, the frequent question, "How do I know which interpreter or interpretation is right?" can be answered with a fair amount of confidence. Part of the answer has to do with being familiar with the history of interpretation. Knowing where certain ideas, theories, questions, and interpretations started from and following their evolution to the present enables one to detect certain ideological, philosophical, social, theological, doctrinal, and moral biases, among other things. Doing this also puts one in a position where they gain the competency to draw their own conclusions. This means that while you are engaging and interacting with the works of scholars and specialists, you will not have to rely solely on them.

Further, you will be more aware of how others may or may not be correctly citing scripture. For example, many people appeal to 2 Thess 3:16–17 to defend their theories of biblical inerrancy. However, it is highly unlikely that many people who do so are even aware that Pauline authorship has been seriously challenged and called into question. Having become aware of such conversations, you might help bring a more nuanced and circumspect view to the conversation. In turn, this may help prevent people from making rash judgments about the text, as well as of one another.

As we have already touched on, the topic of this chapter is indeed an important one and can be incredibly divisive. Even so, the church would do well to address it from time to time; it cannot continue to be swept under the ecclesiastical rug. Being intentional about working through the theological ramifications of the disputed and undisputed letters could be fruitful for local congregations in many ways. Thinking through questions of the inspiration and reliability of scripture, the trustworthiness of God, the social and literary contexts of the ancient world, and the contributions that scholars have made in these areas could even be one way to begin to bridge the gap between the church and academy.

In some respects, the church should request higher levels of scholarship from academics on such serious matters. It is not sufficient for authors to publish lay-oriented commentaries only to gloss over these issues. Further, when a scholar does choose one view over the other, it should be substantiated with solid evidence, not appeals to the majority vote. Hard claims backed by soft research benefit none of us. Scholars, pastors, and laity need to move on from such crude practices! The church and the academy should require higher standards of one another.

Finally, a word about those who hold to views of pseudepigraphy is in order. Whether we agree with, or vehemently reject such notions, it is not our job to bully or demonize people who hold a view contrary to our own. This is true for folks on both sides of the exegetical aisle. It might be kept in mind, too, that as far as I am aware those who subscribe to pseudepigraphal authorship today are not calling for a change in format regarding the accepted twenty-seven documents of the canon. Most of them are even willing to say that the truth of these texts is still important; it remains true and inspired regardless of whether or not Paul said it.

While such claims may not be without their problems and challenges, they are really a far cry from heresy. For example, it remains difficult for many to believe that there were either no filters, checks, or balances in the formation of the Pauline corpus, or that, even if there were, a forgery could have somehow made it through.[67] In the end, and in light of what we have covered in both the first and present chapters, it would seem that the claims of Pauline pseudonymity have not rendered conclusive results—regardless of whether the majority believes this or not! That, in and of itself, is an important point to keep in mind.

9

Our Faith(fulness) or Christ's?

http://michaelhalcomb.com/enteringthefray-pistis.html

"THERE'S A REASON HE is called John the Baptist and not John the Methodist, John the Presbyterian, or John the Episcopalian!" On its own, that sentence sounds like the punch-line of a religious joke. However, several years ago I heard those very words yelled with all seriousness by a traveling evangelist. In the middle of his polemical hellfire and brimstone message, he made this statement in a way that unwaveringly affirmed his own denominational tradition while at the same time delegitimized the others.

Our Faith(fulness) or Christ's?

In the very same scream-ridden sermon, this man also assured listeners that the King James Version of the Bible was the only tried and true, trustworthy translation. Any other version was a work of Satan. The entire message was polarizing and, while full of zeal, ultimately deficient in matters of church history, Christian theology, and translation analyses. The only thing I was sure of after hearing such a message was that I disliked just about everything this so-called evangelist had to say.

The history of Christianity bears witness to the fact that the church has for centuries been enduring translation wars, especially since the rise of modern biblical studies. Soon after I became a Christian, I had an uncle, a King-James-only advocate, who persistently sent anti-NIV tracts and brochures my way; he wanted to prevent me from using a faulty translation of the Bible and asserted that my salvation was hanging in the balance in regards to this issue. While I cringe at such actions today, the traveling evangelist and my uncle were correct that Bible translation should not be taken lightly; their zeal simply overrode their knowledge.

In certain cases, theology can—to some degree—hang in the balance and there are often practical implications and ramifications for accepting one translation over another. Yet, no modern Bible translation has a monopoly on accuracy; every translation has its own issues that need to be addressed. This, however, should not lead us to the fatalistic view that because no perfect English rendering yet exists, the Bible is unreliable and the entire enterprise of biblical studies needs to be chucked out the window.

A better alternative would be to learn the biblical languages and principles of translation and then lend those areas of expertise to the field. Further, consulting scholarly works pertaining to certain words or verses can often easily clarify such issues. There are much better options than simply shrugging off study of the Bible because no perfect English equivalent of the ancient Hebrew, Aramaic, and Greek texts exists. Both the church and academy need more expert translators.

It may be the case, however, that no matter how many experts there are some translation issues will never fully be resolved. In this chapter, we will explore one phrase that, for the last couple of centuries, has not only been given much scholarly time and attention but has also had a profound effect on Christian theology and living. Today, this issue is known as the "*pistis Christou*" debate.

Entering the Fray

TUNING IN

The phrase πίστις Χριστοῦ (*pistis Christou*) is found in a number of passages throughout the New Testament, most notably Rom 3:22, Gal 2:16, and Php 3:9.[1] The debate revolves around translation issues, which two modern English versions of the Bible illustrate quite well:

Gal 2:15 (TNIV)	Gal 2:15 (NET)
"... a person is not justified by observing the law, but *by faith in Jesus Christ* (*pisteōs Christou*)."	"... no one is justified by the works of the law but *by the faithfulness of Jesus Christ* (*pisteōs Christou*)."

On the surface, these two translations may not look terribly different, but upon closer inspection, they most certainly are. Notice that the TNIV is stating that a person is justified before God by *having* or *placing faith* in Jesus Christ. However, the NET is suggesting that persons are justified before God not by way of their own choice to place faith in Jesus Christ, but rather by virtue of the fact that *Jesus Christ himself was faithful* to God. In other words, where the TNIV credits the end-result of justification to human belief, the NET locates it in the fact that Jesus remained faithful to God throughout his life. The two Bible versions are translating the same phrase in dramatically different ways, which have dramatically different theological implications.

Not surprisingly, there is something of a divide among researchers on this issue with many advocates falling on one side or the other. Scholars refer to TNIV's translation choice as the "objective genitive" option and the NET's as the "subjective genitive" translation. The term "*object*ive genitive" is shorthand for saying that Jesus is the "object" of a person's faith. In basic elementary school grammar, we learned that a sentence usually consists of a subject, verb, and object. In this verse the TNIV has humans as the subject. Humans are also carrying out an action, namely, *placing their belief*, which accounts for the verb. Jesus Christ, then, is not the subject but rather the object of the sentence. Humans (subject) place their faith (verb) in Jesus Christ (object). When persons make this choice, the result is that they are justified before God.

However, the NET has Jesus Christ not as the object but rather, the subject. The result: Jesus Christ (subject), through his faithfulness brings about justification (verb) for humans (object). Therefore, to a

Our Faith(fulness) or Christ's?

great degree, the *pistis Christou* debate has to do with whether or not Jesus is the subject or object of the phrase. The trickiest part of making a decision has to do with the fact that in Greek, both translation options are valid. The question then becomes: Is one option more probable or valid than the other? This is precisely where scholars appeal to other grammatical, theological, and contextual factors.

TAKING NOTE

As has already been mentioned, respected scholars fall on both sides of the *pistis Christou* debate. However, some have also attempted to take what I would refer to as a middle ground or even fringe position. Throughout the remainder of this chapter, we will meet scholars from all three groups. More particularly, we will give consideration to the views of a handful of researchers from each of these three perspectives.

Our review begins with the German scholar Johannes Haußleiter (also rendered Haussleiter in many English works), who, although he was not the first researcher to notice that more than one translation option for the phrase *pistis Christou* existed, was one of the earliest modern scholars to deal with the matter head on.[2]

> *Johannes Haußleiter was born in the 1800s. He was an evangelical scholar and earned both PhD and ThD degrees. He was Professor of New Testament Theology and Exegesis at the University of Griefswald, Germany. Haußleiter was a respected scholar and took part in the New Schaff-Herzog Encyclopedia.*

Over the course of about a five year period at the end of the nineteenth century, Haußleiter published two important works in which he argued for the subjective genitive (SG) reading of this phrase.[3] One of his arguments, to which we have already alluded, was that God is shown to be righteous not through the faith of humans but rather the faithfulness of his son, Jesus Christ.

Another point he raises is that if one translates Rom 3:22 as "But the righteousness of God comes through faith in Jesus Christ to everyone who believes" then there is a tautology, that is, an unnecessary repetition. Essentially Paul is made to be saying the same thing with back-to-back statements: humans have "faith in Jesus Christ" and humans "believe in Jesus Christ." The SG translation avoids this problem, for it asserts that "the righteousness of God comes through the faithfulness of Jesus Christ to everyone who believes." The tautology vanishes.

Haußleiter also found a comparative relationship between the phrases "because of Jesus' faith(fulness)" (*ek pisteōs Iēsou*) in Rom 3:26 and "because of Abraham's faith(fulness)" (*ek pisteōs Abraam*) in Rom 4:16. Haußleiter reasoned that in 4:16 the focus is on the faith or faithfulness of Abraham to God. Therefore, if the same phrase is used of Jesus in 3:26, then it must be addressing Jesus' faith or faithfulness to God. For the most part, these are longstanding arguments that have been built upon and nuanced by subsequent proponents of this view.[4]

> Richard Hays was born in 1948. He earned his PhD from Emory University in NT and has received a couple of honorary doctorates. He has an extensive lecturing and publishing record and has received numerous prestigious awards. Hays has also taught New Testament studies at Duke University.

One of the most notable advocates of the SG view is Richard Hays. In his 1982 dissertation, *The Faith of Jesus Christ*, which was edited and republished nearly two decades later, Hays asserts that "'Faith in Christ' is not the most natural translation" of *pistis Iēsou Christou*.[5] While Hays certainly deals with matters of grammar and syntax, his major contribution to the debate comes by way of framing it in the context of a much larger story. Thus, the subtitle of his book, *The Narrative Substructure of Galatians 3:1–4:11*, is quite significant. His overall thesis is: "A story about Jesus Christ is presupposed by Paul's argument in Galatians, and his theological reflection attempts to articulate the meaning of that story."[6]

Hays contends that this overarching story Paul is attempting to articulate is apocalyptic in manner. "Apocalyptic" is simply a reference to Paul's belief that God invaded this evil age, with all of its hostile powers, and overcame it. How did this happen? Jesus Christ trumped this evil world by remaining faithful to God. Therefore, Jesus' faithfulness is to be seen as an apocalyptic rescue for humans; it is a "cosmic story of liberation."[7] For Hays, this is the story that drives Paul; it is the gospel that he is preaching in his letter to the Galatians. *Pistis Christou* must be considered within this larger narrative context.

Paul's claim in Gal 2:21 takes on a quite different meaning. There, Paul writes, "But it is no longer I who live but Christ lives in me. And the life I now live in the flesh I live by the faithfulness of the Son of God, who loved me and gave himself for me." The apostle is speaking about participation in Christ's life and death here. The important thing to note is that Paul is not saying that "he lives now by 'believing in' the Son of God; he has, in fact, just (rhetorically) denied any continuing personal agency at all. Instead, it is now the *pistis* of the Son of God, Jesus Christ's own self-giving faithfulness, that moves in and through him."[8] In Hays's estimation, the SG reading shifts the emphasis away from human initiative to divine participation. Thus, "Insofar as Christian life may be summed up as a 'life of faith,' the individual Christian's faith is a participation in the fidelity of Christ."[9] As such, when "we respond in faith, we participate in an ongoing reenactment of Christ's faithfulness."[10] This is what it means to be Christian.

> Douglas Atchinson Campbell was born in 1961. He earned his PhD from the University of Toronto. He has taught New Testament at Duke University, North Carolina. He has published several works on the life and thought of Paul, including The Quest for Paul's Gospel and The Deliverance of God.

Douglas Campbell also believes that the cosmic, apocalyptic, or eschatological view is central to the conversation. While he has made some compelling grammatical arguments, especially in relation to the ek pisteōs (Rom 1:17a and Hab 2:4) phrase elucidated by Haußleiter, it may well be that one of his strongest contributions to the debate is rooting the revelation of God's righteousness directly in God's sovereignty. In other words, Campbell believes that through Christ's faithfulness, God's righteousness is being revealed. This righteousness forms the content of Paul's message, which is the gospel. Referring to Rom 1:17 and 3:22, Campbell writes that these "programmatic texts state that the faithfulness of Christ—in the broader sense of his obedience, death, and resurrection—has revealed the saving righteousness of God. Moreover, this event is attested by the Prophets, meaning specifically at this point in Romans" that the declaration of Habakkuk 2:4, when applied to Jesus, means "the righteous one by means of faithfulness will live."[11]

This is different, he contends, than the objective genitive (OG) reading, which presupposes that God does not need to reveal his own righteousness to persons—because it is already evident—but rather the offer of salvation. As Campbell says, "To make the eschatological disclosure of God's saving power conditioned upon the believer's faith would be to press the role of anthropocentric faith rather too far. . . . It would be to make the coming of the eschaton dependent upon individual faith, and this is theologically (and practically[!]) ludicrous."[12]

> Peter Bolt was born in 1958. He earned six theological degrees, including a PhD from the University of London (1997). Bolt has served as an ordained minister of the Anglican Church of Australia (Diocese of Sydney) and has taught New Testament Studies at Moore Theological College, Sydney.

Peter Bolt, drawing on the concept of "narrative substructure" popularized by Hays has attempted to show that the Synoptics and Acts lend credence to an SG translation. Here, we shall simply give attention to two passages in Mark and one in Matthew that he finds relevant to the discussion. The first is Mk 11:22. In this verse the expression *echete pistis theou* can be taken as an imperative (a command) or as a simple indicative verb (a statement of reality). If the imperative option is followed, the translation is, "you all have the faithfulness that God has."[13] This is quite different than the indicative rendering, which is, "you all have faith *in* God."[14] Bolt, advocating the SG reading, contends that within the context of the Markan narrative, 11:22 is a statement of "Jesus commending his disciples to the promises of God."[15] In fact, there is no "portion of the Gospel tradition" that "does not show God's faithfulness, as it is brought to fulfillment in Christ."[16] Jesus, then, is an example—and as such a reminder—of God's faithfulness to his covenant promises.

Next, Bolt looks at Mk 9:23, a story concerning a man who brought his sick son to Jesus' disciples for healing. The disciples, however, were incapable of healing the child. When Jesus enters the story and encounters the father's distress and the disciples' inabilities, he says to the father, "all things are possible to the one who believes." Bolt argues that "The flow of action in this account strongly suggests that Jesus was able to do what the disciples could not do, because he is the one who epitomizes 'the one who believes,' and so he does the impossible."[17]

In short, for the same reason that Jesus was able to raise Jairus's daughter from death earlier in the narrative he is able to heal the young boy here: He believes in God's faithfulness and promises. "If this logic is sound, then the lesson drawn from this unit can be extended to the other miracles that Jesus performed in Mark. He is able to work these mighty powers because he himself is a believer."[18] Given the massive amount of miracle material in the Gospel of Mark, if this reading is right—and Bolt urges that it is—then what we have is a "vast amount of material displaying Jesus exercising faith."[19] This may well provide a portion of the narrative substructure for the subjective genitive reading also found in Paul's works.

Another passage that Bolt reviews is Matt 27:43. This is part of the Matthean passion account, wherein Jesus is mocked with the taunt, "he has trusted in God." This remark, made by the religious officials, ironically forms a contrast between Jesus and themselves; in their mocking of Jesus, they are actually inciting themselves and "end up bearing unwitting testimony to another realm of evidence that Jesus is Messiah."[20] This comment "he has trusted God" is "clearly equivalent to 'he has faith in God'" and "the allusion to Psalm 22:8 suggests that Jesus should be seen to be the Messiah because of his previous life of faith and especially because of his faith as he undergoes his greatest trial."[21] Indeed, when one realizes that "Matthew appears to summarize the Messiah's ministry" with this statement from the religious officials, "then we see that this kind of substructure could certainly be deeply embedded in the gospel message and so also underlie the Pauline expression."[22] From his research, Bolt concludes that the Synoptics (and Acts) appear to be natural candidates "for deeply informing Paul's expression 'the faith of Jesus Christ', with the genitive being understood subjectively."[23]

> Luke Timothy Johnson was born in 1943. A native of Park Falls, Wisconsin, he studied at Notre Dame Seminary (BA), St. Meinrad School of Theology (MDiv), Indiana University (MARS), and Yale University (PhD). He also served as a monk for nearly a decade. He has seven children and is married to Joy.

One of Luke Timothy Johnson's major offerings to this discussion seems simple and obvious. He has endeavored to remind translators and interpreters that "Paul can use *pistis* and its cognates in more than one sense."[24] As is the case with most Greek words there are numerous glosses or translation options for the term *pistis*. For example, *pistis* can be viewed as a confession as well as a response to God. It can also refer to obedience to God. Johnson asserts, "If the logic of these distinctions and connections is firm, then one can reach a satisfactory understanding of 'the faith of Jesus' in Paul and see how Rom 5:18–19 explicates Rom 3:21–26."[25]

Stated differently, it is obvious to Johnson that when Rom 3:21–26 is read in light of Rom 5:18–19, where it is stated that "one righteous act resulted in justification and life for all" and "through the obedience of one man the many will be made righteous" then "the point seems clear enough: the righteous deed of Jesus provided the basis for others reaching righteousness (an 'acquittal' for life, or consisting in life)."[26] Even more, "The doing of righteousness here has nothing to do with the response of Christians to Christ, or to the gospel, but everything to do with the response of Jesus to God his Father."[27]

For Paul, there is a "functional equivalence" at work in the terms "faith" and "obedience."[28] Jesus' faith is the "fundamental responsive 'yes' to God."[29] This being the case, it would make little since, "If human beings generally (in Paul's mind) can respond to God only by sin or by faith (by disobedience or obedience), and if Abraham was able to respond to God by faith (which is obedience) and was on that basis justified (Rom 6:16), then Jesus' lack of such response would leave him alone, of all Abraham's children, without faith in God (cf. Rom 4:11–12)."[30] In the end, "The obedience of Jesus is God's way of saving other humans. And by this obedience of Jesus . . . Paul means, simply, Jesus' faith."[31] The point is that in this reading one realizes that "by virtue of the gift of the Spirit the faith of Christians might become like that of Jesus."[32]

Our final two authors to consider in the SG group are Michael Bird and Michael Whitenton. These authors have attempted to show that within the Apostolic Fathers proofs of subjective genitive readings of *pistis Christou* exist. Their contention is that this may lend further credence to the fact that the subjective reading was what Paul had in mind when he wrote. Whitenton does note that, "It is beyond question that some of the early Church Fathers interpreted the πίστις Χριστοῦ constructions primarily in an objective sense."[33] However, there are research gaps that still need to be filled, especially in the earliest works of the Apostolic Fathers.

> Michael R. Whitenton was born in 1983 in Texas. He earned his ThM from Dallas Theological Seminary. His postgraduate work has been carried out at Baylor University, Texas, where he has studied with Bruce W. Longenecker. He also earned a BS in Community Health. He is married to Rachel.

Whitenton argues that scholars have failed to look at a particular pattern at work in the Apostolic Fathers that lends credence to the SG reading. He refers to this as the PGS pattern, which stands for "personal genitive substantive." Essentially, this is a linguist's way of referring to a person's name when it is functioning in Greek as a noun in the genitive case. For English speakers who have not studied foreign languages and are unfamiliar with concepts such as genitives and substantives, this kind of discussion can seem overwhelming and confusing. Therefore, given the rather technical nature of this type of linguistic analysis, we shall only offer a brief summary of his work here.

Basically, Whitenton illustrates that throughout the texts of the Apostolic Fathers, the PSG pattern exists in relation to God, Jesus, and others. In other words, there is a common pattern at work where the context calls for translations such as "the faithfulness of God" (πίστιν Θεοῦ)[34] and "the faith(fulness) of the Lord" (τὴν τοῦ κυρίου πίστιν).[35] Whitenton provides a handful of strong examples to help substantiate his argument. He concludes that there is in fact "evidence from the Apostolic Fathers that would seem to suggest that the early church did refer to the faithfulness of Jesus Christ."[36] Further, there are numerous examples from Hermas that "portray faith as something that is enigmatically mediated through Jesus."[37] The question should be asked as to where the Apostolic Fathers would have learned to think of Jesus in such terms. Whitenton suggests that, "One possible answer is apostolic tradition (both written and oral)."[38] Thus, "we should take seriously at least the possibility that the Apostolic Fathers are, at times, transmitting traditions of a faithful Jesus that they had learned from the work of the apostle Paul himself."[39]

> Michael F. Bird was born in 1974 in Germany and grew up in Ipswich. He earned his PhD from the University of Queensland, Australia. He served in the military as a paratrooper before becoming a lecturer and professor in theology and Bible. He is an Anglican Scholar, is married to Naomi, and has four children.

Whitenton has also written an article with Michael Bird in which the two of them attempt to further demonstrate that the SG reading is the preferred translation of *pistis Christou*. They contend that there are at least eleven occurrences in the Apostolic Fathers where *pistis* "is modified by a genitive that refers to Christ."[40] In the main, however, they appeal to the work of the third-century CE theologian and martyr, Hippolytus of Rome, titled *On Christ and the Antichrist*. In this work Hippolytus seeks to provide readers with a description of the coming antichrist and the effect he will have on the church.

Hippolytus offers his own commentary on a number of New Testament passages but the one that Bird and Whitenton draw attention to is a remark on Rev 12:14. That passage refers to a woman who will be given two great wings, like those of an eagle. In his explanation of this passage, he links the woman's stretched-out, winged arms to the stretched-out arms of Jesus upon the cross. Hippolytus interprets this saying that the woman will possess no other defense "than the two wings of the great eagle, that is to say, the faithfulness of Jesus Christ ('Ιησοῦ Χριστοῦ πίστιν), who in stretching forth His holy hands on the holy tree, unfolded two wings. . . ."[41]

Bird and Whitenton note that, "What is striking is that in this text from Hippolytus we have a subjective genitive construction . . . denoting Jesus' faithfulness, and this is directly related to Jesus' death on the cross."[42] This, they say, appears to be "the clearest reference in the corpus of patristic writings to the saving significance of Jesus' faithfulness as displayed on the cross." As a result, "While Hippolytus derives his remarks about Jesus' faithfulness in death from Revelation, we can credibly correlate his thoughts with what Paul says about Jesus' death as an act of obedience."[43] In this context, "the cross is part of an apocalyptic narrative whereby Jesus' death protects and preserves believers from the messianic woes that are to come upon the church and he is the source of healing for his followers."[44]

Reflecting on the offerings of the aforementioned scholars who advocate an SG translation, we note several distinct emphases.[45] First, the attempt to fit the SG reading within the framework of a broader narrative is important. Second, this narrative substructure is quite apocalyptic and eschatological in form. Seen as an apocalyptic story, Jesus' death becomes a participatory event in and through which humans can be involved in Jesus death. Third, this shifts the emphasis away from the actions of humans to the actions of Jesus; humans are regarded as righteous before God because of Jesus' faithfulness to the Father, not because of their own choices. Finally, this reading appears to resolve a number of the linguistic problems that arise from an OG reading of *pistis Christou* from the New Testament through the Apostolic Fathers.

Despite the appeal of the subjective genitive translation, many prefer the objective genitive rendering "faith in Christ." One of the foremost proponents of this view has been James Dunn. In 1991, he and Richard Hays had a public debate about the matter in Kansas. Several years later,

Our Faith(fulness) or Christ's?

> James D. G. Dunn was born in 1939 and studied at both Glasgow and Cambridge. He has become an incredibly influential scholar within the field of NT studies. He is widely published, and perhaps best known, for his work on the "new perspective" on Paul.

in a book written to honor the academic career of Hays, Dunn admitted in an essay that he agreed with Hays that the driving force behind Paul's theology was a narrative substructure.[46] Dunn also affirmed Hays's contention that Paul had a rich theology of Christians' participation in Christ.[47] What he disagreed with, however, was Hays's hitching of the *pistis Christou* interpretation to these topics because so much should not be "rested on a phrase that is at best allusive and undeveloped... in its usage."[48]

For Dunn, one of the strongest reasons for rejecting the SG reading is the phrase *ek pisteōs* (out of faith), which appears twenty-one times "in the passages in which πίστις Χριστοῦ features most strongly (Rom 3–4; Gal 3)" and is thus "a key phrase in Paul's understanding of his central theme on God's saving righteousness (Rom 1:17; Gal 2:16)."[49] This phrase defines or identifies "individuals (or conduct) by their character," a fact that becomes especially clear when it is set in antithesis to *ek nomou* (out of the law) or like phrases.[50] The point is: "Paul was setting two self-understandings or self-definitions in contrast: those who defined themselves 'out of the law,' that is, by their submission to the law and daily obedience to its commands; and those who defined themselves 'out of πίστις.'"[51] The phrase "'out of faith' carries with it the implication that a trustful commitment to the self-giving Christ can provide a pattern for daily living.... In other words, 'out of faith' answers to the alternative 'out of the law' in a more direct way than 'out of (Christ's) faithfulness' ever can."[52]

Further, the phrase "out of faith" really requires no extra unpacking of meaning, whereas the SG reading does. Additionally, when one considers the fact that in Galatians 3:6–9 Paul uses *ek pisteōs* in reference to both Abraham and Christians this purposeful contrast becomes even more apparent. Here, Dunn should be cited in full:

> "It seems to me that an inescapable conclusion to be drawn from Galatians 3:6–7 is that 'those ἐκ πίστεως' can be reckoned as Abraham's sons precisely and only because they believe as Abraham believed. That is to say, 'those ἐκ πίστεως' is a way of saying 'those who have believed as Abraham believed.' Which must mean that ἐκ πίστεως refers to the Galatians' own πίστις.

Their defining feature, that which causes them to stand out from other Gentiles (and nonbelieving Jews) is their faith."[53]

For Dunn, then, removing "the call of Paul's gospel for faith in Christ," a reading that "fits more snugly" into Paul's expositions, is to remove "one of the central emphases of Paul's gospel—justification by faith alone, by faith in Christ."[54] This leads Dunn to say to Hays, "Sorry Richard," which carries the implication that the SG rendering just cannot bear the weight of its claims.[55] Charles Cranfield is in agreement with his critique. Though Cranfield has a number of ideas worthy of attention, we bring one into focus here.

> Charles Ernest Burland Cranfield was born in 1915. Almost a centenarian, Cranfield served as an army chaplain in WWII, where he ministered to POWs. He was also part of the German Confessing Movement. He studied at theology at Cambridge and later taught at the University of Durham, England.

Like Dunn, Cranfield places a lot of stock in the phrase *ek pisteōs*. Of course, Haußleiter and others had already attempted to render this in the SG sense. Yet, Cranfield challenges such notions. He argues that, in Paul, the term can take on various meanings but that in general, "faith" is that which "allows one to do or not do certain things (Rom 14:1, 2, 22, 23)."[56] There is one aspect of this, says Cranfield, "which has not been given the attention it deserves," namely, that "in its most characteristic Pauline use, faith carries with it what may be called a 'negative' or 'excluding' or indeed a 'sinfulness-admitting' sense."[57] In other words, "To be justified ἐκ πίστεως is to receive as God's free, utterly undeserved gift in Jesus Christ a status of righteousness before him. ἐκ πίστεως excludes all thought of earning that status by anything one can do."[58] Thus, there is a contrast in Paul between justification out of faith and out of works, or out of keeping the law.[59]

For Paul, "To believe in Jesus Christ . . . is to put all one's trust in God's grace in him, to the exclusion of all self-trust and all attempts to justify oneself. It is the attitude of one who knows and confesses that he is a sinner."[60] This "negative function" of faith is found in Paul's appeal to Abraham in Rom 4:17b–21. One of the implications drawn from this passage is that Abraham is portrayed as "ungodly like all the rest of fallen humanity."[61] Seen in this light, it is quite impossible to make the jump from Abraham's faith in God to Jesus' faith in God. Must not one also then reason that just as Abraham was fallen and sinful, so too was

Jesus? Faith presumes fallenness and "was in Paul's mind as strongly associated with the situation of the sinner who knows that he has no ground on which to stand before God except God's own sheer grace in Jesus Christ."[62] Therefore, "it would not be likely to come at all naturally to him to speak of Jesus Christ's πίστις. It would also suggest that we should be wise to hesitate about trying to construct a theology in which Jesus Christ's faith has an important place."[63]

> R. Barry Matlock was born and raised in Nashville, Tennessee. He earned degrees from Lipscomb University and Westminster Theological Seminary respectively. His PhD is from the University of Sheffield, England. Matlock is a fan of the music of Bob Dylan, Hank Williams Jr., and Emmylou Harris.

Barry Matlock also argues that *pistis Christou* is used as a contrastive balance to *ex ergōn nomou* (from works of the Law).[64] We cannot rehearse all of his arguments here but a brief nod to one in particular is in order. Approaching the debate chiefly from linguistic and semantic angles, Matlock attempts to show that the term *pistis* connotes a personal characteristic or quality.[65] Throughout his research, Matlock argues that the SG interpreters, in a sleight-of-hand move, modify the meaning of *pistis* by changing it from a personal characteristic or quality to something resembling an active verb.[66] If proponents of the SG rendering were consistent, argues Matlock, they would actually argue that justification comes from the characteristic of faithfulness that Jesus possesses, they would not tweak this term to mean that in his actions, that is, in his faithful living and faithful dying, justification is achieved.[67]

To offer a crude analogy, it might be like the difference between saying, "The car is beautiful and that is why I like it," and "The car is beautiful when it works." In the first statement, a characteristic or quality of the car is mentioned, which the onlooker believes is inherent to the car itself. The car's beauty is not based upon whether or not it works. However, in the second statement, the meaning is tweaked and takes on something of an active sense; the car's beauty is indeed predicated on the action of working. For Matlock, if Jesus is faithful, then this is an inherent quality or characteristic that is not predicated upon any type of action. As such, this is how the SG interpreters should understand it.

Instead, they modify the meaning and as such, the emphasis is no longer on the inherent faithfulness of Jesus but rather Jesus' faithfulness-unto-death, which has an active, verbal-like sense to it. The move from description to action blurs the lines and is misleading. It should be stated that Matlock is not denying the fact that "faithful-unto-death" is a true statement in Jesus' case. What he is saying, however, is that in the passages where *pistis Christou* and *ek pisteōs* feature prominently, the quality or characteristic of Jesus' faith is not in view and in fact, those passages would make little sense if it were. Taking this alongside other evidences, Matlock maintains that the OG reading is preferred.[68]

> Francis B. Watson was born in 1956. He has published numerous journal articles, monographs, and scholarly books. Watson has held teaching positions at the University of Aberdeen (Scotland), King's College (London), and Durham University (England). His research has focused heavily on Paul and hermeneutics.

Francis Watson has also been a rather vocal opponent of the SG view. For him, the solution to the debate is to be found in four related observations: first, that the theological phrases or "faith formulations" (*ek pisteōs, dia pisteōs, ek pisteōs Christou*, and *ex ergōn nomou*) Paul repeatedly uses all have their origin in the Old Testament passage of Hab 2:4; second, that Hab 2:4 was not read Christologically by Paul; third, that instead, Hab 2:4 was interpreted by Paul as a reference to general humanity, that is, to each individual; and fourth, since Hab 2:4 is a reference to individuals and not the Messiah (or Christ), it should be translated as "The one-who-is-righteous-by-faith will live" and not "The Righteous One will live by faith" (where "The Righteous One" is a Christological title applied to Jesus).[69]

It is unnecessary to recount the many fine particularities of Watson's argument here. What should be given attention, however, is Watson's emphasis on how Paul interpreted Scripture. Part of the confusion has been caused by the word order of Hab 2:4, which is shown below:

ὁ δὲ δίκαιος ἐκ πίστεώς μου ζήσεται

(*ho de dikaios ek pisteōs mou zēsetai*)

For Watson, the whole *pistis Christou* debate is encapsulated in the question of whether or not in Hab 2:4, the phrase *ek pisteōs* (from/by faith), which is situated between the noun *ho dikaios* (righteous one) and the verb *zēsetai* (he will live), is supposed to be linked mainly to the noun preceding it or the verb following it. If *ek pisteōs* points backward, then the Christological reading must be in view, but if it is looking forward, then this is a general reference to individuals. Watson strives to show that nowhere in Paul, or in the New Testament for that matter, is Hab 2:4 read in a messianic or Christological sense.[70]

Instead, all New Testament passages referring to "the Righteous One" (e.g., Acts 3:14; 7:52; or 1 Pet 3:18) are borrowing the title from Isa 53. In keeping with this tradition, Paul would have not read Hab 2:4 Christologically, but in reference to humanity.[71] Therefore, *ek pisteōs* points forward and refers to the fact that "the one-who-is-righteous-by-faith" will live. Within the context of all of Paul's faith formulations, then, the focus is on the faith that believers themselves place in Christ. This faith is what justifies them in God's sight, that is to say, the faith they have placed in Christ makes them heirs of God's promise to life.[72]

> Roy A. Harrisville III, was born in the 1950s. He received his MDiv from Luther Northwestern Seminary (Minnesota) and his PhD in Biblical Interpretation from Union Theological Seminary (New York). He has ministered in the Lutheran Church and published a number of scholarly articles and books.

Our final OG adherent to be considered is Roy Harrisville. Like Bird and Whitenton, he appeals to literature outside the New Testament to help substantiate his views. Harrisville has done extensive searches within the works of ancient authors who pre-date the first century CE as well as research across patristic literature. Against Hays and others who argue that the OG rendering is simply "bad Greek," Harrisville appeals to eight ancient authors whose works seem to suggest otherwise: Aeschines, Eurpides, Herodotus, Demosthenes, Plato, Lysias, Thucydides, Hyperides, and Xenophon.[73] Here, a review of a couple of Harrisville's examples will prove beneficial.

In the much admired ancient drama *Medea*, which is attributed to Eurpides, Harrisville uncovers an OG occurrence. It is located in a statement made by the chorus, who say, "their faith in the gods has no longer held" (*theōn d' ouketi pistis araren*). Here, Harrisville asserts, "the objective genitive reading is plain."[74] Another instance comes by way of the orator Demosthenes, who, in his *Against Leptines* (20.17) refers to "The law, therefore, that removes faith in rewards" (*ho toinun tēn pistin aphairōn tōn dōreiōn nomos*).[75]

Harrisville notes that of the six examples found in Demosthenes, each contains an objective genitive in direct connection with *pistis* or *pisteuō*.[76] After providing a laundry list of examples, he concludes, "These examples should suffice to demonstrate that St. Paul's use of an objective genitive with πίστις was an entirely appropriate Greek construction that native Greek speakers and readers themselves would have been quite used to hearing and reading. Greek orators, philosophers, historians, and poets employed the objective genitive with πίστις. There can be little doubt that they did so because they thought it quite natural, appropriate, and good Greek."[77]

Across patristic literature, Harrisville researched the Fathers' citations of Paul's *pistis Christou* language. He writes, "Since the Fathers who wrote in Greek were closer than we to the apostle in time, culture, geography, and more importantly, language, their witness concerning this debate may be of considerable value."[78] Harrisville has divided his findings into three categories: ambiguous cases, subjective genitive, and objective genitive. There is no need to process the many examples Harrisville provides but in having reviewed the relevant materials, his conclusions are pertinent. He writes:

> "It would seem that when the Fathers talk unequivocally of a subjective faith, they do so in using the phrase πίστις αὐτοῦ. However, when employing the πίστις Χριστοῦ formulation, there is no clear and unambiguous indication of any subjective understanding. The contexts in which the phrase is found admit of no such interpretation. On the other hand, there is clear evidence in both Greek and Latin authors of an understanding of the phrase in an objective sense."[79]

While many interpreters have subscribed to the SG reading, there are also many who, as we have just seen, maintain the more traditional (OG) reading.[80] All of the OG scholars use varieties of evidences to buttress their views. Among other things, they appeal to grammar, context, literary style, tradition, and extra-biblical literature. They are able to meet naysayers on their own turf and find common ground. In the end, however, they vigorously maintain the OG rendering. They do so because they realize that a redefinition of Pauline theology can also mean a redefinition of justification and that is not something to be taken lightly.

Having surveyed key arguments for the SG and OG readings, we now turn our attention to the "middle ground" or "fringe" group. In this final group, we will consider three scholars whose views, if placed on a continuum, are located somewhere between the two previously mentioned groups. We begin with the work of Sam Williams. The breadth of

Our Faith(fulness) or Christ's?

> Sam K. Williams has served as Chair and Professor of Religion at the Colorado College. He has written a number of articles and books, including a commentary on Galatians (ANTC) and also a monograph titled *Jesus' Death as Saving Event: The Background and Origin of a Concept*.

his argument is substantial and need not detain us for long here. Yet, we should note that ultimately, Williams arrives at the view that "the faith of believers is indistinguishable from Jesus' faith. For those who live 'in Christ,' his faith has become their own."[81] As is evident from this statement, one of Williams's foremost contributions to the conversation is the attempt to synthesize some of the material used by the SG and OG sides respectively.

For example, he states that "Paul sometimes distinguishes between *pistis* and *pistis Christou* while at other times he uses the two as virtual equivalents."[82] In fact, he attempts to blur the lines between "the faith of Jesus Christ" (SG) and "faith in Christ" (OG) statements by subsuming them both under the banner "Christ-faith." In addition he writes, "Christian faith is Christ-faith, that relationship to God which Christ exemplified, that life-stance which he actualized and which, because he lived and died, now characterizes the personal existence of everyone who lives in him. Christ is not the 'object' of such faith, however, but rather its supreme exemplar—indeed, its creator."[83] Without a doubt, Williams has many interesting insights and his work is worth consulting first-hand.[84]

> Mark A. Seifrid was born in 1953 in Aurora, Illinois. He earned his BS from the University of Illinois and his MA and MDiv from Trinity Evangelical Divinity School, Illinois. His PhD is from Princeton Theological Seminary. He has also served as a campus minister with the Navigators group.

For now, however, we move on to Mark Seifrid. The views of Seifrid do not seem to be terribly far from those of Williams. For example, Seifrid is quite comfortable using the term "Christ-faith" and he finds value in various portions of both the SG and OG readings.[85] Likewise, he is content to stand somewhere between these two theological poles. One of his most valuable insights is to understand the genitive phrase not as a subjective or objective but rather as a *genetivus auctoris*, that is, a genitive of source.[86] From this vantage point, neither the faith of Christ nor the faith that humans place in Christ is the focus but rather, God himself; this is a theocentric or "God-centered" reading. Seifrid writes, "Faith has its source in the faithfulness of God who promises and fulfills."[87]

It is chiefly "the revelation of God's righteousness" that the apostle has in mind, for "It is the event of the manifestation of God's righteousness within human history which stands at the centre of Paul's interest."[88] Therefore, in contrast with the SG view, "It is not Jesus who acts" but rather "God who acts in Jesus" that is significant.[89] Pushing back against the OG reading, Seifrid claims that "it is properly God who is the object of saving faith. . . . All attention is focused on the God who savingly manifests his righteousness to fallen human beings."[90] As God's Son, Jesus becomes God's agent who is both the source and embodiment of new life. As such, "Christ is thus something more than the object of faith. He is the agent of salvation in all its dimensions. . . . Justification is to be found in this definite place, and no other. As the author of faith, Christ defines faith."[91]

Seifrid believes that the takeaway of such a reading is that it overcomes the shortcomings of both the SG and OG readings. Seifrid writes of the SG view, "Despite its legitimate concern to articulate afresh the connection between doctrine and doing, this approach to Paul has to be judged an exegetical and theological failure."[92] As for the OG approach, it is supplemented by this perspective as it "brings to light a fundamental theological dimension" of Paul's beliefs, namely, that "to believe in Jesus Christ is not first to act, but rather to be acted upon by God in his work in Jesus Christ. It is to know that our faith is the work of another."[93]

> Willis H. Salier was born in 1959 in Broken Hill, Australia. He has earned two degrees in the field of education and four in the area of theology. He earned his PhD from Cambridge University (2003). He has served as Vice Principal and Lecturer at Moore Theological College (Australia). He and his wife Sue have three children.

Lastly, we turn to the work of Willis Salier. His contribution is unique in that he approaches the *pistis Christou* debate from the perspective of John's Gospel. Of course, the phrase *pistis Christou* is never used in John and even more, the noun *pistis* is nowhere to be found. Even so, Salier contends that John's voice still deserves a place at the roundtable. He maintains that hints of both the SG and OG readings are found in John's work, particularly in the notion that Jesus, whom God has sent to reveal his righteousness, carried out the work and mission as God's obedient son.⁹⁴ In John's story, "The accent falls on the Son's obedience."⁹⁵

Having established this, Salier then argues that on the one hand, Jesus' death in John's narrative has an atoning effect. On the other hand, it is "at the singular moment of his death and resurrection" that "Jesus' 'faithfulness' or obedience is displayed" and most sharply brought into focus.⁹⁶ One of the theological conclusions Salier draws from his research is that, within the *pistis Christou* debate, John might help relieve some of the tensions between SG and OG proponents, especially when it comes to each reading's Christological implications. For example, SG proponents have often accused their opponents of focusing on Jesus' divinity, while giving little attention to his humanity. This, they claim, is borderline heresy as it comes close to resembling Docetism. Likewise, OG advocates have accused SG proponents of elevating Christ's humanity at the cost of his divinity, which results in Jesus becoming nothing more than an exemplary figure. In Salier's view, however, "John gives us a model of balance in his presentation of the nature of Christ. . . . Both the obedient action of the Son and the human response believing in the person and work of the Son find their place."⁹⁷

The "middle ground group" label is, I think, an appropriate one. The authors mentioned here have offered provocative and somewhat compelling arguments to substantiate their claims. Perhaps one of the best things these authors have done is place a caution sign before us. They do not find that the evidence leads them to one end of the pendulum or the other, to the thesis or the antithesis, but rather somewhere in the middle. Still, it remains the work of each and every interpreter to judge how the evidence best aligns with the witness of the New Testament. The hope is that all who read this will take that challenge to heart.

In closing, it may be worth mentioning that, as with any major issue in the history of New Testament studies, not everything can be covered in one chapter. As a result, there are many interpreters who have weighed in substantially on the *pistis Christou* debate that did not surface within these pages. Of course, neither this nor any of the other chapters in this book are meant to be exhaustive. As has been reiterated throughout this book, these chapters are meant to be gateways or "first clues." Thus, readers are highly encouraged to consult the sources referenced in the endnotes, as well as the bibliographic materials within each of those works.

Entering the Fray

TAKING ACTION

With the onslaught and continued growth of social media networks throughout the world, fads come as quickly as they go. Twitter even describes the daily fads of its users with the term "trending." On similar sites such as Facebook and YouTube, trends appear one day and vanish the next. Viral videos have the ability to glean millions of views in a day or two and then fall into internet oblivion. Trends and fads are all around.

I say this not to suggest that any of the above views are necessarily fads. Instead, I say it to suggest that when something new does appear in the realm of biblical studies or theology, it is worth pausing and really taking stock. Just as well, this is not to say that because a certain view has dominated the interpretive realm for a long time, it should stand unquestioned. No, our practices, traditions, and long held interpretations are not above question or critique; we should constantly be returning to them to see whether or not they remain firm even under the closest examinations. The *pistis Christou* debate reminds us of this need!

A mature interpreter cannot simply chuck thousands of years of interpretive history out the window to subscribe to the latest and greatest theological fad or idea. Yet, neither can a mature interpreter cling for dear life to a strongly held view without ever stopping to ask questions of it (or let questions be asked of it). Yet, both of these scenarios are quite common. A better approach is found in scrutinizing every new view that comes down the pike as well as every longstanding view that the historical church has affirmed. This is the shared responsibility of students, laity, pastors, and scholars alike.

Another thing that the *pistis Christou* debate reminds us of is the fact that translation is important. As we have seen, entire theological paradigms hinge on how a couple of words are translated. The guild of biblical studies always stands in need of more expert translators and interpreters. While many are content to complain that Bible scholars and preachers do nothing but confuse people (as well as one another), a different route would be to take on the yoke of study and get in those roles and help make them better. Anyone can complain but not everyone can create positive change. The church and academy are both in dire need of more expert exegetes and fewer prooftexters!

Lastly, this debate reminds us that theology is incredibly important. As we have seen, there are at least three distinct ways to understand the *pistis Christou* phrase. Not all of them can be correct; especially when one side is saying just how wrong the other is. Even the so-called happy medium is, in this case, vigorously questioned by many. Some might prefer to just chalk the whole issue up to ambiguity and remain content that something of a stalemate has been reached. The truth is, we cannot simply plead ignorance on this important topic and go about our business. As was stated in the beginning of this chapter, there's simply too much hanging in the balance.

Yet, what is needed in this case is not a group consensus or a majority rule. Instead, both the church and academy need to continually be working through this issue, equipping folks to deal with it in credible and respectable ways. Anything less is just like a vague smoke screen: before too long, people will be able to see right through it. Christians should be able to navigate an issue such as the *pistis Christou* debate without feeling lost or disoriented. A willingness to engage such issues, to persist through the intellectual challenges they posed, loving God with one's whole mind, may be a helpful measure of Christian maturity.

10

A New Perspective on Paul

http://michaelhalcomb.com/enteringthefray-npp.html

ONE OF THE MOST bone-chilling experiences of my life took place at the beginning of 2012 during a study tour in Jerusalem. For lodging, I had been invited by a couple of friends to stay in the guest room of their apartment. One night during my first week there, I was rattled by terrifying screams and thuds; it sounded like someone was being beaten to death. (Neither of my hosts heard the sounds because the husband had removed his hearing aids and the wife wore earplugs while sleeping.) Worried, I woke my hosts to see if we might call the police to intervene.

A New Perspective on Paul

Once awake, they informed me that this was not a case of someone being beaten but rather, this was a woman who frequently lapsed into fits of self-mutilation and yelling. This lady was a Holocaust survivor. Sometimes her spells would last the entire night, up to eight hours; sometimes they occurred two or three times per week. My hosts mentioned that they had attempted, on numerous occasions, to speak with this small, elderly neighbor whose forehead was scar-ridden, but she was not interested in such conversations and preferred to keep to herself. My friends had reasoned that during her fits, she was likely having flashbacks of her days in the concentration camps and that she was probably either inflicting pain upon herself out of guilt for having survived while so many others did not, or that she was expressing her anger toward God for letting her live and suffer for so long.

Like many, I have read about and studied the Holocaust. In fact, one of the high points of my recent trip to Jerusalem was spending time at Oskar Schindler's grave; that was both a joyous and sobering moment for me. Even to this day, I vividly remember reading through *The Diary of Anne Frank* as a teenager and being moved by it. I have seen numerous documentaries—all of which are incredibly difficult to watch—about the Nazi regime and I even had a neighbor once who was an avid collector of Nazi-era weapons. Indeed, one day I hope to visit the hallowed grounds of Auschwitz to pay my respects. Still, the emotions I felt that night in Jerusalem had never been tapped into before; for the next several nights I went to bed fearing that I would once again wake up to those eerie types of screams that should never come out of a human. I was afraid—not really for myself, but for this woman who was reliving so many unspeakable horrors.

I begin this chapter with this story because some proponents of what is known as the "new perspective on Paul" believe that many of the terrors associated with the Holocaust may well have been prevented had Paul's letters been read and interpreted differently. It is sobering to think that this woman has endured a life of agony due, perhaps in great part, to errant theology. While the specific matter of Paul's (and his interpreters') connections to the Holocaust is something that will be given more attention below, for now, let it serve to illustrate the degree of importance that theological discussions may have, not just for our personal lives, but on a global scale.

Entering the Fray

TUNING IN

Unlike the other chapters in this book, here, we will not spend as much time surveying the works of opponents of the new perspective on Paul. Instead we will devote our focus to nearly a dozen of those who have given, and continue to give shape to this strand of scholarship. However, near the end of the chapter, a couple of authors, one who nuances the views of the new perspective and one who rejects it, will be mentioned. Thus, the goal here is to provide a comprehensive picture of the development of this view and to draw attention to some of its significant nuances. Just as well, it is important to bear in mind that this chapter does not provide exhaustive coverage of the matter; not everything that can be said about the new perspective on Paul will be said here! Our manner of proceeding, then, will be to start with Martin Luther in the Reformation era and systematically make our way to studies composed within the new millennium.

We should begin by noting that Martin Luther predated the era of politically correct speech by at least several hundred years. As such, Luther's context (1483–1546 CE) was not one incredibly familiar with beating around the bush or mincing words; it was more common to speak one's views rather straightforwardly—even better if seasoned with rhetorical power and flourish. This is simply a different reality than many of us know and accept today. Political correctness is so deeply embedded in the psyche of our modern societies and cultures that we are prone to take offense at straight speech, even before we've considered the validity of its content.

This point needs to be raised because Martin Luther's comments about Jews were often quite polemical. In fact, a Lutheran denomination has even issued an official statement, explaining, ". . . we deplore and disassociate ourselves from Luther's negative statements about the Jewish people."[1] In large part, this is in response to a work titled *On the Jews and Their Lies*, in which Luther urged rulers and officials to burn the Jews' synagogues, topple their homes, ruin their prayer books, and expel them from the land.[2] Now, it would be one thing if Luther had indicted Jews alone with this sort of rhetoric. However, the fact is, he also criticized his fellow Germans, referring to them as "brutal, furious savages" and among other things, compared them to apes.

A New Perspective on Paul

Just as well, he launched stinging invectives against Christians. Even more, as we all know, he was especially harsh toward Catholics.[3] Interestingly enough, in his last known sermon, Luther said of the Jewish people, "We want to treat them with Christian love and to pray for them, so that they might become converted and would receive the Lord."[4] Rote anti-Semitism is out to completely exterminate Jews, not convert them; Luther cannot wholly be characterized as an anti-Semite, nor can the creation of anti-Semitism in any way be attributed to him as it precedes him by many centuries. It should also be kept in mind that in Luther's polemical letter *On the Lies*, there is mention that he is writing in response to "the Jews who curse us so vilely in their synagogues . . ." This contextual facet tempers some of the one-sided interpretations of Luther and this letter.

In addition, to isolate Luther's unloving statements about Jews from the larger corpus of his rhetoric and to project our own, post-WWII, post-Holocaust sensitivities back on him, is unfair. Further, to single out only his negative statements instead of balancing them with some of the more positive ones is to do him interpretive injustice. To be clear, this is not to excuse any of his remarks, nor is it an attempt to soften or justify them. It is simply a move to help better situate Luther within his own context, with all of its nuances—for better or worse. Having taken these necessary steps, we are now in a better position to make a couple of more points pertinent to the main subject of this chapter. The first of these is quite minor but deserving of attention: Luther was a friar, not a monk.

This is a valuable bit of information when locating Luther in his own context because in his day, friars and monks were quite different. Today these terms, ironically enough, are often used interchangeably. Perhaps the major difference that needs to be acknowledged for our purposes is that monks were stationary while friars had mobility. As one researcher has written, "In the late Middle Ages—Luther's day—monks and friars had two radically different ways of life, two different callings: a life of contemplation versus a life of action; living in secluded monasteries versus preaching in villages; synchronized *ora et labora* versus work in hospitals; prayer versus reason; singing versus arguing."[5]

Blurring the lines between these two ways of life has often caused Luther and therefore his Reformation, to be cast in the wrong light. More to the point, there has been a tendency to paint Luther as a monk instead of a friar because it allows the beginnings of the Reformation to be told in a more dramatic fashion. In the words of one church historian, "I think the real reason [the term] monk is so cherished is that it evokes the quintessential Roman Catholic ascetic" that Luther fled, namely the "black robe, black cloister" and "black and bleak" lifestyle.[6] He is portrayed as leaving this and "coming into light and joy, being lifted out of gloom and doom, leaving behind penance and finding forgiveness. 'Friar' does not come close to ringing the mournful bells of the destitute 'monk.'" Thus, one way to slant the story is to tell it as if Luther "left the miseries of monkdom behind and was converted to a whole new way of salvation."[7] Yet, this is not really the case; Luther was a friar.

Another point commendable to our attention is the fact that while Luther definitely did wrestle with his own spiritual and theological issues internally, this was not the whole story. Luther intensely wrestled with social issues and powers-that-be; he was not confined to a dark room somewhere constantly toiling over his own sins. Again, he did struggle with inner turmoil but this is far from being a way to summarize his entire life. To yank the friar from the social contexts of which he was a part can only lead to misinterpreting him. Even more, this would be to completely miss the nature of his famous *Ninety-Five Theses*, which essentially went viral once drafted and were widely distributed among the public.

In addition, it needs to be remembered that Luther's journey to the *Ninety-Five Theses* did not simply happen overnight; this was a lengthy process in the making. Prior to the *Ninety-Five Theses*, Luther had already been calling for academic reform in schools of theology. Two months prior to penning the *Ninety-Five Theses*, he published a work titled *Against Scholastic Theology*. Luther had long been stewing over the ecclesiastical and theological problems plaguing and confronting him.

Having grown weary of the many issues needing to be dealt with, the proverbial last straw was the Catholic Church's selling of indulgences for the forgiveness of sins. The funds raised were to be used by Pope Leo X to construct Saint Peter's basilica in Rome. This hit home for Luther because funds were being raised in the nearby town of Magdenburg, not far from Wittenburg, where he was teaching and preaching. Thus, his *Ninety-Five Theses* were all focused on the church's selling of indulgences, which is why they were titled *Ninety-Five Theses On The Power Of Indulgences*—a fact lost on many. It was this decisive act that sparked the Reformation, a movement that placed heavy emphasis on the theological tenets of justification and the authority of the Bible—and everyone's right to read and interpret it.

So, why is this section on Martin Luther necessary and what does it have to do with the new perspective on Paul? It is necessary because nearly all researchers who have published works on the new perspective refer back to Luther at some point. Yet, many of those references are often (not always) unfair caricatures. In short, Luther is often pulled out of his context, which greatly slants the telling of both his personal story as well as the story of the Reformation. Additionally, this also affects how one describes the new perspective and where they choose to place their theological stresses or accent marks; this shall become clearer below. It is always good for readers, especially the uninitiated, to be aware of these sorts of things.

Before jumping into the heart of the new perspective and its development, just a few more words are in order. It is definitely an overstatement to either pin the development of Nazism on Luther or to trace it back to him. He certainly made anti-Semitic comments but these did not lead to the rise of Hitler's Third Reich; there were many social factors that contributed to this.[8] It is also something of an overstatement to suggest that, had Luther thought differently, the Holocaust might have been prevented. Again, this is to ignore many of the social and political factors related to those events. It is not too much of a reach, however, to suggest that certain horrors may have been avoided had Luther thought, spoke, and wrote differently. This may be even truer of his later interpreters. Still, it is the case that Hitler read and wrote about Luther. In fact, the Nazi leader hailed him as one of the greatest "statesman," "reformers," and "warriors" ever, who, "if he could be with us, would give us his blessing."[9]

Hopefully, the brief picture of Luther being painted here seems balanced; indeed, the point is not to give an apologetic for him. Instead, the idea is to offer a more nuanced picture of this thinker from the Middle Ages and his lasting theological legacy. Luther was an educated and impassioned friar, a professor and preacher, mobile and outspoken, and socially conscious as well as introspective. Without a doubt, he was also highly influential.

Entering the Fray

Now that we have seen some of Luther's social context, we should turn briefly to his theology. Again, one thing that should not get lost in all of this is the fact that on the religious front, he was railing against both Jews and (German) Catholics; when it came to throwing rhetorical punches, Luther was an equal opportunity employer. He was not raging against the Catholics only. This is worth bearing in mind because in many treatments of the issue, the Catholic Church is singled out.

Luther was not simply equating the Catholic Church of his time with ancient Judaism. He did believe, however, that Jews and Catholics alike were attempting to curry favor with God through their works. Further, he wished for both groups to leave this way of life and commit to (what would be known as) Protestant Christianity.

When it comes to the new perspective on Paul, attention is drawn mostly to Luther's wrestling match with the relationship between God's justice and God's justification. Early on he equated God's justice with the divine wrath that all people would confront; God would mete out punishment for each and every sin of each and every sinner. Yet, he wondered how this could be squared with the idea of justification, the notion that, "God accepts individuals as they trust in him and not on the basis of anything they do or have done."[10]

Luther's breakthrough came when he understood that the goal of Christianity was not to reach the end of life and find out whether God had accepted you or not. Instead, God's acceptance takes place the very moment you trust him; humans are justified already at the beginning of their spiritual journey; as soon as one trusts in God they no longer have a dark cloud of wrathful justice hanging over their heads. This also meant for Luther that his Jewish and Catholic contemporaries, whom he believed to be focusing on "works of the Law" to build up merit with God, were not on the fast track to God's gracious acceptance but rather his divine wrath. Justification comes by faith apart from works (Rom 3:28). Thus, Luther began trumpeting this powerful message wherever he went and to a great degree, this is what formed the centerpiece of his Reformation theology and movement. With this backdrop in view, we are now in a place to turn to the new perspective on Paul, and its development.

A New Perspective on Paul

TAKING NOTE

> Ferdinand Christian Baur was born in 1792 in Schimden, Germany. He was a professor of New Testament at the University of Tübingen for nearly three and a half decades. Both he and his father were pastors. Baur was (and remains) a controversial figure within the fields of biblical studies and church history.

Fast-forwarding ahead a few hundred years from the sixteenth century to the twentieth, we arrive at the work of F. C. Baur.[11] The significance of Baur's work is that his was one of the first analytical studies to offer major pushback against those who had adopted Luther's understanding of Paul. In contrast to the "Lutheran" reading of Paul's letters, especially Romans, Baur asserted that the apostle was not arguing against Jewish legalism. Instead, he was arguing against Jewish particularism. This was a major shift in emphasis because it took "justification by faith" out of the theological spotlight.

In Baur's view, Paul was at odds with his Jewish contemporaries who asserted that one could only attain salvation within the parameters of being identified as a Jew. The apostle railed against this exclusivist approach and instead, asserted that salvation was open to all through Christ apart from taking on Jewish identity markers such as circumcision. For example, in his exposition on Gal 2, Baur remarks that the false teachers, Paul's opposition, desired "to make . . . the salvation of mankind . . . depend entirely on the positive foundation of Judaism."[12] For Baur, then, the main concern is salvation within a Jewish exclusivism paradigm versus salvation within a Christian universalism model.[13]

> Hans Joachim Schoeps was born in 1909 in Berlin. He studied at the universities of Berlin, Marburg, and Heidelberg and earned his doctorate from Leipzig. He taught religion and intellectual history at the University of Erlangen. He opposed Hitler and died in 1980. His resting place is at the Jewish Cemetery in Nuremberg.

Also pushing against the Lutheran understanding of Paul and his epistles was the Jewish historian Hans Schoeps. He maintained that Paul was a rabbinist. His education under Rabban Gamaliel I was shaped, in the main, by the thinking of the rabbinic schools of Palestine. However, there was some Hellenistic influence in the apostle's theology as well. While Schoeps agrees with the notion that specific nuances allowed for a variety of Jewish groups, he argued that Paul stepped outside of those boundaries when he asserted that Jesus was the incarnate Son of God.[14]

Schoeps argues that this is just one proof that Paul misunderstood Judaism; he simply got it wrong. He asserts that this is most evident in Paul's view of the Law. For the rabbis, the Hebrew Torah was understood as Law (*nomos*). However Paul, who followed the Greek version of the Torah (often referred to as LXX or Septuagint), viewed these as a "sum of prescriptions," that is, "a moral way of life prescribed by God."[15] To obey these moral rules would result in life and salvation, while disobedience would result in death and judgment. "Here the notion of Torah has been effectively reduced to the ethical law, a body of demands that, Paul believes, have not been met because of the sinfulness of humankind. Thus righteousness cannot be attained by the works of the law, that is, by human attempts to meet God's demands. Only faith in Christ brings salvation."[16]

This view, Schoeps contends, is in error. Paul's downsizing of the law to a heap of moral platitudes is all the proof one needs to show that Paul did not understand the Jewish position. Schoeps complains, then, "the Christian church has received a completely distorted view of the Jewish law."[17] More astounding than this, however, "is the fact that church theology throughout Christian history has imputed Paul's unacceptability to the Jews to Jewish insensitivity, and has never asked itself whether it might not be due to the fact that Paul could gain no audience with the Jews because from the start he misunderstood Jewish theology."[18] Taken together with Baur, what we have here are two works that shift the emphasis toward both Paul and Judaism within their respective (and related) ancient contexts. Further, this is a decisive move away from Luther's reading of Paul, which was prone to reading the apostle in the setting of the sixteenth-century, instead of first-century, world.

> *Johannes Munck was born in 1904 in Copenhagen. He both earned his ThD from and taught at the University of Copenhagen. He also held a position at the University of Arhaus. He was an ardent opponent of the Tübingen group, strongly opposing their dialectical approach to Paul. He died in 1965.*

In keeping with the notion of situating Paul within his ancient Jewish context, another new perspective scholar, Johannes Munck, sought to show that Paul did not convert from Judaism to Christianity. Or, stated differently, Paul did not abandon Judaism because of the demands of the Law, only to take up the mantle of Christianity. Paul was "called" not "converted" and as such, he was following the pattern set forth by Israel's called-by-God prophets who preceded him. As a result, Paul is to be understood as having been given a place in the salvation-history plan initiated by God.

In Munck's view, Paul believed that God's kingdom was hanging in limbo until the gospel was preached to the Gentiles. He writes, "The fullness of the Gentiles, which is Paul's aim, is the decisive turning-point in redemptive history. With that there begins the salvation of Israel and the coming of Antichrist, and through it the coming of Christ for judgment and salvation, and so the end of the world."[19] There are two points to draw from this pertinent to our discussion here: First, that Paul did not convert from Judaism to Christianity, and second, that Paul is to be viewed as a descendent of the Hebrew prophets, whom God has elected to carry out his plan. Thus, Paul needs to be understood in his proper Jewish milieu.

> Krister Stendahl was born in 1921 in Stockholm, Sweden. He conducted his doctoral work at Uppsala University (Sweden). He was a Bishop in Stockholm and also taught at Brandeis University and served as dean and professor at Harvard Divinity School. Stendahl died in 2008.

An inheritor of Munck's argument was the renowned exegete Krister Stendhal. He aggressively maintained that Luther's reading of his own story into Paul's setting was misguided. Stendahl drew attention to the fact that the "introspective conscience" so familiar to us today, was all but absent from Paul's first-century framework. For example, Paul can at one and the same time speak of being flawless when it came to keeping the Law (Php 3:6), yet how impossible it was to keep the whole Law (Rom 2:17—3:20; Gal 3:10–12). Whereas most modern interpreters read this in a Lutheran fashion, that is, as Paul having an internal struggle, Stendahl contends that it is actually "part of a theological and theoretical scriptural argument about the relation between the Jews and Gentiles."[20]

Paul, then, did not have a crisis of conscience that led him to "convert" from Judaism to Christianity. As Stendhal writes, "Judging from Paul's own writings, there is no indication that he had 'experienced it [conversion] in his own conscience' during his time as a Pharisee. It is also striking to note that Paul never urges Jews to find in Christ the answer to the anguish of a plagued conscience."[21] Indeed, "If that is the case regarding Paul the Pharisee, it is . . . even more important to note that we look in vain for any evidence that Paul the Christian has suffered under the burden of conscience concerning personal shortcomings which he would label 'sins.'"[22]

One must remember, "it was not until Augustine that the Pauline thought about the Law and Justification was applied in a consistent and grand style to a more general and timeless human problem."[23] Seen in this light, then, there is not for Paul, "as we usually think—first a conversion, and then a call to apostleship; there is only the call to work among the Gentiles."[24] What happened to Paul was not a conversion from Judaism to Christianity but rather, a call in likeness with the Hebrew prophets of old—which fell within the wider scope of redemptive history—to lead the Gentiles to faith in Christ.

> William David Davies was born in 1911 in Carmathenshire, Wales. He studied at the universities of Wales (receiving a DD) and Cambridge and was an ordained minister of the Congregational Church. He taught at Yorkshire, Duke, Princeton, and Union, where he was the dissertation supervisor of Ed P. Sanders.

W. D. Davies was adamant too, that Paul was neither converted nor called out of Judaism. Instead, Paul was a devout Pharisee who lived out his Pharisaism, in what he believed to be the truest sense of it, up to his death. The apostle was simply "a Pharisee who had accepted Jesus as the Messiah."[25] In maintaining his Pharisaic heritage, he continued on with the observance of the law but he did not demand that Gentiles do the same. Just as well, the apostle continued to assert the distinct identity and privileges of Israel, for "Despite his noble universalism, he finds it impossible not to assign a special place to his own people."[26] Further, in Paul's view, Christianity is "the fulfillment and not the annulment of Judaism."[27]

For Davies, reading Paul through a Reformation or Lutheran lens distorts our picture of him, his letters, his world, his so-called opponents, and his theology. Were we free from the bonds of Reformation interpretation, we would be able to see easily that within the Judaism of Paul's day there was much debate about "the true interpretation of their common Jewish tradition; this is an in-house, "family dispute" taking place in the first-century, an aspect that is overlooked by modern readers of Paul.[28] The preceding three authors have, in Pauline studies, marshaled strong evidence and leveled robust arguments in attempting to establish the claim that Paul was not a convert from Judaism to

A New Perspective on Paul

Christianity. Instead, he was called by God to preach to the Gentiles, all the while maintaining his own Jewish identity, without forcing it upon his listeners.

> Ed Parish Sanders was born in 1937 in Texas. He earned his ThD from Union Theological Seminary (New York) and has received numerous honorary doctorates. He has taught at McMaster, Oxford, and Duke and has lectured throughout the world. He is a highly respected scholar in the field of NT studies.

By 1977 the stage had been set for E. P. Sanders to capitalize on the notion of a thoroughly Jewish Paul whose message was more concerned with Jewish exclusivism over and against Christian inclusivism than with the Lutheran reading of justification by faith. For Sanders, who is often viewed as the fount from which the new perspective sprang, the notion that Jews were cold legalists obsessed with trying to earn favor with God by keeping the Law and doing good works was patently false. Sanders argued that Jewish law-observing was a grateful response to God; God had elected to give the Jews the Law and covenanted with them to forgive their sins through the merciful provision of atoning sacrifices.

Stated differently, Sanders argued that the Jews of Paul's day understood God as loving, gracious, and forgiving; God elected or chose them as the people to receive his covenant and Law. To obey the Law was a sign of thanks to God for choosing Israel to be his covenant people. To obey the Law was a joyous and delightful act, not a dreaded or dreadful one. Sanders referred to this non-legalistic understanding as "covenantal nomism." He says, "Covenantal nomism is the view that one's place in God's plan is established on the basis of the covenant and that the covenant requires as the proper response of man his obedience to its commandments, while providing means of atonement for transgressions."[29]

Put differently, "Instead of keeping the law to gain acceptance, Jews kept the law in (thankful) response to God's mercies, in order to stay within the covenant God had graciously given them."[30] The emphasis is not on keeping the Law for the purposes of "getting in" on God's good graces, but rather "staying in," which is done through obeying the Law. Sanders has eight spokes in his theological wheel:

1. God elected or chose Israel.

Entering the Fray

2. God gave his elected/chosen people, Israel, the Law. Thus, Torah/Law is a divine gift.

3. God's Law-gift to Israel is a sure sign from God to Israel that they will remain his elected people.

4. Israel's obedience to the Law is their sure sign to God that they will remain his people.

5. In instances of disobedience, Israel will be punished, and in instances of obedience, Israel will be rewarded by God.

6. God's Law-gift provides Israel with means of atonement/sacrifice.

7. When Israel is disobedient and breaches the covenant/breaks the Law, they may atone for their sins via sacrifice.

8. By way of obedience and atonement, as well as God's own mercy, those within the covenant group will ultimately be saved.[31]

This is a far cry from the old portrayals of Judaism as a ruthless, legalistic, religious sect. Covenantal nomism (or Covenantal Law), then, seeks to push beyond such caricatures and attempts to flesh out a theology and lifestyle that is more consonant with ancient Judaism than has often been realized. In turn, readers of the New Testament also get a rather different view of Paul than is often painted. Seen in this light, Sanders's overall aim "to compare Judaism, understood on its own terms, with Paul, understood on his own terms" becomes clear.[32] Because Paul is the virtual rock-star of the New Testament, this also means that Protestant (New Testament-based) Christianity also takes on some significant modifications. We have already seen some of these changes and we shall see more as we continue working through this chapter.

> *James D. G. Dunn was born in 1939 and studied at both Glasgow and Cambridge. He has become an incredibly influential scholar within the field of NT studies. He is widely published and perhaps best known for his work on the "new perspective" on Paul.*

One of the foremost proponents of the new perspective, and actually the scholar who coined the title "New Perspective on Paul," James D. G. Dunn has spent several decades attempting to parse out and fine-tune the various aspects of this approach. We may say that while Dunn was the first to apply the label, his work was not done in a vacuum; it is quite obvious that he had a wide array of predecessors. If these forbears provided the spokes, wheels and framework for the new perspective machine, then Dunn provided the engine. That motor was revved up when Dunn delivered The Manson Memorial Lecture at the University of Manchester in 1982.[33]

Despite acknowledging the important role that Sanders's work had played in Dunn's own thinking, he challenged a number of the points raised by Sanders. Perhaps the most significant of these was the claim that the conclusions of Sanders were actually not too different from the Reformation readings of Paul, they were just redressed in new garb. Dunn wrote, "I must confess that I find Sanders's Paul little more convincing (and much less attractive) than the Lutheran Paul."[34] In mapping out his course, Dunn asserted that the phrase "works of the Law" should be taken in a more sociological sense, that is, it should be understood as referring to "badges" that signify "membership of the covenant people" and thus "mark out the Jews as God's people."[35] Justification, a covenantal category belonging to Jewish theology, was God's way of distinguishing "Jews by birth" from "Gentile sinners" (non-Jews from birth).[36]

For example, in Gal 2:11–15, the consumption of Gentile foods by Jews was viewed by many as a transgression against the God-given badge of Jewish identity (again, marked out by the fact that God had given the Jews the Law). It is worth citing Dunn in full here:

> "The laws on clean and unclean foods do not hold such a central place in the Torah (Lev. 11.1–23; Deut. 14.3–21). But we know that from the time of the Maccabees they had assumed increasing importance in Jewish folklore and Jewish self-understanding. The Maccabean martyrs were remembered precisely as those who 'stood firm and were resolved in their hearts not to eat unclean food' and who 'chose to die rather than to be defiled by food or to profane the holy covenant' (1 Macc. 1.62-3). And the heroes of the popular tales beloved by several generations of Jews, Daniel, Tobit, and Judith, had all shown faithfulness to God precisely by their refusal to eat 'the food of the Gentiles' (Dan. 1.8–16; Tob. 1.10–13; Judith 10.5; 12.1–20). . . . Moreover, from what we know of the Pharisees at the time of Paul, not to mention also the Essenes at Qumran, the maintenance of ritual purity, particularly the ritual purity of the meal table, was a primary concern and major preoccupation. No wonder then that

the men from James were so upset by the slackness of Peter and the other Jewish Christians at Antioch on these matters."[37]

Similarly, throughout Galatians, the issue of Jewish circumcision comes to the surface. Jews receive circumcision (as a badge or marker of God's election), while Gentiles do not. However, some Jewish Christians argued that if Gentiles were going to be included among God's saved covenant people, then they must also don the badge of circumcision. Yet, Paul is adamant about the fact that being justified or "being reckoned a member of God's saved people, is no longer tied to being Jewish. . . . Since the coming of Christ the only identity marker of those who belong to God's people is 'faith in Christ.'"[38] Thus, justification for Paul is dealing, in the main, with the question of how Gentiles can take part in this saving grace that God has offered to Israel.

Another important aspect of Dunn's work that is worth mention here is his understanding of Rom 7:14–25. In light of the work of Munck, Stendahl, and others, Dunn contends that Augustine and Luther interpreted this passage correctly when they understood it as Paul speaking of his "continuing experience as a believer."[39] Such a view, asserts Dunn, squares with the whole of Pauline theology and can be shown to fit nicely within the apostle's views about salvation (soteriology) and the future culmination and final establishment of God's kingdom (eschatology). The pietistic interpretations of these verses, which understand Paul autobiographically—that is, as a Jew transitioning out from under the Law and into Christianity—are quite problematic.[40]

Just as well, the contention that when Paul speaks of "I" in Rom 7 he is speaking of Israel and not himself, does not, in Dunn's view, do justice to the entirety of Paul's theology.[41] However, despite Dunn's disagreement with this suggestion, other new perspective advocates do follow this line of interpretation.[42] For Dunn, the "Already/Not yet tension" within Romans and other portions of Paul's letters underscore "the whole of Paul's soteriology."[43] Further, "In all these cases the two-sided nature of Paul's experience as a believer is clearly evident; the joy of already liberation is balanced by the sigh of frustrated longing for the complete liberty of the sons of God (Rom 8:19–25; 2 Cor 5:1–5)."[44]

These are not the cries "of the non-Christian for the freedom of the Christian; rather it is the cry of the Christian for the full freedom of Christ."[45] To trust in Christ, then, is to embark on the "beginning of a process, a process of dying of the old fleshly nature and dying to the old

A New Perspective on Paul

fleshly nature, a life-long process which will not be completed till the resurrection or transformation of the body."[46] In short, then, "if Rom 7:24 is the believer's life-long cry of frustration, 7:25a is his thanksgiving of eschatological hope, and 7:25b his calm realism for the present in light of both."[47] From this vantage point, there is no need to pit a Jewish Paul against a Christian Paul. In fact, this enables Paul to maintain his Jewish heritage even while submitting to Jesus, whom he believed to be the Messiah.

> Nicholas T. Wright was born in 1948 in England. He received his PhD from Merton College (Oxford) and has served as the Bishop of Durham. Wright has written a number of highly influential books and has appeared on many major television networks as a historical and theological consultant.

We turn next to N. T. Wright, a scholar who has repeatedly added fuel to the new perspective on Paul. Much could be said about Wright's views, but for our purposes here a general overview will do. In relation to Sanders, Wright asserts that ancient Judaism did not follow a "works leads to salvation" schema. Just as well, Paul was not fixated on the notion that his Jewish contemporaries were legalists. In conjunction with Dunn, Wright agrees that the phrase "works of the Law" applies to badges or social boundary markers in relation to God's Law-gift to Israel. In Wright's view, Paul's main question had to do with what defines God's people. With this before us, we review two of Wright's main contributions to the new perspective discussion.

For Wright, rooting God's faithfulness and saving grace in the larger narrative of Israel is important. Whereas his predecessor, Sanders, insisted that Paul's thinking began with the solution of Jesus Christ and worked backward to uncover the problem or plight, Wright argues the opposite. Further, in Wright's estimation, the apostle is not thinking on an individual level but rather in more corporate terms, namely, Israel. Thus, Paul's reasoning begins with Israel's plight, particularly their perpetual state of exile, and is resolved in the Messiah Jesus. As Wright notes, "Nothing less than the framework of covenant theology will do justice to the plight as perceived by Paul. It was real, indubitable, a fact of first-century life. As long as Herod or Pilate ruled over her, Israel was still under the curse of 'exile.' This was in no way a retrojection, imagined out of thin air as the reflex of a new belief or religious experience."[48]

Israel's exile, according to Wright, can be attributed to the fact that she was sinful and double-minded. However, this "critique cannot be reduced to terms of 'human sin, with Israel as a special example' or 'terms of existentialist muddle with the Jews happening to play the leading role in the Sartrean drama."[49] Instead, the heart of the problem is found in "the rebellion of Israel against the covenant purposes of God, seen as the acting out by Israel of the primeval sin of Adam, coming to its full flowering in 'national righteousness,' the meta-sin against which the gospel of the cross struck with its scandalous force, and resulting in Israel's rejection of the gospel."[50] In sum, Israel's plight consisted of her sorry state of exile, which should be "interpreted as a problem about the covenant faithfulness and justice of the creator God who had called her to be his chosen people."[51] In large measure, Israel's problem is characterized as an exclusivist nationalism toward the Gentiles.

Another noteworthy argument of Wright's has to do with justification. He believes that the discussions of justification throughout church history, "certainly since Augustine, got off on the wrong foot—at least in terms of understanding Paul—and they have stayed there ever since."[52] In particular, the belief that "justification by faith" meant for Paul, trying to pull oneself up by their moral bootstraps, attempting to acquire salvation via personal effort, or somehow making themselves good enough for God so that they can get to heaven is completely erroneous.[53] Instead, justification and its related terms are in the first place, covenantal in nature. Thus, the letter to the Romans is not a "statement of how people get saved, how they enter a relationship with God as individuals" rather it is "an exposition of the covenant purposes of the creator God."[54] In short, a covenant is not individual oriented; instead, it is focused on God's people as a whole. Wright offers four keys to his view of justification:

1. It is focused foremost on the covenant declaration that in the future, the true people of God will be vindicated while worshippers of false deities will be proven wrong.

2. It functions similarly to the verdict issued in a law court: "by acquitting someone, it confers on that person the status of 'righteous.' This is the forensic dimension of the future covenantal vindication."[55]

3. This verdict is rendered at the end of history. However, Jesus

came in the middle of history "so that the declaration, the verdict, can be issued already in the present, in anticipation. The events of the last days were anticipated when Jesus died on the cross, as the representative Messiah of Israel, and rose again. . . . The verdict of the last day is therefore now also anticipated in the present, whenever someone believes in the gospel message about Jesus."[56]

4. Thus, all "who believe the gospel of Jesus Christ are already demarcated as members of the true family of Abraham, with their sins being forgiven."[57]

Put differently, "The badge of membership, the thing because of which one can tell in the present who is within the eschatological covenant people, was of course faith, the confession that Jesus is Lord and the belief that God raised him from the dead. . . . 'Faith,' for Paul . . . is not something one does in order to gain admittance into the covenant people. It is the badge that proclaims that one is already a member."[58]

Wright's views on justification have proven quite controversial. Indeed, the great majority of what he has espoused within his view of the new perspective on Paul has met a plethora of critics and challengers. Even so, many recognize in Wright's work a newfound clarity; for them, it is a breath of fresh air in Pauline studies. One who has found a number of points of agreement with Wright is Terence Donaldson. While Donaldson agrees with Munck, Stendhal, Dunn, and Wright on many points, one of the nuances he adds is his claim that Paul's Damascus Road encounter was not where the apostle realized his "call" to the Gentiles. Instead, the events that took place on the Damascus Road were chronologically subsequent to Paul's realization of this fact.

Whereas some have placed Paul's conviction to minister to the Gentiles at the beginning of his Christian experience (so Stendhal), others have placed it later, near the end of Paul's travels (so Watson), and some have even suggested that Paul "converted" into a Gentile community already imbued with this mindset (so Räisänen), Donaldson

> Terence L. Donaldson earned his doctorate in 1982 at Wycliffe. He has taught at the College of Emmanuel and St. Chad (Saskatoon), as well as Wycliffe College. Terry is married to Lois and they have two children. They have lived in Toronto and have participated as members of St. Adrian's Parish.

193

asserts that this was Paul's mentality during his upbringing as a Jew. Donaldson writes:

> "Paul's fundamental conviction—the point of departure for the whole structure [of his convictions]—is the belief that God's intention from the beginning was to work in history toward the salvation of all mankind without distinction. Since this conviction is understood to be integral to Jewish self-understanding, and since there is no indication that this conviction was produced by Paul's Christ-experience in any way, it is probably to be assumed that this was a native conviction, something that shaped his convictional universe on both sides of the Damascus experience."[59]

Four of Paul's underlying convictions are: "(1) faith in Christ is the only entrance requirement for the community, (2) circumcision is not to be required of the Gentiles, (3) Gentiles are to be seen as full members of Abraham's family, and (4) 'an identifiably Jewish group . . . still occupies a legitimate place within the community of believers.'"[60] While this does not completely break from the views of Munck, Stendahl, and others, it certainly issues a serious challenge to them. In the end, however, they do shift the emphasis away from a conversion from Judaism to Christianity, or rote legalism to spiritual freedom.

> Don Garlington, a native to Arkansas, studied at Harding University (Arkansas), Westminster Theological Seminary (Philadelphia), and University of Durham (England). His doctoral supervisor was James D. G. Dunn. He has taught at Trinity Ministerial Academy, Toronto Baptist Seminary, and Tyndale Seminary.

Another active proponent of the new perspective has been Don Garlington, whose work has substantiated many of Sanders's claims, particularly the concept of "covenantal nomism." Garlington has focused much of his attention on the concept of obedience within Pauline theology. He has brought in a number of apocryphal texts to help bolster the claim that faith and obedience are complimentary ideas not antithetical ones. Another aspect of Garlington's work that has been helpful is his spelling out of what the new perspective on Paul is *not*. This may be especially beneficial to those who have simply heard rumors about the new perspective or claims focused on what some perceive to be its pitfalls. Garlington provides seven helpful negations:[61]

1. The new perspective is not an "attack" on the Reformation. Rather, it seeks to remind interpreters that the Reformation itself was precisely spearheaded by a desire to bypass centuries of tradition and return to the original source documents of the Christian faith.
2. The new perspective is not incompatible with the foundational concerns of the Reformers. For example, the mottos of *sola fide*, *sola scriptura*, and *solus Christus* are all maintained.
3. The new perspective is not a purposeful or conscious repudiation of the creeds.
4. The new perspective does not focus solely on sociological ideas, or the new covenant people of God. There is definitely more at stake than this. Soteriology is a major aspect of the new perspective.
5. The new perspective does not deny that within the period of Second Temple Judaism, some held to the theology that works count in the final judgment. However, the real point between Paul and Judaism is Christology, not how works and judgment relate to one another.
6. The new perspective is not an attempt to exonerate ancient Judaism in every regard. There are both "weeds" and "flowers" in the garden of ancient Judaism and these must be kept in proper proportion to one another.
7. The new perspective is not a denial that various religious traditions have adopted self-salvation schemes.

If those are the things that the new perspective on Paul does not represent, then what does it affirm? Garlington maintains that it "is an attempt to understand Paul (and the NT generally) within its own context," it is "rooted in the architecture of biblical eschatology," and that it "is in line with the character of the biblical covenant."[62] Despite the fact that N. T. Wright has concluded that "there are probably almost as many 'New Perspective' positions as there are writers espousing it," Don Garlington has provided exegetes with what are, for the most part, foundational elements of the new perspective. In addition to his work on obedience, these points are helpful for understanding this approach.

Entering the Fray

> Kent L. Yinger was born in 1953. He has studied at Wheaton College (Illinois) and Gordon-Conwell Theological Seminary (Boston), and earned his PhD from Sheffield University. He has taught at George Fox Evangelical Seminary and has participated widely across denominational boundaries.

Our last proponent of the new perspective to be discussed is Kent Yinger. After surveying the works of Sanders, Dunn, and Wright, Yinger offers what he perceives to be six positive results of this perspective. First, he argues that the new perspective affords interpreters a "better grasp on Paul's letters" especially on the topics of good works.[63] Paul was not nervous about Jewish legalism but actually confidently praised the doing of good works. This means that unlike the Lutheran reading, we do not have to "switch gears" when moving from epistle to epistle but instead, we "can see Paul's love of good works running consistently through all he says."[64]

Additionally, the new perspective helps readers avoid "Western individualism" because it reduces "overemphasis on the individual."[65] Yinger contends that within the new perspective, "The gospel is no longer all about my salvation; instead, it is about a new creation (2 Cor 5:17) and a new people. Romans 7 need no longer be primarily about my struggle with Sin, but about Law and Sin in Israel's (or Adam's history)."[66] This is no attempt to remove persons from the picture but instead, a way of shifting them out of the center.

Yinger also maintains that the new perspective reduces anti-Semitic or anti-Jewish attitudes and readings of Paul. In this framework we no longer speak of "inferior Jewish legalism" or of Judaism as a "failed or wrong-headed pattern of religion" but of "Christianity's mother-religion."[67] Likewise, the new perspective makes moving from the Old to New Testament easier. Now "there is considerably more continuity between OT and NT" literature as "Paul's message is not the antithesis of Judaism (or of the OT Law) but is a christologically reconfigured continuation or climax of the same."[68] One result is that Christians can now "read their Old Testaments more naturally."[69]

This perspective also "puts Paul and Jesus on speaking terms."[70] Whereas some have attempted to depict Paul as founding a new religious movement named Christianity, which was a replacement of Jesus' Jewish message, in light of the new perspective this claim no longer holds water. "As some put the matter, Jesus sought the renewal, or

A New Perspective on Paul

reform, of Judaism; Paul abandoned that aim and sought the creation of a world religion encompassing Gentiles."[71] Yinger provides several examples that challenge this, including the notion that "Instead of viewing Pauline grace in competition with gospel discipleship, covenantal nomism shows them forming a harmonious pattern in both Jesus and Paul (and Judaism)."[72] Further, "Both hold to the foundational importance of grace" as well as "obedience to God."[73]

Finally, Yinger contends that the new perspective provides a means of reconciliation between Catholics and Protestants, particularly on the matter of justification. He writes, "Since the Lutheran Reformation's understanding of Paul and justification was one of the major elements leading to the split with Rome, the NPP's re-evaluation of Paul and justification might show the two sides not quite so far apart on this topic as Luther thought."[74] It is interesting that Yinger does not really mention the fact that the new perspective helps reduce nationalistic attitudes, a matter which Dunn and Wright in particular have so emphasized. This is certainly one of the valuable outcomes of this approach.

As was mentioned near the beginning of this chapter, not everyone accepts the new perspective on Paul. Some have built on this foundation and have attempted to push beyond it, without rejecting it wholesale. On such matters, one may consult the work of Lloyd Gaston (often referred to as a proponent of a "hyper-NPP"), among others.[75] Gaston's position is known as the bi-covenantal view. In a nutshell, he claims that within one covenant the Gentiles will be saved by justification through faith and in another covenant the Jews will be saved by obeying Torah.

> Lloyd Gaston has studied at Dartmouth College (BA) and the University of Basel, Switzerland, where he earned his ThD. He has taught at United Theological Seminary, Vancouver School of Theology, and Macalester College. He has served as an ordained minister in the Presbyterian Church, USA.

Therefore, when we read in the NT that Paul went into the synagogues, we should not understand that he went with the intention to preach and convert but rather worship. He was being a faithful Jew. The apostle only preached the gospel to the Gentiles because God's elect, the Jews, were already part of an irrevocable covenant. Whenever Paul criticizes his fellow Jews, he does so on the basis of their desires to exclude Gentiles from God's plan. In short, "what Paul finds wrong with other Jews" is that they do not share in, embrace,

> Mark A. Seifrid was born in 1953 in Aurora, Illinois. He earned his BS from the University of Illinois and his MA and MDiv from Trinity Evangelical Divinity School, Illinois. His PhD is from Princeton Theological Seminary. He has also served as a campus minister with the Navigators group.

or perhaps even understand the content of "his revelation in Damascus."[76]

Unlike Gaston, some have spoken strongly against the new perspective. One treatment, among a growing number who take this position, is given by Mark Seifrid.[77] It is argued aggressively by Seifried that while the new perspective on Paul has a few things right, it is fundamentally wrong in its interpretation of Luther's doctrine of justification. He writes, "Luther's theology of the cross and justification . . . more closely accords with Paul than recent attempts to understand him."[78] Indeed, for Seifried, most of the pushback against the new perspective is because of its de-centering of and flawed understanding concerning Paul's views of justification. In his view, the new perspective's conception of covenantal nomism *a la* Sanders is simply misleading. He contends that, even if it was correct, it can actually be shown to share deep affinities with "the medieval theology to which Luther was reacting."[79] In this sense, Seifrid views the new perspective's two leaders, Dunn and Wright, as dragging interpreters into "blind alleys" because they "follow a path already mislaid" by Sanders.[80] One of the greatest travesties of the new perspective, according to Seifrid, is that he believes it heads in the direction of replacing soteriology with ecclesiology. Thus, he understands himself as one who, in upholding Luther's view of justification, "warns us away from that constant temptation to replace the word of the cross with our community as the vehicle of salvation for the world." When rightly understood, justification "remains the article by which the Church stands or falls."[81]

TAKING ACTION

There is no doubt that the new perspective on Paul is an important matter. Here, I would like to make a case neither for nor against this view but rather, that it needs to be discussed at greater length within our churches as well as academic institutions. It should be more than obvious that unfair caricatures get us nowhere, whether these are coming

A New Perspective on Paul

from those who adopt a new view or those who reject it. Scholarship itself has proven this time and again.

No matter what side of the fence one's congregation or institutions comes down on, exploring the new perspective on Paul will raise a host of issues that are not only deserving of attention, but that have the potential to bear much fruit. In addition to a better understanding of church history, the history of interpretation, and Pauline theology, questions about Christianity's relationship to Judaism will be raised. These discussions can be shaped by explorations into the nature of the covenant, the Law, God's promise to Israel, the sin of Adam and its effects, inclusion in the family of Abraham, concepts of righteousness, justification, obedience, and more. A healthy understanding of these things may go a long way in preventing anti-Judaism or anti-Semitism and instead, provide ways for Christians to foster relationships with their Jewish neighbors. If Christians can do anything to help prevent another Holocaust they should; starting with theology is perhaps the best route to take.

The new perspective also raises questions about the issue of nationalism. This is no light matter. It will inevitably lead to discussions about ethnocentrism, racism, patriotism, immigration issues, and war, among other topics. In today's world, Christians need to know how to work through these issues in an informed way; all believers need to have an informed faith. Being able to address these matters from the perspective of theology helps Christians understand the connection between the Bible, their beliefs, and their lifestyles. Here, we have the potential for very rich discussions to take place and we may find our congregants and students answering the Reformation call to go back to the Bible, although, without bypassing church history.

In light of the previous two topics, conversations about the inclusive and exclusive nature of the gospel and church may surface. In many Western settings, the oxymoronic mantra of "tolerate everyone but the exclusivists" has struck a profound social fear in many. Often, evangelical Christians have found themselves taking many punches in this regard. Of course, this is no reason to create a martyr mentality. Having discussions about the particulars of what it means to be "in" or "out" of the faith are important. They can at one and the same time prevent Christians from being rigidly fundamentalistic and closed-minded, while also providing them with firm ground on which to stand. The reminder that the gospel is and always has been an open invitation, yet has also has drawn boundary lines and markers is important. In some ways, you may find that many yearn to go back to Luther's era, where political correctness was not the driving force behind so much of what is said either in or outside the church.

Finally, it would be beneficial to revisit some of our theological forefathers, perhaps starting with Augustine or Luther. Students and laity will come to realize that thinkers like John Calvin and John Wesley were quite influenced by Luther and Augustine, among others. A journey back through church history will prove helpful for all involved. Stephen Westerholm's *Perspectives Old and New on Paul* may be a great starting place for this.[82] These matters need not be dull, dry, boring, and unrelated to persons' faith. Providing learners with creative ways to explore the church's spiritual and interpretive heritage can be incredibly fulfilling and meaningful. Taking the new perspective on Paul as a particular discussion point, then, may help those in the church and academy move forward in a number of ways.

11

From Peter's House to James's Tomb and Beyond

http://michaelhalcomb.com/enteringthefray-archaeology.html

IN MAY OF 2011, I was in the Ethiopian highlands where I had the opportunity to visit some of the local monks at the city of Debre Libanos. I had met some of these Eastern Orthodox leaders on previous trips but this time I was invited into one of their homes. This was no ordinary home, however, it was a cave. This cave-dwelling Ethiopian had a rug sprawled out on the floor, one rigged-up light bulb hanging from a hook he had mounted into the rock ceiling, and a small plastic bin for storing injera (a local Ethiopian dish).

Entering the Fray

Beyond these things, there was not much to look at; this man pretty much owned nothing. However, I did notice a curtain hanging behind where the man was sitting. It was a nice curtain, quite out-of-place in this small, bland cave. I asked him what purpose the curtain was serving and he replied, "It is covering the door to the Ark of the Covenant; the Ark is back there."

"May I see it?" I proposed. He responded with an immediate, unapologetic, "No!"

There are numerous places in Ethiopia that claim to house the Ark. One of the most famous locations is Bet Giorgi Church (Lalibela), the site where a house of worship has been carved into the ground, earning it the nickname "The Rock Church." Others have alleged that the Ark is stored in the Church of Our Lady Mary of Zion, in Axum. Near the church there is even an official, church-sanctioned, Treasury of the Ark of the Covenant. A casual talk with just about any Ethiopian concerning the Ark will quickly reveal their pride on this topic; they swiftly become apologists on this matter, despite the fact that they have never seen it with their own eyes, viewed photos of it, or met someone who has had the opportunity to look at it.

Many researchers, however, have challenged the claims of the Ethiopians and have offered different hypotheses as to the Ark's whereabouts. To date, however, the original Ark of the Covenant itself has not been recovered. These assertions about the Ark suggest to me that when it comes to archaeological finds, the relics themselves are not brute facts; people attach interpretive meanings and significance to them. In other words, for modern people who are long removed from the original events related to ancient relics, the meaning and value of any artifact is a meaning and value that its respective interpreters assign to it. Thus, it all boils down to how the data is used and interpreted.

When it comes to archaeology related to the Bible, referred to by some as "biblical archaeology," the central aim has often been to validate the Bible itself and to verify its claims by proving that its history, geography, and archaeology are trustworthy. Some contend that if the Bible can indeed be relied upon in terms of history and geography then it must also be theologically dependable. This jump from historical and geographical tracks to theological ones may not be so easy, however. In terms of logic, this may be likened to a "bait-and-switch fallacy," one thing demonstrated to be true creating the expectation that what follows must also be true.

From Peter's House to James's Tomb and Beyond

TUNING IN

To be clear, the truth or trustworthiness of the Bible is not being called into question here. Rather, I am challenging some of the interpretive choices and approaches that researchers make when evaluating artifacts related to the Bible. As archaeologists assign dates to material finds and geological elements, some researchers attempt to match these findings with contemporary biblical events, in order to substantiate the historicity of the biblical narrative. This approach can be problematic, however. Consider an example:

In 1990, under the excavation supervision of Larry Stager at the Philistine site of Ashkelon, a statuette in the form of a silver calf was discovered. The important thing to note is that after this icon was recovered, most of the discussion surrounding it dealt with its age, that is, when it was created/used.[1] Archaeologists dated it to about 1550 BCE and suggested that it was placed in the storeroom of a sanctuary before the destruction of Ashkelon. Based on the fact that it was found in a sanctuary, dated to around 1550 BCE, and seemed to share affinities with the golden calf mentioned in Ex 32:4, some biblical scholars reasoned that this find gave archaeological credence to the historical factuality of the golden calf story in Exodus.

Further, some researchers believed that these deductions provided scholarship with a historical period by which to date the Exodus story.[2] Jacqueline Schaalje, in *Jewish Magazine*, even reinterpreted the silver calf as a "golden" calf to help substantiate the Exodus narrative. She writes, "The 'golden' calf in Ashkelon is a unique find...."[3] The point of this example is not to suggest that archaeology is a fruitless endeavor. Instead, the point is that what persons do interpretively with elements of the past once they are found is of critical importance. Obviously, Schaalje stretched the data to conform to her interpretive direction. While contemporary works of biblical archaeology often follow a scientific and programmatic approach or methodology,[4] their theological motivations render much of the work done (at least in the eyes of secular researchers) subjective and therefore moot.

At the end of the day, it still remains the decision of each researcher how to best interpret the data. Some readings are more probable than others and a strong case can be built in their defense. With all of this in mind, as we proceed in this chapter, it should be made known that my aim here is not to provide readers with an apologetic or defense of archaeological finds and their relationship to the Bible. Instead, the goal is simply to bring to the fore a dozen archaeological discoveries that may have a bearing on our understanding of the New Testament.

TAKING NOTE

In this section the archaeological discoveries that we will review are divided into two categories: "texts and inscriptions," and "ruins and realia." By realia, we simply mean ancient "things." Within each of these categories the finds are listed in the chronological order of their discovery. That said, the bulk of our attention will be given to a single archaeological find, the Gallio inscription, due to the great emphasis placed on it by numerous New Testament scholars.

Additionally, within this chapter, unlike the rest of the book, while the names of scholars who have conducted major research on these artifacts will be mentioned, no biographical sketches will be provided. Instead, graphical sketches of the relics are supplied. At the same time, many general items such as pottery and earthenware, which have provided insight into some of Jesus' teachings, particularly as they relate to rituals and purity, will not be dealt with here. Finally, much could be said about the multitude of finds related to the Herod family but that is simply too much terrain to cover here.[5]

Just as well, during the writing of this chapter it came to my attention that a number of ancient papyri were newly discovered.[6] Perhaps most important among these is a first-century CE text containing Mark's Gospel.[7] Unfortunately, thus far few details about this find have been released to the public. Otherwise, it would have been given significant attention here.

Texts and Inscriptions

Our foray into archaeological finds related to the New Testament begins with what is known as the Gallio Inscription. Gallio is mentioned three times in the New Testament, as well as in several other ancient documents.[8] Acts 18:12, which refers to a point during Paul's ministry in Corinth reads, "And Gallio was the proconsul of Achaia when, with one mind, the Jews rose up against Paul and led him to the judgment seat." 18:14 says, "And when Paul was getting ready to open his mouth, Gallio said to the Jews . . ." Likewise, 18:17 notes, "And the whole crowd turned against Sosthenes, the synagogue ruler, and they were beating him in front of the proconsul; and Gallio was not showing any concern about this."

A sketch of the portion of the Gallio Inscription that contains Gallio's name.

Dating the Gallio Inscription is a tentative matter. At best, we can say that it is likely from a period between 50 CE and 52 CE. Some scholars have suggested that this inscription is the "lynch-pin" or "foundation" of Pauline chronology.[9] This is something of an overstatement, however, because the Gallio Inscription only has bearing on a Pauline timeline as it relates to many other texts, coins, and inscriptions. There is no single item that provides us with "the answer" no matter how badly we wish that were the case. In other words, this ancient relic that is often portrayed as solving one of the most perplexing New Testament riddles is only significant to us if it can be corroborated with many other ancient evidences.

With that in mind, I am going to question what has become almost a consensus in New Testament studies, namely, that Paul was tried before Gallio in 51 CE or 52 CE. For the most part, scholarly works seem to presume these dates. Yet, those same works rarely, if ever, substantiate their claims with evidence. Here, however, I hope to take the opposite route—an evidential one—to arrive at my conclusions. In doing so, I will offer portions of a timeline, which at the end, will provide the big picture.

I begin here by following the claims of two numismatists or "coin experts" that, based on ancient currency, the twenty-sixth and twenty-seventh acclamations of Claudius took place in 49/50 CE. The term "acclamations" here simply refers to honors bestowed upon an official for his outstanding leadership or achievements. Winning a battle or completing a major project might merit an acclamation. Since emperors thoroughly enjoyed being honored, they held these ceremonies frequently. Thus, we add our first piece of data to the timeline:

Dates	Events and Sources
49/50 CE	Claudius receives his twenty-sixth and twenty-seventh acclamations, attested by ancient coins.

In addition to this, we know that Claudius also expelled Jews from Rome in 49 CE, which remained in force until 54 CE when he died. We know this from the ancient author Suetonius who wrote, "Because the Jews constantly made disturbances at the instigation of Chrestus, he expelled them from Rome" (*Claudius*, 25.4), as well as Dio Cassius, who, referring to the same event noted, "As the Jews had flocked to Rome in great numbers and were converting many of the natives to their ways, he banished most of them" (57.18.5a).[10] This comports with the claims of Acts 18:1-3: "After this, he [Paul] left from Athens and went to Corinth. And he found some Jews named Aquila, a native of Pontus who came from Italy (Rome), and his wife Priscilla, because Claudius commanded all of the Jews to leave from Rome. He [Paul] went to them because he was of the same trade as them, and he worked with them. For by trade they were tent-makers."[11]

Claudius died on October 13, 54 CE as Suetonius and others report: "He died on the third day before the Ides of October in the consulship of Asinius Marcellus and Acilius Aviola, in the sixty-fourth year of his age and the fourteenth of his reign" (*Claudius*, 45.1).[12] This information also allows us to mark both the year Claudius was born (10 BCE) as well as the initial year of his reign, which he began just after his nephew and predecessor Caligula was murdered in 41 CE (Suetonius, *Nero*, 34-54).[13] It is important to note for our purposes here that during his rule, Caligula invested in the Roman aqueduct system. In fact, Frontinus, in his work titled *Aqueducts* (1.13), notes that Caligula began this project in the second year of his own reign (38 CE). In the same passage, Frontinus also notes that, "These works Claudius completed on the most magnificent scale, and dedicated in the consulship of Sulla and Titianus, on the first of August in the year 803 after the founding of the city." His date of 803 (counting in a Roman fashion) is the equivalent of 50 CE.[14] Thus, Lucius Salvius Otho "Titianus" and Faustus Cornelius "Sulla" Felix were Roman consuls during the reign of Claudius in 50 CE.[15]

Dates	Events and Sources
10 BCE	Claudius is born.
37 CE	Caligula begins to reign as emperor.
38 CE	Caligula, during his second year in office, begins work on the Roman aqueduct system.
41 CE	Caligula is murdered and his uncle, Claudius, begins to rule.
49 CE	Claudius expels Jews from Rome.
49/50 CE	Claudius receives his twenty-sixth and twenty-seventh acclamations, attested by ancient coins.
50 CE	Claudius completes and dedicates the aqueducts. Titianus and Sulla were Roman consuls.
54 CE	Claudius dies and the Jewish expulsion from Rome ends.

A number of events significant for our timeline here took place during Claudius's time in office. For example, several years into his reign a famine swept across much of the ancient Mediterranean world.[16] While such events happened in different places at different times throughout the centuries, for our purposes here we focus on the one that occurred in 46/47 CE. This famine is mentioned in Acts (11:28, 17:7, 18:2) and by a wide array of other sources.[17] Not long after this, according to coins, Claudius received his twenty-fourth acclamation in 48/49 CE and his twenty-fifth through twenty-seventh acclamations in 49/50 CE.[18] Another important event is the Isthmian games in Corinth, which we know transpired in both 49 and 51 CE.[19]

Entering the Fray

Dates	Events and Sources
10 BCE	Claudius is born.
37 CE	Caligula begins to reign as emperor.
38 CE	Caligula, during his second year in office, begins work on the Roman aqueduct system.
41 CE	Caligula is murdered and his uncle, Claudius, begins to rule.
46/47 CE	A general famine sweeps across the Mediterranean world under the reign of Claudius.
48/49 CE	Claudius receives his twenty-fourth acclamation.
49 CE	Claudius expels Jews from Rome. The Isthmian games take place in Corinth.
49/50 CE	Claudius receives his twenty-fifth, twenty-sixth, and twenty-seventh acclamations, attested by ancient coins.
50 CE	Claudius completes and dedicates the aqueducts. Titianus and Sulla were Roman consuls.
51 CE	The Isthmian games take place in Corinth.
54 CE	Claudius dies and the Jewish expulsion from Rome ends.

Two items from our timeline thus far need to be brought more into focus, namely, the twenty-sixth through twenty-seventh acclamations of Claudius and Gallio's appointment as proconsul of Achaia. Regarding the former, we are aware of a dedicatory inscription on an aqueduct at an Italian port, now referred to by many as the Aqua Claudiua, which reads: "Claudius son of Drusus Caesar Augustus Germanicus Pontifex Maximus, eleventh year of tribunician power, consul for the fifth time, acclaimed emperor for the twenty-sixth time, father of the country."[20] Coinage may place the twenty-sixth acclamation in the eleventh tribunician year (50/51 CE) and the twenty-seventh acclamation in the twelfth tribunician year (51/52 CE).[21]

The numerical references in this inscription have been interpreted in a number of different ways and therefore, it must be borne in mind that what is offered here is tentative. I might also say that while many have made the Gallio Inscription central to Pauline chronology, it may well be the case that pinpointing the numbers on this aqueduct arch could be just as decisive a factor. Also, instead of assuming that Frontinus was erroneous in his dating, as Murphy-O'Connor does, trusting his calculations as is done here is also a very important matter.[22] Regarding the inscription, since it is believed to have been dedicated in 51 CE we can reason that the twenty-seventh acclamation took place either earlier that same year, or as we have suggested, during the previous year in 50 CE.[23]

Enter: the Gallio Inscription. This artifact, also known as the Delphi Inscription, has had a rather patchy history. Discovered in the ancient city of Delphi, there were initially four fragments that were pieced together (1905).[24] Nearly a decade later three more pieces were uncovered (1913) but they were not added to the original until over sixty-five years later, when a couple of additional pieces were also included (1970).[25] When all nine fragments are fit together they may produce the following reconstructed text:

> Claudius Caesar Augustus Germanicus, twelth year of tribunician power, acclaimed emperor for the twenty-sixth time, father of the country, sends greetings to [. . .]. For long have I been well-disposed to the city of Delphi and solicitous for its prosperity, and I have always observed the cult of the Pythian Apollo. Now since it is said to be destitute of citizens, as my friend and proconsul L. Iunius Gallio recently reported to me, and desiring that Delphi should regain its former splendor, I command you (sing.) to invite well-born people also from other cities to come to Delphi as new inhabitants, and to accord them and their children all the privileges of the Delphians as being citizens on like and equal terms. For if some are transferred as colonists to these regions [. . .][26]

Of major interest to us are the notes concerning Claudius's twenty-sixth acclamation and of course, the mention of Gallio. We see that the relationship between these two pieces of information place Gallio as proconsul during the twenty-sixth acclamation of Claudius. According to our timeline, this means that Gallio was serving in this capacity in 50 CE. Now, we also know from Seneca that Gallio only served about half of his term due to illness: "For I remember master Gallio's words when he was getting a fever in Achaia but boarded ship at once, insisting that the disease was not from his body but from the place" (Seneca, *Letters*,

Entering the Fray

104.1).[27] So, we posit here a timeframe of about six months in office for Gallio. Our timeline now gets updated as follows:

Dates	Events and Sources
10 BCE	Claudius is born.
37 CE	Caligula begins to reign as emperor.
38 CE	Caligula, during his second year in office, begins work on the Roman aqueduct system.
41 CE	Caligula is murdered and his uncle, Claudius, begins to rule.
46/47 CE	A general famine sweeps across the Mediterranean world under the reign of Claudius.
48/49 CE	Claudius receives his twenty-fourth acclamation.
49 CE	Claudius expels Jews from Rome. The Isthmian games take place in Corinth.
49/50 CE	Claudius receives his twenty-fifth, twenty-sixth, and twenty-seventh acclamations, attested by ancient coins.
50 CE	Claudius completes and dedicates the aqueducts. Titianus and Sulla were Roman consuls. Gallio assumes the role of proconsul of Achaia. However, he only served about half of his one-year tenure in office.
51 CE	The Isthmian games take place in Corinth.
54 CE	Claudius dies and the Jewish expulsion in Rome ends.

In the letter from Seneca, referenced above, it was mentioned that Gallio boarded a boat. In the ancient world, travel by boat was not really possible during the winter months. From the end of October to the end of February, seas were rarely traversed.[28] Acts tells us that Gallio was in Corinth (Acts 18:12–17). This must have been between the years of the Isthmian games of 49 and 51 CE, that is, in the year 50 CE. Since Paul was brought before Gallio, this means that Paul was also in Corinth in 50 CE. Acts also tells us that Paul stayed on in Corinth for about eighteen months, plus a few weeks (Acts 18:11, 18). The question we ask now is: When did Paul arrive at and leave Corinth? Or, when did his eighteen-month stint begin and when did he leave?

If we date the Jerusalem Council at 49 CE, and allow that Paul took a boat up to the Phrygia-Galatia (South Galatia) region (Acts 16:1–10) and then traveled through Asia Minor from March, 49 CE to September, 49 CE, this gives him six months of travel and allows him enough time to cross over by boat from Troas into Macedonia, landing at Samothras just before winter (16:11). He arrived at Neapolis and then went into Philippi and spent some time there (16:11). At the beginning of 50 CE he traveled by land, south through Amphipolis, Apollonia, Thessalonika, Berea, and Athens (Acts 16:11—17:34).

In the spring of 50 CE, perhaps the month of March, he arrived in Corinth. Gallio was serving from March/April, 50 CE to September, 50 CE. It was during this period that Paul was tried. If he stayed on for just over 18 months and first arrived in March/April of 50 CE that means that he left Corinth in the fall of 51 CE, perhaps in September or October, just before sea travel ended. This puts him at Ephesus and then Caesarea Maritima and Jerusalem just before the start of winter (Acts 18:21–22). This also means that he was in Corinth during the Isthmian games of 51 CE. It is possible that he, Aquila, and Priscilla sold tents and leather goods to those who attended the games. In the end, the data may lead us to the tentative timeline below:

Dates	Events and Sources
10 BCE	Claudius is born.
37 CE	Caligula begins to reign as emperor.
38 CE	Caligula, during his second year in office, begins work on the Roman aqueduct system.
41 CE	Caligula is murdered and his uncle, Claudius, begins to rule.
46/47 CE	A general famine sweeps across the Mediterranean world under the reign of Claudius.
48/49 CE	Claudius receives his twenty-fourth acclamation.

| 49 CE | Claudius expels Jews from Rome. The Isthmian games take place in Corinth.

Paul attends the Jerusalem Council. From there he travels to the Phrygia-Galatia region, then along the coast of Asia Minor all the way to Troas, where he boards a boat to Macedonia. |
|---|---|
| 49/50 CE | Claudius receives his twenty-fifth, twenty-sixth, and twenty-seventh acclamations, attested by ancient coins. |
| 50 CE | Claudius completes and dedicates the aqueducts. Titianus and Sulla were Roman consuls.

Gallio assumes the role of proconsul of Achaia. However, he only served about half of his one-year tenure in office.

Paul travels from Macedonia southward into Greece. In the spring (March or April) he arrives in Corinth, and not too long after this he is brought before Gallio.

In the fall and before winter commences and prevents travel, Gallio leaves Corinth. |
| 51 CE | The Isthmian games take place in Corinth.

In the fall and before winter commences and prevents travel, Paul leaves Corinth. He arrives at Neapolis just before winter and travels to Caesarea Maritima, and then to Jerusalem. |
| 54 CE | Claudius dies and the Jewish expulsion in Rome ends. |

At this point we shift our attention from the Gallio Inscription to the 1929 recovery of the Erastus Inscription. We should preface our discussion of this relic by making it known that there is considerable debate among researchers as to whether or not the Erastus mentioned in the New Testament is the same Erastus mentioned in this inscription. In fact, it is not even clear that within the New Testament all of the mentions of Erastus refer to the same person. This lack of clarity exists in part because Erastus was a very common name in the ancient world; in addition to appearing nearly one-hundred times in Latin and Greek texts, at least one other inscription containing this name has been found.[29] Further, because the front of the Erastus Inscription is missing, the artifact could have originally contained the name Eperastus, which was also quite common. If Eperastus is the name on the original inscription then this discovery is certainly not connected to the New Testament.[30]

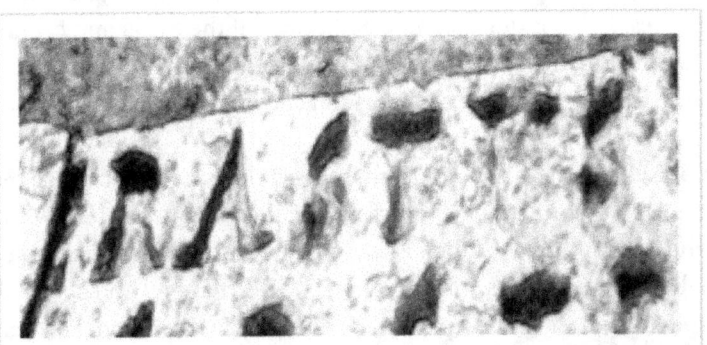

A sketch of the portion of the Erastus Inscription that contains the name Erastus.

There are at least two other matters which muddy the waters: the claim that the Erastus Inscription is not from the first but second century, and a possible disconnect between the term used in the New Testament to describe Erastus and the man described on the ancient stone. Concerning the former, Steven Friesen, in conjunction with Charles Williams, an archaeologist who oversees Corinthian excavations, claims that this inscription was situated within a plaza, or at the foot of steps one would walk up to enter the plaza. The floor of the plaza covers an ancient latrine, dated to the Hardianic period, which suggests the inscription "can not have been laid earlier than the second quarter of the second century CE."[31] In other words, the latrine beneath the plaza dates to the second century. If it were one of the first things constructed in the plaza then the inscription near the steps was likely placed later.

Entering the Fray

Regarding the triple use of the name Erastus in the New Testament (Acts 19:22; Rom 16:23; 2 Tim 4:20), so as not to get off track, we focus here on the mention in Romans. In Rom 16:23 we read, "You all greet Erastus the *oikonomos*." There has been considerable debate, spanning decades, as to how to understand the term *oikonomos*; a handful of fascinating suggestions have been made but those need not detain us here.[32] What is important is that for the most part, this term is either understood as referring to a social elite in ancient Corinth who joined Paul's congregation, or a poor man, who was not a believer and therefore not active in Paul's church. There are compelling arguments from both sides.[33] This is quite significant because if the social and economic statuses of Erastus could be recovered, it might provide more insight into the makeup of Paul's churches in general, and the congregation in Corinth in particular.

Based on the discussions among scholars at this point, it seems wise to resist connecting the Erastus of the New Testament with the Erastus Inscription. As much as we might like to know more about the social makeup of Paul's congregations, we need not rely on strained interpretations of Erastus to provide us with this information. Further, we need to take seriously the claims of Friesen that as Western interpreters who live in a society focused on upward mobility, we may well be reading our own social and economic ideas back into these matters.

To this, I would add that among many Christians there is often a deep desire to connect the New Testament to artifacts, so as to ground the text in a more concrete and less abstract reality. Because of this we often stretch the data, ignore important details, and overlook significant pieces of information. This, however, cannot be called honest research. Therefore, until more solid evidence surfaces, we need not rush to connect the dots of the text with ancient relics; the New Testament does not stand or fall, nor does it lose any credibility, if the Erastus Inscription is not directly connected to it.[34]

Before proceeding to another inscription, we bring into view two important text collections, namely, the Nag Hammadi Codices (NHC) and the Dead Sea Scrolls (DSS). While the DSS have enjoyed more popularity, it is believed that the NHC were discovered first. Both sets of texts are named after the locations in which they were found and both are reported as having been stumbled upon by pastoralists or rural workers. The NHC were found in 1945 in Upper Egypt near the town of Nag Hammadi. A local farmer, Muhammad Ali al-Samman, was digging for good fertilizing soil and ended up unearthing a large jar with a bowl inside.

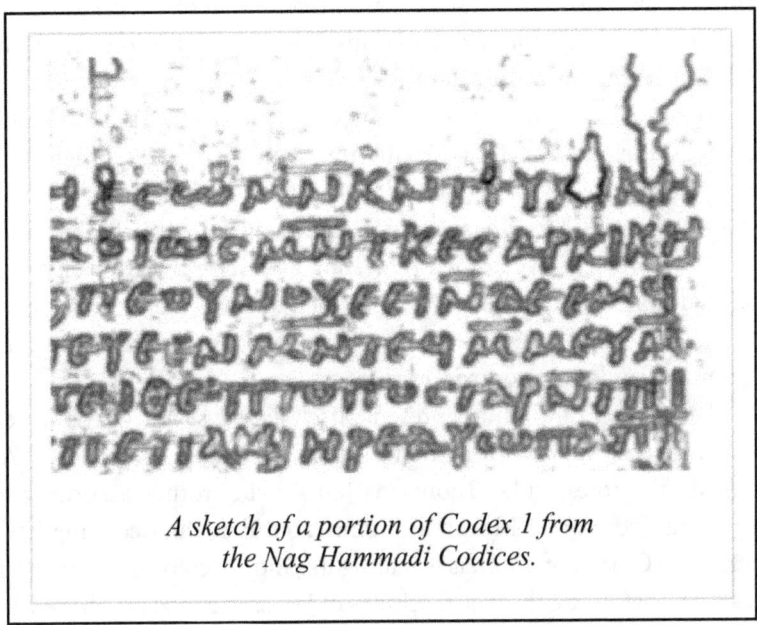

A sketch of a portion of Codex 1 from the Nag Hammadi Codices.

Supposedly he conducted his digging in the Pacomian cemetery, which is situated at the foot of the Djebel el Tarif cliff. Contained within the bowl was a collection of thirteen leather codices or bound books, which are dated to the fourth century CE.[35]

Due to a number of circumstances, it took nearly two decades before the general public would be able see photographic reproductions of these texts. Instrumental in bringing this to fruition was James Robinson, a leading Nag Hammadi researcher, who later published the first English version of these ancient Coptic texts.[36] It is believed that these works were composed in Greek and later translated into the Coptic versions uncovered. All told, it took almost thirty-five years to see the NHC in print form.

These works have been popularized in large measure by Bart Ehrman and Elaine Pagels.[37] Among the NHC are what these and other scholars refer to as the gnostic Gospels. Ehrman and Pagels contend that the Gnostics were a Christian group whose voice and literature was essentially suppressed and quieted by domineering church leaders. Just as well, they claim that because this is the case, it is likely that in these works we find some of the truest and most authentic teachings of Jesus. Of the fifty-two works contained in the NHC, the Gospel of Truth, the Gospels of Thomas, Philip, and The Egyptians, the Apocryphon of John, and the Wisdom of Jesus Christ are central in this regard.

Even so, from the six works just mentioned the one that has likely garnered the most attention from New Testament researchers is the Gospel of Thomas, which contains 114 proverbs, parables, and teachings attributed to Jesus. While fragments of this document had been discovered in various locations at prior points in history, it was not until the NHC findings that the text was made available in full.[38] Some interpreters have argued that Thomas can be traced back to an oral tradition from as early as 50 CE, which moves it from the realm of late heresies to the realm of earliest Christianity. Such claims, however, are tenuous and quite controversial.

The Gospel of Thomas "presents itself as 'the secret words which the living Jesus spoke and Didymus Judas Thomas wrote down.'"[39] As Sean Martin notes, Judas Thomas is Jesus' twin brother according to Syrian tradition. . . ."[40] Martin also points out that, "In declaring itself 'secret', the Gospel of Thomas is nailing its Gnostic colours to the mast: these, it is saying, are the true teachings of Jesus, intended for 'those who have ears to hear.'"[41] Regardless of the stance once takes on the authority of texts like the Gospel of Thomas, anyone interested in New Testament studies should read and be familiar with these ancient works.[42]

It is no exaggeration to say that the Dead Sea Scrolls have received quite a bit more attention than the NHC. Our first modern encounter with the DSS is traced back to two Ta'amra Bedouin shepherds who, while walking through the Qumran Cave area located in the Dead Sea region of Israel, found these scrolls. As the story goes, Muhammad Abu-Dieb and a friend were searching for a lost sheep when they happened upon a cave whose door was partially blocked. One of the men picked up a rock and threw it into a cave and thereafter he heard something shatter. They went into the cave and found a broken jar that had contained several scrolls, including the Isaiah Scroll, the Habakkuk Commentary, and the Community Rule. This led to explorations in other nearby caves and over the next twelve years, numerous scrolls turned up.

From Peter's House to James's Tomb and Beyond

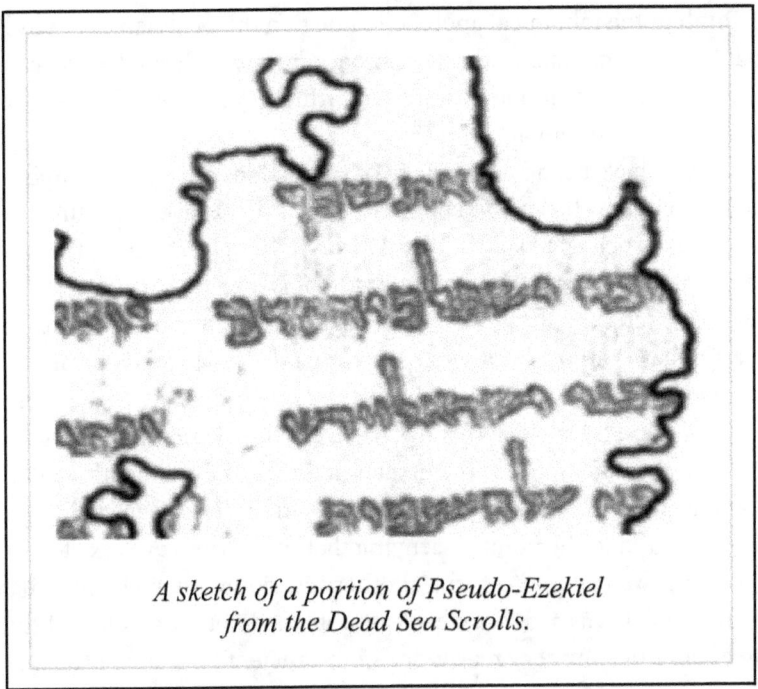

A sketch of a portion of Pseudo-Ezekiel from the Dead Sea Scrolls.

The DSS contain Hebrew, Aramaic, and Greek texts. Some of these 972 works are apocryphal or non-canonical, others discuss traditions having to do with various sects or biblical figures, and a number are concerned with rules and prayers. Most notably, with the exception of Esther, all of the Old Testament books are included among the DSS. One of the texts that has received the most attention is The Book of War, which in its discussion of the battle between good and evil, sheds light on aspects of ancient battles from clothing to prayers to rituals, and the roles that community leaders assumed.

It is often assumed that the DSS contain New Testament documents, which is not the case; there are no New Testament documents among the DSS.[43] This, however, does not mean that they are unimportant or unrelated to the New Testament. In fact, one of the major payoffs is that "The scrolls make a major contribution to our understanding of the Second-Temple period and reveal the religious practices of this period in a different light. . . . They enlighten us about a pivotal period in the development of Judaism and Early Christianity, and monotheism in general."[44] Zvi Gal has written, "The scrolls reflect the major change that Judaism underwent in this period, from a faith based on the law of Torah to the rabbinical approach known in the Mishnah. The scrolls enable us to understand the Jewish background of Early Christianity, as it is reflected in similar customs and rituals, such as baptism and the partaking of communal meals."[45]

There have been a wide range of suggestions as to who composed the DSS and how they ended up in the caves. There have been a number of scholars, such as Eleazar Sukenik, who have suggested that Qumran was occupied by a social/religious sect that is directly connected to the caves and scrolls.[46] It has also been argued that Qumran once served as a military outpost.[47] Others have contended that the Qumran villa belonged to an affluent family from the city of Jerusalem who stored the texts there.[48] One idea that has received a lot of attention is that this was where a sect known as the Essenes made their dwelling; these then, would be the Essene libraries.[49] Such contentions have been challenged, however, even to the point of denying that the Essenes ever existed.[50]

Here, we bring into focus another inscription, namely, the Pilate Stone or Pilate Inscription. This limestone inscription was found during a series of summer excavations in the ancient port city of Caesarea Maritima in 1961. At least half of the text is missing and the stone appears to have been removed from a wall and reused and fitted into a staircase.[51] Given the tarnished nature of the inscription, the textual reconstructions of scholars vary.[52] What is legible of the remaining Latin is arranged in three lines as follows: "S TIBERIEVM / . . . NTIVS PILATVS / . . . ECTVS IVDA E."[53] Géza Alföldy, arguing that Pilate was conducting major work in this seaport city, reconstructs and translates the inscription to read: "Seaman's Tiberium / Pontius Pilate / Prefect of Judea."[54]

A sketch of a portion of the Pilate Inscription.

It is possible that Pilate was attempting to curry favor with Tiberius and erected a building in his honor, naming it after him.[55] Josephus describes the port city as "built of fine materials" and having a "fine structure." He claims that its "subterranean vaults and cellars had no less of architecture bestowed on them than had the buildings above ground" and that "Herod built there a theater of stone and on the south quarter, behind the port, an amphitheater capable of holding many men" (*Antiquities*, 15.9.6). Elsewhere he says that in the city there were "many arches" and this is a place "where mariners dwelt" frequently (*Wars*, 1.21.5–7). Josephus has a low opinion of Pilate and paints him as a cause of disturbances among the Jews, particularly by allowing Jerusalem to be tainted with idolatrous acts and images (*Wars*, 2.9.2–3; *Antiquities*, 18.3.1).

Philo also appears to have a negative view of Pilate referring to him as a man of "cruel, stubborn and inflexible" disposition whose time in office was marked by corruption to the tune of "bribes, insults, thefts, riots, pointless beatings, exactions without trial, and ongoing and very tortuous cruelty" (*Legatio ad Gaium*, 38). This is not exactly the way that he is portrayed in the New Testament but neither is it too far of a stretch, since we hear in the New Testament of Pilate slaying a number of Galileans (Lk 13:1). Further, he did concede to the crowds during Jesus' trial and this ultimately led to the murder of an innocent man (Mt 27:18; Mk 15:10; Lk 23:4, 14–16, 33). Even so, we should remember that Philo and Josephus both had agendas in mind when they were writing, which, in playing down Pilate, may have scored them favor from those officials who despised Pilate.[56] The New Testament writers also had agendas and this must not be forgotten.

There are at least three important things that the Pilate Inscription has provided for discussions about the New Testament. First, it helps substantiate the "historical Pilate" and roots him squarely in history.[57] Secondly, the inscription provides us with data beyond textual sources for Pilate.[58] Thirdly, the Pilate Inscription helps fill out the historical picture of Caesarea Maritima, both above ground and below water.[59]

The final three discoveries we bring into view in this section are all tombs or ossuaries: the James Ossuary, the Jesus Family Tomb, and the Caiaphas Tomb.[60] It should be kept in mind that a tomb is the structure that holds ossuaries while an ossuary is a box-like coffin that was designed to hold bones. Hershel Shanks provides a helpful note on the ancient context surrounding ossuaries.

> "For about a hundred years at the turn of the era, chiefly in Jerusalem, an unusual burial custom developed—the reburial of the bones of the deceased in smallish, rectangular bone boxes called ossuaries. During the period of the Israelite monarchy, from the tenth through sixth centuries BCE, special concern was also expressed for the bones of the deceased. But they were not reburied in ossuaries. At that time in Jerusalem, it was customary to lay the deceased on a rock-cut burial bench in a burial cave; after about a year, when the flesh had decayed, the bones were deposited with the bones from previous burials in a repository under the stone burial bench. Some scholars have speculated that this is what is meant by the Biblical phrase to be 'gathered to their fathers (Jdg 2:10; 2 Kgs 22:20) or 'buried with his fathers' (2 Kgs 8:24) or 'slept with his fathers' (2 Kgs 13:13).... Ossuaries were used, however, in the late Second Temple period, which ended with the Roman destruction of the Temple in 70 CE."[61]

The James Ossuary has something of a mysterious back story. Unlike many other relics unearthed during excavations, this piece was supposedly bought on the archaeological "black market" around 1976 by an antiquities collector named Oded Golan.⁶² However, it was almost three decades later (2002) when the James Ossuary came to the scholarly world's attention. In particular, Golan invited André Lemaire to view and study the burial box.⁶³

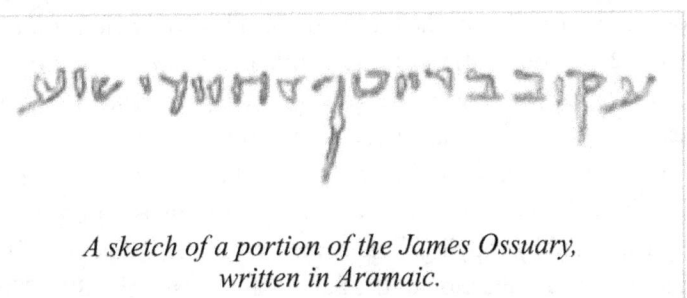

A sketch of a portion of the James Ossuary, written in Aramaic.

What made this ossuary so interesting was an Aramaic inscription on the outside which (transliterated here) read: *ya'akov bar yosef akhui diyeshua*. This is translated to "James, the son of Joseph, the brother of Jesus."⁶⁴ Essentially, there are three major views on this ossuary:

1. It is completely authentic and refers back to the Jesus of the New Testament.
2. It is wholly inauthentic and perhaps a forgery.
3. It is partially legitimate, that is, the box is authentic but the inscription may be a later addition.

There has been a flurry of literature published on this find and there is no way to cover all of that here. Instead, I will simply provide some of the claims espoused by each view.

We have already mentioned André Lemaire who contends that the James Ossuary is authentic and provides us with the earliest artifact relating back to Jesus and his existence. He concludes this based on the shape of the letters, which fit the "approximate date" of 20 BCE–70 CE and can likely be narrowed down to "the last decades before the Roman destruction of Jerusalem in 70 CE," which "was the exact period when James, the brother of Jesus, would have died."⁶⁵ Further, after thorough examinations in the labs of the Geological Survey of Israel, six samples of both the limestone and patina, along with two samples of attached soil, were studied using high-tech machinery. Lemaire notes that after this, the scientists concluded in a letter to Hershel Shanks that, "[T]he patina does not contain any modern elements (such as modern pigments) and it adheres firmly to the stone. No signs of the use of a modern tool or instrument was [sic] found. No evidence that might detract from the authenticity of the patina and the inscription was found."[66]

Despite these claims, others have suggested that the James Ossuary is not authentic.[67] One of the more notable places this view is espoused is in the 2009 compilation of essays titled *Resurrecting the Brother of Jesus: The James Ossuary and the Quest for Religious Relics*. In that work, for example, Byron McCane begins by noting that even if the ossuary had been authentic, it would not "have told us anything we did not already know."[68] Further, McCane asserts that this is a forgery, which was constructed by copying three names out of the Catalogue of Jewish Ossuaries in the Collection of the State of Israel (see nos. 396, 570, and 573) and then combining them with the aid of a scanner and computer. Following this, the newly linked epitaphs were engraved on the box.[69] Within the same book, one of McCane's co-authors, Jonathan Reed argued that this forged relic brings to light the academy's lust for "archaeoporn" and in addition, reveals "the limitations of artifactual proof texting that have plagued biblical archaeology since its inception."[70]

Finally, there are some who take a middle-ground approach. For example, Eric Meyers has contended that the burial box is authentic but he questions the inscription and other details. He has suggested that "the front side on which the inscriptions was incised looked suspicious because it had been cleaned to its original whitish limestone coloring and because the incision of parts of the inscription looked recent."[71] Just as well, he has noted that "the patina in particular looked as if it had been applied intentionally and was not the result of natural weathering over time." Additionally, "the application of dirt taken from a specific location with hot or even cold water was easy to do and could create the impression of being original."[72]

Meyers has also questioned certain paleographical elements of the ossuary. Interestingly, Meyers has also suggested that through conversations with archaeologists and a certain store-owner who previously worked along Jerusalem's Via Dolorosa, he has learned that the box was sold in the 1990s and did not originally contain the phrase "brother of Jesus." Meyers relays the story about an archaeologist visiting the shop: "The archaeologist noted an ossuary nearby his [the shop owner's] chair

From Peter's House to James's Tomb and Beyond

and inquired about it. The dealer brought it closer and showed him the inscription on it, 'James, son of Joseph,' and said that this was his retirement pension."[73]

As we can see from the views of these three researchers alone, there is quite a bit of disagreement about the James Ossuary's authenticity. It may indeed be the case that the box tells us little about the ancient world or earliest Christianity. However, if the ossuary were to finally be proven authentic, the "inscription would constitute the most direct archaeological evidence found to date of the historical person of Jesus, Christianity's founder" and "the earliest known artifact to mention him."[74] However, there may simply be too much ambiguity surrounding this relic to come to such conclusions.

Another ossuary relevant to our discussion here is the 1980 discovery known as either the Jesus Family Tomb or the Talpiot/Talpiyot Tomb. It bears the name "Talpiyot" because it was found just outside the Old City (Jerusalem) in the neighborhood of East Talpiyot. The Talpiyot Tomb is a cave-like structure that contained ten ossuaries, six of which were marked by script or text. The tomb was first located when the Solel Boneh Construction Company of Israel "was clearing away rubble with a bulldozer after having dynamited a section in the Jerusalem suburb of Talpiot."[75] Today the location sits in the middle of an apartment complex.

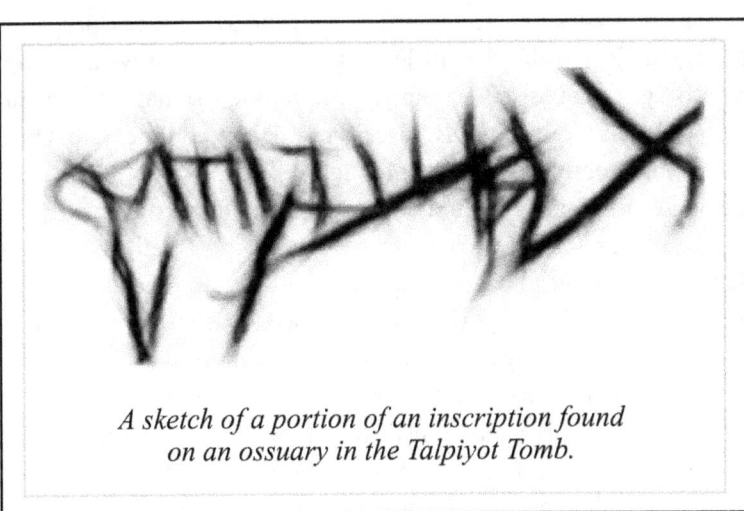

A sketch of a portion of an inscription found on an ossuary in the Talpiyot Tomb.

Inscribed separately on a handful of the ossuaries were the following epithets: Jesus son of Joseph, Judah son of Jesus, Matia, Joseh,

Mariamne Mara, Maria.[76] This has led some researchers, such as James Tabor and Simcha Jacobovici, to suggest that this was the family tomb of Jesus Christ. Tabor even sees this as evidence of a Jesus dynasty.[77] This led to further speculation that the Jesus and Mariamne (or translated Mary) here were husband and wife and had a son together name Judah. Just as well, since bones were recovered in these boxes, it led to the conclusion that if this was the Jesus of Christianity, he must not have been resurrected—his body is still here. Of course, this is a rather radical reinterpretation of the story of the Jesus of the New Testament.

Many scholars have signed a declaration asserting that they believe there is no relationship between this ossuary and the Jesus of Christianity. A couple of compelling arguments against this connection are given by archaeologist Shimon Gibson: The suggestion that the Mariamne is that of Mary Magdalene is based on the Acts of Philip, a fourth-century CE text and a comment by Hippolytus from the second century CE. However, the ossuary containting these remains can read "Mariame kai Mara" which would "imply that remains of two female individuals were kept in the ossuary, a mother and daughter, or perhaps two sisters."[78] In addition, the name Josheh is actually just an abbreviated form of Joseph, who was mentioned on one ossuary as the father of Jesus. This Joseph is probably the father of both Jesus and Judah alike, not merely the former.[79]

Gibson writes, "Hence, if we discount the Mariamne=Mary Magdalene and [Joseh]=brother of Jesus connections, then we are simply left with a group of ossuaries bearing common Jewish names of the first century CE. As a result of this, there is nothing to commend this tomb as the family tomb of Jesus."[80] One might ask also why these ossuaries bear no Christian symbols and how, like much of Christian history, the location of this tomb was not turned into or identified as a place of sacred or holy pilgrimage among Christians. These and other unanswered questions have left many unconvinced by the claims that these ossuaries are in any way connected to the Jesus of the New Testament.[81]

The last item to be discussed in this section is the famed Caiaphas Tomb, which was discovered in North Talpiyot in 1990 while the Peace Forest was under excavation.[82] The tomb housed a number of ossuaries including the one that is often attributed to Caiaphas, the high priest. Also known as "Ossuary Six," this burial-box was ornately decorated and covered by an orange lid. Inside, were "partial remains of six people:

a sixty-year-old male, an adult woman, two infants, and two children."[83] On the outside of the ossuary were two inscriptions, presumably inscribed after the structure had been set in place because it appears that "the scribe had to force his hand down the narrow gap between the ossuary and the wall and the resulting scrawl is difficult to decipher. On the narrow side the inscription reads Yehosef bar (son of) Qp', on the longer side Yehosef bar (son of) Qyp.'"[84] The name Qyp' resembled the name Qapha, which was found on nearby ossuaries, which had been housed in the same tomb. Due to the fact that Aramaic uses no vowels but only consonants, the name can be pronounced as Qayapa, which in English is rendered Kaiapha, from whence we get Caiaphas.

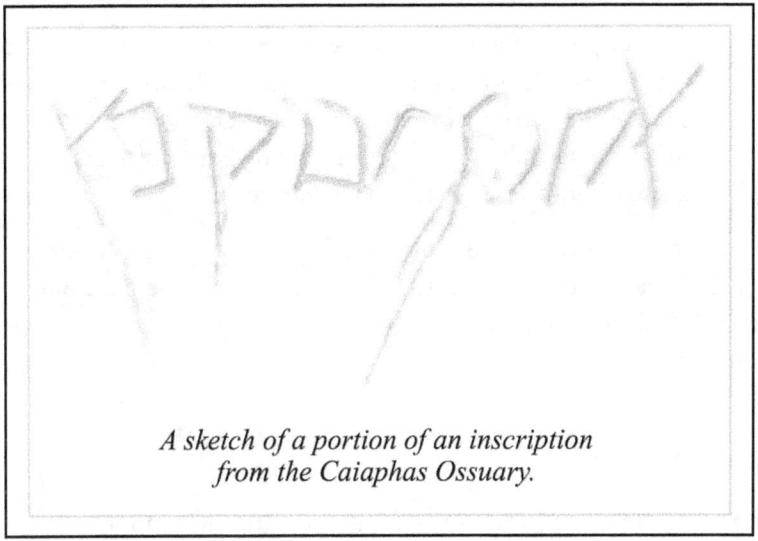

A sketch of a portion of an inscription from the Caiaphas Ossuary.

Josephus comments that there was a high priest named "Joseph Caiaphas" who was "called Caiaphas" (*Antiquities,* 18.2, 3). Following that clarification Josephus proceeds in his narrative to use neither the first name Joseph, nor the double-name Joseph Caiaphas, but the surname Caiaphas. This comports with numerous New Testament passages (Mt 26:3, 57; Lk 3:2; Jn 11:49, 18:13, 14, 24, 28; Acts 4:6). These verses note that Caiaphas was indeed a Jewish high priest who, in conjunction with Pilate, executed Jesus.

As with the archaeological finds mentioned already there are those who believe that the Caiaphas Ossuary belongs to the high priest mentioned in the New Testament and those who do not. Helen Bond has surveyed the literature and concludes that "it is possible" that the connection to the New Testament is valid.⁸⁵ The four major doubts that have been expressed are:

1. Neither the ossuary nor the tomb contain any reference to this man's high priestly status.
2. Beyond the one ossuary, the tomb itself is quite ordinary, which might have been odd if Caiaphas were a wealthy man. Indeed, his father-in-law's tomb, which has been recovered, was quite ornate.
3. There was a coin found in one of the ossuaries. Putting coins in burial boxes was a pagan practice, not a Jewish one. Since Caiaphas was a Sadducee, this practice raises important questions.
4. The scripts on the ossuaries, namely qp' and qyp' can "only be pronounced the same way" and therefore refer to the same person, "if the name were Qopha."⁸⁶ However, one could attribute this to a spelling mistake or an abbreviation of sorts, which means that this is inconclusive evidence.

In her final analysis Bond writes, "We will never know for sure, but the bones of the sixty-year-old male may well have been our one tangible link with a man who played a crucial part in the history of humankind...."⁸⁷

Ruins and Realia

In this section our focus turns from texts and inscriptions to ruins and realia. In particular, we are going to briefly consider the following items: The Shroud of Turin, Peter's House, the Pool of Siloam, and the Migdal (or Magdala) Synagogue. The story of the Shroud of Turin, a linen in which some believe Jesus was buried, miraculously containing his bodily imprint, is one shrouded in scandal. Its name comes from the city in which it is housed, namely, Turin, Italy where it is kept in the Cathedral of St. John the Baptist. Initially, however, it was stationed in Lirey, France and was known as the Shroud of Lirey. First brought to the public's attention around 1353, the supposed burial-cloth has been relocated numerous times.⁸⁸

From Peter's House to James's Tomb and Beyond

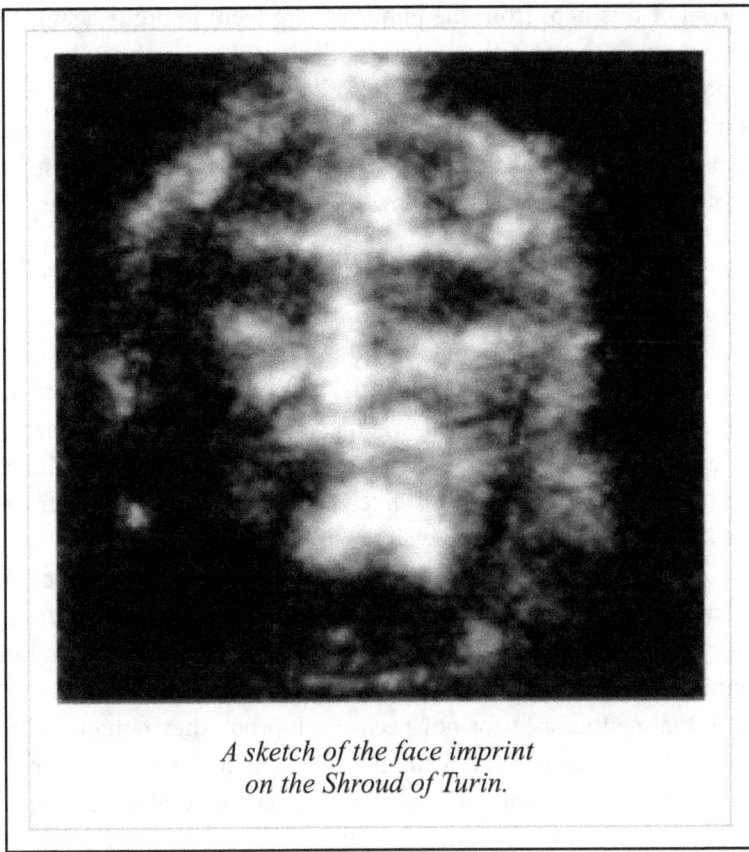

A sketch of the face imprint on the Shroud of Turin.

This was no archaeological find in the sense of the ossuaries or inscriptions mentioned above, yet, given the attention it has attracted it is worth including in this section. While the relic had been on display in its early history, it was not until 1898 and 1931 that the wider public had the opportunity to see photos of it. In fact, one thing that calls the authenticity of the cloth into question is the fact that for thirteen centuries the cloth went unmentioned.[89] Could one person or even more, an entire religious movement, have kept the linen quiet for this long? Would not the church have put this on display or deemed it a pilgrimage site? Why is this bodily impression on the shroud not mentioned by the writers of the New Testament, particularly the Gospel writers? When the tomb was entered why wasn't the imprint noted by the disciples, recorded, and passed on?

These questions, however, are only the tip of the iceberg. The claims of forgery announced by the church early on and the forced removal of this item from the public sphere seem to argue against its authenticity.[90] The fact that none of Christianity's enemies have attempted to destroy the relic might also be suggestive. Scientific claims about blood and pollen samples as well as the type of linen itself, which has been carbon-dated to 1260–1390 CE, have been all been used to discount the claims that this belongs to Jesus or even a first-century CE Israeli context at all.[91]

Some have also found that the supposed blood-stains actually contain traces of paint.[92] Despite the fact that some photographers have asserted that the shroud contains what is similar to a photographic negative and not a positive and that the fades and blurs could not have been created by an artist, such arguments have met their challengers and carry little weight.[93] In light of this shroud's history and the research conducted on it, it is most likely that this piece cannot be traced back to the historical Jesus or even the first-century CE.

Thus, its main value for Christians may be that it leads them to reflect devotionally on the death and resurrection of Jesus. Even the Catholic Church has stored away the shroud taking the view that, "any attempt to confirm the life, death, or resurrection of Jesus contravenes a faith that neither asks for nor needs such proof, they remain unperturbed by the scientists and their tests, recalling it was the Savior himself who reminded Thomas (Jn 20:29): 'You believe because you can see me. Happy are those who have not seen and yet believe.'"[94]

We turn away from the contentious cloth to something more set in stone, namely, an ancient house located in Capernaum. Not far from a second-century CE synagogue that has been unearthed, this home, referred to by many as the "House of St. Peter," was first acknowledged by two Franciscan archaeologists in 1968 and then their later contemporaries.[95] Since the archaeological history is quite elaborate and has been covered in depth elsewhere, here we shall simply mention a number of the reasons why some believe this to be the house of St. Peter. We turn first to the New Testament.

From Peter's House to James's Tomb and Beyond

A reconfigured sketch based on a sign in Capernaum at the site of Peter's house.

It is rather clear from the New Testament itself that Peter had family in Capernaum. Indeed, Mk 1:29–30 notes, "And next, going out from the synagogue, he entered into the house of Simon and Andrew with James and John. And the mother-in-law of Simon was in lying in bed with a fever. . . ." (cf. Mt 8:14–16). Many identify this same house as the one mentioned in Mk 2:1, which is located in Capernaum.[96] Concerning Jesus, Matthew wrote, "And leaving Nazareth he went and he settled/lived in Capernaum in the mountains of Zebulon and Naphtali" (4:13). We also know that Jesus preached in the synagogue at Capernaum (Mk 1:21; Jn 6:54–58). Obviously, Jesus spent time in the ancient town of Capernaum. Did he, however, dwell for a period in the house that archaeologists have uncovered? James H. Charlesworth offers at least six observations as to why he thinks it is likely:[97]

1. Peter lived in Capernaum, as the New Testament notes.

2. This house that has been excavated is the only house in this area of Galilee that has been identified by archaeologists, pilgrims, and other early traditions as Peter's home.

3. An octagonal basilica was placed over sacred places in the Holy land. Over time, a basilica was placed over this house and by the

time of the sixth century it was already being celebrated as St. Peter's place.

4. Within the home itself archaeologists have noted the different types of rooms and the structural updates made over time. For example, the central room in the house was plastered and this act dates to the first-century CE.

5. Christian graffiti dated to the second century CE was discovered on the first-century CE plaster. It is even possible that one of the graffiti pieces bears the name "Peter." This is not attributed to the hand of Peter, but possibly to someone identifying this as his place. It could have also simply been tourist graffiti.

6. The narrow basalt walls of this home probably could have only supported at thatched roof, which is what is described in Mk 2:1–12.

In light of these comments, James Strange notes that while it is not possible to prove beyond the shadow of a doubt that this was Peter's home, there is "a considerable body of circumstantial evidence" that "does point to its identification as St. Peter's house."[98] Further, in a curious contrast he writes, "Though we moderns search for proof, that hardly mattered to those ancient pilgrims who scratched their prayers on the walls of the house-church in the belief that this was, indeed, St. Peter's house. So, for that matter, what 'proof' does a modern pilgrim need?"[99] Murphy-O'Connor agrees with this notion, stating that, "The most reasonable assumption is the one attested by the Byzantine pilgrims, namely, that it was the house of Peter in which Jesus may have lodged (Mt 5:20). Certainly, nothing in the excavations contradicts this identification."[100]

Even so, others are a bit more cautious in their conclusions. Jonathon Reed, for example, argues that the house is "of marginal concern to the nature and character of Capernaum at the time of Jesus."[101] Leslie Hoppe, weighing in on the matter writes, "Archaeology cannot provide all the answers that we would like. It would be fascinating to know whether the house beneath the octagonal church did in fact provide shelter to Jesus while he stayed in Capernaum. The archaeological evidence is not sufficient to provide a definitive answer."[102]

The next discussion piece is the Pool of Siloam, which was first discovered in 2004 and is located near the Old City of Jerusalem in the

Silwam area. It was stumbled upon during attempts to access and repair a broken sewage pipe. The pool, mentioned in the New Testament and other ancient literature, received water from the nearby Gihon Springs, which was carried through what is now referred to as the Siloam Tunnel. This tunnel is dated to Iron Age II (1000–550 BCE) but the pool itself is believed by some to have been built in the first century BCE and done away with around 70 CE.

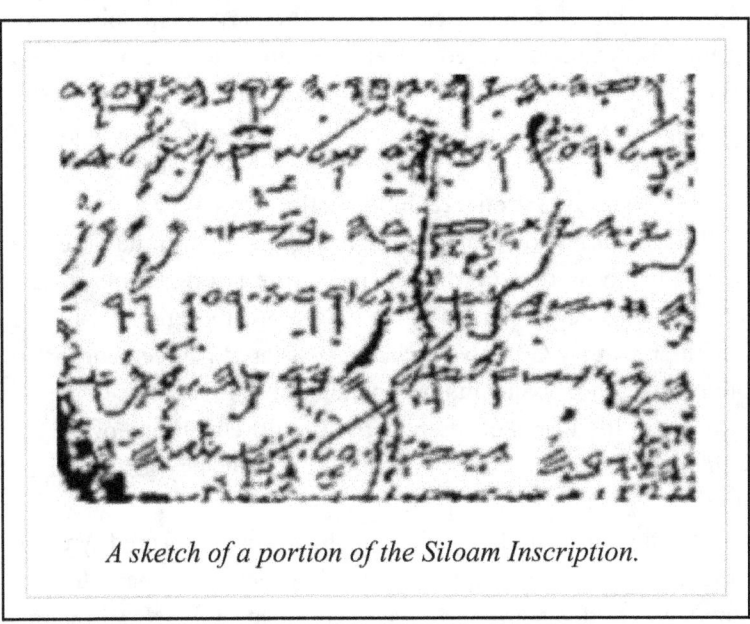

A sketch of a portion of the Siloam Inscription.

Within the New Testament, Siloam is mentioned by both Luke and John. In Lk 13:14 there is a reference to "the tower in Siloam." Since work commenced on this excavation, at least two towers have been discovered.[103] In Jn 9:7, Jesus is reported as having told a blind man to go wash "in the pool of Siloam." This pool, not far from the Temple, likely served as a *mikveh*, that is, a ritual bath for cleansing.[104] In fact, steps leading up toward the Temple have been uncovered. The Pool of Siloam also functioned as a fresh water source and may have, at one time or another, been used as a swimming pool.[105] In the Old Testament the prophets Isaiah (8:6) and Hezekiah (3:15) both mention the waters of Siloam (*Shiloah* in Hebrew). Josephus noted that the pool was outside the wall and mentions several other details as well, all of which comport with the archaeological findings (*Wars,* 5.4.1; 5.6.1; 5.9.4; 5.12.2).

The site excavations, which have been led by Eli Shukrun and Ronny Reich, have led to coin discoveries, which help date the pool to the Hasmonean Period.[106] They have also been able to conclude that at one point, the pool was at least 225 feet in width.[107] Unfortunately, some interpreters have emphasized only what they perceived to be theological or symbolic aspects of this story, without giving any credence to—though not necessarily denying—the notion that it may have happened in an actual historical place.[108] Their argument: John's Gospel is primarily symbolic or theological in nature and therefore, the event at the Pool of Siloam (Jn 9:1–11) is no exception. It should be stated however, those who do acknowledge this pool should not simply swing the pendulum the other way and ignore the theological aspects in favor of the historical ones. Both are important![109]

Today, excavations on the Pool of Siloam continue. There will likely be much more data to be shared in the future. However, at this point, while some scholars disagree on the precise function of the site in the first century CE, most archaeologists are in agreement that this is indeed the Pool of Siloam mentioned in both testaments of the Bible as well as in the works of Josephus. This will remain one of the more significant finds in the history of biblical archaeology for centuries to come.

Our final item to discuss here is the newly discovered synagogue in the ancient city of Magdala, which is believed by many to be the hometown of one of several Marys mentioned in the New Testament, most obviously, Mary Magdalene—or more precisely, Maria(m) of Magdala.[110] Researchers have dated the synagogue, found in 2009, to the first century CE and it has even been suggested that this structure was in use prior to the destruction of the Jerusalem Temple in 70 CE.[111] If this is the case, some have speculated that Mary may have attended the synagogue in her hometown, a well-known port city in its day. One may speculate also that Jesus, who traveled throughout Capernaum teaching and preaching, might have visited this site.

A sketch of a portion of a decorated stone in Magdala containing a menorah and pitchers.

The study of synagogues among archaeologists and New Testament scholars has been quite contentious. Some have even maintained that the entire concept of synagogues as buildings in the ancient world is errant; synagogues were religious groups, not buildings.[112] To offer a rather simplistic analogy, this is much like the stock phrase heard in many evangelical churches today that "the church is not a building it is a group of believers." However, with the discovery of numerous ancient synagogue structures, such claims hardly hold water. These edifices, dating back even to the third century BCE, are often characterized by elaborate decorations, impressive facades, and usually face in the direction of Jerusalem.[113]

In the New Testament, Mary is mentioned in all four Gospels and each time bears her town name. According to the Gospels of Matthew (28:1–10) and John (20:14–18), Mary is the first person to have seen the risen Jesus. In Luke's account she had seven demons driven out of her (Lk 8:1–3). In all three Synoptics she is listed as one of the women at Jesus' crucifixion (Mt 27:55; Mk 15:41; Lk 8:3).

Throughout history, Mary has been portrayed as a prostitute, though this is likely a misguided interpretation. Such depictions can be found in Andrew Lloyd Webber's 1970s musical "Jesus Christ Superstar," Franco Zeffirelli's movie "Jesus of Nazareth," and "The Last Temptation of the Christ," by Nikos Kazantzakis. Rosemary R. Reuther has contended that these representations are rooted "in orthodox Christianity to primarily displace the apostolic authority claimed for women through her name."[114] Jane Schaberg agrees noting that to paint Mary in such a way is to not only create a legend but downplay a "major witness to the crucial data of Christianity, especially the resurrection."[115]

If Mary of Magdala could be connected to the synagogue, this may help temper some of the criticisms against her. Indeed, unless some explicit data surfaces proving this to be the case, such links will likely remain tenuous and speculative. The same goes for placing Jesus at this location. What is of great value to us at this point is that more light is being shed on synagogues in the first century. In turn, through artwork, architecture, and other realia, we can begin to add to our understanding of ancient Judaism. As a result, we are better able to understand the social and cultural worlds behind and in the New Testament.

TAKING ACTION

In this chapter we have looked at a dozen archaeological discoveries relevant to the New Testament. We have seen, however, that relating a number of these directly to the New Testament can be untenable or highly questionable. Yet, there are a few finds that do come to bear on the witness of the New Testament. As interpreters we have truly only entered the fray here. Even so, it is important that we take any claims relating archaeological evidence to the New Testament with the utmost seriousness. We might even take our cues from Paul, who, though he was not speaking about archaeology, suggested that we examine everything carefully. In a world where "archaeoporn" has become a growing industry, we need to be careful about what we do and do not subscribe to, whether on television, in a book, or in an academic or church setting.

For example, it should be clear enough from this chapter that the neither the Bible nor Christianity stands or falls on archaeological finds. While there will likely always be both radical and fundamentalist interpretations of archaeological data, we need to realize that archaeology cannot prove or disprove Christianity, but rather it can only illustrate the New Testament. By that we mean that it can help us understand the world in which the New Testament was situated. Archaeology's main value for us is that it helps us understand the cultural practices, daily living habits, societal norms, community mores, etc., of the first century

CE. In turn, these things help us understand the New Testament and its claims in their ancient context.

Something else that should be clear from this chapter is that not all archaeological discoveries are created equal. Some are legitimate, some illegitimate, and others questionable. The truth is, the stones do not always cry out the way we would like or want them to. That is a point that we must respect because we are not called to be archaeological ventriloquists who make artifacts say or mean things that they never intended to say or mean. This reminds me of one of my first trips to the Mediterranean world, where I had the opportunity to visit many of the sites mentioned in the New Testament. During that trip I began to grow frustrated with the leader, a New Testament scholar, who persistently doubted the meanings assigned to many of the ancient sites or relics by other interpreters. I desperately wanted some of what I was seeing to validate the New Testament.

Looking back I realize that some of my anxiety, while stemming from a passion for the Bible, was quite ill-founded. Today I am much more cautious about connecting the dots between ancient artifacts and the New Testament. Of course, I am not suggesting that connections do not exist; the Gallio Inscription is but one proof of that. What I am saying, however, is that we need not be in a rush to defend or prove the Bible by way of archaeology because ultimately that is not where we, as interpreters of the New Testament, find value in our task. This is a point that needs to be understood by Christians in academic institutions as well as churches.

It would be wonderful to see schools and congregations take greater interest in archaeology and how it comes to bear on the Bible. Many institutions and congregations even offer frequent trips to ancient sites to take part in digs. More than anything we need to understand the big picture of the New Testament; we need to understand the world it grew out of and described because this is what will help us really get a grasp on our sacred text and allow it to get a more firm grasp on us. So, there is certainly value in the archaeological enterprise. The important thing is that we keep that value where it is supposed to be, so that we do not become rigid fundamentalists or extremist handlers and interpreters of the data.

12

Approaching Revelation

http://michaelhalcomb.com/enteringthefray-revelation.html

IT WOULD NOT BE an overstatement to say that many twenty-first-century Americans have a doomsday mentality. Terms such as "apocalypse" or "Armageddon" are common within the vernacular. In fact, an entire subculture has been constructed around an end-of-the-world mentality, whose devotees are known as "preppers." The nickname essentially refers to people who are prepped or prepared for end-time events. They often build multi-million-dollar, underground bunkers stocked with food, water, and weapons so that when a great day of wrath comes, they can retreat to these supposedly indestructible safe houses and live on.

As in 1999, the year before the so-called Y2K outage, folks living in 2011 started prepping for the end of the world in 2012. Many have held the view that an ancient Mayan calendar predicted the world's end and as such, sought to be prepped and readied. Even with the failed predictions of a Christian evangelist in 2011 that the rapture and Armageddon were going to take place, there are still many caught up in the religious fervor. Marketers, playing off these fears, have started to cash-in on the hype by selling apocalyptic clothing, apps, books, and even promises to care for pets after their owners are raptured.

Just days before I set to work on this chapter, within the time span of a week, two sets of tornadoes ripped through Kentucky, followed only several days later by snow, and then a few days after that, temperatures in the eighties. Some posting on Facebook believed that these events were signs that Christ's return was near. This apocalyptic rhetoric became even more intensified when just after this, school shootings took place in the neighboring state of Ohio, and an earthquake rocked Mexico. These "signs" sent people back to their Bibles looking for ancient prophecies that might be just coming true in their midst.

These events tend to make certain individuals want to escape from this world and its harsh realities. They want Jesus to return so that they can "fly away" and be spared from all of the heartache. In short, their religious motivations are undergirded and driven by fear. Perhaps this is to be expected. After all, most of us want to lead comfortable, pain-free lives. Where better to do that than in heaven where there will be no more tears? Besides, isn't that what Christianity is really about anyway: getting to heaven? Isn't the escape from Judgment Day what believers are promised in biblical texts like Revelation?

TUNING IN

The book of Revelation has always been swirled in controversy. Many, such as Martin Luther, have even questioned whether or not it should be kept in the New Testament. This is the case because its mysterious language and imagery has often left readers befuddled. Why is the text so cryptic? What is it trying to say? Was the ancient author under the influence of some kind of hallucinogen when he was writing? Why couldn't the author have just been straightforward? These are all questions I have heard asked, whether in jest or seriousness.

Entering the Fray

The general bewilderment with Revelation suggests that most readers have no idea where to begin with this text. Indeed, many don't even begin with the text itself, but rather a certain theological paradigm they have been exposed to within their churches, seminaries, or the literature they have been engaging. For example, when I bring up the book of Revelation with many of my friends, the first question they ask me is, "Are you pre-trib, trib, post-trib, preterist, historicist, futurist, idealist, dispensational, progressive dispensational, premillenial, post-millineal, panmillenial, or amillenial?" Many other monikers could be added to this list.

This, however, is not the proper place to begin in our encounter with Revelation. Indeed, my own rule of thumb is that when Revelation comes up in a conversation beginning with the above question, it is likely best for me not to discuss the matter any further. Why? Because the minute I open my mouth, I will be pigeon-holed or backed into a corner, and a fruitless debate will ensue.

A more effective starting point is with the question of genre. One's view of Revelation should flow from an understanding of the type of ancient literature this is. Actually, this holds true for any literature we read. When we read a novel, we don't read it the same way we do a laundry list. When we encounter poetry, we do not engage it the same way we would a business memo. We know that an encyclopedia is meant to be understood differently than a memoir. Genre is key! This is particularly true when we read the closing book of the New Testament.

Whatever genre we understand Revelation to be should give shape to how we read and interpret it. In turn, this should give shape to how we empathize with what it is attempting to say, make sense of its meaning, and theologize its contents. It is my view that if, from the beginning, we can shift many of our conversations about Revelation away from preformatted theological paradigms to genre, our dialogues will bear fruit rather than disdain. Being able to talk to—instead of past—one another is the first and perhaps most important step when it comes to matters such as these.

Here, then, we will look at a handful of leading views concerning the genre of Revelation, namely: letter, liturgy, drama, narrative, prophecy, and apocalypse. Some authors also contend that at points, some of these categories overlap. We will look at each of these in turn, reviewing only several of the leading proponents of each view. Along the way we will encounter some scholarly vocabulary, which we will also need to

Approaching Revelation

define and make sense of. While I do have my own view on the genre of Revelation, which is a rather nuanced version of Bruce Malina's thesis (mentioned below), I do not find it necessary to push my judgments here. It seems more appropriate to simply initiate the conversation and provide some of the relevant research, which should set you on the way to forming your own conclusions. That, after all, is part of what makes engaging the Bible and its related literature so much fun.

TAKING NOTE

As with each of the other chapters in this book, here I must be incredibly selective in which authors to review. Inevitably, I have omitted what some believe to be significant works that deserve mention, which is likely true. Yet, it is simply untenable to cover all of the relevant literature here. To reiterate, the function of this book is to act as a "first clue" to accessing the details of significant discussions among scholarly researchers. A second step, then, would be to consult these works directly and then the bibliographical materials contained within them; this will enable readers to take themselves deeper into the issues. It might seem helpful to define several terms here, such as eschatology, apocalyptic, prophecy, etc., however, given the fact that there are no set or wholly agreed upon definitions of these terms by scholars, it will prove most beneficial to simply describe each interpreter's view on their own. In doing so, particular uses of these and other terms will become clearer.

We begin our journey into the genre question of Revelation by engaging current rather than dated research, not least because contemporary works often discuss and draw upon the studies that precede them.

> *Richard Bauckham was born in 1946 in London. He studied at the University of St. Andrews, Scotland, and later taught there. He also served in teaching and research capacities at Clare College, St. John's College, and Ridley Hall, Cambridge. In addition to his many scholarly works he has also written two children's books.*

Our first claim worthy of acknowledgement is that Revelation is a circular letter. As we shall see, however, there are a variety of nuances when it comes to this hypothesis.

Richard Bauckham contends that as a circular letter, Revelation would have been passed around through a host of ancient churches or congregations. Its aims, then, are quite general and capable of covering a number of issues in a

239

wide variety of different contexts and settings. Perhaps most important among Bauckham's arguments is the claim that many misreadings of Revelation "have resulted from neglecting the fact that it is a letter."[1] It is the "special character of a letter as a literary genre" that "enables the writer to specify those to whom he or she is writing and to address their situation as specifically as he or she may wish."[2] If Revelation is a circular letter, then "John has employed an apparently original method of writing" that "speaks as specifically as could be desired" to each of the seven churches mentioned in chapters 2–3.

Thus, the "seven messages provide seven different introductions" to the rest of the work and suggest that John has designed a text that "very unusually, is intended to be read from seven explicitly different perspectives."[3] In particular, this is a prophetic letter, meant to address "the worldwide tyranny of Rome, and, even more broadly" the "cosmic conflict of God and evil" as understood from a first-century CE context.[4] Given the variety of situations mentioned, this letter is not to be understood, in the main, as a text that, in its entirety, was "written for the consolation and encouragement of Christians suffering persecution. . . ."[5] The uncritical acceptance of this view, in Bauckham's opinion, leads to disparate misunderstandings of both the parts and the whole of Revelation.

> Gregory K. Beale was born in 1949 in Dallas, Texas. He earned his ThM from Dallas Theological Seminary and his PhD from the University of Cambridge. He has held positions at numerous schools including Westminster Theological Seminary. In 2004 he served as president of the Evangelical Theological Society.

Whereas Bauckham asserts that Revelation is a prophetic letter, Gregory Beale contends that it is an apocalyptic one. By apocalyptic, Beale means an "end-time judgment of cosmic evil and consequent establishment of the eternal kingdom."[6] Revelation, then, has an "already and not yet" dual nature about it; the judgment and establishing of the eternal kingdom has commenced but it has not yet been finalized. Likewise, evil is already under assault but it has not yet been eradicated. The future hope of God's conquering of evil should encourage the recipients of the letter who comprise a "confused church living in the midst of compromise and doubt."[7]

For Beale, this "apocalyptic letter" aims to address "problems among the seven churches by appealing to both their present and future share in Christ's blessings."[8] Though Beale acknowledges that

Approaching Revelation

Revelation also contains prophetic features, he contends that the duality prevalent in other ancient apocalyptic works shapes the entire structure of Revelation.

In particular, he is interested in how the church within the old creation, that is, the church in chapters 2–3, contrasts with the church of the new creation in 21:9—22:5. For example, the false prophets of 2:2 correspond to, and contrast with, the twelve true apostles of 21:14. Likewise, the Christians who dwell where Satan's throne is (2:13) run parallel and counter to the Christians who dwell where God's throne is (22:1). These and numerous other antithetical parallels form an *inclusio* or bracket for the whole of the letter.[9] In between, there are five recapitulations (repeated parallel visions) loosely based on the format of the book of Daniel, which "signal the broad structural divisions" of the apocalyptic letter (4:1—8:1; 8:2—11:19; 12:1—14:20; 15:1—16:21; 17:1—21:8).[10]

> M. Eugene Boring was born in 1938. He earned his PhD from Vanderbilt University. Boring's ordination took place with the Christian Church (Disciples of Christ). Boring has written numerous commentaries and has translated nearly a dozen theological works from German into English.

Eugene Boring, on the other hand, views the whole of Revelation as a letter, particularly, a pastoral letter. He notes that the author, John, chose the letter form for the same reasons that the apostle Paul did, namely, because "He has something important to say which he cannot say personally to the congregations because he is absent . . . the letter is a substitute . . ."[11]

For Boring, the fact that Revelation is a letter has at least four important implications:

1. This was "written to specific Christians in a specific place, time, and situation" that is, first-century CE Asia Minor (modern-day Turkey).

2. Given the specific nature of this letter, it was not a general or circular letter.

3. It "was not written to us" today.[12] In short, John was aware that "the readers to whom he directed his letter would know when it was written—their own time—and the situation it presupposed—their own situation."[13]

4. This letter, which was meant to be read aloud, would not have been handled by its earliest hearers in a private setting. Instead,

it was meant to be heard during a church gathering, and read by the worship leader. As such, it was not heard as or understood to be "the last book of the Bible" or even "a book at all" but rather, a letter—which also contained letters.[14]

Grasping the fact that Revelation follows the ancient letter format should help prevent interpreters from falling prey to the "current pop-eschatology misunderstanding of Revelation as a book of long-range predictions forecasting events in our own time. . . ."[15] It also helps correct the erroneous view that biblical prophecy is to be understood as long-range prediction. "The future John announces . . . is always either the immediate future of his first-century readers (e.g., 2:10) or the ultimate future of the victory of God at the end of history (e.g., 21:1—22:5), which John perceived as near at hand."[16] Revelation, then, is not a "book" of predictions but rather, a letter "written to first-century readers who were expected to understand it" otherwise "it would have been meaningless to its first readers and would not have been a letter to them at all."[17]

> Austin Marsden Farrer was born in 1904 in London, England. He was raised in the Baptist tradition by his father who was a preacher, but eventually became an Anglican. He studied at Balliol College, Oxford, and later became Fellow and Chaplain of Trinity College, Oxford. He died unexpectedly in 1968.

While Boring's claim that Revelation was meant to be read within the context of a worship setting is not too distant from the views of Austin Farrer, ultimately, Farrer does not see Revelation as a letter. Instead, he sees it as a document that follows the worship schedule of a Jewish liturgy. It should be mentioned that the notion of Revelation as liturgy has become quite popular within the last few decades. Here, we shall only look at three works in this category, which means that we are only touching the tip of the iceberg of such studies.

For Farrer, the author of Revelation, St. John, sees the Scriptures as arranged in calendrical patterns. Put differently, "he sees them artificially arranged in the Jewish sacred calendar, with its feasts and lessons. . . ."[18] It is this pattern that the ancient author has in mind when he arranges and composes his own work. The result is that Revelation is structured after the Jewish festal calendar. Further, Farrer argues that the numerous OT references and images that were occasionally read during weekly and festal synagogue gatherings were ultimately taken up by John and recycled—or given a "rebirth"—for Christian worship.

Approaching Revelation

In particular, Farrer understands Revelation to be based on a twelve-point diagram, structured around the Zodiac. This Zodiac, however, is not circular but squared or diamond-shaped and has three levels: jewels/colors, tribes of Israel, and Zodiac characters/narratives.[19] Farrer believes that it is this diagram that "supplies the answer" to much of the confusion surrounding the interpretation of Revelation. In his view, it shows how John keeps "so many concerns in mind" at once such as "following the symbolical week and the sacred year, the scheme of traditional eschatology, of Christ's prophecy, and of multiple Old Testament [typologies]."[20] Farrer refers to this diagram with the name "Pleroma," by which he means the revelation that discloses the fullness of the "life of God."[21] In the end, for Farrer, Revelation becomes a grand theological poem rooted in the Jewish sacred calendar and based on a three-tiered, diamond-shaped diagram, which was modified to fit within the context of ancient Christian liturgy. To be sure, Farrer's thesis is quite dense and at times rather tough to follow. Even so, he has managed to raise many questions about Revelation that have caused researchers to reevaluate this ancient text, and therefore his work ought to be taken seriously.

> Philip C. Carrington was born in 1892. He studied at Christ's College, Canterbury and the University of Canterbury. He was ordained as an Anglican priest and served many years leading Boy Scout troops. He held positions at St. Barnabas Theological College and Bishop's University. He died in 1975.

Another scholar who has taken note of a Jewish liturgical influence on Revelation is Philip Carrington. Writing prior to Farrer, even though Farrer never cites him, Carrington contended that the poem of Revelation, which is lovelier than the poetic works of Samuel Coleridge and has a greater sense of melody, rhythm, and composition than the masterpieces of Bach, was born out of Jewish liturgy.[22] More specifically, Carrington has argued that it borrowed heavily from the temple liturgy. He notes, "The author of the Revelation frequented the temple, and loved its liturgy" which "forms the background of the whole poem."[23]

The most borrowed portion of the temple liturgy in Revelation is the daily sacrifice. Carrington deals with this at length and we cannot review his work in great depth here. It is enough, however, to point out that for him, it is the sacrifice that functions as the basis for the Christian liturgy that John imagines and creates. Thus, "Revelation follows

243

Entering the Fray

the events of the daily sacrifice with variations suggested by the ritual Day of Atonement."[24] Christian worship, then, becomes "Sacrificial Worship . . . based on Hebrew ritual, and no doubt reflects the custom of St. John's own day," which was subsequently "followed in every Eucharistic liturgy of the Catholic Church."[25]

> Barbara Wootten Snyder earned her PhD in 1991 from the Department of Near Eastern Studies at the University of California at Berkeley. Snyder earned her AB from UC Riverside (1976) and her MDiv from Gordon-Conwell Theological Seminary (1982). She has written several works on the Apocalypse.

While a host of liturgical views concerning Revelation have been put forth by scholars, one last piece of research to be mentioned here belongs to Barbara Snyder. For Snyder, Revelation is a large *chiasm*, that is, it is presented in an a-b-c-c-b-a pattern where the main themes are laid out and then repeated in inverted order. According to Snyder, this framework comes from the temporal context of the end-time Feast of Tabernacles.[26] The following outline illustrates her view:

SNYDER'S THEORY OF CHIASTIC STRUCTURE IN REVELATION

A. Apocalypse, Epistle, Prophecy (Rev 1:1–20)
  B. Vision of the saints on earth (2–3)
    C. Judgment meeting of the heavenly Sanhedrin (4–5)
      D. Seven seals (6:1—8:1)
        E. Seven trumpets (8:2—9:21)
          F. Theophany related to land and sea (10)
            G. War against saints on earth (11)
            G. War against dragon in heaven (12)
          F. Counter-theophany related to land and sea (13)
        E. Seven proclamations (14)
      D. Seven bowls (15–16)
    C. Judgment meeting of heavenly Sanhedrin on messianic reign (17—20:15)
  B. Vision of the saints in heaven (21:1—22:5)
A. Apocalypse, Epistle, Prophecy (22:6–21)

A description of this feast which was certainly celebrated in John's era, the first century CE, began with the opening and reading of the Torah scroll, followed by the burning of incense, then the blowing of trumpets over the offering, the pouring out of water and wine libations over the offerings, singing and dancing, and finally, the pouring out of the bowls.

> David Edward Aune was born in 1939. He earned both a BA and MA from Wheaton, an MA from the University of Minnesota, and a PhD from the University of Chicago. He has taught at St. Xavier University, Loyola University, and the University of Notre Dame. He has published extensively in the field of NT studies.

Another author who believes that Revelation was likely meant to function within the context of liturgy is David Aune. He has written extensively on Revelation, including a massive three-volume commentary, along with numerous other works. In his view, "The Apocalypse of John" was "explicitly intended for public presentation, possibly within the setting of Christian worship," which ultimately allowed it to serve a "cultic function."[27] In Aune's view, Revelation, like most ancient texts, was written for the ear, that is, "expressly for public, oral performance."[28] As such, "Orality played an explicit role in the composition of the Apocalypse of John, for the entire document" was "intended for oral performance before Christian congregations."[29] For Aune, then, Revelation is a performed liturgy sharing similarities with ancient drama.

> Edward White Benson was born in 1829 in Highgate, Birmingham. He earned his BA at Trinity College, Cambridge and was chosen by Prince Albert to be the first headmaster of Wellington College, Berkshire. He later became the Sometime Archbishop of Canterbury. Benson died in 1896.

Like Aune, who remains cautious while locating Revelation alongside ancient dramas, Edward Benson, who had written nearly a century earlier, held similar reservations. However, for Benson, it seemed more obvious that Revelation followed the ancient format of "acts and scenes."[30] Indeed, it is this structure that he believes guides the story and its characters, choruses, vivid descriptions, voices, and visions. Benson writes that the scenes and acts had "passed before the eye of the Seer on an almost unlimited stage wider than the commonly visible world."[31] In short, Revelation is a "spiritual drama."[32] As a spiritual drama, it was penned under the assumption that "in the Christian Congregation there will be Readers and Hearers" who come under its influence.[33]

> James Lowell Blevins was born in 1936. He was a native of Hot Coal, West Virginia. He earned degrees from Duke University, Eastern Baptist Theological Seminary, and Southern Baptist Theological Seminary, where he later taught. He suffered a severe bout of diabetes and died in 2004.

If both Aune and Benson expressed caution when approaching Revelation on dramatic terms, James Blevins is quite the opposite. In Blevins's view, Revelation is "a prophetic message in the form of Greek tragic drama."[34] It was composed some time during the reign of Domitian (81–96 CE) and was written with an eye toward being performed in the theater at Ephesus, where John conducted his ministry. This is most obvious in the fact that Revelation's sevenfold patterns—letters, seals, trumpets, bowls, plagues, etc.—correspond to the only ancient theater containing seven windows ever excavated, namely, the Ephesian amphitheater.[35]

As a result, "Every time a festival gathering was held there [the Ephesian theater], the number seven was before the populace. The seven windows were the dominant features of the architecture of the theater building. The main purpose of the windows or *thuromata* was to effect the presentation of scenery in Greek drama. . . . This suits well many of the scenes in Revelation."[36] Additionally, Blevins argues that prose would have been "woefully inadequate" to capture the essence of Revelation.[37] Blevins has even recreated a script complete with stage settings, entrances and exits, etc., which correspond to the play of Revelation. In Belvins's view, this "Greek drama made the prophetic message more appealing to a Greek community," particularly the Greek community of Ephesus.[38]

> A native of taught Christian Studies and New Testament Calgary, Alberta, Canada, Gilbert Desrosiers taught at ICI University (now Global University) in Irving, Texas. After nearly three decades of religious study and teaching theology, Desrosiers became an atheist. He published his work on Revelation in 2000.

Gilbert Desrosiers also takes note of the dramatic aspects of the story but does not necessarily classify it as a drama. Instead, he places more focus on the narrative shape and character of Revelation. Put differently, for Desrosiers, Revelation is a story stocked with all of the main ingredients of a good tale: actors, major characters, minor characters, a setting, a plot, climactic events, and most importantly a beginning, middle, and end.[39] The story has two major sections (1:9—3:22 and 4:1—22:5) bracketed between a prologue (1:1–8) and an epilogue (22:6–21).⁴⁰ Given that Revelation is a narrative, it is no problem for Desrosiers, unlike Boring or those who believe that it is an epistle, to refer to it as a "book."⁴¹ For Desrosiers the main plot orbs around the dual issues of judgment and salvation.⁴²

> James Lynn Resseguie was born in 1945 in Buffalo, New York. He earned his AB from the University of California, his MDiv from Princeton Theological Seminary, and his PhD from Fuller Theological Seminary. He is a Presbyterian and has served in various capacities at Winebrenner Theological Seminary.

James Resseguie also approaches Revelation from a narrative point-of-view. For him, there are two important aspects that undergird his approach. First, he believes that there is an "organic unity" to John's story. In other words, the work "is a unified whole. The parts cannot be understood without understanding the whole."⁴³ Second, "close readings of the complexities and nuances of the text, taking note of the structure, rhetoric, setting, characters, point of view, plot, and the narrator's style and his repertoire" are central to his narrative approach.⁴⁴ Overall, Resseguie sees Revelation as having a "U-shaped plot" where the top, "stable condition, is represented by the protagonists—God (4:1–11) and the one like a son of man (1:12–20)."⁴⁵ However, there are "seeds of instability" present "within the narrative, sending the U-shaped trajectory downward to disaster. The world is in rebellion and requires a messianic repair. Evil in the guise of the dragon, the beast, and the land beast runs rampant."⁴⁶

After hitting the bottom of the "U-shaped plot" a reversal occurs and the ascension to victory, in light of the cross, begins to take place. Now, "The seven-eyed, seven-horned, slaughtered-yet-risen Lamb takes the scroll and begins the work of messianic repairs to the cosmos. Christians are enlisted in this work through active resistance to the norms, values, and beliefs of the beast and Babylon. . . . The upward movement of the U is marked by active resistance to Babylon, patient endurance, and holding fast to the testimony of Jesus (13:10; 14:12)."⁴⁷ In light of this, "The world at large is called to change directions also, to repent and to give 'glory to the God of heaven' (11:13). The top of the U, the new stable condition, is the safe arrival of God's pilgrim people to the new promised land, the new heaven and the new earth, the new Jerusalem."⁴⁸

Richard Hays has also picked up on the notion of active resistance. In fact, Hays refers to Revelation as a resistance narrative. More specifically, it is a "visionary document of resistance to an idolatrous sociopolitical order" that repeatedly calls the church "to vigilance and discernment."[49] Hays attempts to recreate both the narrative thought and ethical worlds of Revelation. It is no surprise, then, to find comments such as "Revelation must reimagine the world."[50] Of course, Hays himself is imagining the reimagination but his approach is quite creative. He notes, "The book's imaginative power annihilates the plausibility structure on which the status quo rests and replaces it with a vision of a new world. The authority of the Roman Empire is thereby delegitimated, and the way is prepared for the community to receive the truth about God's coming order."[51] In the end, functioning as a resistance narrative means that Revelation is ultimately a "critique of the prevailing false political order," which is itself "a critique of the unjust and oppressive use of wealth and power."[52]

> *Richard Hays was born in 1948. He earned his PhD from Emory University in NT and has received a couple of honorary doctorates. He has an extensive lecturing and publishing record and has received numerous prestigious awards. Hays has also taught New Testament studies at Duke University.*

> *Frederick David Mazzaferri was born in 1942 in Australia. While his initial field of study was telecommunications, he eventually earned a degree in theology from the University of Aberdeen in 1986. He is a Seventh-day Adventist and maintains interest in cosmology, digitronics, and mathematics.*

Frederick Mazzaferri also sees Revelation as a narrative but in his view, it is a "Prophetic Call Narrative" based on Old Testament precedents such as Zechariah, Daniel, and especially Ezekiel. In the Old Testament, the standard formula for a prophet to commence his work was a divine confrontation, an introductory word, and a commission. These calls were often laced with vision reports, oracles, and other spiritual or ecstatic events. "The prophet is Yahweh's spokesman, addressing his people directly. He delivers Yahweh's crucial, conditional word to meet their urgent need, in the hope that they may respond for their own well-being."[53] In his research, Mazzaferri concludes that in the biblical tradition, to be prophetic means to be less about prediction and symbolism and more

Approaching Revelation

about "revelational visions, exposition of Scripture, teaching, exhorting, comforting, [and] strengthening."[54]

Whereas Mazzaferri has understood Revelation as a prophetic story or narrative, there have also been positions put forth by other interpreters who see it as a prediction-fulfillment type of device. This predictive prophecy schema has become incredibly popular in Western Christianity by dispensationalist teachers like Tim LaHaye, one of the creators of the *Left Behind* series of novels. Central to dispensational theology are the events of the so-called rapture and tribulation. Of course, the New Testament teaches that one day, Jesus will return. For Dispensationalists, however, prior to the "Second Coming" there will be a time when Jesus returns secretly and all "believers" (true Christians) will be evacuated from planet earth and non-believers will be left behind.[55] Some believe that the rapture will take place before the tribulation, others contend that it will happen during the tribulation, and still others argue that it will happen after the tribulation period (hence the labels "pre-trib," "trib," and "post-trib"). For LaHaye, the rapture is imminent and "That is why we share Christ with as many people as possible—so they will be ready for the rapture. . . . While no one knows 'that day and hour' (Matthew 24:36), we certainly can recognize the 'season' in which we are now living."[56]

> Timothy F. LaHaye was born in 1926 in Detroit, Michigan. He earned a BA from Bob Jones University and a DMin from Western Seminary. He founded San Diego Christian College and donated 4.5-million dollars to Liberty University to build a School of Prophecy (2002), of which he is the president.

The tribulation will consist of seven years of tribulations and hardships. There is time for repentance during this period but life will be terrible and the earth will eventually and finally be destroyed. For Tim LaHaye, as predictive prophecy, Revelation describes the events preceding the rapture, the sufferings during the tribulation, and those things that happen after the tribulation. Therefore, it is something like a guidebook for charting church and world history; it has, hidden beneath its layers, clues as to when "the end" will be. It is replete with mysterious codes that need to be solved and riddles that hold the key to being prepared for the rapture and tribulation. In LaHaye's own words, "Prophecy is history written in advance."[57]

Entering the Fray

> Bruce J. Malina is a professor at Creighton University. He earned his Doctor of Sacred Theology from the Studium Biblicum Franciscanum in Jerusalem as well as a Doctor of Theology from the University of St. Andrews (Scotland). He is a founder of The Context Group and has published extensively.

For Bruce Malina, however, nothing could be farther from the case. In Malina's view, Revelation is an ancient astral prophecy. This position is based on the premise that the prophet John had an "initial, ecstatic vision while considering the vault of the sky."[58] For Malina, a social scientist and cultural anthropologist, the key to understanding Revelation begins with detaching it from one's modern presuppositions about life, the world, and the Bible. He is worth citing in full here:

> "Modern readers might find it difficult to recapture the first-century sense of the sky. Most of us know that the ancient earth-centered perception of the encapsulating sky was displaced by a sun-centered conception of the world (16th–18th c.), which was in turn, dissolved by a galaxy-centered point of view (18th–19th c.). This last model itself has given way to a non-centered sky system (20th c.). Consequently, we must recover some adequate ancient model of an earth-centered total system of the universe to be considerate readers of Revelation."[59]

While Malina's work has traces of the works of Farrer, Carrington, and others who acknowledge the role of the Zodiac in antiquity, our main reason for mentioning it here is that Malina proposes a unique understanding of prophecy. As astral prophecy, Revelation is concerned with ancient reports of prophets and seers interacting with "star-related, celestial personages and the outcomes of that interaction."[60] Thus, these accounts "might describe both the initial circumstances of such interactions (i.e., visions, dreams, ecstasies and other altered states of consciousness), the interactions proper (what the prophet or seer hears and sees, i.e., alternative realities, the very secrets to be revealed), as well as the outcomes of the interactions (impact or meanings of celestial phenomena)."[61]

One result of this type of approach to Revelation, as Malina puts it, is that "It seems quite certain that ancient Mediterraneans were not future-oriented at all. In other words, there is nothing in the book of Revelation that refers to the future."[62] In John's account, "Even the new Jerusalem is descending right now! The reason for this is that the author

Approaching Revelation

of the book and his audience were concerned with their present and with those dimensions of human living immediately rooted in their present...."[63] For Malina, all of the mishandling of Revelation is rooted in our fundamental misunderstanding of the cosmic orientation of ancient peoples. Once this is recaptured, not only will Revelation be approached more accurately and responsibly, in addition John the Seer's focus "on the god of the sky as the true center of the cosmos" will help reorient us "into our proper place in creation."[64]

While there are many nuanced understandings of Revelation and its relation to the Hebrew prophets, some researchers have attempted to place it within the genre known as apocalyptic literature. For example, G.K. Beale, who has already been mentioned, believes that Revelation is apocalyptic, that is, an intensified form of prophecy or prophetic speech. More specifically, he believes that the "apocalyptic-prophetic nature of Revelation" can be defined as "God's revelatory interpretation (through visions and auditions) of his mysterious counsel about past, present, and future redemptive-eschatological history, and how the nature and operation of heaven relate to this."[65] Put differently, as an apocalyptic-prophetic text, Revelation is about why and how God revealed his eternal plan of salvation and what earthly and heavenly beings have to do with it. Cast in the mold of a letter (see above for more on this), the hope behind Revelation is to "motivate the audience to change their behavior in light of the transcendent reality of the book's message."[66]

> J. Nelson Kraybill was born in 1954 in Elizabethtown, Pennsylvania. He earned his BA from Goshen College, his MDiv from Princeton, and his PhD from Union Theological Seminary. He has pastored Prairie Street Mennonite Church and served as the president of Associated Mennonite Biblical Seminary.

While J. Nelson Kraybill sees the author of Revelation, John, as a prophet, ultimately he views Revelation as an apocalypse. For Kraybill, the very first word of Revelation, the term *apocalypsis*, refers to "an unveiling." More specifically, Kraybill argues that on the one hand "John's vision unveils the Roman Empire, showing it to have become a violent beast that usurps devotion belonging to God."[67] On the other hand, "Revelation also unveils the nature of divine love, made known by a Lamb that was slain. Humanity must choose between allegiance to the beast and allegiance to the Lamb."[68] As a genre, then, the Apocalypse is a divine unveiling about divine truths and worldly anti-truths that humans must choose between. While Revelation can be understood as a prophecy, that function is ultimately subsumed under the apocalyptic genre. Therefore, anything prophetic has little to nothing to do with "forecasts of the distant future" and is more focused on providing "spiritual insight into the writer's immediate circumstances."[69]

> Adela Yarbro Collins was born in 1945. She earned her BA at Pomona College, and both her MA and PhD at Harvard University. She has held appointments at the Universities of Notre Dame, Chicago, and Yale. She has also served as the president of the Society of New Testament Studies. She is married to Dr. John J. Collins.

For Adela Yarbro Collins, taking Revelation as an apocalypse means understanding that it is literature that was "evoked by a crisis."[70] Collins is of the opinion that the crisis that led John to write Revelation was that he found himself in a context where "A new set of expectations had arisen as a result of faith in Jesus as the Messiah and of belief that the kingdom of God and Christ had been established."[71] These expectations created a "political tension between the adherents of the kingdom of God and those of the kingdom of Caesar (11:15; 12:10; 16:10; 17:18). Both claim dominion over the whole earth and eternal rule."[72] Revelation seeks to strike fear of Roman power into its hearers. As Collins notes, Revelation's "vivid images are certainly designed more to evoke terror than to allay it."[73] However, these frightening images are resolved in the Apocalypse's claim that "judgment and salvation" are on the horizon and thus, "Feelings of fear and resentment are released by the book's repeated presentations of the destruction of the hearers' enemies . . . the persecutors are destroyed by divine wrath and the persecuted are exalted to a new glorious mode of existence."[74]

> Elisabeth Schüssler Fiorenza was born in 1938. She earned her MDiv from the University of Würzburg and her ThD from the University of Münster. She has taught at Harvard University and has also served as president of both the Society of Biblical Literature and the American Academy of Arts and Sciences.

Elisabeth Schüssler Fiorenza also views Revelation as an apocalypse. However, for her, "apocalyptic" is "to be understood not as a literary container or a theological qualification but as a rhetorical practice."[75] As apocalyptic rhetoric, Revelation "invites the audience to participate in the visions and auditions of the seer. It utilizes conventional

Approaching Revelation

imagery and traditional symbolism as a shared code to allow mutual understanding between seer and reader. . . . It is mythological-fantastic language. . . . [it] speaks about the past, present, and future in mythological language and images."[76] In the main the rhetoric of Revelation reveals that its "central theological concern is not apocalyptic speculation on the course of history or the provision of an exact schedule for the end-time events. Rather, Revelation's central problem and topic is the issue of power and justice."[77]

For Fiorenza, the rhetorical world of Revelation's visions unveils that fact that "Christians have been liberated and appointed to be the representatives and agents of God's power and empire on earth. Therefore, they are locked into a struggle with Babylon/Rome, whose imperial powers are the agents of the demonic and destructive power of Satan."[78] It is the "empire-status of Christians" that "generates Revelation's rhetorical problem as a question of power and justice. Revelation's central query is: To whom does the earth belong? Who is the ruler of this world? The book's central theological symbol is therefore the throne, signifying either divine and liberating or demonic and death-dealing power."[79]

Nearing the end of this section and looking back, we realize that many different reading strategies have been employed in attempting to understand Revelation. Some approaches share similarities, some stand in stark contrast, and some overlap. We have seen, for example, how Beale's work mixes a few of the reading strategies together. Sean Kealy takes this view as well. In his view Revelation is an epistle meant to be read in liturgy that is both prophetic and apocalyptic in nature. As a letter, it provides a "personal and pastoral touch" and reveals its concern "with the real historical situations of the churches of the time."[80] As such, during liturgy, "The visions of heavenly realities" which "are directly related to earthly events" would draw hearers into thanksgiving and worship.[81] As a prophecy written in the tradition of Israel's prophets, it enabled its hearers to "survive the collapse of all their human institutions" and "to find some meaning in the disasters they were experiencing."[82] Being

> Sean P. Kealy was born in 1937 in Thurles, Republic of Ireland. He earned his BSS and LSS from the Biblical Institute of Rome, his BD and STL from Gregorian University, Rome, and his BA and MA from University College, Dublin. He has taught at a number of seminaries, colleges, and universities.

253

Entering the Fray

an apocalypse, it sought to provide "assurance of lasting victory to the faithful, to point out that the persecution, turbulence and warfare" were simply "the darkest hour before the dawn."[83]

> Craig S. Keener was born in 1960. He earned his BA from Central Bible College, his MDiv from Assemblies of God Theological Seminary, and his PhD from Duke University. He has taught at both Palmer and Asbury Theological Seminary. He is married to Medine and has a son, David.

Sharing Kealy's mixed approach to Revelation, Craig Keener writes, "To be sure, most of Revelation belongs to a mixture of apocalyptic and prophetic genres."[84] Indeed, "A forced choice between 'apocalyptic' and 'prophetic' genres . . . is pointless. . . . Later apocalypses could also consider themselves 'prophecy' (e.g., 4 Ezra 12:42), so it is not surprising that Revelation does the same (1:3; 22:7, 10, 18–19)." Further, Revelation is "framed as a letter."[85] In particular, "it is a letter to specific first-century churches" and therefore its symbolism should be interpreted "in light of symbols these churches would have understood."[86] Acknowledging these aspects of Revelation should keep us safe from the danger of reading "modern doctrinal agendas" into this ancient work.[87]

TAKING ACTION

While I was writing this chapter my daughter, who, at the time was finishing preschool, brought home a calendar of events for her spring semester. The first thing I noticed on the calendar was the following note: "Wear Sandals and a Robe." I looked next to the note and realized that it was referring to an Easter-week event where someone impersonating Jesus was going to visit her school; they wanted the children to dress up for the festivities. Written next to the note in the date box was: "Tuesday, April 3: Jesus is coming!" I had to chuckle at that. Of course, I could have interpreted it as an end-time prediction, but when I sent my daughter off to school on Tuesday, April 3, I did so without the expectation that I would never see her again because the "second coming" was at hand. Put differently, I did not believe that my child's teacher was predicting the world's end.

However, there are Christians who have a habit of committing exactly such genre confusions. Yet, the truth is, every so-called prophet who has every attempted to pin a date on Jesus' return or the end of

Approaching Revelation

the world has been wrong; there is a one hundred percent failure rate! This should give us pause when we hear folks in our own time claiming that they have figured it all out and have cracked the doomsday code. This is especially the case when it comes to Revelation! It is one thing to try to predict the end of time but it is another thing to drag Revelation into the discussion. Despite there being a number of genre options to choose from when approaching Revelation, one thing that all should be able to agree on—even though not all do!—is the fact that this biblical work is first and foremost a first-century text written to and for first-century persons.

This, however, does not mean that Revelation is irrelevant to modern Christians. Still, we do not need to resort to fanatic, decontextualized readings to find significance; we can tap into the meaning(s) of Revelation even while maintaining our integrity as interpreters. To be sure, Revelation can be difficult to "get." Its language, imagery, and claims, however understood, can even seem difficult to believe. Yet, any way we slice it, we must not hear or see it as a call to abandon this world or this life. It is not a guidebook on how to escape this world. Instead, we should see it as a call to place our allegiance in God and devote ourselves to his kingdom.

When I reflect on these matters, I am reminded of a story that the Methodist Bishop William Willimon tells. He reports that one day, a young philosophy student came into his office and expressed that he was losing his faith. Willimon asked him to say more and the student remarked, "I no longer am able to believe in the virgin birth of Jesus." After that, Willimon remarked, "Well, what is it? Tuesday? I seem to believe in the virgin birth today, but who knows where I'll be on Wednesday? The point is not what you or I happen to believe, it's what the church believes, the Bible asserts. Relax, maybe it will come to you when you are older." The student replied, "But how can I be a Christian when I can't believe this doctrine?"

Willimon answered, "Look, I hate to tell you, but the virgin birth is not the strangest thing we are going to ask you to believe . . . next we're going to ask you to turn the other cheek rather than turn violent, to look across a communion table and believe these strangers are sisters and brothers, to start thinking that the poor and the outcast are really royalty. We start you out on the virgin birth because we think if you can believe that without choking, we can eventually get you to swallow the really important, really essential stuff about Jesus."[88]

We might replace the virgin birth doctrine in this story with Revelation. Indeed, while Revelation is full of strange ideas and images, even strange beliefs, it is not the strangest thing that Christians are asked to believe. Read from certain perspectives, it may well be asking us—just as it may have been asking its original audiences—to examine our true allegiances, to turn the other cheek, to share communion with "strangers" and to bring justice to the outcasts of the world. It may be calling us to once again put Christ at the center of our cosmos and to shun the idolatries surrounding and influencing us. If these conclusions are accurate, then it is high time to stop twisting and bending Revelation to meet outlandish modernist interpretations.

It has been suggested in this chapter that whether in the churches or academies of today, a way forward when approaching Revelation is to begin by discussing matters of genre. This will help us better understand one another and help prevent us from simply talking past and/or judging one another based on preconceived theological paradigms and presuppositions; it will provide us with familiar grounds, perhaps even common grounds, as starting points for our discussions. This will also aid us in handling Revelation with a greater sense of interpretive integrity. In short, it will save us from acting as if this ancient work was written with only us modern folks in mind and had no real relevance for first-century persons. We must acknowledge that it is bordering on the height of modern arrogance to suggest that Revelation was irrelevant to its first-century audiences and only meant to speak to Christians thousands of years later.

In short, while Revelation continues to have implications for Christians today, those implications can only flow out of what this text meant two thousand years ago. To treat the text any other way is to treat it unethically as an interpreter and to do damage to it. This fact needs to be recaptured by modern readers of Revelation and wholly embraced. Otherwise, we will not only do damage to the text, but may even continue to use the text to do damage to others in its name. We must realize that such actions fly directly in the face of what Revelation seeks and has sought to say and do, namely, to bring glory and honor to Almighty God who is on the throne.

Conclusion

It is said that John Wesley, when he wished to show a girlfriend a good time, would read treatises on theology and church history to her. Needless to say, Wesley did not do so well in that department. While *Entering the Fray* offers a lot of valuable information, it is probably not the type of book you would want to take on a first date. Second or third date . . . maybe! If you are a theology geek like me, it might just impress you to find that your significant other totes around a book such as this one. This book, however, was not written for lovers; it was written for those who wish to dive deeper into the interpretation of, and interpretive issues related to, the New Testament.

As such, this book has covered a wide variety of topics that, over the course of history, have helped give contour to the New Testament and the many diverse understandings that exist today. We have reviewed the development of the canon, the significance of New-Testament-related archaeological discoveries, the importance of Paul and his letters, matters pertaining to the historical Jesus and the Gospels, questions about Revelation, and more. We have, without a doubt, covered a lot of ground! It should be kept in mind, as I have stated several times, this book is neither meant to be an exhaustive account of New Testament studies nor the last word; instead, it is best understood as a work that provides a "first clue" for digging deeper into the topics explored in detail here, as well as their related issues.

Throughout, I have striven to keep these rather dense matters accessible for non-specialists. That's because, in the main, this work has been written with students, clergy, and laity in mind. Even so, my hope is that it will also find a welcome home in the libraries of scholars as well. I have also endeavored to show the relevance that each issue under discussion has both in and outside of the academic world. The "Taking Action" sections reveal that these conversations, which often begin with scholarly inquiry, are in no way meant to be relegated to the scholarly

Conclusion

realm; after all, their implications and consequences are eventually put before students, pastors, and persons in the pews. To that pragmatic end, I hope that you have found this book helpful and edifying.

In closing, I would like to state that while I have written from a particular perspective, namely out of an evangelical tradition, I have attempted to steer clear from lapsing into apologetics. Of course, I have offered my own opinions and suggestions and quite expectedly, I have also questioned a number of views. Mostly, I have attempted to be as fair as possible when it comes to hearing views that affirm the faith on the one hand, or are antagonistic towards it on the other. I have not silenced anyone. I think that is something from which all readers will benefit.

I will note that I have not approached this book with the oft-found mindset in seminaries and universities that a person's faith must be destroyed and rebuilt before it can be a substantive faith. Instead, I have made every effort to provide readers with more of an informed faith than they had before they began reading. From this standpoint, I believe that this volume is a great resource for anyone interested in the New Testament, regardless of whether they happen to be in or outside the walls of the academy or church. In closing, then, I hope that *Entering the Fray* will not only help bridge some of the divide that exists between the church and academy, but also be a resource that readers can return to time and again, for understanding, clarity, and edification. May it be!

Timeline

http://michaelhalcomb.com/enteringthefray-home.html

THE FOLLOWING TIMELINE CONTAINS the sketches of the scholars seen throughout this book. They are listed in chronological order by each scholar's birth year. On several occasions, precise dates could not be recovered and estimates had to be provided. The primary purpose of this timeline is to provide an overview of the succession of biblical scholarship within the last few hundred years. A secondary function of this timeline is to help consolidate the information that you have learned in the preceding twelve chapters. A third aim of this resource is to provide you with a quick-reference tool for your studies. Those scholars mentioned in chapter 11, such as Hershel Shanks, Joseph Fitzmeyer, J. H. Charlesworth, etc., were not listed in scholarly sketches and thus, are not included in this timeline. Likewise, additional scholars have been cited in endnotes, which are not included here. You may consult the endnotes for more details on their works. Last names are in bold, so as to make searching easier.

Timeline

1694   Hermann Samuel **Reimarus** was born in 1694 in Hamburg. He served most of his professional career at the Gymnasium Johanneum in his hometown, where he also taught oriental languages. He was an avid Deist and challenged the historical foundations of the traditional Christianity of his day.

1717   Johann David **Michaelis** was born in 1717 in Halle, Germany. He was the son of C.B. Michaelis, a prominent professor at Halle. He was an extraordinary philologist and linguist who exerted much influence in biblical studies. He taught at the University of Göttingen for many years. He died in 1791.

1725   Johann Salomo **Semler** was born in 1725 at Saalfeld, Thuringa. He grew up among German Lutheran pietists. Semler published nearly three hundred scholarly works in his life. He both attended and taught at the University of Halle. A controversial figure of his day, he was often referred to as the father of German rationalism.

1731   Edward **Evanson** was born in 1731 at Warrington, Lancashire. As a child, he was educated by his uncle and in his teenage years he studied classics at Emmanuel College, Cambridge. He was an ordained minister but after preaching a controversial Easter sermon in 1771, he lost that post. Evanson died in 1805.

1745   Johann J. **Griesbach** was born in 1745 in Butzbach, Germany. He earned several degrees and spent the majority of his career at the University of Jena. In 1976, two-hundred years after the publication of his Greek synopsis of the Gospels, scholars remembered him by hosting the J.J. Griesbach Bicentenary Colloquium.

1752   Johann Gottfried **Eichorn** was born in 1752 in Dorrenzimmern, Germany. He studied under Johann D. Michaelis at Göttingen, where he would later assume the role of professor. He was a prominent OT scholar but also lectured on the NT and in fact, published an introductory textbook on the NT. He died in 1827.

1761   Heinrich **Paulus** was born in 1761 in Leonberg, Württemberg. He served as a professor of exegesis, church history, theology and oriental languages at a variety of institutions including the universities of Jena, Würzburg, and Heidelberg. Paulus was a Lutheran rationalist and a very controversial figure in his day.

1780 Wilhelm M.L. **De Wette** was born in 1780 at Ulla, Germany. He was raised Lutheran as his father was a pastor, but later in life Wilhelm defected from the faith. He remarried after losing his first wife, who died during childbirth. He studied at the University of Jena and later taught at the University of Basel.

1792 Ferdinand Christian **Baur** was born in 1792 at Schimden, Germany. He was a professor of New Testament at the University of Tübingen for nearly three and a half decades. Both he and his father were pastors. Baur was (and remains) a controversial figure within the fields of biblical studies and church history.

1804 Matthias **Schneckenburger** was born in 1804 in Talheim, Germany. His father was a farmer and businessman and his brother, Max, was a well-known scholar. Matthias was a prominent Lutheran pastor and theologian in his day. He taught New Testament and theology at the University of Bern.

1808 David Friedrich **Strauss** was born in 1808 in Ludwigsburg. He studied at Tübingen and then returned to his alma mater, Stift, where he taught philosophy. He was a pupil of the famed F.C. Baur and is remembered as one who, in his day, challenged the traditional views of the foundations of Christianity.

1809 Bruno **Bauer** was born in 1809 at Eisenburg, Germany. He studied at the University of Berlin and was classmates with the controversial Karl Marx. Bauer was very conservative at the beginning of his career but over time, became a very controversial figure, especially when, in 1852, he rejected the "historical Jesus."

1814 Eduard Gottlob **Zeller** was born in 1814 at Kleinbottwar, Germany. He studied under Georg W.F. Hegel at the University of Tübingen. He taught at the universities of Bern, Marburg and Heidelberg respectively. He was an ardent opponent of Christianity during his lifetime. He died at Stuttgart in 1908.

1822 Albrecht Benjamin **Ritschl** was born in 1822 at Berlin. His father was an evangelical pastor. Ritschl studied at the universities of Bonn and Halle, receiving his doctorate from the latter.

Timeline

He lectured at Göttingen for twenty-five years, where he taught Church History and the History of Dogma. He died in 1889.

1823 Ernest **Renan** was born in 1823 in Tréguier, France. He studied at the Issy-les-Moulineaux Seminary and later accepted a teaching position at Vendôme. From the early years of his teenage life, Renan was marked as a sophisticated thinker. Like many of his contemporaries, he became a controversial figure.

1828 Joseph Barber **Lightfoot** was born in 1828 at Liverpool. He graduated with a Doctor of Divinity in 1851 from Trinity College in Cambridge. He served as the Bishop of Durham for a decade. He helped produce the Revised Version of the Bible as well as a translation of the Apostolic Fathers. He died in 1889.

1829 Edward White **Benson** was born in 1829 at Highgate, Birmingham. He earned his BA at Trinity College, Cambridge and was chosen by Prince Albert to be the first headmaster of Wellington College, Berkshire. He later became the Sometime Archbishop of Canterbury. Benson died in 1896.

1830 Eduard **Lekebusch** was born in 1830. He was a pastor of two churches in the northern state of Schleswig-Holstein in Germany. Lekebusch earned a doctorate in theology and it is not clear as to whether he published much beyond his book that investigaes the composition and origin of Acts. Lekebusch died in 1892.

1837 Franz Camille **Overbeck** was born in 1837 at St. Petersburg, Russia. He was a close friend of Friedrich Nietzche and a Protestant theologian. He studied at the universities of Leipzig, Göttingen, Berlin and Jena respectively. His antagonism toward Christianity made him a very controversial figure. He died in 1905.

1838 Theodor **Zahn** was born in 1838 at Mörs. He was a German Lutheran theologian with deep interests in both the New Testament and patristics. He studied and taught at the University of Göttingen in addition to several other prominent institutions. He died in 1933 having published and lectured extensively throughout Germany.

1842 Willem Christiaan **van Manen** was born in 1842 at Noordeloos,

Netherlands. He, his father, and his grandfather, were all pastors in the Dutch Reformed Church. He studied at Utrecth and was later a professor in Early Christian literature and New Testament Exegesis at Leiden University. He died in 1905.

1843   William **Sanday** was born in 1843 in England. He taught at Oxford and also served at Hatfield Hall (Durham) in the late 1800s and then moved on to Christ Church where he stayed until his passing in the early 1900s. Sanday was well known in Anglican circles and is remembered as a tenacious speaker and author.

1850s-1860s   Johannes **Haußleiter** was born in the 1800s. He was an evangelical scholar and earned both the PhD and ThD degrees. He was Professor of New Testament Theology and Exegesis at the University of Griefswald, Germany. Haußleiter was a respected scholar and took part in the *New Schaff-Herzog Encyclopedia*.

1851   Karl Gustav "Adolf" von **Harnack** was born in 1851 at Dorpat (Tartu), Estonia. The son of a professor of homiletics and church history, he blossomed as a leading European Protestant scholar. He taught at a number of major universities including Leipzig, Marburg, Giessen and Berlin. He died in 1930.

1851   Sir William Mitchell **Ramsay** was born in 1851 at Glasgow, Scotland. He studied at the University of Aberdeen as well as St. John's College, Oxford. He taught at the former of these institutions for twenty-five years. To this day, Ramsay's work remains influential. He died in 1939.

1857   Adolf **Jülicher** was born in 1857 Falkenberg Germany and grew up as a Lutheran. He studied at the University of Berlin and later spent most of his academic career teaching at the University of Marburg. Jülicher is perhaps remembered by scholars foremost for his rejection of allegorical interpretations of parables.

1859   F.G.E. Wilhelm (or William) **Wrede** was born in 1859 in Hanover. He grew up a Lutheran and like his father, served in Lutheran ministries. Wrede both studied and taught in Göttingen and was a member of the History of Religions School, which consisted of many prominent theologians of the 1800-1900s.

Timeline

1863 Johannes **Weiss** was born in 1863 and was the son of the noted NT exegete Bernhard Weiss. He was also the son-in-law of the prominent liberal theologian Albrecht Ritschl. He both earned a degree from and taught at Göttingen. Weiss helped pave the way for future discussions of eschatology and Christian origins.

1865 Arthur S. **Peake** was born in 1865 at Leek, Staffordshire. He was raised a Methodist and continued in that tradition throughout his life. He studied at Oxford and taught at a number of colleges and universities, including the University of Manchester. Peake was also active in the 1927 Lausanne Conference.

1870s-1910s Hans Jürgen **Ebeling** was a German theologian and philosopher. He was heavily influenced by Immanuel Kant and is one of the lesser known voices among modern scholars within messianic secret research. Ebeling was very active in speaking out against communist socialism in his day and was also a devout Catholic.

1874 Dr. Burnett H. **Streeter** was born in 1874 in London. He received his PhD at Queen's College (Oxford) and later became a professor at Oxford University. His works on the synoptic Gospels, ancient manuscript traditions, and text-critical matters have all been widely influential in the field of biblical studies.

1875 Albert **Schweitzer** was born in 1875 in Germany and was raised a Lutheran. He was broadly educated and earned his doctorate from the University of Strasbourg. He was a major contributor to historical Jesus studies but perhaps best remembered for leaving a life of biblical scholarship to be a medical doctor in rural Africa.

1876 Karl **Adam** was born in 1876 in Bavaria. He received his doctorate from the University of Munich and was ordained into the Catholic priesthood in 1900. He has left a controversial legacy as many have acknowledged a pro-Nazi agenda in his works. He published frequently and held several academic positions.

1877 Walter **Bauer** was born in 1877 at Königsberg, Prussia. He earned his doctorate from the University of Marburg. He taught in several academic settings but spent most of his career at Georg Augusta University in Göttingen. One of his best known works, *BDAG*, is still widely used today. He died in 1960.

Timeline

1883   Martin F. **Dibelius** was born in 1883 in Dresden in the church parsonage where his parents lived. His mother died while he was a young boy, which drew him close to his father. He earned a PhD from Tübingen and a ThD from Berlin, where he also taught. He is also remembered for challenging Nazi dominance.

1883: Henry Joel **Cadbury** was born in 1883 at Philadelphia. He was raised within the Quaker tradition. He earned his PhD from Harvard University, where he later taught for two decades. He accepted the Nobel Peace prize in 1947 on behalf of a British humanities organization he served alongside of. He died in 1974.

1883   Julius Daniel **Schniewind** was born in 1883 in Elberfeld. He studied in Bonn, Halle, Berlin and Marburg. He earned his doctorate from Halle in 1925. He served as a chaplain in WWI and later—after being embroiled in much theological and religious controversy—as a hospital chaplain. He taught in a variety of universities and colleges.

1884   Rudolf **Bultmann** was born in 1884 in Germany and raised as a Lutheran. He studied at Tübingen, Berlin and Marburg. He researched under J. Weiss and is remembered by many for his demythologizing (removing of the mysterious/myth-like portions) of the NT. Bultmann long been viewed as a polarizing scholar.

1884   Alfred E.J. **Rawlinson** was born in 1884. He studied at Dulwich College and Oxford. He taught at Keble College and Christ Church, both in Oxford. He underwent ordination in 1910 and served as the Bishop of Derby for over two decades. He was a renowned NT scholar and Anglican churchman and theologian.

1887   Vincent **Taylor** was born in 1887 in Lancashire, England. He earned his doctorate from the University of London and later taught at Wesley College (Leeds). He was a very active Methodist preacher and teacher. In addition, he was a member of the prestigious Fellowship of the British Academy.

Timeline

1890   Ernst **Löhmeyer** was born in 1890 in Dorsten, Westphalia. He was raised a Lutheran and later earned his ThD at Berlin and then a PhD at Erlangen. In 1946, Soviet NKVD agents kidnapped Löhmeyer, imprisoned, tried, and later executed him on false charges. After being kidnapped he was never seen again.

1891   Karl Ludwig **Schmidt** was born in 1891 in Frankfurt. He earned his doctorate from Berlin University. He served in the Polish army and was badly injured, which led to his discharge and return to academia. Schmidt is remembered as both a founder of the Form Criticism School and as an anti-Nazi protestor.

1891   Frederick C. **Grant** was born in 1891. He earned Sacred Theology Doctorate and served as a professor at Union Theological Seminary and president at Western Theological Seminary. He published widely on the Gospels and was a pioneer in researching Mark in relation to orality. He also served on the translation board of the RSV.

1892   Philip C. **Carrington** was born in 1892. He studied at Christ's College, Canterbury and the University of Canterbury. He was ordained as an Anglican priest and served many years leading Boy Scout troops. He held positions at St. Barnabas Theological College and Bishop's University. He died in 1975.

1900   John **Knox** was born in 1900 at Frankfort, Kentucky. He studied at Emory University (BD) and earned his PhD from the University of Chicago, both of which, in addition to Union Theological Seminary, he would later teach at. Originally a Methodist pastor, later in life he was ordained in the Episcopal Church.

1903   Hans E.F. **von Campenhausen** was born in 1903 at Rosenbeck. He studied at Heidelberg, Marburg and Göttingen respectively. He signed the "Commitment of the Professors at German Universities to Adolf Hitler and the Nazi State" in 1933. He taught at Greifswald, Vienna and Heidelberg. He died in 1989.

1904   Austin M. **Farrer** was born in 1904 in Hampstead (London, England). He studied at St. Paul's School in London. He was a prominent and often controversial Anglican theologian and churchman, who served as a deacon, priest, and chaplain. He and the theologian C.S. Lewis shared a close friendship.

Timeline

1904   Johannes **Munck** was born in 1904 at Copenhagen. He both earned his ThD from and taught at the University of Copenhagen. He also held a position at the University of Aarhus (also Arhaus). He was an ardent opponent of the Tübingen group, strongly opposing their dialectical approach to Paul. He died in 1965.

1905   Günther **Bornkamm** was born in 1905 in Görlitz, Germany. He earned his PhD from the University of Marburg where he studied under R. Bultmann. He was a member of the Confessing Church, which spoke out against the Nazi regime. He served as a soldier in WWII and later taught at the University of Heidelberg.

1906   Ernst **Käsemann** was born in 1906 in Westphalia, Germany. He earned degrees from the universities of Bonn, Tübingen and Marburg respectively. He was a student of R. Bultmann who is often remembered for resisting German socialism and Hitler. This led to his arrest and imprisonment by the Gestapo in 1937.

1909   Hans Joachim **Schoeps** was born in 1909 at Berlin. He studied at the universities of Berlin, Marburg, and Heidelberg and earned his doctorate from Leipzig. He taught religion and intellectual history at the University of Erlangen. He opposed Hitler and died in 1980. His resting place is at the Jewish Cemetery in Nuremberg.

1910   Frederick Fyvie **Bruce** was born in 1910 at Elgin, Scotland. He was heavily influenced by William Ramsay while studying at the University of Aberdeen. He later started the biblical studies department at the University of Manchester. A prolific author, he published thousands of works. He died in 1990.

1911   William David **Davies** was born in 1911 at Carmathenshire, Wales. He studied at the universities of Wales (receiving a DD) and Cambridge, and was an ordained minister of the Congregational Church. He taught at Yorkshire, Duke, Princeton and Union, where he was the dissertation supervisor of Ed P. Sanders.

Timeline

1914   Philipp **Vielhauer** was born in 1914 at Cameroon, to pietistic missionary parents from Switzerland. He studied under Rudolf Bultmann and Martin Dibelius, among others. He was put out of his church in Baden when, in the 1930s, he refused to take Hitler's oath. Later drafted and wounded in war, he had a metal plate placed in his head.

1914   Rudolf **Schnackenburg** was born in 1914 in Würzburg, Germany. He earned his PhD from Breslau. He was a respected scholar and Catholic priest, who taught at a number of institutions but spent most of his career at Maximilians University in Würzburg. Upon retirement he served as a nursing home chaplain.

1914   Edward C.F.A. **Schillebeeckx** was born in 1914 in Antwerp, Belgium. He earned his doctorate from Sorbonne and later assumed a number of teaching roles at various academic institutions including the Catholic University of Nijmegen in the Netherlands. He is remembered as a creative and controversial theologian.

1914   Bruce Manning **Metzger** was born in 1914 at Middletown, Pennsylvania. He earned his BA from Lebanon Valley College and his ThB, MA, and PhD from Princeton, where he taught. His wife Elizabeth's father was the third president of Princeton. He had two sons, John and James. He died 4 days after his birthday in 2007.

1915   Hans Georg **Conzelmann** was born in 1915 at Talfingen, Germany. He studied at the universities of Marburg and Tübingen, earning his doctorate from the latter. He taught at Tübingen, Heidelberg, Zurich and Göttingen. He fought in World War II where he received serious injuries. He died in 1989.

1915   Donald **Guthrie** was born in 1915 in England. He earned all of his degrees (BD, ThM, and PhD) from the University of London. He was a lecturer and principal at London Bible College (now London School of Theology) and published a number of prominent New Testament works. He died in 1992.

1915   Kurt **Aland** was born in 1915 at Berlin-Steglitz, Germany. He studied at Friedrich-Wilhelms University and later taught at a number of institutions, including Münster. He was once arrested by the Marxist regime on charges of trafficking watches. He was married twice, had three children and died in 1991.

1915 Charles Ernest Burland **Cranfield** was born in 1915. Now nearly a centenarian, earlier in life Cranfield served as an army chaplain in WWII, where he ministered to POWs. He was also part of the German Confessing Movement. He studied at theology at Cambridge and later taught at the University of Durham, England.

1915 Markus **Barth** was born in 1915 at Safenwill in the Canton Aargau. The son of the Reformed pastor and incredibly influential theologian Karl Barth, Markus made a name for himself within the field of New Testament scholarship and theology. He taught at the University of Basel in Switzerland. He died in 1994.

1919 Willi **Marxsen** was born in 1919 in Kiel. He served as a soldier in WWII and later studied theology in Kiel, where he earned his doctorate. He was active in the church and held several academic positions. Marxsen was interested in the relationships between the Church, Christian identity, and Christian living.

1920 Norman **Perrin** was born in 1920 in England. He earned his ThD from the University of Göttingen where he studied under Joachim Jeremias. Perrin taught at Emory for a short time and then moved to the University of Chicago Divinity School. He died at the age of 56 as a revered interpreter of the Gospels.

1921 Dennis Eric **Nineham** was born in 1921. He has served as an ordained priest and chaplain, and earlier in life, he studied at The Queen's College (Oxford). He has held positions at Keble College (Oxford) and the universities of Bristol, Cambridge and London respectively. He has a wide range of expertise in both theological and biblical studies.

1921 Krister **Stendahl** was born in 1921 at Stockholm, Sweden. He conducted his doctoral work at Uppsala University (Sweden). He was a Bishop in Stockholm and also taught at Brandeis University and served as Raymond E. Brown Chair in Biblical Studies and theology at St. Mary's Seminary in Baltimore. Stendahl died in 2008.

Timeline

1923   Brevard **Childs** was born in 1923 at South Carolina. He was raised a Presbyterian and earned degrees from the University of Michigan (BA, MA), Princeton Theological Seminary (BD) and the University of Basel (ThD). He was married to Ann, whom he met while studying in Basel. He died in June of 2007.

1924   Géza **Vermes** was born in 1924 in Hungary. He studied in Budapest and later earned his ThD from the Catholic University of Leuven. He was raised Roman Catholic and even served in the priesthood but left the church in 1957 to reaffirm his Jewish identity. He taught for over two decades at Oxford University.

1926   Timothy F. **LaHaye** was born in 1926 at Detroit, Michigan. He earned a BA from Bob Jones University and a DMin. from Western Seminary. He founded San Diego Christian College and donated $4.5 million to Liberty University to build a School of Prophecy (2002), of which he is the president.

1926   Robert "Bob" W. **Funk** was born in 1926 in Indiana. He studied at Butler University, Christian Theological Seminary and earned his PhD from Vanderbilt University. For the majority of his career, Funk was a polarizing and controversial figure, a mantle that his Westar Institute and The Jesus Seminar carry-on today.

1927   Dr. Michael D. **Goulder** was born in 1927. He was educated at Trinity College (Oxford) where he studied under Austin Farrer. He was awarded an honorary doctorate from Trinity College during a lecture series on the synoptic Gospels and Q. He spent most of his academic career at the University of Birmingham.

1927   Ben **Meyer** was born in 1927. He studied all over the world and received his doctorate from The Universita Gregoriana. He held positions at several esteemed institutions including McMaster University. He wrote several significant works on the Historical Jesus, hermeneutics and philosophy.

1930   Colin John **Hemer** was born in 1930. He earned his doctorate under F.F. Bruce at the University of Manchester in 1965. He taught at Manchester as well as Sheffield and served as the librarian at Tyndale House for a few years. He also lectured in Turkey and Australia. He was also an avid bird-watcher. He died in 1987.

1930s Dr. Jack Dean **Kingsbury** was born in the 1930s in California. He earned his doctorate from the University of Basel. He has served much of his career as a professor at Union Theological Seminary (VA) and has written extensively on the Gospels. Kingsbury is heralded by many as a pioneer in biblical literary criticism.

1930s-1940s Bruce J. **Malina** was a professor at Creighton University. He earned his Doctor of Sacred Theology from the *Studium Biblicum Franciscanum* in Jerusalem as well as a Doctor of Theology from the University of St. Andrews (Scotland). He is a founder of The Context Group and has published extensively.

1931 Morna D. **Hooker** was born in 1931. She earned her Doctor of Divinity from Cambridge (the first female to do so). In addition to being bestowed with numerous scholarly awards such as the Burkitt Medal, she has held a number of academic positions and has been an active preacher within the Methodist Church.

1931 Burton L. **Mack** was born in 1931. He earned his PhD in NT Studies and the History of Religions from the University of Göttingen. Mack held a position for a number of years as the John Wesley Professor of NT at Claremont School of Theology (CA). Mack has been a controversial scholar throughout his career.

1932 Dr. Wayne A. **Meeks** was born in Aliceville, Alabama in 1932. He earned his PhD from Yale University and has, among other places, taught at Indiana, Emory and Yale Universities respectively. He has published extensively in the area of NT studies and has remains an active in the Presbyterian Church.

1934 John Dominic "Dom" **Crossan** was born in 1934 in Ireland. He earned his Doctor of Divinity at Maynooth College, whereafter his studies led him around the world and to resign from the Catholic priesthood. He taught at DePaul University for two and a half decades.

1934 I. Howard **Marshall** was born in 1934. He earned his PhD from the University of Aberdeen (Scotland), where he later taught and became Professor Emeritus. Marshall has lectured all over the world including in Prague, Cairo and the Ukraine. His wife Maureen Yeung is president of Evangel Seminary in Hong Kong.

1935   Dr. Robert H. **Stein** was born in 1935. He earned his doctorate from Princeton Theological Seminary. He has written many works on the Gospels and Jesus. He has taught in a number of institutions including Bethel Theological Seminary (Minnesota) and Southern Baptist Theological Seminary (Kentucky).

1936   James Lowell **Blevins** was born in 1936. He was a native of Hot Coal, West Virginia. He earned degrees from Duke University, Eastern Baptist Theological Seminary, and Southern Baptist Theological Seminary, where he later taught. He suffered a severe bout with diabetes and died in 2004.

1937   Ed Parish **Sanders** was born in 1937 in Texas. He earned his ThD from Union Theological Seminary (New York) and has received numerous honorary doctorates. He has taught at McMaster, Oxford, and Duke and has lectured throughout the world. He is a highly respected scholar in the field of NT studies.

1937   Sean P. **Kealy** was born in 1937 at Thurles, Republic of Ireland. He earned his BSS and LSS from the Biblical Institute of Rome, his BD and STL from Gregorian University, Rome, and his BA and MA from University College, Dublin. He has taught at a number of seminaries, colleges, and universities.

1938   Elisabeth Schüssler **Fiorenza** was born in 1938. She earned her MDiv from the University of Würzburg and her ThD from the University of Münster. She has taught at Harvard University and has also served as president of both the Society of Biblical Literature and the American Academy of Arts and Sciences.

1938   M. Eugene **Boring** was born in 1938. He earned his PhD from Vanderbilt University. Boring's ordination took place with the Christian Church (Disciples of Christ). Boring has written numerous commentaries and has translated nearly a dozen theological works from German to English.

Timeline

1939 Vernon K. **Robbins** was born in 1939. He earned both his MA and PhD from the University of Chicago. He is currently a professor at Emory University in Atlanta, Georgia but has also taught in Norway and South Africa. He currently leads the Rhetoric of Religious Antiquities (RRA) group.

1939 David Edward **Aune** was born in 1939. He earned both a BA and MA from Wheaton, a MA from the University of Minnesota, and a PhD from the University of Chicago. He has taught at St. Xavier University, Loyola University, and the University of Notre Dame. He has published extensively in the field of NT studies.

1939 Dr. James D.G. **Dunn** was born in 1939 and studied at both Glasgow and Cambridge. He has become an incredibly influential scholar within the field of NT studies. He is widely published and perhaps best known for his work on the new perspective on Paul.

1940s-1950s Sam K. **Williams** has served as Chair and Professor of Religion at the Colorado College. He has written a number of articles and books, including a commentary on Galatians (ANTC) and also a monograph titled *Jesus' Death as Saving Event: The Background and Origin of a Concept*.

1940s-1950s Lloyd **Gaston** has studied at Dartmouth College (BA) and the University of Basel, Switzerland, where he earned his ThD. He has taught at United Theological Seminary, Vancouver School of Theology, and Macalester College. He has served as an ordained minister in the Presbyterian Church, USA.

1940 Dr. Graham N. **Stanton** was born in 1940 and passed away in 2009. He earned his PhD at Westminster College and served as a professor at Cambridge University. Stanton wrote broadly on Jesus, the Apostle Paul, and 2nd century (CE) literature. He received numerous awards and was highly-esteemed among his peers.

1941 Harry Y. **Gamble** was born in 1941. He earned degrees from Wake Forest (BA), Duke (MDiv) and Yale (MA, PhD) respectively. He has served as Professor and Chair of Religious Studies at the University of Virginia and has published several works related to early church history. He is married to his wife Tamara.

Timeline

1942 Marcus J. **Borg** was born in 1942. He earned his DPhil from Oxford University. He taught for decades at the Oregon State University and has held the position as Canon Theologian at Trinity Episcopal Church in Portland. As a prolific member of the Jesus Seminar, Borg's work has been very controversial.

1942 Lee Martin **McDonald** was born in 1942. He earned his ThM from Harvard University and his PhD from the University of Edinburgh in Scotland. He has authored/edited over twenty books and hundreds of articles. He has served in several American Baptist churches as well as the U.S. Army Reserve's chaplaincy.

1942 John P. **Meier** was born in 1942 in the Bronx, New York. He earned his SSD (Doctorate in Sacred Scripture) from the Biblical Institute (Rome). He has spent most of his academic career at the University of Notre Dame (Indiana). Meier is a Catholic priest and a highly respected scholar in NT and theological studies.

1942 Frederick David **Mazzaferri** was born in 1942 at Australia. While his initial field of study was telecommunications, he eventually earned a degree in theology from the University of Aberdeen in 1986. He is a Seventh-day Adventist and maintains interest in cosmology, digitronics, and mathematics.

1943 Elaine **Pagels** was born in 1943 in Palo Alto, California. A student of the history of religions, she also studied dance at Martha Graham's studio. She earned her PhD from Harvard University where she studied under Helmut Koester. She teaches at Princeton Theological Seminary and is married.

1943 Luke Timothy **Johnson** was born in 1943. A native of Park Falls, Wisconsin he studied at Notre Dame Seminary (BS), St. Meinrad School of Theology (MDiv), Indiana University (MARS) and Yale University (PhD). He also served as a monk for nearly a decade. He has seven children and is married to Joy.

1944 Andrew T. **Lincoln** was born in 1944 at Wolverhampton, England. He earned his BD from Westminster Theological Seminary, Philadelphia and both his MA and PhD from Trinity

College, Cambridge. He has taught at several prominent universities such as Sheffield, Toronto and Gloucester.

1945 Adela Yarbro **Collins** was born in 1945. She earned her BA at Pomona College and both her MA and PhD at Harvard University. She has held appointments at the Universities of Notre Dame, Chicago, and Yale. She has also served as the president of the Society of New Testament Studies. She is married to Dr. John J. Collins.

1945 James Lynn **Resseguie** was born in 1945 at Buffalo, New York. He earned his AB from the University of California, his MDiv from Princeton Theological Seminary, and his PhD from Fuller Theological Seminary. He is an Anglican scholar and has served in various capacities at Winebrenner Theological Seminary.

1946 Richard **Bauckham** was born in 1946 at London. He studied at the University of St. Andrews, Scotland, and later taught there. He also served in teaching and research capacities at Clare College, St. John's College, and Ridley Hall, Cambridge. In addition to his many scholarly works he has also written two children's books.

1947 William J. **Abraham** was born in Northern Ireland in 1947. He is ordained in the United Methodist Church and teaches at Perkins School of Theology. He earned his BA at the Queen's University of Belfast, his MDiv from Asbury Theological Seminary, and his DPhil at Regent's Park College.

1948 Dr. Nicholas T. **Wright** was born in 1948 in England. He received his PhD from Merton College (Oxford) and has served as the Bishop of Durham. Wright has written a number of highly influential books and has appeared on many major television networks as a historical and theological consultant.

1948 Dr. Richard **Hays** was born in 1948. He earned his PhD from Emory University in NT and has received a couple of honorary doctorates. He has an extensive lecturing and publishing record and has received numerous prestigious awards. Hays has also taught New Testament studies at Duke University.

1948 Maarten J.J. **Menken** was born in 1948 at Leiden, Netherlands.

He earned both a MA and PhD in theology from the University of Amsterdam. He has taught at several institutions such as Tilburg University (Netherlands) & Catholic Theological University (Utrecth). His research focuses on the NT's use of the OT.

1949   Gregory K. **Beale** was born in 1949 at Dallas, Texas. He earned his ThM from Dallas Theological Seminary and his PhD from the University of Cambridge. He has held positions at numerous schools including Westminster Theological Seminary. In 2004 he served as president of the Evangelical Theological Society.

1950s-1960s   Barbara **Wootten** Snyder earned her PhD in 1991 from the Department of Near Eastern Studies at the University of California at Berkeley. Snyder earned her AB from UC Riverside (1976) and her MDiv from Gordon-Conwell Theological Seminary (1982). She has written several works on the Apocalypse.

1950s-1960s   Ched **Myers** is a native Californian. He earned a BA from the University of California at Berkley and an MA from Graduate Theological Union. He has served as adjunct faculty at numbers institutions including Fuller Theological Seminary. He and his wife Elaine work with Bartimaeus Cooperative Ministries in California.

1950s-1960s   Margaret Y. **MacDonald** was born in the 1950s-1960s. She earned her BA from Saint Mary's University (1983) and her doctorate from the University of Oxford (1986), where she held a Commonwealth scholarship. She has taught at the universities of Ottawa and St. Francis Xavier.

1950s-1960s   Don **Garlington**, a native to Arkansas, studied at Harding University (Arkansas), Westminster Theological Seminary (Philadelphia), and University of Durham (England). His doctoral supervisor was James D.G. Dunn. He has taught at Trinity Ministerial Academy, Toronto Baptist Seminary and Tyndale Seminary.

1950s-1960s   Terence L. **Donaldson** earned his doctorate in 1982 at Wycliffe. He has taught at the College of Emmanuel and St.

Chad (Saskatoon), as well as Wycliffe College. Terence is married to Lois and they have two children. They have lived in Toronto and have participated as members of St. Adrian's Parish.

1950s-1970s   A native of Calgary, Alberta, Canada, Gilbert **Desrosiers** taught Christian Studies and New Testament at ICI University (now Global University) in Irving, Texas. After nearly three decades of religious study and teaching theology, Desrosiers became an atheist. He published his work on Revelation in 2000.

1950s   Dr. Rikki E. **Watts** was born in the 1950s. A native Australian, Watts has several degrees including one in aeronautics. He traveled for some time with *Cirque du Soleil* conducting scientific analyses for their shows. He has also worked with IBM. He holds a degree in Philosophy, Art history and Sociology. He teaches at Regent College.

1950s   Roy A. **Harrisville** III, was born in the 1950s. He received his MDiv from Luther Northwestern Seminary (Minnesota) and his PhD in Biblical Interpretation from Union Theological Seminary (New York). He has ministered in the Lutheran Church and published a number of scholarly articles and books.

1951   Dr. Ben **Witherington** III, was born in North Carolina in 1951. He earned his DPhil from Durham University (England) and is a prolific publisher. He has written a commentary on every book of the NT and appeared on many major television networks. Currently, he teaches at Asbury Theological Seminary.

1951   Dr. John S. **Kloppenborg** was born in 1951. He earned his PhD from the University of St. Michael's College. He has taught in a number of academic institutions throughout the world, with much of that time being spent at the University of Toronto (Canada). He is a general editor of the IQP (International Q Project).

1953   Kent L. **Yinger** was born in 1953. He has studied at Wheaton College (Illinois) and Gordon-Conwell Theological Seminary (Boston), and earned his PhD from Sheffield University. He has taught at George Fox Evangelical Seminary and has participated widely across denominational boundaries.

Timeline

1953   Mark A. **Seifrid** was born in 1953 at Aurora, Illinois. He earned his BS from the University of Illinois and both his MA and MDiv from Trinity Evangelical Divinity School, Illinois. His PhD is from Princeton Theological Seminary. He has also served as a campus minister with the Navigators group.

1954   J. Nelson **Kraybill** was born in 1954 in Elizabethtown, Pennsylvania. He earned his BA from Goshen College, his MDiv from Princeton, and his PhD from Union Theological Seminary. He has pastored at Prairie Street Mennonite Church and served as the president of Associated Mennonite Biblical Seminary.

1955   Craig L. **Blomberg** was born in 1955 at Rock Island, Illinois. He earned his PhD in New Testament from Aberdeen University, Scotland. He has taught at Palm Beach Atlantic College and Denver Seminary. He was also a research fellow with Tyndale House, in England. He has a wife, Fran, and two children

1955   Bart D. **Ehrman** was born in 1955. He studied at Wheaton College (BA) and received both his MDiv and PhD from Princeton Theological Seminary, where he studied under the renowned text-critic, Bruce Metzger. Ehrman has two children and is married to Dr. Sarah Beckwith, an English teacher at Duke University.

1955   Dr. Michael **Gorman** was born in 1955. He received his MDiv and PhD from Princeton Theological Seminary. He is currently acting Raymond E. Brown Chair in Biblical Studies and Theology at St. Mary's Seminary in Baltimore. He is a well-known and respected Pauline scholar who lectures and teaches in churches worldwide.

1956   Francis B. **Watson** was born in 1956. He has published numerous journal articles, monographs, and scholarly books. Watson has held teaching positions at the University of Aberdeen (Scotland), King's College (London), and Durham University (England). His research has focused heavily on Paul and hermeneutics.

1958   Peter **Bolt** was born in 1958. He earned six theological degrees, including a PhD from the University of London (1997). Bolt has served as an ordained minister of the Anglican Church of

Australia (Diocese of Sydney) and has taught New Testament Studies at Moore Theological College, Sydney.

1959 Willis H. **Salier** was born in 1959 at Broken Hill, Australia He has earned two degrees in the field of education and four in the area of theology. He earned his PhD from Cambridge University (2003). He has served as Vice Principal and Lecturer at Moore Theological College (Australia). He and his wife Sue have three children.

1960s Pieter F. **Craffert** was born in the 1960s in Natal, South Africa. He earned his doctorate from the University of South Africa (Unisa). He has also studied with Gerd Theissen at the Karl Ruprecht University in Heidelberg, Germany. Craffert is an active member of The Context Group.

1960 Craig S. **Keener** was born in 1960. He earned his BA from Central Bible College, his MDiv from Assemblies of God Theological Seminary, and his PhD from Duke University. He has taught at both Palmer and Asbury Theological Seminary. He is married to Medine and his son is David.

1961 Douglas **Atchinson** Campbell was born in 1961. He earned his PhD from the University of Toronto. He has taught New Testament at Duke University, North Carolina. He has published several works on the life and thought of Paul, including *The Quest for Paul's Gospel* and *The Deliverance of God*.

1963 Jonathan L. **Reed** was born in the 1963 in Minneapolis. He earned his PhD from the Claremont Graduate School, where he studied with Burton Mack. He has taught in numerous academic institutions and has appeared on many major television networks like ABC, CNN & NatGeo as an archaeological consultant.

1967 Dr. Mark **Goodacre** was born in 1967 in Leicestershire, England. He earned his DPhil at the University of Oxford. He has taught at the University of Birmingham (England) and also Duke University (North Carolina). Goodacre has published extensively on the synoptic Gospels and Q.

1970s R. Barry **Matlock** was born and raised in Nashville, Tennessee. He earned degrees from Lipscomb University and Westminster

Timeline

Theological Seminary respectively. His PhD is from the University of Sheffield, England. Matlock is a fan of the music of Bob Dylan, Hank Williams, Jr. and Emmylou Harris.

1970   David **Watson** was born in 1970. He has served in the Methodist Church as an ordained minister. He studied at Texas Tech, Perkins School of Theology and went on to earn his PhD from Southern Methodist University (TX). He has served as a professor of NT and academic dean at United Theological Seminary (OH).

1974   Michael F. **Bird** was born in 1974 at Germany and grew up in Ipswich. He earned his PhD from the University of Queensland, Australia. He served in the military as a paratrooper before becoming a lecturer and professor in theology and Bible. He is an Anglican scholar, is married to Naomi and has four children.

1975   Anthony **Le Donne** was born in 1975. He earned his PhD from the University of Durham where he studied with James D.G. Dunn and John Barclay. He has taught NT and Second Temple Judaism at Lincoln Christian University and has an interest in historiography in relation to Historical Jesus research.

1983   Michael R. **Whitenton** was born in 1983 at Texas. He earned his ThM from Dallas Theological Seminary. His postgraduate work has been carried out at Baylor University, Texas, where he has studied with Bruce W. Longenecker. He also earned a BS in Community Health. He is married to Rachel.

Notes

Chapter 1: The New Testament and the Others

1. For an insightful discussion on this topic, see Frances M. Young, *Biblical Exegesis and the Formation of Christian Culture* (Peabody, MA: Hendrickson, 2002). It should be noted here that in addition to gathering biographical data via email, Facebook, and similar types of personal correspondences, for the "Scholarly Sketches" found throughout this book, on occasion, I also consulted Donald K. McKim, *Dictionary of Major Biblical Interpreters* (Downers Grove, IL: InterVarsity Press, 2007), *Dictionary of Biblical Interpretation*, vol. 1, A-J, ed. J. H. Hayes (Nashville, TN: Abingdon, 1999), and *Dictionary of Biblical Interpretation*, vol. 2, K-Z, ed. J. H. Hayes (Nashville, TN: Abingdon, 1999).
2. Steven R. Fischer, *A History of Reading* (London: Reaktion Books, 2003), 83.
3. Anthony J. Mills, "A Penguin in the Sahara," *Archeological Newsletter of the Royal Ontario Museum* 2 (March, 1990), 37.
4. For more examples and resources, see Lee M. McDonald, *The Origin of the Bible: A Guide for the Perplexed* (London: T&T Clark, 2011), esp. 192-98.
5. Various scholars have suggested different criterion. It is unnecessary to deal with each and every view here. For an in-depth discussion of this topic, see Bruce M. Metzger, *The Canon of the New Testament: Its Origin, Development, and Significance* (Oxford: Oxford University Press, 1997), 251-88. Here, I am following the work of McDonald, *The Origin*, 208-230. For more on the debate concerning the date of the Muratorian Canon, see: Albert C. Sundberg, Jr., "Canon Muratori: A Fourth Century List," in *Harvard Theological Review* 66 (1973): 1-41 and his review of Metzger's, *The Canon of the New Testament* in the *Journal of the American Academy of Religion* 60/2 (1992): 350-355; Everett M. Fergson, "Canon Muratori: Date and Provenance," in *Studia Patristica* 18 (1982): 677-83; and G. M. Hahneman, *The Muratorian Fragment and the Development of the Canon* (OMS; Oxford: Oxford University Press, 1992).
6. For Luther's views, see *Luther's Works* (vol. 35; St. Louis: Concordia, 1963), 395-99. When it comes to John Calvin, many reason that since he wrote extensive works on every Old Testament work except Ezekiel, and every New Testament work except for 2 John, 3 John, and Revelation, he must have questioned their placement in the canon. This is not enough evidence, however, to suggest that he wanted to ban them from the canon, and researchers must be careful not to overreach in their interpretations of the evidence here. For a much fuller discussion of these matters, see Roger Nicole, "John Calvin and Inerrancy" *Journal*

Notes

of the *Evangelical Theological Society* 25/4 (December, 1982): 425–42. For Zwingli's thoughts, see Huldrych Zingli, Emil Egli, and Georg Finsler, *Huldreich Zwinglis Sämtliche Werke: einzig vollständige Ausgabe der Werke Zwinglis Bd. II* (Corpus reformatorum 89; Zürich: Theologischer Verlag, 1982).

7. For Erasmus's views on this topic, see his annotations *ad Apoc.* 22.12.
8. Johann S. Semler, *Abhandlung von freier Untersuchung des Canons*, 4 Vols. (Halle: Hemmerde, 1771–75).
9. Theodor Zahn, *Forschungen zur Geschichte des neutestamentlichen Kanons und der altkirchlichen Literatur*, 10 vols. (Erlangen: Deichert; Leipzig: Böhme, 1881–1929); and *Geschichte dees neutestamentlichen Kanons*, 2 vols. (Erlangen, Deichert; Leipzig, Böhme, 1888–92).
10. Several of Harnack's most important works are as follows: Adolf von Harnack, *Lherbuch der Dogmengeschichte* (Freiburg: i. B., Mohr (Siebeck), 1886–89); and *Die entstehung des Neuen Testaments und die wichtigsten Folgen der neuen Schöpfung* (Leipzig: Hinrichs, 1914).
11. Walter Bauer, *Rechtgläubigkeit und Ketzerei im ältesten Christentum* (Tübingen: Mohr, 1964).
12. Kurt Aland, *The Problem of the New Testament Canon*. (CST; London: A.R. Mowbray & Co., 1962), 19.
13. Ibid.
14. Ibid.
15. For example, see Dennis C. Duling, *The New Testament: History, Literature, And Social Context*, 4th ed. (Canada: Thomson Wadsworth, 2003), 57.
16. Brevard S. Childs, *The New Testament As Canon: An Introduction* (Valley Forge, PA: Trinity Press Intl., 1994).
17. Hans von Campenhausen, *The Formation of the Christian Bible*, trans. J. A. Baker (Philadelphia, PA: Fortress, 1972).
18. Harry Y. Gamble, *The New Testament Canon: Its Making and Meaning* (Philadelphia, PA: Fortress, 1985), 12.
19. Ibid., 18.
20. Lee M. McDonald, *The Formation of the Christian Biblical Canon* (Peabody, MA: Hendrickson, 1995), 142.
21. McDonald, *The Biblical Canon: Its Origin, Transmission, and Authority* (Peabody, MA: Hendrickson, 2007), 429. See also Peter Balla, *Challenges to New Testament Theology: An Attempt to Justify the Enterprise* (WUNT 2:95; Tübingen: Mohr Siebeck, 1997), 86–146."
22. Ibid.
23. Luke T. Johnson, *The Writings of the New Testament: An Interpretation* (Philadelphia, PA: Fortress Press, 1990), 545.
24. William J. Abraham, *Canon and Criterion in Christian Theology* (Oxford: Oxford University Press, 2006), 55.
25. Ibid.
26. Ibid.

Notes

Chapter 2: Different Methods to the Madness

1. For discussions of the sixteenth and eighteenth centuries in relation to modern interpretive approaches, see Allan K. Jenkins and Patrick Preston, *Biblical Scholarship and the Church: A Sixteenth-Century Crisis of Authority* (Burlington, VT: Ashgate Publishing Company, 2007); and Michael C. Legaspi, *The Death of Scripture and the Rise of Biblical Studies* (Oxford: Oxford University Press, 2010).
2. Morna D. Hooker, *The Gospel According to Saint Mark* (BNTC; Peabody, MA: Hendrickson, 1991), 33.
3. Bruce M. Metzger, *A Textual Commentary on the Greek New Testament*, 2nd ed. (Stuttgart: German Bible Society, 1994), 62.
4. Dennis E. Nineham, *The Gospel of St. Mark* (PGC; New York: The Seabury Press, 1968), 55.
5. Rikki E. Watts, *Isaiah's New Exodus in Mark* (Grand Rapids, MI: Baker, 1997), 56.
6. Willi Marxsen, *Mark the Evangelist: Studies on the Redaction History of the Gospel* (Nashville, TN: Abingdon, 1969), 25.
7. Ibid., 149.
8. Ibid., 149–50.
9. Jack D. Kingsbury, *The Christology of Mark's Gospel* (Philadelphia, PA: Fortress Press, 1983), 51.
10. Brevard S. Childs, *The New Testament As Canon: An Introduction* (Valley Forge, PA: Trinity Press Intl., 1994).
11. Childs, *The New Testament*, 86.
12. Ibid.
13. Ibid., 86–87.
14. Bruce J. Malina and Richard L. Rohrbaugh, *Social-Science Commentary on the Gospels* (Minneapolis, MN: Fortress, 1992), 174–75.
15. This definition is taken from Robbins's website, which was accessed on Tuesday, January 31, 2012 at http://www.religion.emory.edu/faculty/robbins/SRI/defns/s_defns.cfm. The definition is actually a bit more complex. Here is the dictionary entry in full, which reveals some of the intricacies and nuances of his approach: "Socio-Rhetorical Interpretation: An approach to literature that focuses on values, convictions, and beliefs both in the texts we read and in the world in which we live. It views texts as performances of language in particular historical and cultural situations. It presupposes that a text is a tapestry of interwoven textures, including inner texture, intertexture, social and cultural texture, ideological texture, and sacred texture. A major goal of socio-rhetorical interpretation is to nurture an environment of interpretation that encourages a genuine interest in people who live in contexts with values, norms, and goals different from our own."
16. Vernon K. Robbins, *Jesus the Teacher: A Socio-Rhetorical Interpretation of Mark* (Minneapolis: MN: Fortress, 2009), 29. Interestingly, Robbins has stated repeatedly in publications that he created and coined the term "socio-rhetorical" in the year 1984. See for example his following works where he makes this claim: "Beginnings and Developments in Socio-Rhetorical Interpretation" (May 1, 2004) accessed on 06.01.12 at http://www.religion.emory.edu/faculty/robbins/Pdfs/SRIBegDevRRA.pdf; "Socio-Rhetorical Interpretation" in *The Blackwell Companion to the New Testament*, ed. D.E. Aune (Malden, MA: Wiley-Blackwell, 2010), 192–219; and a review of "What's in the Word: Rethinking the Socio-Rhetorical Character

Notes

of the New Testament," in *Review of Biblical Literature* 06 (2012). However, I have shown that nearly half a dozen published works prior to the year 1984 used this term. See E.W. Mechling, *From Paradox to Parody: A Socio-Rhetorical Theory of Counter-Institutional Movement Organizations, Applied to Free Clinic Movement* (PhD Diss.; Temple University, 1979); Eric R. Weisman, *The Rhetoric of Holocaust Survivors: A Dramatistic Perspective* (PhD Diss.; Temple University, 1980), endnote #36 of chapter 2; *Handbook of Political Communication*, eds. D. D. Nimmo and K. R. Sanders (Beverly Hills, CA: Sage Publications, 1981), 438, 439; *Explorations in Rhetoric: Studies in Honor of Douglas Ehninger*, eds. D. Ehninger and R. E. McKerrow (Glenview, IL: Scott-Foresman, 1982), 32, 34, 35; D. M. Lessing, *Documents Relating to the Sentimental Agents in the Volyen Empire* (New York: Knopf, 1983), 164. It is more correct then, to say that while Robbins did not create or coin the term, he possibly was the first to introduce it to those in the field of biblical studies. For more on this matter, see the post "'Socio-Rhetorical'— Did Vernon Robbins Create the Term?" (06.0712) at my website http://www.michaelhalcomb.blogspot.com/2012/06/socio-rhetorical-did-vernon-robbins.html.

17. For more on the inscription, see W. Dittenberger, *Orientis graeci inscriptiones selectae* 2, no. 458 (Hildesheim: Olms, 1960), 48–60, here line 41–42.
18. Ben Witherington III, *The Gospel of Mark: A Socio-Rhetorical Commentary* (Grand Rapids, MI: Eerdmans, 2001), 70. "While Witherington uses the term "socio-rhetorical" to describe his work, his publications also appear to have close affinity to the "historical rhetorical criticism" model used by Hans D. Betz, *Galatians: A Commentary on Paul's Letter to the Churches in Galatia* (Philadelphia, PA: Fortress, 1979) and Margaret M. Mitchell, *Paul and the Rhetoric of Reconciliation: An Exegetical Investigation of the Language and Composition of 1 Corinthians* (Louisville, KY: WJK, 1993)."
19. Ched Myers, *Binding the Strong Man: A Political Reading of Mark's Story of Jesus* (Maryknoll, NY: Orbis, 2006), 123.
20. Ibid., 123–24.
21. Ibid., 124.

Chapter 3: From Paul's Gospel to the Four Gospels

1. Graham N. Stanton, *Jesus and Gospel* (Cambridge: Cambridge University Press, 2004), 51.
2. Wayne A. Meeks, *The Origins of Christian Morality: The First Two Centuries* (New Haven, CT: Yale University Press, 1993), 196.
3. Richard B. Hays, *The Faith of Jesus Christ: The Narrative Substructure of Galatians 3:1—4:11* (BRS; Grand Rapids, MI: Eerdmans, 1984), 30.
4. N. T. Wright, *The New Testament and the People of God* (Minneapolis, MN: Fortress Press, 1992), 79.
5. Ben Witherington III, *Paul's Narrative Thought World: The Tapestry of Tragedy and Triumph* (Louisville, KY: WJK, 1994), 2.
6. James D. G. Dunn, "Whose Story?" in *Narrative Dynamics in Paul: A Critical Assessment*, ed. B. W. Longenecker (Louisville, KY: WJK, 2002), 217–30.

7. Richard B. Hays, *The Faith of Jesus Christ: The Narrative Substructure of Galatians 3:1—4:11* (BRS; Grand Rapids, MI: Eerdmans, 1984); and "Is Paul's Gospel Narratable?" *Journal for the Study of the New Testament* 27.2 (2004): 217–39.
8. Michael J. Gorman, *Cruciformity: Paul's Narrative Spirituality of the Cross* (Grand Rapids, MI: Eerdmans, 2001), 93.
9. Luke T. Johnson, *The Real Jesus: The Misguided Quest for the Historical Jesus and the Truth of the Traditional Gospels* (New York: HarperCollins, 1996).
10. Ibid., 154.
11. Contra Gorman's claims, see Joseph H. Hellerman, *Reconstructing Honor in Roman Philippi: Carmen Christi as Cursus Pudorum* (SNTSMS 132; Cambridge: Cambridge University Press, 2005). Hellerman contends that this is not an early Christian hymn, but rather that Paul made it up while writing this epistle. Thus, it is an "occasional" part of Paul's later, not a "traditional" part of early Christian liturgy.
12. Hyam Maccoby, *The Mythmaker: Paul and the Invention of Christianity* (New York: Harper & Row, 1986). It may well be worth noting that Luke Timothy Johnson, in his more recent work titled *Among the Gentiles: Greco-Roman Religion and Christianity* (New Haven, CT: Yale University Press, 2009), appears to move in quite a different direction than some of his earlier publications such as *Real Jesus*. Whether one agrees or disagrees with his earlier or later views, this certainly demonstrates both the dynamic nature of biblical studies as well the importance of continual research and reflection.

Chapter 4: What Do You Mean by "Synoptic Problem?"

1. Reprint: Burnett H. Streeter, *The Four Gospels: A Study of Origins, Treating the Manuscript Tradition, Sources, Authorship, & Dates* (Eugene, OR: Wipf & Stock, 2008). R.H. Lightfoot, *History and Interpretation in the Gospels* (London: Hodder & Stoughton, 1935), 27-28, n.1, has questioned the origin of the designation "Q" saying: "It seems now to be assumed that the symbol Q originated in Germany, as being the first letter of the German Quelle, source. Dr Armitage Robinson, however, in conversation with the pesent writer maintained in all seriousness that he himself was the first to use the symbol, and for an enitrely different reason. In lecturing at Cambridge on the sources of the gospels, in the 'nineties of the last century, he was in the habit, he said, of alluding to St Mark's gospel as P (reminiscences of St Peter), and so the presumed sayings-document as Q, simply because Q was the next letter after P in the alphabet. His contention, therefore, was that some of his hearers carried his method across the North Sea, and that German scholars, having adopted the symbol Q from him, soon found an explanation for it, which to them no doubt seemed both more satisfactory and more rational. Dr Robinson emphasized that no designation of the sayings-document by the symbol Q appeared in German writings until after the period of his lectures at Cambridge, and that the now common explanation of the symbol would be found to be still later. If, as Dr Burkitt informs me, Wellhausen was the first in Germany to use the symbol Q, it is possible to date accurately its appearance in print in that country, since the first edition of his *Einleitung*, in which it appears, was published in 1903. His commentaries on the synoptists began to appear in the same year."

Notes

2. Austin M. Farrer, "On Dispensing with Q" in *Studies in the Gospels: Essays in Memory of R.H. Lightfoot*, ed. D. E. Nineham (Oxford: Blackwell, 1955), 55–88.
3. Michael Goulder, *Midrash and Lection in Matthew* (London: SPCK, 1974); "On Putting Q to the Test," *New Testament Studies* 24 (1978): 218–24; "Farrer on Q," *Theology* 83 (1980): 290–95; "Is Q a Juggernaut?" *Journal of Biblical Literature* 115 (1996): 667–81; and "Self Contradiction in the IQP" *Journal of Biblical Literature* 118 (1999): 506–17. See also Christopher A. Rollston, *Gospels According to Michael Goulder: A North American Response* (Harrisburg, PA: Trinity Press Intl., 2002).
4. Mark Goodacre, *The Synoptic Problem: A Way Through the Maze* (TBS 80; Sheffield: Sheffield Academic Press, 1996); "Fatigue in the Synoptics," *New Testament Studies* 44 (1998): 45–58; "A Monopoly on Marcan Priority? Fallacies at the Heart of Q," *Society of Biblical Literature Seminary Papers 2000* (Atlanta: Society of Biblical Literature, 2000), 583–622; and *The Case Against Q: Studies in Markan Priority and the Synoptic Problem* (Harrisburg, PA: Trinity Press Intl., 2002).
5. John S. Kloppenborg, *The Formation of Q: Trajectories in Ancient Wisdom Collections* (Minneapolis: Fortress Press, 1987); *Q Parallels: Synopsis, Critical Notes & Concordance* (F&F; Salem, OR: Polebridge Press Westar Institute, 1998); *The Critical Edition of Q: A Synopsis Including the Gospels of Matthew and Luke, Mark and Thomas with English, German and French Translations of Q and Thomas* (Hermenia; Minneapolis, MN: Fortress Press, 2000); *Excavating Q: The History and Setting of the Sayings Gospel* (Minneapolis, MN: Fortress Press, 2000); and *Q, the Earliest Gospel: An Introduction to the Original Stories and Sayings of Jesus* (Louisville, KY: WJK, 2008).
6. Augustine, *The Harmony of the Gospels* (1.2).
7. Johann J. Griesbach, *A Synopsis of the Gospels of Matthew, Mark & Luke* (Halle: 1776).
8. Robert H. Stein, *The Synoptic Problem: An Introduction* (Grand Rapids, MI: Baker 1994), and *Studying the Synoptic Gospels: Origin and Interpretation*, 2nd ed. (Grand Rapids, MI: Baker Academic, 2001); William R. Farmer, *The Synoptic Problem* (Macon, GA: Mercer University Press, 1981); and *The Gospel of Jesus: The Pastoral Relevance of the Synoptic Problem* (Louisville, KY: WJK, 1994). For another take on this matter, specifically from the viewpoint of orality and oral traditions, see James D.G. Dunn, *Jesus Remembered: Christianity in the Making* (vol. 1; Grand Rapids, MI: Eerdmans, 2003) who builds on the work of Kenneth E. Bailey, "Middle Eastern Oral Tradition and the Synoptic Gospels," in *Expository Times* 106/12 (Spring, 1995): 363-367. See also Dennis Ingolfsland, "Jesus Remembered: James Dunn and the Synoptic Problem," in *Trinity Journal* 27 (Fall, 2006): 187-197.

Chapter 5: Did Jesus Try to Keep a Messianic Secret?

1. William Wrede, *Das Messiasgeheimnis in den Evangelien: Zugleich ein Beitrag zum Verständnis des Markusevangeliums* (Göttingen: Vandenhoeck & Ruprecht, 1901). For the English edition see William Wrede, *The Messianic Secret*, trans. J. C. G. Grieg (Cambridge: James Clarke & Co., 1971). One of Wrede's precursors, Heinrich E. G. Paulus, had written about the concept of the messiah to a great degree in the early 1800s. You can read about Paulus at the beginning of the next chapter.

2. Adolf Jülicher, *Neue Linen in der Kritik der evangelischen Uberliefrung* (Giessen: Alfred Töpelmann, 1906).
3. Albert Schweitzer, *Das Messianitäts-und Leidensgeheimis: Eine Skizze des Lebens Jesu* (Tübingen: J. C. B. Mohr, 1901); or *The Mystery of the Kingdom of God: The Secret of Jesus' Messiahship and Passion*, trans. W. Lowrie (New York: Macmillan, 1950); and *The Quest of the Historical Jesus: A Critical Study of its Progress from Reimarus to Wrede*, trans. W. Montgomery (New York: Macmillan, 1948; original 1906).
4. William Sanday, *The Life of Christ in Recent Research* (New York: Oxford University Press, 1907), 74.
5. Ibid.
6. Ibid., 75.
7. Ibid.
8. Johannes Weiss, *Christ: The Beginning of Dogma*, trans. V. D. Davis (Boston, MA: American Unitarian Association, 1911), 22.
9. Martin Dibelius, *Die Formgeschichte des Evangeliums* (Tübingen: J. C. B. Mohr, 1919), and *From Tradition to Gospel* (London: 1934).
10. Karl L. Schmidt, *Der Rahmen der Geschichte Jesu* (Berlin: 1919).
11. Rudolf Bultmann, *Die Geschichte der synoptischen Tradition* (Göttingen: Vandenhoeck und Ruprecht, 1921).
12. Arthur S. Peake, "The Messiah and the Son of Man" in *The Bulletin of the John Rylands Library* 8/1 (January, 1924), 65.
13. Ibid., 67.
14. Ibid., 76.
15. Julius Schniewind, *Das Evangelium nach Markus* (Göttingen: Vandenhoeck und Ruprecht, 1933).
16. Ernst Löhmeyer, *Galiläa und Jerusalem* (FRLANT 52; Göttingen: Vandhoeck & Ruprecht, 1936), 12.
17. H. J. Ebeling, *Das Messiasgeheimnis und die Botschaft des Marcus-Evangelisten* (BZNW 19; Berlin: Töpelmann, 1939).
18. Frederick C. Grant, *The Gospel of the Kingdom: The Haskell Lectures* (New York: Macmillan, 1940); and *The Earliest Gospel: The Cole Lectures* (New York: Abingdon-Cokesbury Press, 1943).
19. Alfred E. J. Rawlinson, *St. Mark* (WC; London: Methuen, 1949).
20. Vincent Taylor, *The Gospel According to St. Mark* (London: Macmillan, 1952), 147.
21. Ibid.
22. Willi Marxsen, *Mark the Evangelist*, trans. R. A. Harrisville (Nashville, TN: Abingdon Press, 1959).
23. Karl Adam, *The Christ of Faith: The Christology of the Church* (New York: Mentor Omega, 1962), 138–39.
24. Ben F. Meyer, *The Aims of Jesus* (London: SCM, 1979).
25. Ben F. Meyer, "Master Builder and Copestone of the Portal: Images of the Mission of Jesus," *Toronto Journal of Theology* 9 (1993): 196.
26. Jack D. Kingsbury, *The Christology of Mark's Gospel* (Philadelphia, PA: Fortress Press, 1983).
27. Burton Mack, *A Myth of Innocence: Mark and Christian Origins* (Philadelphia, PA: Fortress, 1988), 289.
28. Ibid.

Notes

29. Heikki M. Räisänen, *The "Messianic Secret" in Mark's Gospel*, trans. C. Tuckett (Edinburgh: T & T Clark, 1990).
30. Morna Hooker, *The Gospel According to Saint Mark* (BNTC; Peabody, MA: Hendrickson, 1991), 67.
31. N. T. Wright, *Jesus and the Victory of God. Christian Origins and the Question of God* (Vol. 2; Minneapolis, MN: Fortress, 1996).
32. David F. Watson, *Honor Among Christians: The Cultural Key to the Messianic Secret* (Minneapolis, MN: Fortress Press, 2010).
33. For a great resource on messianic research see James L. Blevins, *The Messianic Secret in Markan Research, 1901-1976* (Washington, DC: University Press of America, 1981).
34. Wrede wrote this on January 2, 1905 to Adolf von Harnack. See Martin Hengle and Anna M. Schwemer, *Der messianische Anspruch Jesu und die Anfänge der Christologie: vier Studien* (Tübingen: Mohr Siebeck, 2001), ix.

Chapter 6: ReQuesting Guides on the Quest for Jesus

1. Hermann S. Reimarus, *Fragments*, ed. C. H. Talbert (LJS; Philadelphia, PA: Fortress Press, 1970; original 1778).
2. Albert Schweitzer, *The Quest of the Historical Jesus*, trans. D. Nineham (Minneapolis, MN: Fortress Press, 2001), xiii.
3. Heinrich Paulus, *Das Leben Jesu als Grundlage einer reinen Geschichte des Urchristentums* (2 Vols.; Heidelberg: C. F. Winter, 1828).
4. David F. Strauss, *The Life of Jesus Critically Examined* (Philadelphia, PA: Fortress Press, 1972; original 1835/36).
5. Ernest Renan, *The Life of Jesus* (New York: Brentano's, 1863), 237.
6. Ibid., 179-80.
7. See Schweitzer, *The Quest of the Historical Jesus*.
8. Rudolf K. Bultmann, *Jesus* (Berlin: Deutsche Bibliothek, 1926), 6.
9. Ernst Käsemann, "The Problem of the Historical Jesus," in *Essays on New Testament Themes* (Naperville, IL: Alec R. Allenson, 1964), 15-47.
10. Günther Bornkamm, *Jesus of Nazareth* (New York: Harper & Row, 1960), 13.
11. Norman Perrin, *Rediscovering the Teaching of Jesus* (New York: Harper & Row, 1976); and *Jesus and the Language of the Kingdom: Symbol and Meaning in New Testament Interpretation* (Philadelphia, PA: Fortress Press, 1976).
12. Hans Conzelmann, *Jesus* (Philadelphia, PA: Fortress Press, 1973). See also his earlier essay, "The Method of the Life-of-Jesus Research" in *The Historical Jesus and the Kerygmatic Christ: Essays on the New Quest of the Historical Jesus*, eds. C. E. Braaten and R. A. Harrisville (Nashville, TN: Abingdon Press, 1964), 54-68.
13. Rudolf Schnackenburg, *Rückfrage nach Jesus*, ed. K. Kertelge (Freiburg: Herder, 1974), 194-220.
14. Edward C.F.A. Schillebeeckx, *Jesus: An Experiment in Christology* (New York: Seabury Press, 1979).
15. Géza Vermes, *Jesus the Jew: A Historian's Reading of the Gospels* (London: Collins, 1973).

16. See, for example, Vermes, *The Gospel of Jesus the Jew* (Newcastle: University of Newcastle upon Tyne, 1981); *Jesus and the World of Judaism* (London, SCM Press, 1983); and *The Religion of Jesus the Jew* (Minneapolis, MN: Fortress Press, 1993).
17. E. P. Sanders, *Jesus and Judaism*, (Philadelphia, PA: Fortress Press, 1985), 58.
18. Ibid., 319–20.
19. Mary Rourke, "Cross Examination," *Los Angeles Times*, (24 February 1994): E1, E5.
20. Burton Mack, *A Myth of Innocence: Mark and Christian Origins* (Philadelphia, PA: Fortress, 1988), 96.
21. John D. Crossan, *The Historical Jesus: The Life of a Mediterranean Jewish Peasant* (New York: HarperCollins, 1992), esp. 216, and *Jesus: A Revolutionary Biography* (New York: HarperCollins, 1995), 139–52.
22. See Marcus J. Borg, "From Galilean Jew to the Face of God: The Pre-Easter and Post-Easter Jesus" and "The Historical Study of Jesus and Christian Origins," in *Jesus at 2000*, ed. M. J. Borg (Boulder, CO: Westview Press, 1997); *The God We Never Knew: Beyond Religion to a More Authentic Contemporary Faith* (San Francisco: HarperSanFrancisco, 1997); "The Historian, the Christian, and Jesus," *Theology Today* 52 (1995): 6–16; *Meeting Jesus Again for the First Time: The Historical Jesus and the Heart of Contemporary Faith* (San Francisco: HarperSanFrancisco, 1994); and "An Orthodoxy Reconsidered: The End-of-the-World Jesus," in *The Glory of Christ in the New Testament*, eds. L. D. Hurst and N. T. Wright (Oxford: Clarendon Press, 1987). Borg has published many other works on the historical Jesus as well.
23. Ben Witherington III, *The Christology of Jesus* (Minneapolis, MN: Fortress Press, 1990); *Jesus, Paul, and the End of the World: A Comparative Study in New Testament Eschatology* (Downers Grove, IL: InterVarsity Press, 1992); *The Jesus Quest: The Third Search for the Jew of Nazareth* (Downers Grove, IL: InterVarsity Press, 1995); and *Jesus the Sage: The Pilgrimage of Wisdom* (Minneapolis, MN: Fortress Press, 1994).
24. John P. Meier, "The Present State of the 'Third Quest' for the Historical Jesus: Loss and Gain," *Biblica* 80 (1999): 487.
25. N. T. Wright, *Jesus and the Victory of God: Christian Origins and the Question of God* (Vol. 2; Minneapolis, MN: Fortress Press, 1997), 239.
26. Ibid., 163.
27. Pieter F. Craffert, *The Life of a Galilean Shaman: Jesus of Nazareth in Anthropological-Historical Perspective* (Matrix: The Bible in Mediterranean Context; Eugene, OR: Cascade, 2008).
28. Anthony Le Donne, *Historical Jesus: What Can We Know and How Can We Know It?* (Grand Rapids, MI: Eerdmans, 2011), 8.

Chapter 7: Can Luke's Acts be Trusted?

1. For a good discussion of this specific topic, see James W. Aageson, "The Pastoral Epistles, Apostolic Authority, and the Development of the Pauline Scriptures" (5–26), Robert W. Wall, "The Function of the Pastoral Letters within the Pauline Canon of the New Testament: A Canonical Approach" (27–44), "When and How was the Pauline Canon Compiled? An Assessment of Theories" (95–128), and Mark Harding, "Disputed and Undisputed Letters of Paul" (129–168) in *The Pauline Canon*, ed. S. E. Porter (PS 1; Leiden: Brill, 2004).

Notes

2. John Bradshaw, "It Is Written" on channel 27 WKYT, Lexington, KY viewed on 02/05/2012.
3. For a number of resources which offer very helpful reviews of most of the scholars mentioned in this chapter, see Arthur Cushman McGiffert, "The Historical Criticism of Acts in Germany" in *The Beginnings of Christianity: The Acts of the Apostles*, vol. 2, eds. F. J. Foakes-Jackson and K. Lake (London: Macmillan and Co., 1922), 363–95; A. T. Robertson, *Luke the Historian in the Light of Research* (New York: Scribner's Sons, 1930); Henry J. Cadbury, *The Book of Acts in History* (New York: Harper & Brothers Publishers, 1955); A. J. Mattill Jr., *Luke as a Historian in Criticisms Since 1840* (Ann Arbor, MI: University Microfilms, 1959); A. J. and Mary Mattill, *A Classified Bibliography of Literature on the Acts of the Apostles* (Leiden: Brill, 1968); W. Ward Gasque, *A History of the Interpretation of the Acts of the Apostles* (Peabody, MA: Hendrickson, 1989); Colin J. Hemer, *The Book of Acts in the Setting of Hellenistic History*, ed. C. H. Gempf (Winona Lake, IN: Eisenbrauns, 1990); Mark Alan Powell, *What are They Saying About Acts?* (Mahwah, NJ: Paulist Press, 1991), esp. 80–95; and François Bovon, *Luke the Theologian: Fifty-five Years of Research* (1950–2005), trans. K. McKinney (Waco, TX: Baylor University Press, 2nd rev. edn. 2006). The outline of the middle portion of this chapter is influenced by the work of Gasque. See also, Thomas E. Phillips, *Paul, His Letters, and Acts* (LPS; Peabody, MA: Hendrickson, 2009).
4. As has been restated throughout this book, not every interpreter who speaks on every issue can be listed. For more resources on Acts, see the works in the preceding note as well as the following: Joel B. Green and Michael C. McKeever, *Luke-Acts and New Testament Historiography* (IBRB 8; Grand Rapids, MI: Baker, 1994), and Joel B. Green, *The Theology of the Gospel of Luke* (NTT 3; Cambridge: Cambridge University Press, 1995). Among many others, see also Stanley E. Porter, *The Paul of Acts: Essays in Literary Criticism, Rhetoric, and Theology* (WUNT 115; Tübingen: Mohr Siebeck, 1999), and Bruce Chilton, *Rabbi Paul: An Intellectual Biography* (New York: Doubleday, 2004).
5. Wilhelm M. L. de Wette, *Lehrbuch der historisch-kritischen Einleitung in die Bibel alten und Neuen Testaments: zweyter Teil: Die Einleitung in das Neue Testament enthaltend* (Berlin, 1826; 5th ed., 1847), 204–7.
6. Ibid., 202–4.
7. Ferdinand Christian Baur, *Paul, the Apostle of Jesus Christ, His Life and Work, His Epistles and His Doctrine: A Contribution to the Critical History of Primitive Christianity*, 2 vols, ed. E. Zeller, trans. A. Menzies (2nd ed. London: Williams & Norgate, 1876), 84.
8. Ibid.
9. Matthias Schneckenburger, *Uber den Zweck der Apostelgeschichte* (Bern: Ch. Fischer, 1891).
10. Eduard Zeller, *Die Apostelgeschichte nach ihrem Inahlt und Ursprung kritisch Untersucht* (Stuttgart: Carl Mäcken, 1854).
11. Gasque, *History*, 44.
12. Zeller, *Die Apostelgeschichte*, 364–488.
13. See Martin Dibelius, *Studies in the Acts of the Apostles*, eds. H. Greeven, trans. M. Ling (New York: Scribners, 1956).
14. Ernst von Haenchen, *Die Apostelgeschichte: Neu Übersetzt und Erklärt* (Göttingen: Vandenhoeck & Ruprecht, 1959), 45.

15. Philipp Vielhauer, "On the 'Paulinism' of Acts," in *Studies in Luke-Acts*, ed. L. E. Keck and J. L. Martyn, trans. W. C. Robinson Jr. and V. P. Furnish (Nashville, TN: Abingdon, 1966).
16. Ibid., 36–37.
17. Hans Conzelmann, *The Theology of St. Luke* (New York: Harper & Row, 1960).
18. Clare K. Rothschild, *Luke-Acts and the Rhetoric of History: An Investigation of Early Christian Historiography* (WUNT 175; Tübingen: Mohr Siebeck, 2004), 42.
19. Hans Conzelmann, "Luke's Place in the Development of Early Christianity," in Keck and Martyn (eds.), *Studies*, 302–3.
20. One may find many details of Franz Camile Overbeck's views in the introductions of Zeller's *Die Apostelgeschichte* and de Wette's *Lehrbuch*.
21. John Knox, *Chapters in a Life of Paul* (New York: Abingdon-Cokesbury, 1950), 19.
22. Ibid. See also, John Knox, "'Fourteen Years Later': A Note on the Pauline Chronology," *Journal of Religion* 16 (1936): 341–49; and "The Pauline Chronology," *Journal of Biblical Literature* 58 (1939): 15–29.
23. John Dominic Crossan and Jonathan L. Reed, *In Search of Paul: How Jesus's Apostle Opposed Rome's Empire with God's Kingdom* (San Francisco: HarperSanFrancisco, 2004).
24. Ibid., 17.
25. Ibid., 19.
26. Albrecht Ritschl, *Die Entstehung der altkatholischen Kirche: eine kirchen- und dogmengeschichtliche Monographie* (Bonn: A. Marcus, 1857), 128–29.
27. Von Eduard Lekebusch, *Die Composition und Entstehung der Apostelgeschichte von Neuem untersucht* (Gotha: Perthes, 1854).
28. Joseph Ernest Renan, *History of the Origins of Christianity*, vols. 2–3 (London: Mathieson & Company, ca. 1890).
29. Joseph Barber Lightfoot, "Discoveries Illustrating the Acts of the Apostles," in *Essays on the Work Entitled "Supernatural Religion"* (London: Macmillan, 1889), 291–302; and *Dictionary of the Bible*, vol. 1 (London, 1893), 25–43. Additionally, see many of Lightfoot's commentaries on the Pauline epistles.
30. Gasque, *History*, 190–92, has a great discussion of these matters.
31. On this topic, it is interesting to read the work of Charles Kingsley Barrett, *Luke the Historian in Recent Study* (London: Epworth, 1960). Barrett's thesis is that Luke cannot really be discredited due to some of his historical anachronism where he reads the state of his own, present-day church back on to the narrative of Acts.
32. Sir William Mitchell Ramsay, *The Bearing of Recent Discovery on the Trustworthiness of the New Testament* (London: Hodder & Stoughton, 1915), 78–79.
33. Ibid., 80.
34. Ibid., 81.
35. For more on this, see Sir William Mitchell Ramsay, *The Church in the Roman Empire Before A.D. 170* (London: Hodder & Stoughton, 1893), *St. Paul the Traveler and the Roman Citizen* (London: Hodder & Stoughton, 1896), and *Historical Commentary on St. Paul's Epistle to the Galatians* (London: Hodder & Stoughton, 1899).
36. Adrian N. Sherwin-White, an expert on the Roman Empire and Roman law also believed that Acts was historically credible. In his book *Roman Society and Roman Law in the New Testament: The Sarum Lectures 1960–1961* (Oxford: Clarendon Press, 1963), he argued that "the confirmation of historicity is overwhelming" and should, without a doubt, be trusted. He criticized Bible scholars stating that their

Notes

reluctance to accept Acts is "absurd." Indeed, "Roman historians have long taken it for granted" (189). Even so, F. F. Bruce, "The Acts of the Apostles: Historical Record or Theological Reconstruction," in *Aufstieg und Niedergang Der Romischen Welt*, eds. H. Temporini and W. Haase (II.25.3; Berlin: Walter De Gruyter, 1985) claimed that Acts and Galatians were "impossible to harmonize" (2580), speaking mainly of matching Gal 1:18–20 with Acts 9:26–29. Further, Paul J. Achtemeir, *The Quest for Unity in the New Testament Church* (Minneapolis, MN: Fortress Press, 1987) has concluded that these unsolvable discrepancies are proof enough that Acts should be engaged on a theological level, not a historical one (75).

37. A controversial suggestion regarding the language of Acts was put forth by Charles Cutler Torrey, *The Composition and Date of Acts* (HTS 1; Cambridge, MA: The University of Harvard Press, 1916). He argues that Acts 1:1—15:35 is the Greek translation of an Aramaic original by an unknown Judean whose aim was to recount the beginnings and growth of the Christian church. Eventually, Luke picked this translation up, added it to his own materials (the remainder of Luke through chapter 28) and proceeded to share the final, redacted product.
38. Adolf von Harnack, *Die Apostlegeschichte, Beträge zur Einleitung in das Neue Tesament* 3 (Leipzig: J.C. Hinrichs, 1908), 222. Here I borrow the translation of Gasque, *History*, 334, n84.
39. Here again, I borrow the translation of Gasque, *History*, 335, n89.
40. Kirsopp Lake and Henry J. Cadbury, *The Beginnings of Christianity: The Acts of the Apostles*, vol. 4, eds. F. J. Foakes-Jackson and K. Lake (London: Macmillan and Co., 1933), 208.
41. Henry J. Cadbury, *The Book of Acts in History* (London: Adam and Charles Black, 1955). See also *The Making of Luke-Acts*, 2nd ed. (Peabody, MA: Hendrickson, 1999).
42. Hemer, *Book of Acts*, 66.
43. Ibid., 86.
44. Ibid., 86–87.
45. F. F. Bruce, *The Acts of the Apostles*, 2nd ed. (London: 1952), 15. See also Bruce's *Commentary on the Book of Acts* (NIC/NLC; Grand Rapids, MI: 1952).
46. Bruce, *Acts of the Apostles*, 263.
47. I. Howard Marshall, *Luke: Historian and Theologian* (CEP; Grand Rapids, MI: Zondervan), 18.
48. Ibid., 38.
49. Ibid., 75.

Chapter 8: Paul: Disputed or Undisputed?

1. For a critique of F. C. Baur on this matter, see Clare K. Rothschild, *Hebrews as Pseudepigraphon: The History and Significance of the Pauline Attribution of Hebrews* (WUNT 235; Tübingen, Mohr Siebeck, 2009), 127–29, who, as the title of her book suggests, accepts Hebrews as pseudepigraphal. Even so, she does not shy away from using the term forgery as a descriptor.
2. It is interesting, in light of this, to consider the remark in 2 Pet 3:16: "Just as he does also in all of his letters, that is, speaking in them about these things that are

Notes

difficult to understand, things which the ignorant and unstable distort—as they also do to the rest of the scriptures—to their own destruction."

3. Among scholars there has been a debate as to whether or not in antiquity an "epistle" was distinguished from a "letter." Here, however, the terms will be used interchangeably. For more on this, see the classic work of Adolf Deissmann, *Light from the Ancient East: The New Testament Illustrated by Recently Discovered Texts of the Graeco-Roman World* (London: Hodder & Stoughton, 1910), 232–46. See also William G. Doty, "The Classification of Epistolary Literature," *Catholic Biblical Quarterly* 31 (1969): 183–99.

4. See for example, Lee A. Johnson, "Paul's Epistolary Presence in Corinth: A New Look at Robert W. Funk's Apostolic *Parousia*," *Catholic Biblical Quarterly* 68/3 (July, 2006): 481–501.

5. For a discussion of this, see Donald Guthrie, *New Testament Introduction* (Downers Grove, IL: InterVarsity Press, 1970), 643–84.

6. The second edition (1805) is cited here: Edward Evanson, *The Dissonance of the Four Generally Received Evangelists and the Evidence of Their Respective Authenticity Examined*, 2nd ed. (Gloucester: D. Walker, 1805), 336.

7. See especially F. C. Baur, *Paul the Apostle of Jesus Christ, His Life and Work, His Epistles and Doctrine: A Contribution to the Critical History of Primitive Christianity*, vol. 2, trans. A. Menzies and E. Zeller (London: Williams and Norgate, 1875), 35–105.

8. Andrew T. Lincoln and A. J. M. Wedderburn, *The Theology of the Later Pauline Letters* (NTT; Cambridge: Cambridge University Press, 1993), 83. In the same volume, Lincoln's co-author, A. J. M. Wedderburn, appeals twice to majority consensus concerning the claim that Paul did not write Colossians (4 n3 and 20 n53).

9. Ibid., 83–84.

10. Lincoln says, for example, "Ephesians has many lengthy sentences . . . which extend by means of relative and participial clauses. It strings together prepositional phrases and has a fondness for synonyms, which it links by genitival constructions or piles together for emphasis" (84).

11. Andrew T. Lincoln, *Ephesians* (WBC 42; Dallas, TX: Word, 1990), lxxii.

12. Markus Barth, "Conversion and Conversation: Israel and the Church in Paul's Epistle to the Ephesians," *Interpretation: A Journal of Bible & Theology* 17 (January, 1963): 3.

13. Ibid.

14. Ibid.

15. Ibid. See also, Markus Barth, *Ephesians: Introduction, Translation, and Commentary on Chapters 1–3* (YABC 34a; New York: Doubleday and Co. Inc., 1974); and *Ephesians: Translation and Commentary on Chapters 4–6* (YABC 34b; New York: Doubleday and Co. Inc., 1974).

16. One of the earliest commentators to deny Pauline authorship of Ephesians was Ernst Theodor Mayerhoff. See his work *Der Brief an die Colosser mit vornehmlicher Berücksichtigung der drei Pastoralbriefe* (Berlin: Schultze, 1838).

17. Margaret Y. MacDonald, *Colossians and Ephesians* (Sacra Pagina 17; Collegeville, MN: Liturgical Press, 2008), 7.

18. Ibid., 7–8.

19. Ibid., 8.

20. Craig L. Blomberg, *From Pentecost to Patmos: An Introduction to Acts Through Revelation* (Nashville, TN: B&H Publishing Group, 2006), 287.

Notes

21. Ibid., 288.
22. Ibid.
23. Ibid.
24. See Johann Ernst Christian Schmidt, "Vermutungen uber die beiden Briefe an die Thassalonicher," in *Bibliothek für Kritik und Exegese des Neuen Testaments*, vol. 2 (Hadamar: 1801), 380–86; David Nicolaus Berdot, *Exercitatio theologica-exegetica in epistulam Pauli ad Titum* (Halle: Orphanotropheum, 1703); and Paul Anton, *Exegetisch Abhandlung der Pastoralbriefe St. Pauli* (Halle: 1753–1755).
25. Maarten J. J. Menken, *2 Thessalonians* (NTR; London: Routledge, 1994), 38.
26. Ibid., 39.
27. Ibid.
28. Ibid., 31.
29. Ibid.
30. Ibid., 32.
31. Ibid.
32. Ibid., 43.
33. Ibid.
34. Guthrie, *Introduction*, 573.
35. Ibid., 572.
36. Ibid.
37. Ibid.
38. Ibid.
39. Ibid., 573.
40. Ibid., 579.
41. For more on this, see Luke T. Johnson, *The First and Second Letters to Timothy: A New Translation with Introduction and Commentary* (AYBC 35a; New York: Doubleday, 2001), 13.
42. I. Howard Marshall, *The Pastoral Epistles* (ICC; Edinburgh: T&T Clark, 1999), 1. Marshall collaborated on certain portions of this book with P. H. Towner.
43. Ibid., 57.
44. Ibid.
45. Ibid., 57–58.
46. Ibid., 84.
47. Ibid. Given the absolute language used by Marshall here, it is interesting that he subtitles this portion of the chapter "Theoretical Possibilities."
48. Ibid., 58. Marshall holds this view despite the fact that, at one point, he concludes that the principal difficulty for anyone who accepts Pauline authorship "is to offer a convincing explanation of how the PE could have been composed in or around the same time as the other, undoubtedly genuine letters of Paul with their different language and style" (74).
49. Ibid., 85.
50. Ibid., 92.
51. Luke T. Johnson, *The First and Second Letters to Timothy: A New Translation with Introduction and Commentary* (YABC 35a; New York: Doubleday, 2001), 55–56. Later, Johnson cites Schleiermacher in 1807 and Eichorn in 1812 as two of the first scholars to begin this trend (63).
52. Ibid., 58.
53. Ibid.

54. Ibid., 63
55. Ibid.
56. Ibid., 92.
57. Ibid., 94.
58. Ibid., 95.
59. Ibid., 96.
60. Ibid., 97.
61. Ibid.
62. Ibid.
63. Ibid.
64. Ibid., 98.
65. Ibid., 90.
66. F. W. Farrar, *The Bible: Its Meaning and Supremacy* (London: 1901), 145.
67. On the matters of the composition, collection, and formation of the Pauline Canon as well as the topic of pseudepigraphy, see—among other volumes and in addition to those already listed in this chapter—the following works: Albert E. Barnett, *Paul Becomes A Literary Influence* (Chicago: The University of Chicago Press, 1941); Gordon J. Bahr, "Paul and Letter Writing in the Fifth Century," *Catholic Biblical Quarterly* 28 (1966): 465–77; *Apostolic History and the Gospel: Biblical and Historical Essays Presented to F. F. Bruce on his 60th Birthday*, eds. W. W. Gasque and R. P. Martin (Grand Rapids, MI: Eerdmans, 1970); Richard N. Longenecker, "Ancient Amaneuses and the Pauline Epistles," in *New Dimensions in New Testament Study*, eds. R. N. Longenecker and M. C. Tenney (Grand Rapids, MI: Zondervan, 1974), 281–97; Harry Gamble, "The Redaction of the Pauline Letters and the Formation of the Pauline Corpus," *Journal of Biblical Literature* 94 (1975): 403–18; John L. White, "Saint Paul and the Apostolic Letter Tradition," *Catholic Biblical Quarterly* 45/3 (1983): 433–44; Anthony Kenny, *A Stylometric Study of the New Testament* (Oxford: Clarendon Press, 1986); Raymond F. Collins, "Glimpses Into Some Local Churches of the New Testament Times," *Laval théologique et philosophique* 42/3 (1986): 291–316; Richard Bauckham, "Pseudo-Apostolic Letters," *Journal of Biblical Literature* 107/3 (September, 1988): 469–94; David L. Mealand, "Positional Stylometry Reassessed: Testing A Seven Epistle Theory of Pauline Authorship," *New Testament Studies* 35 (1989): 266–86; Walter Schmithals, *Paul & the Gnostics*, trans. J. E. Steely (Nashville, TN: Abingdon, 1992); *The Deutero-Pauline Letters: Ephesians, Colossians, 2 Thessalonians, 1-2 Timothy, Titus*, ed. G. Krodel (PC; Minneapolis, MN: Fortress, 1993); David Trobisch, *Paul's Letter Collection: Tracing the Origins* (Minneapolis, MN: Fortress, 1994); Jerome Murphy-O'Connor, *Paul the Letter-Writer: His World, His Options, His Skills* (GNS 41; Collegeville, MN: The Liturgical Press, 1995); David L. Mealand, "The Extent of the Pauline Corpus: A Multivariate Approach," *Journal for the Study of the New Testament* 59 (1995): 61–92; Matthew Thekkekara, *The Letters of St. Paul: The Face of Early Christianity* (Bangalore: Kristu Jyoti Publications, 1997); John B. Polhill, *Paul & His Letters* (Nashville, TN: B&H Publishers, 1999); William O Walker Jr., *Interpolations in the Pauline Letters* (JSNTSS 213; London: Sheffield Academic Press, 2001); Mark Harding, *What Are They Saying About The Pastoral Epistles?* (WATSA; Mahwah, NJ: Paulist Press, 2001); M. Luther Stirewalt Jr., *Paul, The Letter Writer* (Grand Rapids, MI: Eerdmans, 2003); George K. Barr, *Scalometry and the Pauline Epistles* (JSNTSS 261; London, T&T Clark, 2004); E. Randolph Richards,

Notes

Paul and First-Century Letter Writing: Secretaries, Composition and Collection (Downers Grove, IL: InterVarsity Press, 2004); Edwin D. Freed, *The Apostle Paul and his Letters* (London: Equinox, 2005); Stephen Finlan, *The Apostle Paul and the Pauline Tradition* (Collegeville, MN: The Liturgical Press, 2008); Brevard S. Childs, *The Church's Guide for Reading Paul: The Canonical Shaping of the Pauline Corpus* (Grand Rapids, MI: Eerdmans, 2008); *Pseudepigraphie und Verfasserfikition in fruhchristlichen Briefen*, eds. J. Frey, J. Herzer, M. Janssen, and C. K. Rothschild (WUNT 246; Tübingen: Mohr Siebeck, 2009), esp. 333–62; Richard I. Pervo, *The Making of Paul: Reconstructions of the Apostle in Early Christianity* (Minneapolis, MN: Fortress, 2010); and *The Early Reception of Paul*, ed. K. Liljeström (PFES 99; Helsinki: Finnish Exegetical Society, 2011).

Chapter 9: Our Faith(fulness) or Christ's?

1. It should be kept in mind that the specific phrase *Pistis Christou* is used as a synonym with a number of related phrases that have varied spellings such as: *pisteōs Iēsou* (Rom 3:26), *pisteōs Christou* (Gal 2:16 and Php 3:9), and *pisteōs Iēsou Christou* (Gal 2:16, 3:22 and Rom 3:22).
2. See for example James Macknight, *A New Literal Translation from the Original Greek of All the Apostolic Epistles* (London: Longman and Hurst, 1795), esp. 32, 40, 44, 71–72, 288, 294, and 349. See also J. P. Lange and F. R. Fay, *The Epistle of Paul to the Romans*, 2nd ed., trans. J. F. Hurst, P. Schaff, and M. B. Riddle (New York: Charles Scribner's Sons, 1869), esp. 129.
3. Johannes Haußleiter, *Der Glaube Jesu Christi und der christliche Glaube: Ein Beitrag zur Erflärung des Römerbriefs* (Leipzig: Georg Böhme, 1891); and "Was versteht Paulus unter christlichem Glauben?" in *Griefswalder Studien: theologische Abhandlungen Hermann Cremer zum 25 jährigen Professorjubiläum*, ed. S. Oettli (Gütersloh: C. Bertelsmann, 1895), 159–82.
4. Many commentaries and articles bring Haußleiter's views to the surface. For a concise description of these matters, see Paul Pollard, "The 'Faith of Christ' in Current Discussion," *Concordia Journal* 23/3 (July, 1997): 214–15.
5. Richard B. Hays, *The Faith of Jesus Christ: The Narrative Substructure of Galatians 3:1—4:11* (SBLDS 56; Chico, CA: Scholars Press, 1983), 162. Cf. the second edition *The Faith of Jesus Christ: The Narrative Substructure of Galatians 3:1—4:11* (TBRS; Grand Rapids, MI: Eerdmans, 2002).
6. Hays, *The Faith* (2002), xxiv.
7. Ibid., xxxix.
8. Richard B. Hays, "The Letter to the Galatians: Introduction, Commentary, and Reflections," in *The New Interpreter's Bible: Second Corinthians-Philemon*, vol. 11 (Nashville, TN: Abingdon Press, 2000), 244.
9. Hays, *The Faith* (2002), li.
10. Ibid., 211.
11. Douglas A. Campbell, "The Faithfulness of Jesus Christ in Romans 3:22," in *The Pistis Christou Debate: The Faith of Jesus Christ: Exegetical, Biblical, and Theological Studies*, eds. M. F. Bird and P. M. Sprinkle (Peabody, MA: Hendrickson, 2009), 70–71.

12. Douglas A. Campbell, "Romans 1:17—A Crux Interpretum for the ΠΙΣΤΙΣ ΧΡΙΣΤΟΥ Debate," *Journal of Biblical Literature* 1113 (1994): 273.
13. Peter G. Bolt, "The Faith of Jesus Christ in the Synoptic Gospels and Acts," in *The Pistis Christou Debate: The Faith of Jesus Christ: Exegetical, Biblical, and Theological Studies*, eds. M. F. Bird and P. M. Sprinkle (Peabody, MA: Hendrickson, 2009), 212.
14. Ibid.
15. Ibid.
16. Ibid., 213.
17. Ibid., 215.
18. Ibid.
19. Ibid.
20. Ibid., 217.
21. Ibid.
22. Ibid.
23. Ibid., 222.
24. Luke T. Johnson, "Rom 3:21–26 and the Faith of Jesus," *Catholic Biblical Quarterly* 44/1 (January, 1982): 81.
25. Ibid., 81.
26. Ibid., 89.
27. Ibid.
28. Ibid., 86.
29. Ibid., 87.
30. Ibid.
31. Ibid., 89.
32. Ibid.
33. Michael R. Whitenton, "After ΠΙΣΤΙΣ ΧΡΙΣΤΟΥ: Neglected Evidence from the Apostolic Fathers," *Journal of Theological Studies*, NS, 61/1 (April, 2010): 83.
34. Ignatius, *To the Ephesians* (16:2).
35. Polycarp, *To the Philippians* (4:3), and Hermas, *Visions* (4:1:8), *Mandates* (11:4), and *Similitudes* (6:1:2 and 6:3:6).
36. Whitenton, *After*, 108.
37. Ibid.
38. Ibid.
39. Ibid.
40. Michael F. Bird and Michael R. Whitenton, "The Faithfulness of Jesus Christ in Hippolytus's *De Christo et Antichristo*: Overlooked Patristic Evidence in the Πίστις Χριστοῦ Debate," *New Testament Studies* 55 (2009): 555.
41. Ibid., 559.
42. Ibid.
43. Ibid., 560.
44. Ibid., 561.
45. On this view, see also Gerhard Kittel, "πίστις Ἰησοῦ Χριστοῦ bei Paulus," *Theologischen Studien und Kritiken* 79 (1906): 419–36; Rudolf Bultmann, *Theology of the New Testament*, vol. 2, trans. K. Grobel, (New York: Charles Scribner's Sons; 1954); and Karl Barth, *The Epistle to the Romans*, 6th ed., trans. E. C. Hoskyns (London: Oxford University Press, 1933).
46. James D.G. Dunn, "ΕΚ ΠΙΣΤΕΩΣ: A Key to the Meaning of ΠΙΣΤΙΣ ΧΡΙΣΤΟΥ," in *The Word Leaps the Gap: Essays on Scripture and Theology in Honor of Richard*

Notes

B. Hays, eds. J. R. Wagner, C. K. Rowe, and A. K. Grieb (Grand Rapids, MI: Eerdmans, 2008): 352–56.
47. Ibid., 356.
48. Ibid., 357.
49. Ibid., 358. See: Rom 1:17 (2x); 3:26, 30; 4:16 (2x); 5:1; 9:30, 32; 10:6; 14:23 (2x); Gal 2:16; 3:7, 8, 9, 11, 12, 22, 24; 5:5.
50. Ibid., 359.
51. Ibid.
52. Ibid.
53. Ibid., 361.
54. Ibid., 366.
55. Ibid.
56. Charles E. B. Cranfield, *On Romans and Other New Testament Essays* (Edinburgh: T&T Clark, 1998), 96.
57. Ibid.
58. Ibid.
59. Ibid., 96–97.
60. Ibid., 97.
61. Ibid.
62. Ibid.
63. Ibid.
64. R. Barry Matlock, "Detheologizing the Pistis Christou Debate," *Novum Testamentum* 42 (2000): 20–23.
65. Ibid., esp. 6–17.
66. Ibid., 14–16.
67. Ibid., 11.
68. See also R. Barry Matlock, "Saving Faith: The Rhetoric and Semantics of πίστις in Paul," in *The Pistis Christou Debate*, 3–90.
69. Francis Watson, "By Faith (of Christ): An Exegetical Dilemma and its Scriptural Solution," in *The Pistis Christou Debate*, 147–55.
70. Ibid., 155–63.
71. Ibid., 159.
72. Ibid., 162–63.
73. Roy A. Harrisville III, "Before ΠΙΣΤΙΣ ΧΡΙΣΤΟΥ: The Objective Genitive As Good Greek," *Novum Testamentum* 48/4 (2006) 354–58.
74. Ibid., 354.
75. Ibid.
76. Ibid., 355.
77. Ibid., 356.
78. Roy A. Harrisville III, "ΠΙΣΤΙΣ ΧΡΙΣΤΟΥ: Witness of The Fathers," *Novum Testamentum* 36/3 (1994): 234.
79. Ibid., 240–41.
80. Among numerous others, see also James Barr, *The Semantics of Biblical Language* (Oxford: Oxford University Press, 1961), 161–205; Arland J. Hultgren, "The Pistis Christou Formulation in Paul," *Novum Testamentum* 22/3 (1980): 248–63; and Mark Elliot, "Πίστις Χριστοῦ in the Church Fathers and Beyond," in *The Pistis Christou Debate*, 277–90.

81. Sam K. Williams, "Again *Pistis Christou*," *Catholic Biblical Quarterly* 49/3 (1987): 446.
82. Ibid., 447.
83. Ibid., 446.
84. It is also worthwhile to consult Donald B. Garlington, "The Obedience of Faith in the Letter to the Romans: Part I: The meaning of *hupakoe pisteos* (Rom 1:5; 16:26)," *Westminster Theological Journal* 52 (1990): 201–24; "The Obedience of Faith in the Letter to the Romans: Part II: The Obedience of Faith and Judgment by Works," *Westminster Theological Journal* 53 (1991): 47–52; "The Obedience of Faith in the Letter to the Romans: Part III: The Obedience of Christ and the Obedience of the Christian," *Westminster Theological Journal* (1993): 87; and *The Obedience of Faith: A Pauline Phrase in Historical Context* (WUNT 2/38; Tübingen: Mohr Siebeck, 1991).
85. Mark A. Seifrid, "The Faith of Christ," in *The Pistis Christou Debate*, 145.
86. Ibid., 137.
87. Ibid., 140.
88. Ibid., 141.
89. Ibid.
90. Ibid.
91. Ibid., 144.
92. Ibid., 146.
93. Ibid.
94. Willis H. Salier, "The Obedient Son: The 'Faithfulness' of Christ in the Fourth Gospel," in *The Pistis Christou Debate*, 224–37.
95. Ibid., 225.
96. Ibid., 233.
97. Ibid., 236–37.

Chapter 10: A New Perspective on Paul

1. This statement was officially issued in 1983 by The Lutheran Church-Missouri Synod and can readily be found online.
2. This was written by Luther in 1543 and can now be found in vol. 47 of his works. For more on this matter, see Timothy F. Lull, "Luther's Writings," in *The Cambridge Companion to Martin Luther*, ed. D. K. McKim (Cambridge: Cambridge University Press, 2003), 39–61.
3. See Uwe Siemon-Netto, "The Synod's response," in The Lutheran Witness 123/4 (April, 2004): 14–15, *The Fabricated Luther: The Rise and Fall of the Shirer Myth* (St. Louis, Minn.: Concordia Publishing House, 1995); and *The Fabricated Luther: Refuting Nazi Connections and Other Modern Myths*, 2nd ed. (St. Louis, Minn.: Concordia Publishing House, 2007).
4. See vol. 51 of Luther's works.
5. Kenneth Hagen, "So You Think Luther Was a Monk? Stop It!" *Logia: A Journal of Lutheran Theology* 19/2 (Eastertide, 2010): 37.
6. Ibid.
7. Ibid.

Notes

8. For research which claims direct links between Luther and Hilter, see William L. Shirer, *The Rise and Fall of the Third Reich* (New York: Simon & Schuster, 1960); Richard Seigmann-Gall, *The Holy Reich: Nazi Conceptions of Christianity, 1919-1945* (New York: Cambridge University Press, 2003); and Emily Paras, "The Darker Side of Martin Luther," *Constructing the Past* 9/1/4 (2008): 1–12.
9. Adolf Hitler, *Mein Kampf* (New York: Houghton Miffllin Company, 1971), 213. See also Peter F. Wiener, *Martin Luther: Hitler's Spiritual Ancestor* (Cranford, NJ: American Atheist Press, 1999), ix–x.
10. James D. G. Dunn and Alan M. Suggate, *The Justice of God: A Fresh Look at the Old Doctrine of Justification by Faith* (Grand Rapids, MI: Eerdmans, 1993), 1.
11. Stephen Westerholm, *Perspectives Old and New on Paul: The 'Lutheran' Paul and His Critics* (Grand Rapids, MI: Eerdmans, 2004) 101–16, begins his discussion of modern criticism with the works of Wilhelm Wrede, *Paul* (Boston: American Unitarian Association, 1908) and Albert Schweitzer, *The Mysticism of Paul the Apostle* (New York: Seabury Press, 1931), and surprisingly overlooks F. C. Baur. Just as interesting is the fact that N. T. Wright, *What Saint Paul Really Said: Was Paul of Tarsus the Real Founder of Christianity?* (Grand Rapids, MI: Eerdmans, 1997), 12–14 begins not with Baur but with Albert Schweitzer, *Paul and His Interpreters: A Critical History* (London: Adam and Charles Black, 1912) and then jumps straightaway to Rudolf Bultmann, *Theology of the New Testament*, 2 vols., trans. K. Grobel (New York: Charles Scribners Sons, 1951–1955). Wright points out that Schweitzer was one of the first to assert that justification was not at the center of Paul's writings and theology (13).
12. Ferdinand C. Baur, *Paul the Apostle of Jesus Christ: His Life and Works, His Epistles and Teachings*, vol. 1, trans. Rev. A. Menzies (London: Williams & Norgate, 1875), 261–62.
13. Francis Watson discusses some of Baur's views as well as those of Sanders, Dunn, et al. in his *Paul, Judaism, and the Gentiles: Beyond the New Perspective*, rev. ed. (Grand Rapids, MI: Eerdmans, 2007), 27–56.
14. For more on this, see Westerholm, 123–28.
15. Hans Joachim Schoeps and Harold Knight, *Paul: the Theology of the Apostle in Light of Jewish Religious History* (Philadelphia, PA: Westminster, 1961), esp. 29 and 188.
16. Westerholm, 128.
17. Schoeps, 261–62.
18. Ibid.
19. Johannes Munck, *Paul and the Salvation of Mankind* (Richmond: John Knox Press, 1960), 49.
20. Krister Stendahl, "The Apostle Paul and the Introspective Conscience of the West," *Harvard Theological Review* 56/3 (July, 1963): 200–2.
21. Ibid., 202.
22. Ibid.
23. Ibid., 205.
24. Ibid.
25. William D. Davies, *Paul and Rabinnic Judaism: Some Rabbinic Elements in Pauline Theology* (New York: Harper & Row, 1970), 71. The original edition was published three years earlier in 1967.
26. Ibid., 74–75.

27. William D. Davies, "Paul and the Law: Reflections on Pitfalls in Interpretations," in *Paul and Paulinism*, eds. M. D. Hooker and S. G. Wilson (London: SPCK, 1982), 12.
28. William D. Davies, "Paul and the People of Israel," *New Testament Studies* 24 (1977–78): 22.
29. Ed P. Sanders, *Paul and Palestinian Judaism* (Philadelphia, PA: Fortress, 1977), 75.
30. Michael B. Thompson, *The New Perspective on Paul* (GBS 26; Cambridge: Grove Books Limited, 2010), 8.
31. Here I am following Kent L. Yinger, *The New Perspective on Paul: An Introduction* (Eugene, OR: Wipf and Stock, 2011), 30–31.
32. Sanders, *Paul*, xi.
33. James D. G. Dunn, "The New Perspective on Paul," given as The Manson Memorial Lecture delivered at the University of Manchester, England, November 4, 1982. The original document can readily be located online at a number of websites and an updated form can be found in James D. G. Dunn, *Jesus, Paul, and the Law: Studies in Mark and Galatians* (Louisville, KY: Westminster John Knox, 1990), 183–214, and *The New Perspective on Paul*, rev. ed. (Grand Rapids, MI: Eerdmans, 2008), 99–120.
34. Dunn, "The New Perspective" (original lecture), 4.
35. Ibid., 8.
36. Dunn, *Jesus, Paul, and the Law*, 190.
37. Dunn, "The New Perspective" (original lecture), 7.
38. Yinger, *New*, 23.
39. James D. G. Dunn, "Romans 7:14–25 in the Theology of Paul," in *Essays on Apostolic Themes: Studies in Honor of: Howard Ervin*, ed. P. Elbert (Peabody, MA: Hendrickson, 1985), 50.
40. Ibid., 49–52.
41. Ibid., 49–58. He is referring mainly to W. G. Kümel, *Römer 7 und die Bekehrunng des Paulus* (Leipzig: Hinrichs, 1929), esp. ch. 4.
42. See for example, Yinger, 60–63.
43. Dunn, "Romans 7," 59.
44. Ibid.
45. Ibid., 64.
46. Ibid., 68.
47. Ibid., 70.
48. N. T. Wright, *The Climax of the Covenant: Christ and the Law in Pauline Theology* (Minneapolis, MN: Fortress, 1991), 261. See also, *What Saint Paul Really Said*.
49. Ibid.
50. Ibid.
51. Ibid.
52. Wright, *What Saint Paul Really Said*, 115.
53. Ibid., 113.
54. Ibid., 131.
55. Ibid.
56. Ibid.
57. Ibid.
58. Ibid., 132.

Notes

59. Terence L. Donaldson, *Paul and the Gentiles: Remapping the Apostle's Convictional World* (Minneapolis, MN: Fortress, 1997), 157.
60. These views can be found in full within *Paul and the Gentiles*, 125-26. Here, I cite the nice summary provided by Gerhard H. Visscher, *Romans 4 and the New Perspective on Paul: Faith Embraces the Promise* (SBL 122; New York: Peter Lang, 2009), 31.
61. Don Garlington, *In Defense of the New Perspective on Paul: Essays and Reviews* (Eugene, OR: Wipf and Stock, 2005), 9-14.
62. Ibid., 2-8.
63. Yinger, 87.
64. Ibid., 88.
65. Ibid.
66. Ibid.
67. Ibid.
68. Ibid., 89.
69. Ibid.
70. Ibid., 90.
71. Ibid., 91.
72. Ibid.
73. Ibid.
74. Ibid., 92-93.
75. See also Heikki Räisänen, *Paul and the Law* (WUNT 29; Tübingen, Mohr Siebeck, 1987), John G. Gager, *Reinventing Paul* (Oxford: Oxford University Press, 2000); Simon J. Gathercole, *Where is Boasting? Early Jewish Soteriology and Paul's Response in Romans 1-5* (Grand Rapids, MI: Eerdmans, 2002); and "What Did Paul Really Mean?" *Christianity Today* 51 (August, 2007): 22-28 and Francis Watson, *Paul, Judaism, and the Gentiles*.
76. Lloyd Gaston, *Paul and the Torah* (Vancouver: University of British Columbia Press, 1987), 140.
77. See also Bultmann, *Theology of the New Testament*; Charles E. B. Cranfield, "St. Paul and the Law," *Scottish Journal of Theology* 17 (1964): 43-68; *A Critical and Exegetical Commentary on the Epistle to the Romans*, 2 vols. (ICC; Edinburgh: T&T Clark, 1975-1979); Peter Stuhlmacher, *Gottes Gerechtigkeit bei Paulus* (FRLANT; Göttingen: Vandenhoeck & Ruprecht, 1965); "'Das Ende des Gesetzes': Über Ursprung and Ansatz der paulinischen Theologie," *Zeitschrift für Theologie und Kirche* 67 (1970): 14-39; Ernst Käsemann, *Perspectives on Paul* (Philadelphia, PA: Fortress, 1971); *Commentary on Romans* (London: SCM, 1980); Seyoon Kim, *The Origin of Paul's Gospel* (WUNT; Tubingen: J. C. B. Mohr (Paul Siebeck) 1981); *Paul and the New Perspective: Second Thoughts on the Origin of Paul's Gospel* (Grand Rapids, MI: Eerdmans, 2002); Andrew A. Das, *Paul, the Law, and the Covenant* (Grand Rapids, MI: Hendrickson, 2001); Stephen Westerholm, *Perspectives Old and New on Paul*.
78. Mark A. Seifrid, *Christ, Our Righteousness: Paul's Theology of Justification* (Downers Grove, IL: InterVarsity Press, 2000), 74.
79. Mark A. Seifrid, "Blind Alleys in the Controversy over the Paul of History," *Tyndale Bulletin* 45 (1994): 74.
80. Ibid., 75.
81. Ibid, 95.

82. Stephen Westerholm, *Perspectives Old and New on Paul: The 'Lutheran' Paul and His Critics* (Grand Rapids, MI: Eerdmans, 2004).

Chapter 11: From Peter's House to James's Tomb and Beyond

1. For an overview of this story, see Eric H. Cline, *Biblical Archaeology: A Very Short Introduction* (Oxford: Oxford University Press, 2009), 55-58.
2. The statuette was found by Stager in the layer of Bronze II debris at the Ashkelon site.
3. Jacqueline Schaalje, "Archaeology in Israel: Ashkelon" at http://www.jewishmag.com/41mag/ashkelon /ashkelon.htm. Accessed 06.20.11.
4. See for example George A. Smith, *The Historical Geography of the Holy Land* (London: Hodder & Stoughton, 1894). See also Lyman Coleman, *An Historical Geography of the Bible* (Philadelphia, PA: E. H. Butler & Co., 1850); Gershon Galil, Zekharyah Kalai, and Moshe Weinfeld, *Studies in Historical Geography and Biblical Historiography* (SVT 81; Leiden: Brill, 2000); Edwin Aiken, *Scriptural Geography: Portraying the Holy Land* (London: I.B. Taurus, 2010); Zekharyah Kalai, *Historical Geography of the Bible: The Tribal Territories of Israel* (Jerusalem: Magness Press, 1986); and Howard F. Vos, *Wycliffe Historical Geography of Bible Lands* (Grand Rapids, MI: Hendricksen, 2003).
5. For example, the wine jug inscribed with Herod's name, the tomb of Herod, Masada and its many artifacts, etc., could all be discussed. A great starting point for these matters are Yadin Roman, *Masada: Kings' Stronghold, Zealots' Refuge* (ERETZ Ha-Tzvi, Inc., 1997). See also, National Geographic Channel, *Herod's Lost Tomb*. DVD. Directed by Madman Entertainment. Australia, 2010.
6. The list is said to include fragments of Heb 11, 1 Cor 8-10, Matthew, Rom 9-10, and Luke from 2 CE along with a fragment of Mark from 1 CE. Thanks to Dr. Fred Long of Asbury Theological Seminary for this data. CNN also reported on this at http://www.youtube.com/watch?v=Hs6PmAvzQj0. Accessed online on 03.06.12.
7. This appears to be part of "The Green Project" which can be read about at http://explorepassages.com/collection. Accessed online on 03.06.12.
8. See for example, *Prosopographia Imperii Romani saec.* II, eds. E. Groag, A. Stein, L. Petersen, M. Heil, and K. Wachtel (Leipzig: Walter de Gruyter, 1933), 237, Tacitus, *Annals* [15.73], *Sylloge Inscriptionum Graecarum*, eds. W. Dittenberger and F. F. H. von Gaertringen (Leipzig: Hirzel, 1915-1924), 801D.
9. See Jerome Murphy-O'Connor, *St. Paul's Corinth: Texts and Archaeology* (Wilmington, DE: Michael Glazier, Inc., 1983), 143. See also Joseph A. Fitzmyer, *The Acts of the Apostles* (YABC 31; New York: Doubleday, 1998) who claims that the Gallio Inscription "supplies a rare peg on which to hang . . . absolute chronology" (621). For more on Paul during the reign of Claudius see F. F. Bruce, "Christianity Under Claudius," *Bulletin of the John Rylands Library* 44 (March, 1962): 309-26.
10. Many New Testament scholars have attempted to equate Suetonius's statement with Dio 60.6.6-7. See for instance Gerd Luedemann, *Paul, Apostle to the Gentiles: Studies in Chronology* (Philadelphia, PA: Fortress, 1984). However, Dixon Slingerland, "Suetonius Claudius 25.4 and the Account in Cassius Dio," *Jewish Quarterly Review* 79/4 (1989): 305-22; "Suetonius Claudius 25.4, Acts 18, and Paulus Orosius' *Historium adversum pagans* libri VII: Dating the Claudian Expulsion(s) of the Roman Jews," *Jewish Quarterly Review* 83/1-2 (1992): 127-44;

Notes

"Chrestus: Cristus?" in *The Literature of Early Rabbinic Judaism: Issues in Talmudic Reaction and Interpretation*, ed. A. J. Avery-Peck, (Lanham, MD: University Press of America, 1989), 133–44; and "Acts 18:1–17 and Luedemann's Pauline Chronology," *Journal of Biblical Literature* 109/4 (1990): 686–90, has shown the problems that relating these two texts creates. He contends that 60.6.6-7 refers to an attempted return of the Jews to Rome in which they were turned away "again." Thus, 57.18.5a refers to the initial event.

11. For more on this see David A. Cineira, *Die Religions-Politik Des Kaisers Claudius Und Die Paulinische Mission* (HBS; Freiburg: Herder, 1999), 212–14. It is curious that Cineira appears to adopt a date of 51–52 CE for Gallio being in office but still says (my translation): "At some point between (51–52 CE) Paul must have confronted Gallio. If we go back eighteen months, i.e., up to the period that Paul stayed in Corinth, we will see that Paul came to Corinth in the winter of 49–50, where Priscilla and Aquila, since the late autumn of 49 CE had without a doubt already set up shop" (212).

12. See also, Tacitus, *Annals* 12.69, 13.2.6; Suetonius, *Nero* 9; and Dio 60.35.2–4.

13. See also Dio Cassius, *Roman History* 60.6.6.

14. See Josiah Osgood, *Claudius Caesar: Image and Power in the Early Roman Empire* (Cambridge: Cambridge University Press, 2011).

15. For some discussion of texts, images, and dates of Roman Imperial Coinage (RIC) among other data, see http://wildwinds.com/coins/ric/claudius/i.html. Database accessed online on 03.06.12. For other data, see Gaston Deschamps and Georges Cousins, "Emplacement et ruines de la ville de Kys en Carie," *Bulletin de correspondance hellénique* 11 (1887): 306–7; *L'Année épigraphique* 147 (1973), 149 (1973), and 155 (1973) = Giordano 187 no. 6 (1971); C. Zangemeister, *Corpus Inscriptionum Latinarum* (1898), IV. 3340 tab. IV, IV. 5512, and XCI .1 = Smallwood no. 295.

16. For a plethora of sources related to this matter, see Kenneth S. Gapp, "Notes: The Universal Famine Under Claudius," *Harvard Theological Review* 28/4 (October, 1935): 258–65.

17. Some scholars believe that the "revelation" referred to in Gal 2:1–2, which piqued Paul's interest in going to Jerusalem, may be related to a vision of a famine. On this, see Ben Witherington III, *Grace in Galatia: A Commentary on Paul's Letter to the Galatians* (Grand Rapids, MI: Eerdmans, 1998), 131–35.

18. H. A. Seaby, *Roman Silver Coins*, vol. 2, 3rd ed., Rev. R. Loosley (London: Seaby, 1979), 7. See also David R. Sear, *Roman Coins and Their Values*, 4 vols. (London: Spink, 2000), 370–71. For great renderings of many of these important Claudian coins, see Richard J. Plant, *Roman Base Metal Coins: A Price Guide* (Torquay: Rotographic/Predecimal, 2006), 14–15; and *Roman Silver Coins: A Price Guide* (London: Rotographic, 2006), 32.

19. For a discussion of the Isthmian Games in relation to Paul see Oscar Broneer, "Paul and the Pagan Cults at Isthmia," *Harvard Theological Review* 64 (1971): 169–87; and "The Apostle Paul and the Isthmian Games," *Biblical Archaeologist* 25 (1962): 1–31. See also Allen B. West, *Corinth VIII, Part II: Latin Inscriptions, 1896–1926* (Corinth Series; New Jersey: American School of Classical Studies at Athens, 1931), esp. 31, 54, and 70–2. In addition, see Daniel J. Geagan, "Notes of the Agonistic Institutions of Roman Corinth," in *Greek, Roman and Byzantine Studies* 9 (1968): 71–75.

20. Part of the trouble here is that different researchers have translated/interpreted the first and third sets of numbers differently (the middle number, that is, "consul for the fifth time" appears uncontested. However, scholars have argued that tribunician power here can refer either the ninth, tenth, eleventh, or twelfth year. Likewise, for the imperial acclamation, the twenty-second, twenty-third, twenty-fourth, twenty-fifth, twenty-sixth, and twenty-seventh have been suggested. It fits nicely within our timeline if we accept the eleventh tribunician year, consul for the fifth time, and the twenty-sixth acclamation to have all taken place in 50 CE. This, then, would also avoid the conclusion of Murphy-O'Connor, *St. Paul's Corinth* (143) that Frontinus (*Aq.* 1.13) was wrong on account of scribal error. For several among a host of different interpretations see: David Braund, *Augustus to Nero: A Sourcebook on Roman History, 31 BC–AD 68* (London: Croom Helm, 1985), 86; Brian W. Jones and R. D. Milns, *The Use of Documentary Evidence in the Study of Roman Imperial History* (SAC; Syndey: Sydney University Press, 1984); J. S. Wacher, *The Coming of Rome* (BBC; London: Routledge & Kegan Paul, 1979); and Robert K. Sherk, *The Roman Empire: Augustus to Hadrian* (New York: Cambridge University Press, 1988), 100. For this and other reconstructed texts and inscriptions see M. P. Charlesworth, *Documents Illustrating the Reigns of Claudius & Nero* (Cambridge: Cambridge University Press, 1939); and E. Mary Smallwood, *Documents Illustrating the Principates of Gaius Claudius & Nero* (Bristol: Bristol Classical Press, 1984).

21. Again, I am following Seaby, *Roman Coins* here.

22. Contra Mark Humphries, *Early Christianity* (CF; London: Routledge, 2006), 130.

23. See especially A. A. Barrett, "Claudius' British Victory Arch in Rome," *Britannia* 22 (1991): 15–16; and Barbara Levick, *Claudius* (New Haven, CT: Yale University Press, 1990), 72.

24. Emile Bourguet, *De rebus Delphicis imperatoriae aetatis capita duo* (Montpellier: C. Coulet et. Fils, 1905).

25. For more on the piecing together of these fragments, see A. Brassac, "Une inscription de Delphes et la chronologie de saint Paul," *Revue Biblique* 22 (1913): 36–53; A. Plassart, "L'inscription de Delphes mentionnant le proconsul Gallion," *Revue des Etudes Greques* 80 (1967): 372–78; J. H. Oliver, "The Epistle of Claudius which mentions the Proconsul Junius Gallio," *Hesperia* 40 (1971): 239–40; and Murphy-O'Connor, *St. Paul's Corinth*, 141 and 173–76.

26. See Murphy-O'Connor, *St. Paul's Corinth*, 141–42.

27. See also Pliny, *Natural Histories* 31.62.

28. See Acts 27:9, 28:11; Pliny, *Natural Histories*, 2:47; Suetonius, *Claudius* 18; Josephus, *Jewish Wars*, 2:200–3.

29. See D. I. Pallas and S. Dantis, "Ἐπιγραφές ἀπὸ τὴν Κόρινθον," *Ephemeris Archaiologike*. Athens. (1977): 75–76, no. 19; P. M. Fraser and E. Matthews, *A Lexicon of Greek Personal Names* (Oxford: Oxford University Press, 1987). This lexicon is now online and its databases can be accessed and searched at http:// www.lgpn.ox.ac.uk/database/lgpn.php. Accessed online on 03.07.12. See also Andrew D. Clarke, "Another Corinthian Erastus Inscription," *Tyndale Bulletin* 42/1 (May, 1991): 146–51; Justin Meggitt, "The Social Status of Erastus (Rom 16:23)," *Novum Testamentum* 23 (1996): 218–23; and *Paul, Poverty and Survival* (Edinburgh: T&T Clark, 1998), 139–40, n. 345; A. D. Rizakis, S. Zoumbaki, and M. Kantirea, *Roman Peloponnese I: Roman Personal Names in the Social Context*

Notes

(Achaia, Arcadia, Argolis, Corinthia and Eleia) (Athens: Kentron Hellenikes kai Romaikes archaiotetos, ethnikon Hidryma Erunon, 2001), no. 651.

30. See Meggitt, "The Social Status" (218–23); and Steven J. Friesen, "The Wrong Erastus: Ideology, Archaeology, and Exegesis," in *Corinth in Context: Comparative Studies on Religion and Society*, eds. S. J. Friesen, D. N. Schowalter, and J. C. Walters (Leiden: Brill, 2010), 231–56.
31. Friesen, "Wrong Erastus," 242.
32. For example, the terms *agoranomos, aedile*, and *quaestor*, among others, have all been candidates. Most notably see Gerd Theissen, *The Social Setting of Pauline Christianity: Essays on Corinth* (Philadelphia, PA: Fortress Press, 1982), esp. 81–83. See also Friesen, "Wrong Erastus."
33. For those who view Erastus as a social elite of Paul's church, see Theissen, *The Social Setting*; David J. K. Gill, "Erastus the *Aedile*," *Tyndale Bulletin* 40 (1989): 293–301; Clarke, "Another Corinthian Erastus," and John K. Goodrich, "Erastus, Quaestor of Corinth: The Administrative Rank of ὁ οἰκονόμος τῆς πόλεως (Rom 16.23) in an Achaean Colony," *New Testament Studies* 56 (2010): 90–115; and "Erastus of Corinth (Romans 16.23): Responding to the Recent Proposals on his Rank, Status, and Faith," *New Testament Studies* 57 (2011): 583–93. For those who understand Erastus to be poor and unrelated to the Pauline mission, see Meggitt, *Paul, Poverty and Survival*; as well as Friesen, "Wrong Erastus."
34. Already in 1931, two years after the discovery of the Erastus Inscription, Henry J. Cadbury, "Erastus of Corinth," *Journal of Biblical Literature* 50 (1931): 42–58 was denying that this was a reference to the Erastus of the New Testament.
35. For more on this see Paul Foster, *The Apocryphal Gospels: A Very Short Introduction* (New York: Oxford University Press, 2009), 26–60.
36. James M. Robinson, *The Nag Hammadi Library in English* (CGLP; New York: Harper & Row, 1977).
37. See for example, Bart D. Ehrman, *Lost Scriptures: Books That Did Not Make it Into the New Testament* (New York: Oxford University Press, 2003); *Lost Christianities: The Battle for Scripture and the Faiths We Never Knew* (New York: Oxford University Press, 20003); *The Lost Gospel of Judas Iscariot: A New Look at Betrayer and Betrayed* (New York: Oxford University Press, 2006); and with Zlatko Pleše, *The Apocryphal Gospels: Texts and Translations* (New York: Oxford University Press, 2011). See also Elaine H. Pagels, *The Johannine Gospel in Gnostic Exegesis: Heracleon's Commentary on John* (Nashville, TN: Abingdon Press, 1973); *The Gnostic Paul: Gnostic Exegesis of the Pauline Letters* (Philadelphia, PA: Fortress Press, 1975); *The Gnostic Gospels* (New York: Random House, 1979); *Beyond Belief: The Secret Gospel of Thomas* (New York: Random House, 2003); and with Karen L. King, *Reading Judas: The Gospel of Judas and the Shaping of Christianity* (New York: Viking, 2007); and also with Charles W. Hedrick, *Nag Hammadi Codices XI, XII, XIII* (Leiden: E.J. Brill, 1990).
38. I am referring here to the earlier 1897 discovery of the Oxyrhynchus Papyri. For more on this, see Stephen J. Patterson, "The Oxyrhynchus Papyri: The Remarkable Discovery You've Probably Never Heard Of," *Biblical Archaeology Review* 37/2 (March/April, 2011): 8 Pp.
39. Sean Martin, *The Gnostics: The First Christian Heretics* (Harpenden, Herts: Pocket Essentials, 2006), 80.
40. Ibid.

Notes

41. Ibid., 80–1.
42. The works of April DeConick are quite insightful when it comes to these matters. See April D. DeConick, *Recovering the Original Gospel of Thomas: A History of the Gospel and Its Growth* (London: T&T Clark, 2005); *The Original Gospel of Thomas in Translation: With A Commentary and New English Translation of the Complete Gospel* (JSNTSS 287; London: T&T Clark, 2005); *The Thirteenth Apostle: What the Gospel of Judas Really Says* (New York: Continuum, 2007); and *The Codex Judas Papers*, ed. A. D. DeConick (NHMS 71; Leiden: Brill, 2009).
43. Some have suggested that two portions of Mark's Gospel, namely, Mk 4:28 (=7Q6), 6:52–53 (=7Q5), and a fragment of James 1:23–24 (=7Q8), along with 1 Tim 3:16 (=7Q4) have been found but these claims are highly contentious. For more on this, see J. O'Callaghan, "Papìros neotestamentarios en la vueva 7 de Qumrân?" *Biblica* 53 (1972): 91–100. For a discussion of those who agree and disagree with O'Callaghan, see J. A. Fitzmeyer, *The Dead Sea Scrolls: Major Publications and Tools for Study* (SBLRBS 20; Atlanta, GA: Scholars Press, 1990), 168–72; and Robert H. Gundry, "No NU in Line 2 of 7Q5: A Final Disidentification of 7Q5 with Mark 6:52–53," *Journal of Biblical Literature* 118 (1999): 698–707.
44. Zvi Gal, *Qumran: Scrolls in the Desert* (Israel: Ostracon Press, 2010), 21.
45. Ibid., 22.
46. Eleazar Lipa Sukenik, *The Dead Sea Scrolls of the Hebrew University* (Jerusalem: Magnes Press, Hebrew University, 1955). See also, Roland de Vaux, *Archaeology and the Dead Sea Scrolls* (SL; London: Oxford University Press, 1973); *The Message of the Scrolls* (New York: Simon and Schuster, 1957), 1958; Yigael Yadin, *The Scroll of War of the Sons of Light Against the Sons of Darkness* (London: Oxford University Press, 1962); *The Temple Scroll: The Hidden Law of the Dead Sea Sect* (New York: Random House, 1985); and with Chaim Rabin, *Aspects of the Dead Sea Scrolls* (Jerusalem: Magnes Press, Hebrew University (1965); Magen Broshi, *Psalms Scroll from Qumran* (Jerusalem: Israel Museum, 1986); *The Shrine of the Book* (Jerusalem: Israel Museum, 1991); and with James C. VanderKam, *Qumran Cave 4. XIV: Parabiblical Texts, Part 2* (Oxford: Clarendon Press, 1995); Ben-Zion Eshel, *The Dead Sea Region* (Jerusalem: Kiryath-Sepher, 1958); and Hanan Eshel, *The Dead Sea Scrolls and the Hasmonean State* (Jerusalem: Yad Ben-Zvi Press, 2008). Additionally, see James H. Charlesworth, *Caves of Enlightenment: Proceedings of the American Schools of Oriental Research Dead Sea Scrolls Jubilee Symposium (1947–1997)* (ASOR; North Richland Hills, TX: BIBAL Press, 1998).
47. David Stacey, "Some Archaeological Observations on the Aqueducts of Qumran," *Dead Sea Discoveries* 14/2 (2007): 222–43; and "Seasonal Industries at Qumran," *Bulletin of the Anglo-Israel Archaeological Society* 26 (2008): 7–29.
48. Yizhar Hirschfeld, *Qumran in Context: Reassessing the Archaeological Evidence* (Peabody, MA: Hendrickson, 2004).
49. Norman Golb, *Who Wrote the Dead Sea Scrolls? The Search for the Secret of Qumran* (New York: Scribner, 1995). For more on this, see some of the works listed three notes back as well.
50. See Rachel Elior, *Zikaron u-nešiyah: sodan šel megilot Midbar Yehudah* (Jerusalem: Mekon Wan Lir bi-Yerushalayim, 2009).
51. See Helen K. Bond, *Pontius Pilate in History and Interpretation*. Doctoral thesis, Durham University. Available at Durham E-Theses Online: http://etheses.dur.ac.uk/967/ (1994), esp. 35–36; and the later publication of this dissertation *Pontius Pilate in History and Interpretation* (Cambridge: Cambridge University Press).

Notes

52. For various renderings, see E. Weber, "Zur Inschrift des Pontius Pilatus," *Bonner Jahrbücher* 171 (1971): 194-200; A. Degrassi, "Sull'iscrizione di Ponzio Pilato," *Rendiconti dell' Accademia Nazionale dei Lincei, ser. 8: classe di Scienze morali, storiche e filologiche* 19 (1964): 59-65; S. Bartina, "Poncio Pilato en una inscripción monumentaria Palestinense," *Cultura bíblica* 19 (1962): 170-75; C. Gatti, "A propositio di una rilettura dell'epigrafe di Ponzio Pilato," *Aevum* 55 (1981): 13-21; A. Frova, "L'iscrizione di Ponzio Pilato a Cesarea," *Rendiconti dell'Istituto Lombardo* 95 (1961): 419-34; L. Boffo, *Iscrizioni greche e latine per lo studio della Bibbia* (Brescia: Paideia Editrice, 1994), 217-33; J. P. Lémonon, *Pilate et le gouvernement de la Judée: texts et monuments* (Eb; Paris: J. Gabalda, 1981); V. Burr, "Epigraphischer Beitrag zur neuren Pontius-Pilatus-Forschung," in *Vergangenheit, Gegenwart, Zukunft*, ed. W. Burr (Würzburg: Echter, 1972), 37-41; G. Labbé, "Ponce Pilate et la munificence de Tibère: l'inscription de Césarée," *Revue des études anciennes* 93 (1991): 277-97; and "Ponce Pilate," in *Palestine in the Time of Jesus: Social Structures and Social Conflicts*, ed. K. C. Hanson and D. E. Oakman (Minneapolis, MN: Fortress, 1998), 78; G. Alföldy, "Pontius Pilatus und das Tiberieum von Caesarea Maritima," *Scripta Classica Israelica* 18 (1999): 85-108; I. Di Stefano Manzella, "Pontius Pilatus nell'iscrizione di Cesarea di Palestina," in *Le iscrizioni dei cristiani in Vaticano: Materiali e contribute scientific per una mostra epigrafica*, ed. I. Di Stefano Manzella (ISS 2; Vatican City: Edizioni Quasar, 1997), 209-15.
53. Here, the backslashes represent a new line.
54. Alföldy, "Pontius Pilatus" (106-7); Craig A. Evans, "Excavating Caiaphas, Pilate, and Simon of Cyrene: Assessing the Literary and Archaeological Evidence," in *Jesus and Archaeology*, ed. J. H. Charlesworth (Grand Rapids, MI: Eerdmans, 2006), 336-37 follows this view.
55. For more on this see A. Raban and E. Linder, Caesarea, the Herodian Harbour," *International Journal of Nautical Archaeology and Underwater Exploration* 7 (1978): 238-43; R. L. Hohlfelder, "Caesarea Beneath the Sea," *Biblical Archaeology Review* 8/3 (1982): 42-47, 56; and with J. P. Oleson, A. Raban, R. L. Vann, "Sebastos, Herod's Harbour at Caesarea Maritima," *Biblical Archaeologist* 46 (1983): 133-43; L. Vann, "Herod's Harbor Construction Recovered Underwater," *Biblical Archaeology Review* 9/3 (1983): 10-14.
56. A handful of texts from Tacitus have also been used to shed light on Pilate, namely *Annals* 1.80; 2.6, 83; 4.5; and *History* 5.9.
57. So Keith N. Schoville, "Top Ten Major Archaeological Discoveries of the Twentieth Century Relating to the Biblical World," *Stone-Campbell Journal* 4 (Spring, 2001): 21-22.
58. Steven Feldman and Nancy E. Roth, "The Short List: The New Testament Figures Known to History," *Biblical Archaeology Review* 28/6 (November/December, 2002): 34-37.
59. Jerry Vardaman, "A New Inscription Which Mentions Pilate As 'Prefect,'" in *Journal of Biblical Literature* 81 (1962): 70-1.
60. Craig A. Evans, *Jesus and the Ossuaries: What Jewish Burial Practices Reveal About the Beginning of Christianity* (Waco, TX: Baylor University Press, 2003), 91-115, lists at least seven ossuary discoveries not mentioned here that are related to New Testament studies: The Nicanor Ossuary Inscription (1902), the Jesus Son of Joseph Ossuary (1926), the Alexander Son of Simon Ossuary (1941), the Qorban Ossuary (1956), the Yehohanan Ossuary (1968), and the House of David Ossuary

(1971). I would add to these the already mentioned Herod's Tomb discovered in 2007 and possibly the Tomb of Annas (2000).
61. Hershel Shanks, *In the Temple of Solomon and the Tomb of Caiaphas* (Washington, DC: Biblical Archaeology Society, 1993), 35.
62. Golan was subsequently arrested on suspicion of fraud and taken to trial under accusations leveled by the Israeli Antiquities Authority, who released a statement asserting that the ossuary was fake. Notes from the trial can be obtained at the following link: http://www.bibleinterp.com/PDFs/Authenticity_Letter.pdf. Accessed online on 03.08.11.
63. Hershel Shanks and Ben Witherington III, *The Brother of Jesus: The Dramatic Story & Meaning of the First Archaeological Link to Jesus & His Family* (San Francisco: HarperSanFrancisco, 2003), esp. 11–14.
64. William D. Barrick, "Curiosities or Evidence? The James Ossuary and the Jehoash Inscription," *Master's Seminary Journal* 14/1 (Spring, 2003): 2.
65. André Lemaire, "Burial Box of James the Brother of Jesus: Earliest Archaeological Evidence of Jesus Found in Jerusalem," in *Biblical Archaeological Review* 28/6 (November, 2002): 24–33.
66. André Lemaire, "Epigraphy—and the Lab—Say It's Genuine," in *Biblical Archaeology Review* 28/06 (November/December, 2002): 28–29.
67. See Jodi Magness, "Ossuaries and the Burials of Jesus and James," *Journal of Biblical Literature* 124/1 (2005), who asserts that "the controversy surrounding the 'James ossuary' reflects a fundamental and widespread misconception about the function and social context of ossilegium in the late Second Temple period Judaism. There should be no controversy. Even if the inscription is authentic and is not a modern forgery, this ossuary did not contain the bones of James the Just, the brother of Jesus" (154).
68. Byron R. McCane, "The Bones of James Unpacked," in *Resurrecting the Brother of Jesus: The James Ossuary Controversy and the Quest for Religious Relics*, eds. R. Byrne and B. McNary-Zak (Chapel Hill, NC: University of North Carolina Press, 2009), 26.
69. Ibid., 26–29.
70. Jonathan L. Reed, "Objects, Faith, and Archaeoporn," in *Resurrecting the Brother of Jesus*, 204.
71. Eric Meyers, "The James Ossuary Yet Again" accessed online on 03.08.12 at http://www.bibleinterp.com/articles/Ossuary_Again.shtml.
72. Ibid.
73. Eric Meyers, "Well-known Israeli Archeologist Casts More Doubt on Authenticity of James Ossuary" accessed online on 03.08.12 at http://www.bibleinterp.com/articles/Meyers_More_Doubt.shtml. See also remarks made by Frank M. Cross in the work of Joseph Green, "Here at Six Divinity Avenue," *Semitic Museum News* 6/2 (February, 2003): 5; and Paul V. M. Flesher, "The Aramaic Dialect of the James Ossuary Inscription," *Aramaic Studies* 2/1 (2004): 37–55.
74. Flesher, "The Aramaic Dialect," 38.
75. René A. López, "Does the Jesus Family Tomb Disprove His Physical Resurrection?" *Bibliotheca Sacra* 165 (October-December, 2008): 427.
76. Ibid.
77. Simcha Jacobivici and Charles Pellegrino, *The Jesus Family Tomb: The Evidence Behind the Discovery No One Wanted to Find* (San Francisco, CA: HarperOne, 2007), 213–34. James D. Tabor, *The Jesus Dynasty: The Hidden History of Jesus,*

Notes

His Royal Family and the Birth of Christianity (New York: Simon and Schuster, 2006), once asserted that Jesus was not married and that such claims were "short on evidence" and little more than "gripping fiction" (4). Since 2006, however, he has changed his mind. For more on this see Lopez, "Does the Jesus Family Tomb Disprove," esp. 432–33.

78. Shimon Gibson, "Is the Talpiot Tomb Really the Family Tomb of Jesus?" *Near Eastern Archaeology* 69/3–4 (2006): 23.
79. Ibid.
80. Ibid.
81. Robert M. Price, "A Crowded but Empty Tomb: The Skeptical Eye," *Humanist* 67/3 (May/June, 2007) has asserted that the James Ossuary and the Jesus Family Tomb findings either stand or fall together. He notes, "Both identifications depend upon name and population statistics. Both sets of artifacts have the same physical characteristics, such as patina quality. . . . the James ossuary and others very likely come from the same recently documented site. . . . And at Talpiot, there were empty spaces set aside for three more ossuaries. . . . One thing's for sure: you have no business appealing to the James box as proof of a historical Jesus if you don't also accept a larger family unit including Mrs. Christ and their progeny" (46). A number of works have been written to disprove the claims of Jacobivici and others. See for example, Darrell L. Bock and Daniel B. Wallace, *Dethroning Jesus: Exposing Popular Culture's Quest to Unseat the Biblical Christ* (Nashville, TN: Thomas Nelson, 2007), 193–213; Dillon Burroughs, *The Jesus Family Tomb Controversy: How the Evidence Falls Short* (Ann Arbor, MI: Nimble, 2007); Gary R. Habermas, *The Secret of the Talpiot Tomb: Unravelling the Mystery of the Jesus Family Tomb* (Nashville, TN: Broadman & Holman, 2007); *Buried Hope or Risen Savior: The Search for the Jesus Tomb*, ed. Charles L. Quarles (Nashville, TN: Broadman & Holman, 2008); James R. White, *From Toronto to Emmaus: The Empty Tomb and the Journey from Skepticism to Faith* (Birmingham, AL: Solid Ground Christian, 2007).
82. Shanks, *In the Temple*, 35.
83. Helen K. Bond, *Caiaphas: Friend of Rome and Judge of Jesus?* (Louisville, KY: Westminster John Knox, 2004), 5.
84. Ibid.
85. Ibid., 7–8.
86. Ibid., 8.
87. Ibid. See also Rainer Metzner, *Kaiphas Der Hohepriester jenes Jahres: Geschichte und Deutung* (AJEC 75; Leiden: Brill, 2010) who suggests that the connection is "unwahrscheinlich" (unlikely) (176). Additionally, see Z. Greenhut, "The Caiphas Tomb in the North Talpiyot, Jerusalem," *Atiqot* 21 (1992): 63–71; and "Burial Cave of the Caiphas Family," *Biblical Archaeology Review* 18/5 (1992): 28–36; and W. Horbury, "The Caiaphas Ossuaries and Joseph Caiaphas," *Palestine Exploration Quarterly* 126 (1994): 32–48.
88. Joe Nickell, *Relics of the Christ* (Lexington, KY: University Press of Kentucky, 2007), esp. 122–38.
89. Ibid.
90. See Robert A. Wild, "The Shroud of Turin: Probably the Work of a 14th Century Artist or Forger," *Biblical Archaeology Review* 10/2 (March/April, 1984): 30–46.

91. Walter C. McCrone, "The Shroud Painting Explained" and Gary Vikan, "Debunking the Shroud: Made by Human Hands," *Biblical Archaeology Review* 24/29 (November, 1998), 27–30. See also G. Fazio, G. Mandaglio, and M. Manganaro, "The Interaction Between Radiation and the Linen of Turin," *Radiation Effects & Defects in Solids* 165/5 (May, 2010): 337–42; Raymond N. Rogers, "Studies on the Radiocarbon Sample from the Shroud of Turin," *Thermochimica Acta* 425/1 (2005): 189–94 and J. A. Kohlbeck and E. L. Nitowksi, "New Evidence May Explain Image on Shroud of Turin: Chemical Test Link Shroud to Jerusalem," *Biblical Archaeological Review* 12/4 (July/August, 1986): 18–29. Additionally, see Christopher Chippindale, "Tempting Providence with the Turin Shroud?" *History Today* 37/9 (September, 1987): 5–6; and Suzanne F. Singer, "Has the Shroud of Turin Been Dated—Finally?" *Bible Review* 5/2 (April, 1989).
92. Ibid.
93. See however, John White, "Is the Shroud of Turin Authentic?," *New American* 26/10 (May, 2010), who quotes Ray Rogers, a physical chemist who has suggested that something miraculous happened in conjunction with this linen saying, "I am forced to conclude that the image was formed by a burst of radiant energy—light if you like" (38). See also, John C. Iannone, *The Mystery of the Shroud of Turin: New Scientific Evidence* (New York: Alba House, 1998); and Wendy Miller, "Shroud of Turin—What it Is and Where It's Been," *Biblical Archaeology Review* 12/4 (July/August, 1986). See also Dan Porter's website in conjunction with STURP at http://www.shroudstory.com/. Accessed online on 03.09.12.
94. V. Bortin, "Science and the Shroud of Turin," *Biblical Archaeologist* 43/2 (March, 1980): 117.
95. See V. Corbo, *Cafarnao I* (SBF 19; Jerusalem: Franciscan Printing Press, 1974); S. Loffreda, *Cafarnao II* (SBF 19; Jerusalem: Franciscan Printing Press, 1974); A. Spijkerman, *Cafarnao III* (SBF 19; Jerusalem: Franciscan Printing Press, 1975); and E. Tesa, *Cafarnao IV* (SBF 19; Jerusalem: Franciscan Printing Press, 1972).
96. The Greek, however, may allow this to be read as Jesus' own home, instead of the home of Simon and Peter.
97. James H. Charlesworth, "Jesus Research and Archaeology: A New Perspective," in *Jesus and Archaeology*, ed. J. H. Charlesworth (Grand Rapids, MI: Eerdmans, 2006), 49–50.
98. James F. Strange, "Has the House Where Jesus Stayed in Capernaum Been Found?: Italian Archaeologists Believe They Have Uncovered St. Peter's Home," in *The Galilee Jesus Knew* (Washington, DC: Biblical Archaeology Review, 2008), 87.
99. Ibid.
100. Jerome Murphy-O'Connor, *The Holy Land*, 4th ed. (Oxford: Oxford University Press, 1998), 220.
101. Jonathon L. Reed, *Archaeology and the Galilean Jesus: A Re-examination of the Evidence* (Harrisburg, PA: Trinity, 2000), 143.
102. Leslie J. Hoppe, *What Are They Saying About Biblical Archaeology?* (New York: Paulist Press, 1984), 75.
103. Hershel Shanks, "Jerusalem Update: 2, 700-Year-Old Tower Found?" *Biblical Archaeology Review* 26/5 (September/October, 2000): 39–41. See also research on the Siloam Inscription: Simon B. Parker, "Jerusalem's Underground Water Systems: Siloam Inscription Memorializes Engineering Achievement," *Biblical Archaeology Review* 20/4 (July/August, 1994) 20–38; Hershel Shanks, "Please Return the Siloam Inscription to Jerusalem," in *Biblical Archaeology Review* 17/3

Notes

(May/June, 1991): 58–60; and "Jerusalem Explores and Preserves Its Past: Is the Siloam Channel Referred to in Chronicles and Isaiah?" *Biblical Archaeology Review* 7/4 (July/August, 1981).

104. Shanks, "Please Return."
105. Yoel Elitzur, "The Siloam Pool—'Solomon's Pool'—Was A Swimming Pool," *Palestine Exploration Quarterly*, 140/1 (2008): 17–25. See also Hershel Shanks, "Ritual Bath or Swimming Pool?" *Biblical Archaeology Review* 34/3 (May/June, 2008).
106. Hershel Shanks, "The Siloam Pool: Where Jesus Cured the Blind Man," *Biblical Archaeology Review* 31/5 (September/October, 2005): 16–23.
107. Ibid.
108. See for example, the work of Bruce Grigsby, "Washing in the Pool of Siloam—A Thematic Anticipation of the Johannine Cross," in *Novum Testamentum* 28/3 (1985): 227–35. Even more, see Oyeronke Olajubu, "Reconnecting with the Waters: John 9.1–11," in *The Earth Story in the New Testament*, eds. N. C. Habel and V. Balabanski, (EB 5; London: Sheffield Academic Press, 2002), 115.
109. See D. Moody Smith, "John: Historian or Theologian?" *Bible Review* 20/5 (October, 2004): 22–31; and Hershel Shanks, "How Historical is the Gospel of John?" *Biblical Archaeology Review* 31/5 (September/October, 2005).
110. The Israeli Antiquities Authority released an official press report, which can be accessed online at http://www.antiquities.org.il/article_Item_eng.asp?sec_id=25&subj_id=240&id=1601&module_id=#as. Accessed online on 03.09.12. See also Hershel Shanks, "Exclusive! Major New Excavation Planned for Mary Magdalene's Hometown," *Biblical Archaeology Review* 33/5 (September/October, 2007): 52–55.
111. Joey Corbett, "New Synagogue Excavations in Israel and Beyond," *Biblical Archaeology Review* 37/4 (July/August, 2011): 52–59.
112. See Howard Clark Kee, "The Transformation of the Synagogue after 70 C.E.: Its Import for Early Christianity," *New Testament Studies* 36 (1990): 1–24; "The Changing Meaning of Synagogue: A Response to Richard Oster," *New Testament Studies* 40 (1994): 281–83; "Defining the First-Century CE Synagogue: Problems and Progress," *New Testament Synagogues* 41 (1995): 481–500; and *Evolution of the Synagogue*, eds. H. C. Kee and L. Cohick (Harrisburg, PA: Trinity Press, 1999), 7–26. Additionally, see Richard A. Horsley, *Archaeology, History, and Society in Galilee: The Social Context of Jesus and the Rabbis* (Valley Forge, PA: Trinity, 1996), 145; *Galilee: History, Politics, People* (Valley Forge, PA: Trinity, 1995), 222–37; and H. A. McKay, *Sabbath and Synagogue: The Question of Sabbath Worship in Ancient Judaism* (EPRO 122; Leiden: Brill, 1994); and "Ancient Synagogues: The Continuing Dialectic Between Two Major Views," *Currents in Research: Biblical Studies* 6 (1998): 103–42.
113. Mordechai Aviam, *Ancient Synagogues in the Land of Israel* (Jerusalem: ERETZ Magazine, 1997), 4–7.
114. Rosemary R. Reuther, *Women-Church* (San Francisco, CA: Harper & Row, 1985), 286 n1.
115. Jane Schaberg, "How Mary Magdalene Became a Whore," *Bible Review* 8/5 (October, 1992): 30–7; and with Melanie Johnson-DeBaufre, *Mary Magdalene Understood* (New York: Continuum, 2006).

Chapter 12: Approaching Revelation

1. Richard Bauckham, *The Theology of the Book of Revelation* (NTT; Cambridge: Cambridge University Press, 1994), 12.
2. Ibid., 13
3. Ibid., 14.
4. Ibid., 15.
5. Ibid.
6. Gregory K. Beale, *The Book of Revelation* (NIGTC; Grand Rapids, MI: Eerdmans, 1999), 141.
7. Ibid., 144–45.
8. Ibid., 134.
9. Ibid.
10. Ibid., 135–36.
11. M. Eugene Boring, *Revelation* (Interpretation; Louisville, KY: John Knox Press, 1989), 7.
12. Ibid.
13. Ibid, 9.
14. Ibid., 6.
15. Ibid., 24.
16. Ibid.
17. Ibid.
18. Austin Marsden Farrer, *A Rebirth of Images: The Making of St. John's Apocalypse* (Albany, NY: State University of New York Press, 1986), 8.
19. Ibid., 220.
20. Ibid., 306–7.
21. Ibid., 310.
22. Philip C. Carrington, *The Meaning of the Revelation* (London: SPCK, 1931), xvii.
23. Philip C. Carrington, "The Levitical Symbolism in Revelation," in *Days of Vengeance*, ed. D. Chilton (Fort Worth, TX: Dominion Press, 1987), 233. But see also his *The Meaning of the Revelation*, esp. 381–94; and "Astral Mythology in the Revelation," *Anglican Theological Review* (July 1, 1931): 289–305.
24. Carrington, "Levitical Symbolism," 241.
25. Ibid., 241–42.
26. Barbara Wooten Snyder, "Combat Myth in the Apocalypse: The Liturgy of the Day of the Lord and the Dedication of the Heavenly Temple" (PhD diss.; Berkeley, CA: University of California at Berkeley, 1991), 207–41.
27. David E. Aune, "The Apocalypse of John and the Problem of Genre," *Semeia* 36 (1986): 81. See also his three volumes in the Word Biblical Commentary series: *Revelation 1-5*, *Revelation 6-16*, and *Revelation 17-22* (WBC A-C; Nashville, TN: Thomas Nelson, 1997–1998).
28. Aune, "The Apocalypse," 78.
29. Ibid.
30. Edward White Benson, *The Apocalypse: An Introductory Study of the Revelation of St. John the Divine: Being a Presentment of the Structure of the Book and of the Fundamental Principles of Its Interpretation* (London: Macmillan and Co., 1900), 3.
31. Ibid., 6.

Notes

32. Ibid., x.
33. Ibid., 14.
34. James L. Blevins, "The Genre of Revelation" *Review & Expositor* (June 1, 1980): 393.
35. James L. Blevins, *Revelation As Drama* (Nashville, TN: Broadman Press, 1984).
36. Blevins, "The Genre," 398.
37. Ibid., 394.
38. Ibid., 396.
39. Gilbert Desrosiers, *An Introduction to Revelation: A Pathway to Interpretation* (CBSS; New York: Continuum, 2000), esp. 10–19.
40. Ibid., 22.
41. Ibid.
42. Ibid.
43. James L. Resseguie, *The Revelation of John: A Narrative Commentary* (Grand Rapids, MI: Baker Academic, 2009), 17.
44. Ibid., 18.
45. Ibid., 45.
46. Ibid.
47. Ibid., 45–46.
48. Ibid., 46.
49. Richard B. Hays, *The Moral Vision of the New Testament: Community, Cross, new Creation: A Contemporary Introduction to New Testament Ethics* (Edinburgh: T&T Clark, 1997), 181.
50. Ibid., 183.
51. Ibid.
52. Ibid.
53. Frederick David Mazzaferri, *The Genre of the Book of Revelation from a Source-Critical Perspective* (Beiheft 54; Berlin: De Gruyter, 1989), 381. Interestingly, Mazzaferri argues, "The term, NT apocalyptic, is inappropriate, even if a genre exists, since it has no canonical members. Suggested members are disparate, or too late either to have influenced John or to evince a common stock of tradition he may have tapped" (382).
54. Ibid., 209.
55. Tim F. LaHaye, "The Second Coming: A Two-Phased Event," in *The Popular Handbook on the Rapture: Experts Speak Out On End-Times Prophecy*, eds. T. F. LaHaye, T. Ice, and E. E. Hindson (Eugene, OR: Harvest House, 2011), 53–58.
56. Ibid., 58.
57. Tim F. LaHaye and Thomas Ice, *Charting the End Times: A Visual Guide to Understanding Bible Prophecy* (Eugene OR: Harvest House, 2001), 11.
58. Bruce J. Malina, *On the Genre and Message of Revelation: Star Visions and Sky Journeys* (Peabody, MA: Henrickson, 1995), 1.
59. Ibid., 3.
60. Ibid., 19.
61. Ibid.
62. Ibid., 266.
63. Ibid.
64. Ibid., 267.
65. Beale, *Revelation*, 38.
66. Ibid., 39.

67. J. Nelson Kraybill, *Apocalypse and Allegiance: Worship, Politics, and Devotion in the Book of Revelation* (Grand Rapids, MI: Brazos, 2010), 22.
68. Ibid.
69. Ibid.
70. Adela Yarbro Collins, *Crisis and Catharsis: The Power of the Apocalypse* (Philadelphia, PA: Westminster, 1984), 84.
71. Ibid., 106.
72. Ibid., 142.
73. Ibid., 153.
74. Ibid., 154.
75. Elizabeth Schüssler Fiorenza, *Revelation: Vision of a Just World* (PC; Minneapolis, MN: Fortress, 1991), 24.
76. Ibid., 25.
77. Ibid., 117.
78. Ibid., 119.
79. Ibid., 120.
80. Sean P. Kealy, *The Apocalypse of St. John* (MBS 15; Wilmington, DE: Michael Glazier, 1987), 53.
81. Ibid.
82. Ibid., 49.
83. Ibid., 52.
84. Craig S. Keener, *Revelation* (NIVAC; Grand Rapids, MI: Zondervan, 2000), 74.
85. Ibid.
86. Ibid.
87. Ibid., 75.
88. William H. Willimon, *Why I Am a United Methodist* (Nashville, TN: Abingdon, 1991), 40–41.

www.ingramcontent.com/pod-product-compliance
Lightning Source LLC
Chambersburg PA
CBHW050609300426
44112CB00013B/2145